milestones in

mass communication research

milestones in

mass

communi

cation
research

media effects

Shearon Lowery *Florida International University*

Melvin L. De Fleur *University of Miami*

Longman
New York & London

Milestones in Mass Communication Research: Media Effects

Longman Inc., 1560 Broadway, New York, N.Y. 10036
Associated companies, branches, and representatives
throughout the world.

Developmental Editor: Gordon T. R. Anderson
Editorial and Production Supervisor: Ferne Y. Kawahara
Manufacturing Supervisor: Marion Hess
Composition: Bi-Comp, Incorporated
Printing and Binding: Fairfield Graphics

Library of Congress Cataloging in Publication Data
Lowery, Shearon.
  Milestones in mass communication research.
  Includes index.
  1. Mass media.   2. Mass society.   I. De Fleur,
Melvin L. (Melvin Lawrence), 1923–   .   II. Title.
HM258.L68   1983   302.2′34   82-14043
ISBN 0-582-28352-3
ISBN 0-582-28353-1 (pbk.)

Manufactured in the United States of America

contents

foreword

Why do people examine the past? In some cases it is no more than an antiquarian fascination with the things and ideas of former times. Such fascinations maintain a lively trade in antiques and memorabilia. But this book, *Milestones in Mass Communication Research*, is far from being just a contribution to intellectual nostalgia. For any student or practitioner of mass communication this is an essential look at eleven milestone books in the mainstream of mass communication research.

While the examination of these eleven books stretching from the 1920s to the present may provide a bit of pleasant nostalgia, more importantly, examination of these key books will provide an understanding of the present. Specifically, this guided tour of the 50-year trail stretching behind current mass communication research efforts will help explain contemporary emphasis on some topics and continuing gaps in our knowledge of other topics. This well-organized tour by Shearon Lowery and Melvin De Fleur will help explain why the laissez-faire nature of scientific inquiry does not always provide intellectual closure or definitive answers for practical, everyday mass communication problems and situations.

While history may not repeat itself, examination of the past does clarify the present and place it in context. Sometimes the context is one of *constraint*. Historical changes in people's opinions, beliefs and lifestyles, or in the variety of mass media content, may render the scientific axioms of one era totally inoperative in another! Other times, the setting revealed by an examination of the past is one of *continuity*, not in the particulars, but in the general patterns of behavior and events. In this sense, history does sometimes repeat itself—at least in the abstract!

One of the first milestones examined in this book, *The People's Choice* by Paul Lazarsfeld, Bernard Berelson and Hazel Gaudet, offers examples of both continuity and constraint. This pioneering study of the 1940 Presidential election is the source of numerous empirical generalizations traditionally cited as part of our basic knowledge of mass communication. However, recent criticism shows that their validity as universal statements about the mass communication process is constrained by the time and place of the supporting empirical research—Erie County, Ohio in 1940. A number of these empirical generalizations about mass communication and public affairs are limited to the historical era prior to television when the vast majority of voters strongly identified with the Democratic and Republican parties.

However, on some occasions, close attention to the historical context of our empirical research reveals the very opposite of time-bound constraints. Previous scholarly work by one of the authors of this book, Melvin De Fleur, documented the historical continuity in the patterns of evolution and diffusion of the various mass media. Beginning with newspapers in the nineteenth century and continuing with film, radio, and television during this century, all mass media have displayed similar patterns as they appeared and spread through society. De Fleur has traced the rise of each new medium from the convergence of new social conditions with technological developments to displace the dominion of older, established media.

Discovery of repeating patterns is one of the fruits of historical review. In the absence of broad, abstract theoretical descriptions of mass communication—and, consequently, the absence of empirical research flowing from rigorous hypothetico-deductive models—historical examination is one of our most fruitful strategies.

A Cumulative Enterprise

Whether examination of the past reveals continuity or discontinuity in our empirical generalizations about the uses and effects of mass communication, there is an even more fundamental reason for looking back. Science is a cumulative enterprise. Each new endeavor is a creative effort building on past efforts. Science is not a series of discrete, isolated achievements. It is ongoing. Good science does not rest on its achievements. A good study opens the door to many new studies. One of the criteria used to evaluate scientists is the number of subsequent works citing their work. By that criterion each of the eleven books selected by Lowery and De Fleur receive exceptionally high marks! Good science whets the creative appetite and sharpens the questions probed in subsequent investigations. Any question which can be fully answered in a study or two is a poor question!

As science moves forward it leaves a trail of empirical investigations and theoretical writings, including a few milestones. Close examination of this historical trail will sharpen our understanding of the present—and of the future! Lowery and De Fleur note:

> The past is always the principal guide used by science for the future. . . . Most of the time it represents the foundation on which the cutting edge of current conceptualization rests as it presses forward.

Science represents steady building and occasional innovation. It is too bad that science popularly is regarded in terms of discoveries and breakthroughs. Anyone who approaches these eleven mass communication research milestones from that popular perspective will leave disappointed. But while these are not dramatic, grandiose breakthroughs, they are key milestones along the trail of patient and methodical accumulation of information about mass communication and its role in our society. Each of these eleven works set in motion dozens of subsequent investigations aimed at clarifying and detailing our understanding of mass communication.

For the most part, social science research is the gradual process of making explicit and clear that which was implicit and vague in previous thought. In some sciences with long historical traditions, well-developed paradigms, and large numbers of contributors, this evolution of the explicit from the implicit occurs continuously. But in mass communication research, which Lowery and De Fleur date from the 1920s and which granted its first indigenous PhDs only in the 1950s, the historical trail zigs and zags across contributing disciplines and across central research questions. Although ongoing programs of research have appeared in the last decade or so, even now there remain many different perspectives of mass communication. People see many different things when they turn their attention to the mass media. The richness of the collection assembled here by Lowery and De Fleur is the richness of these perspectives. While the absence of closure in these descriptions and explanations of mass communication is sometimes frustrating, it is best regarded, Lowery and De Fleur say, as an embarrassment of riches.

Salvation and Despair

Among the illustrations of the vast differences in how people regard mass communication are the *salvation* and *despair* syndromes, which over time repeatedly have been attached to each of the mass media. Typically, the salvation syndrome appears just ahead of, or simultaneous with, the diffusion of a new communication medium. In their turn, newspapers, film, radio, television, and all the new technologies now waiting on the horizon have been hailed as the salvation of civilization. Their potential contributions to wider and richer education, greater civic participation, and other noble social goals have been loudly touted. Seldom have these blue-sky projections been fulfilled. At some subsequent point in time, disillusionment has set in, and many have indicated the mass media as a prime source of social evils. Four of the milestone works examined here stem, at least in part, from despair over the social consequences of various mass media.

From the Payne Fund studies of film in the 1930s to contemporary concern over sex and violence on television there has been major social and scholarly concern about the impact of mass communication on the behavior of children.

This concern across half a century with mass communication and children illustrates a major aspect of the sociology of knowledge as it relates to the development of mass communication research. As Lowery and De Fleur note in this book:

> A central proposition of the sociology of knowledge is that in the search for new understandings, the problems that are investigated . . . are heavily influenced by the times in which the knowledge is sought.

While this may be generally true for all science, and particularly so for the social sciences, it is especially so for mass communication research. The eleven milestones examined here are much more a product of their times than the result of basic research or theoretical inquiry into how mass communication works.

Origins of the Milestones

This essay is not the setting for a full examination of the intellectual and historical roots of mass communication research, nor even of eleven milestones along the way. But some broad categorical sources of the shaping influence on these eleven major works should be noted in passing in the hope of stimulating more detailed thought and historical inquiry.

Four categories account in large measure for the origins of the eleven milestones. The first category already has been noted—concern over the social impact of mass media on children. Beginning with Payne Fund studies in the 1930s and continuing through the contemporary federal government reports on television, mass communication and the socialization of children has emerged as a major subdiscipline in mass communication research. Four of the milestones in this book are part of this subfield's heritage.

Closely akin to the concerns over media impact is a second category, prosocial manipulation. In many ways this is the reverse side of the coin in category one. Rather than being concerned with harm, the concern here is using the media for social good. In an earlier time, when the term had less of a pejorative meaning, this side of the coin would be described as social engineering. In any event, in these first two categories there is a desire to promote the public interest and advance the social good. Three of the milestones fall into this category—World War II research on the American soldier, Hovland's search for a scientific rhetoric, and efforts at tracing the diffusion of civil defense messages through interpersonal networks.

A third category of shaping influences arises from the investigation of specific social issues and events. Here fall the intriguing study of the "Invasion from Mars," the benchmark survey of Erie County during the 1940 Presidential election, and the work of the National Commission on the Causes and Prevention of Violence during the turbulent 1960s. While each of these milestones also addresses important general questions about mass communication, each is strongly rooted in its specific historical setting. Perhaps it is this strong strain of event-oriented research which made journalism schools feel especially comfortable with mass communication research as it emerged as a distinct discipline with graduate degrees and specialized research journals during the last 25 years.

The three categories suggested so far to account for major influences in the origins of mass communication research cover ten of the eleven milestones. The one remaining book, Elihu Katz and Paul Lazarfeld's *Personal Influence*, appears to be the only one stemming almost entirely from a general theoretical orientation. Even here, critics of the Left contend that such work, as well as most American mass communication research, stems from an administrative perspective, an interest in prosocial manipulation designed to perpetuate the existing mass media structure. Whether *Personal Influence*—and other pieces of mass communication research—stem from general inquiry and basic theoretical concerns or from a narrow, subservient administrative perspective is a question which readers must examine for themselves.

Historical scrutiny of the mass communication research literature will yield more complex and detailed descriptions of the primary influences defining scholarly research on the mass media than clearly is possible in this essay. The four nominal categories suggested as roots for the milestones in this volume, or more extensive critiques of the administrative perspective, are but part of a larger set of historical hypotheses which must be examined. In any event, it is clear that a number of forces other than intellectual curiosity and general theoretical inquiry have shaped the field.

General Theory and Specific Inquiries

It is now commonplace to say that human behavior is more complex than the phenomena of physical and biological science. But there is another complication making broad theoretical inquiry difficult and historical sensitivity essential. In mass communication the present is always moving!

While the forces of gravity or molecules of basic elements are little changed over recent millenia, the mass media of the 1980s are vastly different from those of our childhood. If there is to be a mass communication science, it must be cumulative in two senses. First, it should be conceptually and intellectually cumulative just as all science is. But it also must be historically cumulative.

This necessity to be historically cumulative sets a limit on the general theoretical nature of our knowledge and maintains a permanently key place for milestone research focused on specific situations of the moment. In other words, Wilbur Schramm's description of mass communication research as a crossroads where many pass but few tarry, may continue to be at least partially true forever. Since the time of that original statement by Schramm, a number of institutions have located themselves at the crossroads and begun to produce an indigenous mass communication research product rather than simply bartering goods from other disciplines. But the constantly shifting nature of mass communication, technologically, socially, and behaviorally, most likely means that the marketplace of ideas in mass communication research will remain a mixture of contributors from many intellectual perspectives.

Future Trends

To project what this mix of intellectual entrepreneurs will be for the remainder of this century, it is necessary to speculate about the most likely social trends which will shape both the mass media and the research about them. Lowery and De Fleur begin *Milestones in Mass Communication Research* with a review of the major social trends which launched mass communication in the nineteenth century. The master trends were industrialization, urbanization, and modernization. Contemporary society is now in the midst of new departures in all these areas, trends which intimately involve and affect mass communication as we have known it.

For some time now we have been a post-industrial society with the concomitant characteristics of a declining proportion of blue collar workers, a rising proportion of working women, and major increases in levels of education.

Urbanization to a considerable degree now means suburbanization with all its implications for sense of community and the distribution of mass communication services.

While lifestyles are continuously evolving, this is a period of accelerated change, influenced in part by changes in the workplace, home, and neighborhood, and most importantly, the mass media.

These trends will shape much of the mass communication research undertaken in the immediate decades ahead. Full exploitation of these rich opportunities for scholarship, or even just understanding what kinds of contributions research is likely to make to this social transition, demands close scrutiny of past mass communication research efforts, especially the milestone contributions of the seminal works presented here.

Maxwell McCombs
Syracuse University

acknowledgments

1

developing frameworks for studying mass communication

What have been the major research studies that have shaped thinking about the nature and influence of mass communication in the United States? A somewhat arbitrary answer to this question is given in the present book by our summaries of eleven large-scale research projects, the findings of which have been published in book form over the last half century. Why were these particular studies chosen rather than a number of potential alternatives? The selection may have been arbitrary, but it was by no means capricious. The studies we have identified as milestones in communication research have made important contributions to the development of the field in at least one of three ways: Some led researchers to conceptualize the process of mass communication in a new and important way; others introduced innovative methodological procedures or strategies that made a difference in how future research was conducted; several played a particularly important part in shaping public beliefs about the nature of media influences. At least a few did all three. All the studies selected represent attempts to study the media within the framework of science. Science can take many forms, ranging from experimental strategies of the laboratory to the controlled observations of the field observer or the clinician.

As a means of developing reliable and valid knowledge about some subject matter, science is in an *ideal* sense both innovative and cumulative. Supposedly, it breaks new ground with every study and moves the cutting edge of theory and method in a systematic way. Each new theoretical development is tested definitively and accepted or rejected as a valid description and explanation of the events under study. Presumably science also retests its findings so that it is self-policing and only those conclusions that have been found to be reliable remain in the accumulating body of knowledge.[1] Unfortunately, things do not work out so neatly in the real world. Studies are undertaken for a variety of reasons, with varying levels of sophistication. Some move the stream forward; others merely muddy its waters.

As a developing field, the study of mass communication has been particularly unsystematic. Because they came from a variety of disciplines, communication researchers in the past have almost never coordinated their efforts or built upon the results of previous research. Seldom have they been willing to abandon a theory because someone else's data failed to support it. Many investigations have been carried out simply because there was a substantial amount of money to do so and the public wanted answers to some policy question. Many of those questions were not theoretically significant. In other words, media research did not move forward in a neat and orderly way following the ideal model of science. Our selection of milestone studies had to take this situation into account. The resulting progression of studies, therefore, represents a kind of "mixed bag" of research efforts that played various roles in the development of our contemporary understanding of the process and effects of mass communication in modern society.

In spite of this unsystematic development, earlier studies did have at least *some* influence on later ones, and they represent the intellectual heritage of the present discipline. Over the years there were identifiable changes in basic conceptualizations. There has also been an increase in the level of sophistication of methods and techniques used in media research. Generally, these advances paralleled developments in the social and behavioral sciences, mainly psychology and sociology. It is the purpose of the present chapter to present a brief overview of the progression of the general theoretical frameworks that have been used over the last half century for the study of mass communication. The chapter also presents a brief discussion of the changes in methodological strategies and procedures that have played a part in the conduct of media studies.

An essential beginning point for understanding the development of frameworks for the study of mass communication is to review the meaning of the term *mass society*. It is from this concept that came such derived terms as "mass" audience, "mass" media, and (of course) "mass" communication. Once the nature of this rather complex set of ideas has been clarified, the underlying thinking behind early theories of mass communication can be understood. This understanding sets the stage for changes in our central theories of the effects of mass communication that occurred both as a result of media research and findings from the parent social and behavioral sciences. Following the clarification of these theoretical issues in order to provide guidelines for the review of specific research efforts, the growth of the media of mass communication is briefly traced, as these developments have occurred in American society.

CONCEPTUALIZING MASS SOCIETY

The term "mass," as used in "mass" society is, as we have noted, the intellectual source from which we obtain the concepts of "mass" media and "mass" communication. Unless the mass concept is thoroughly understood, in both its historical and contemporary perspectives, theories about the nature and effects of mass communication cannot be fully grasped. It does not refer merely to large numbers. Many so-called mass societies happen to have large populations. However, the underlying features that distinguish this type of society from other forms (e.g., traditional society) have to do with the relationships between their members rather than the size of their populations. This idea of mass as a form of societal organization emerged from a century and a half of theoretical analyses by a number of pioneer social scientists. It remains important in the public's beliefs about the power and influence of the media.

The concept of mass society emerged from the study of fundamental social changes that took place in society over the last two centuries. These changes altered drastically the relationships that members of society have with others as they carry on their everyday lives. The changes were subtle, complex, and profound. It is not easy to capture their essential nature in a brief review. However, we can begin by summarizing the master trends that shaped the emerging mass society.

The Master Trends

Prior to the late eighteenth century, western society was what sociologists call "traditional" in its organization. It was changing only slowly. People remained rooted to the land, and agriculture was almost everyone's principal preoccupation. The production of goods from wood, metal, leather, and cloth was in the hands of individual artisans and craftsmen. There were a few cottage industries and entrepreneurs, but no factories and no vast systems for distribution and consumption of manufactured products. Water, wind, and muscle were the sources of power used to operate the few machines that existed.

In terms of social organization, people were tied to each other through family and kinship, loyalties to local rulers, or through deeply established beliefs, customs, and traditions that guided their behavior in almost all aspects of social life. Communication between people was, for the vast majority, a matter of word-of-mouth. Books were being printed, but only a few people were sufficiently affluent or literate to use them. Early forms of the newspaper had appeared in some cities, but they played little part in the daily affairs of the population at large.

By the end of the century, major changes that would drastically restructure this traditional type of society were beginning. The development and spread of mass communication would be part of those changes, but almost every aspect of social life was to undergo alteration. In retrospect, we can identify three master trends that were, and continue to be, at the heart of the change from traditional to modern society. These are *industrialization, urbanization,* and *modernization.* As the new society was developing, each of these trends had a profound influence on social relationships, material culture, social norms and the thoughtways of individuals.

Industrialization   Generally speaking, the Industrial Revolution began as the eighteenth century came to a close. It was not a sudden transition but a gradual acceleration of processes of change that had begun much earlier. The idea of producing goods for entrepreneurs to market was well-established in Europe long before the mid-1700s. Developments in science and engineering were about to yield new power sources and machinery. The next major step was to combine investment capital with the new machines that could spin, weave, grind, stamp, and cut with a stamina and precision that no craftsman could match. With these devices replacing human hands and muscles, goods could be produced far more rapidly, uniformly, and cheaply than ever before. Steam power derived from wood or coal soon replaced other sources of energy and transformed one industry after another.

Such applications spread through the western world all during the nineteenth century, and soon a great variety of manufactured goods was being produced. The social significance of this process is that it greatly changed relationships between people in terms of their work. Earlier, human beings made things for each other. The artisan or craftsman performed or controlled all phases of the production process, from assembling raw materials to selling the finished product to his customer. In the new industrial order, the process of production was divided into a host of mini-steps, with machines doing most of the more demanding tasks. The human being became a kind of appendage to the machine, working at the machine's pace, feeding it raw products, or taking its finished goods away to be marketed by impersonal systems to unknown customers. In his classic analysis, Marx maintained that this system resulted in serious *alienation* of the industrial worker, not only from the work itself but from other people and even from himself.[2]

The industrial labor force required people with minimal skills who could be hired for minimal pay. They had to be free from traditional obligations to lands and landlords so that they could work when they were needed. In England, much earlier, many peasants had been evicted from their farms by the Enclosure Acts; they constituted just such a pool of free labor. It became clear quite early that using such workers was better than using slaves (who were available at the time). Even though the workers had to be paid, they could be dismissed in slack periods, which in the long run minimized the costs of production. In other countries there were somewhat similar poorly educated and unskilled populations that could make up an industrial labor force. In the United States, immigrants who had been driven out of other countries were welcomed as they entered at the "bottom of the ladder" in the mines, mills and factories. Even many of those who went first to the farms later migrated to towns and cities to become part of the new labor force.

Two additional elements were especially significant in shaping the emerging social order. These were the *factory system* and the *corporation*. The factory system was a direct result of the economic advantages of "shop production." This meant housing the machinery, labor, and stages of the manufacturing process under one roof. Plants were located, logically enough, where materials, labor, and transportation could easily come together. The social significance of the early factory system was that new communities developed around the sites—communities with no history or traditions of their own. They drew their residents from diverse sources. Social relationships in such areas, even outside the plant, tended to be culturally rootless and personally anonymous.

As factories, marketing enterprises, transportation systems, and financial institutions grew larger, the importance of the corporation became increasingly clear. Corporations, as legal entities for sharing risks and protecting shareholders from personal liability, had existed prior to industrialization, but it was the spread of this form of sociolegal organization that made the industrial society possible. The majority of early factories were often financed by a single individual, or at most by a few partners or a family. But as industrial and commercial activities increased in scope, larger and larger amounts of capital were required. Through the sale of shares, it was possible to obtain funds from hundreds or even thousands of owners willing to risk their capital for a proportionate part of the profits.

The significance of the development of the corporate structure and the great expansion in the size of industrial–commercial groups is that they brought a new dependence on *bureaucracy* as a form of social organization. A small group can be informal and depend upon intuitive understanding of its rules and tasks in order to achieve its goals. A group of thousands, designed to achieve the goals of a factory, a retail chain, or even a newspaper, must be far more impersonal in its structure. Groups organized as bureaucracies are deliberately designed to achieve clear-cut goals in a rational and efficient manner. Aside from all of the bad jokes about bumbling bureaucrats and snarls of red tape, bureaucracy, in principle, is the most effective way in which large-scale social enterprises can be conducted. A bureaucratic group has written rules; the activities of each person's position are carefully set forth; patterns of power and authority are clearly defined; the system of rewards and punishments is specified in contractual agreements. There are no real alternatives to this form of social organization for enterprises of large scope. For this reason, we live in an age of bureaucracy. All large-scale activities in contemporary society—manufacturing, commercial, educational, military, religious, sports, medical, and recreational —are carried out by groups that are bureaucratically organized. About the only exceptions are our families and friends.

Needless to say, the new types of human relationships resulting from the growth of bureaucracy were very different than the older forms based on friendship, kinship, or traditional loyalty. As the traditional society gave way to the industrial order, the bonds that united people were based less and less on such sentiments and more and more on the impersonal obligations of the legal contract.[3] People still had families and friends, but the increasingly mobile, differentiated, and bureaucratized society was one that tended to reduce close personal ties between people rather than strengthen them.

Urbanization   The social controls that traditional people exercise over each other decline sharply with the changes mentioned. People's customs and other rules for behavior give way to more formal means of control through civil or restitutive law and criminal justice systems with police, courts, and penal institutions. Deviant behavior becomes increasingly common as the older rules lose their force. The second master trend that has played a part in the emergence of mass society is urbanization. Defined very simply, urbanization is a process by which an increasing proportion of the population of a given area live in towns and cities. In the history of mankind, it is a relatively recent phenomenon. While human life in various forms goes back millions of years, people have been city dwellers for only a short part of that time. For example, the first known cities were established a mere 7,000 years ago.[4] We think of Europe today as highly urbanized. However, 150 years ago it was still overwhelmingly rural. As late as the beginning of the nineteenth century, only three percent of the world's people lived in communities of 5,000 or more.[5] Today, urbanization is one of the most significant trends of modern life. Even in the new world, cities reach 15 million or more (e.g., Mexico City). Dozens of cities in the United States have exceeded one million inhabitants. Today, less than five percent of the U.S. population is still in farming, and only about a quarter of the population lives in rural areas. These trends are very much in evidence in other parts of the globe. Some countries are considerably more urbanized than the United States.

This explosion in urban growth began and kept pace with the industrial revolution. But while the two master trends are closely linked, they are not simply different ways of looking at the same thing. In many areas, urbanization has proceeded without industrialization. Other areas have become industrialized without significant changes in the proportion of the population that is urban. The social significance of urbanization is that it changes the quality of life. Above all, it brings unlike people together. In the early days of industrialization, uprooted farm people were drawn to the new factory towns to seek work. They were joined there by others from different parts of the country and by people from the slums of established cities. These people did not relate to each other easily because of their social and psychological differences. Whereas the earlier rural and traditional social order was based on clear conceptions of the rules of social behavior, life in the new cities was characterized by a confusion of the rules, customs, and traditions, a condition called *anomie*.

The process of bringing unlike people together was accelerated greatly in the United States by heavy immigration from other lands. Not only were rural people going to the city to seek their fortunes, but millions of foreigners were arriving to enter at the bottom of the social ladder. The population of the United States grew very rapidly during the late nineteenth and early twentieth centuries as national policy sought to fill vacant land. A veritable tidal wave of immigration brought poorly educated and economically deprived people to the new world. Emma Lazarus' words inscribed at the base of the Statue of Liberty captures the essential characteristics of this inflow of humanity:

> Give me your tired, your poor,
> your huddled masses yearning to breathe free,
> the wretched refuse of your teeming shore—
> send these, the homeless, tempest-tossed to me:
> I lift my lamp beside the golden door.

And so they came. They poured in from northern, southern, and eastern Europe; from Asia and Africa; from Mexico and the dozens of lands to the south. They settled mainly in the cities, entered at the bottom of the labor force, and began their struggle upward. They spoke different languages, followed different customs, and subscribed to different values. They developed prejudices toward each other; called each other by bad names; discriminated against each other, and sometimes fought each other in the streets. All the while, those who had arrived earlier deplored and rejected the later arrivals. The end product was what August Comte had called "a multitude of separate corporations."[6] They split up into enclaves where language and customs could be maintained and where dislike and distrust of "the others" could be kept alive. Emotion and sentiment became more significant than reason and rationality in decisions about behavior. As time went on, many of those who had entered at the bottom did move up the social ladder. The majority did not. The industrial labor force, its related commercial activities, and the opportunities provided by public education provided the basis for upward mobility for some and social differentiation for all. Urbanization, in other words, created great differences between people. These differences provided no basis for the older and traditional bonds, based on loyalty, trust, and fealty, to develop again and keep people together. The new social order was what Ferdinand Tönnies called the *Gesellschaft*.[7] Trust was replaced by *distrust*. In a society of distrust, the contract rather than the handshake becomes the principal basis for regulating obligations between people.

Modernization As industrialization and urbanization continued, the lifestyles of the inhabitants of modern societies underwent change. Hundreds and even thousands of *innovations* were adopted. Inventive people designed machines for every conceivable purpose. By the turn of the century, the industrial order was producing an incredible array of devices that the ordinary family could purchase and use. These ranged from basics, such as tools and clothing, to the exotic, such as ointments for bust development or electric devices guaranteed to restore hair on bald heads. Mechanical innovations—indoor plumbing, central heat, the automobile, refrigeration, electric lights, and so on—had an impact on every aspect of life. Not only were the objects of everyday use undergoing change, but the very rhythm and meaning of life were different. Time scheduling assumed a new importance. Work, play, meals, education and even worship started and stopped according to the clock.

Industrialization and urbanization had already created differences between people. Modernization was a force toward even greater distinctions. Material lifestyles, based on consumption of the products of the new industries, were quite different at each level in the stratification system. Rich people had always lived differently than poor people, but the emerging industrial order brought a tremendous new diversity of goods. Those at the highest economic level could engage in conspicuous consumption and surround themselves with amenities never dreamed of by the affluent in more traditional societies.

Many of these new products served as status symbols and were adopted as quickly as possible by those who could afford them. Those lower in the system looked on with envy or used the new time-payment plans to acquire what they could. Between the economic elite at the top and the destitute poor at the bottom stretched numerous middle levels identified mainly by their patterns of consumption of the goods of modern society. In this way, modernization created another basis for social differentiation in addition to those stemming from regional, ethnic, and religious sources.

The process of modernization is closely linked with the growth of the mass media. Populations undergoing modernization not only increase their consumption of goods but their use of print, film, and broadcast media. Generally, they undergo a corresponding increase in literacy which has an influence on their perceptions and participation in government.

Modern societies, then, are media-dependent societies. Their populations make use of the media for achieving a great many goals that are handled differently in the traditional society. The media provide information critical to economic, political, religious, and educational decisions in ways that are totally different from preindustrial societies. This flow of information further breaks people away from traditional ways of life and thrusts them into constantly changing ways of thinking about family obligations, sexual mores, basic values and other central features of human existence.

Contemporary Society as Mass Society

Our review of the master trends underlying the transition from traditional to contemporary society has emphasized increases in social differentiation and psychological isolation in urban-industrial populations brought about by such factors as bureaucracy, contracts, migration, stratification, and the spread of innovation. It is said that all of these individual and social forces have worked to set people apart far more than to bring them together. The master trends, in one form or another, led social theorists of the last century to conceptualize the urban–industrial society as a *mass* society. The term "mass" in this context refers not to numbers but to a distinctive pattern of social organization, more precisely, a process of changing social organization that occurs when industrialization, urbanization, and modernization increasingly modify the social order. In other words, "mass" society emerges when the following changes take place:

1. Social differentiation in the society *increases* because of the growing division of labor, the bureaucratization of human groups, the mixing of unlike populations, and differential patterns of consumption.
2. The effectiveness of informal social controls *erodes* as the influence of traditional norms and values declines, leading to increases in the incidence of deviant behavior.

3. The use of formal social controls (the contract, restitutive law, and criminal justice systems) *rises* as the new impersonal society develops.
4. Conflicts *increase* because of social differences between people with opposing values and lifestyles.
5. Open and easy communication as a basis of social solidarity between people becomes *more difficult* because of social differentation, impersonality and distrust due to psychological alienation, the breakdown of meaningful social ties, and increasing anomie among the members.

Does this theoretical description provide an accurate picture of society today? Clearly it does not. There is much more to contemporary society than this portrayal of people psychologically and socially isolated from each other. Yet, the idea remains important. The concept of mass society is significant for the study of the media for two reasons. First, in spite of the fact that the theoretical picture it provides of contemporary society is overdrawn, we can recognize at least some of these trends around us. We *have* undergone industrialization, urbanization, and modernization. Life in contemporary society is very different because of these changes than it was in the "good old days" of traditional society. The ideas embedded in the conceptualization of mass society do provide an understanding of at least some of the features of life in the urban–industrial social order. But more important, it was this conceptualization of mass society that dominated the thinking of those intellectuals who were first concerned about the effects of the new mass media.

As each new medium came into the society and was adopted for widespread use, there was an increasing level of concern about the influences of the mass communication process. As the newspapers and, later, films and broadcasting were increasingly criticized for their presumed undesirable influences, the idea that members of the mass society could easily be controlled by powerful media troubled the critics. It was assumed that the isolated and alienated individual was at the mercy of those who could control the media. The media were thought to have great power because of the absence of other competing social and psychological influences on people.

THE SPREAD OF THE MEDIA IN MASS SOCIETY

Our contemporary forms of mass communication emerged as a part of the development of mass society. The new media—newspapers for the ordinary citizen, movies as a form of family entertainment, radio and television as devices of daily use at home—were products of industrialization and modernization.[8] They would not have been possible without the gathering together of large audiences resulting from urbanization. There was no single date that marks the beginning of the age of mass communication, but it came with the development of the first mass newspaper. Print as a medium of communication had been around for centuries but it was the mass newspaper that brought printed information to the ordinary citizen of the industrializing society. Magazines, film, and broadcast media followed later as social changes as well as scientific and technological advances made them possible.

Print

The techniques of writing have ancient roots. This skill was invented independently in several places in the world at various times. This important ability to communicate using written symbols spread slowly over the centuries as alphabets became increasingly standardized, and as lighter and more portable surfaces became available. The printing press and the process of manufacturing paper were important technological advances that eventually led to the use of print as a *mass* medium. However, it was not until the early part of the nineteenth century that ordinary people began to have direct experiences with the printed word.

Books, of course, are the oldest print medium. They were first produced by a press with moveable type in 1456. For centuries they remained a medium for the elite. Few ordinary people were literate, and still fewer could afford to buy a book even if they could read it. Increasingly, however, the use of books spread among the better educated segments of the society. Then, as education itself became more commonplace, the use of books increased until in the nineteenth century they became a mass medium. Today, they remain our most respected medium in terms of their use as college textbooks, works of literary merit, scholarship, or scientific importance. They are also a very popular medium in the form of cheap paperbacks produced for all taste levels.

The mass newspaper got its start in 1834 in New York when a printer put together a power press, a scheme for financing the paper through advertising, and a bureaucratic organization for gathering the news and distributing the paper. Earlier, there had been newspapers for the educated minority, but the new daily paper was aimed at those for whom literacy was a relatively new experience. By the time the first mass newspaper appeared, urbanization was well under way. Industrialization had produced a working class that was not tied to agriculture, and modernization had brought free public education to the children of the new industrial labor force. The new venture was profitable beyond the dreams of its publisher, and within months he had numerous imitators. Soon there was a mass newspaper in every major city and the age of mass communication had begun.

The newspaper spread rapidly in the United States, not only in a geographic sense but in its increasing adoption by the public. Great newspaper empires were founded by pioneer journalists, such as William Gordon Bennett, Horace Greeley, and William Randolph Hearst. By the end of the century, the newspaper was not only a deeply established mass medium; it was "the only game in town." It had no real competitors until the growth of the movies and the development of broadcasting. The peak of newspaper usage in the United States was during the decade 1910–1920 (the period of World War I). Circulations were at an all-time high in terms of the number of daily newspapers produced and consumed per household. For example, in 1910 more than 1.3 daily newspapers were sold per household in the United States. Since that time, the newspaper has declined steadily but slowly. Today, the number of competing newspapers has been greatly reduced; the majority are owned by large newspaper chains and circulation has dropped to about 0.8 per household.[9] However, the newspaper, with millions of daily readers, remains a major mass medium in contemporary society.

Magazines have a shorter history than either books or newspapers. Late in the last century printing techniques and postal services had developed to a point where mass-circulation magazines were possible. Modernization had raised the literacy level and the magazine provided a supplement to the briefer accounts of the newspaper. During the late nineteenth century and the first half of the twentieth, most magazines were aimed at a large and general readership. With circulations in the millions, they were a significant mass medium. In more recent times the general and large-circulation magazines have all but disappeared. Today, there are some 10,000 different periodicals produced in the United States, but for the most part they are aimed at very specialized categories of readers. As social differentiation has increased, it is no longer financially profitable to produce a magazine that will appeal to everyone. Magazines now focus on interest groups; there is a magazine for every taste, hobby, and activity. These magazines range from *Skin Diver* and *Model Train* to *Penthouse* and *Gourmet*. Readership is high because issues are often passed on to others to be read again and again. Taken as a whole, magazines constitute a major mass medium, even though their readership is scattered across thousands of specialized topics and interests.

Film

As a mass medium, the film has had a relatively short history. While its technological roots lie in the distant past, it became a form of recreation for ordinary people in society less than a century ago. The lens, critical to both photography and projection, was understood and used as early as 600 B.C. However, the idea of projecting shadow images onto a screen through a transparency was not to become a reality until the 1600s. Then, as science moved slowly forward, the basic chemistry of photography was developed, and the light-sensitive photographic plate became available. It was not until 1839 that the first actual photographs were made, to astonish the world with their vivid detail. Progressing from still to motion pictures required an understanding of the physiology of the visual senses and the psychology of perceiving motion from a series of rapidly projected photographs. By the beginning of the 1900s, simple moving pictures of brief duration were being shown to paying audiences and the stage was set for the movies to become a major mass medium.

The first family-oriented motion picture theaters were the simple and crude "nickelodeons." By 1910 there were some 10,000 such exhibition halls in various cities of the United States, and early motion picture production studios were supplying a variety of silent films for their use. But it was during the next decade that the movies blossomed into a major mass medium. More attractive theaters were built. Movies became longer and told stories. The star system was invented: sex gods and goddesses of the screen enthralled millions of fans. Although the movies were silent until about 1927, they were a major form of weekly entertainment for some 90 million as the 1920s came to a close.

The Golden Age came between 1930 and 1940. Movies had no competitors. The sale of tickets per household was at an all-time high of about 2.5 per week for every household in the United States. (Currently it has dropped to a mere 0.27 per household per week.) The decline of the movies began when television started to reach the majority of households in the United States. At first, the black-and-white broadcasts made only minor inroads in the movie industry. Later, as color television brought free talking pictures into all corners of the nation, the popularity of the movies dropped greatly. Movies remain today mainly because they are a relatively inexpensive form of entertainment for children and young people of dating age. The film industry also makes money producing movies for the insatiable television industry. Yet, the future of the movies is less than clear. As TV increases its flexibility with new forms of cable and subscription broadcasts, the number of entertainment choices for most Americans will expand. Indeed, this expansion of choices will probably also occur in most other countries as satellites make broadcasts increasingly available. Therefore, the fate of the movies in their traditional form remains to be seen.

Broadcasting

The idea of instantaneous communication over long distances had fired the imagination of thinkers for centuries. It was not until 1844, however, that the dream was realized. In that year Samuel F. B. Morse sent a message along a copper wire between Washington, D.C. and Baltimore, Maryland to open the era of telecommunication. By the end of the century, radio waves had been discovered by Heinrich Hertz and adapted to a wireless telegraph by Guglielmo Marconi. When the waves were suitably interrupted to produce coded signals, they could telegraph information across vast distances without wires.

Transmission of the human voice was accomplished via the wireless telegraph by 1906, when a few additional devices (e.g., the vacuum tube) were added. The age of broadcasting had been made possible. However, at that time, radio was by no means a mass medium for household reception, but was used by military and commercial interests for a variety of purposes. A few amateurs were able to receive the signals at home, but the idea that radio could become a mass medium for ordinary people had not yet reached its time.

It was not until the early 1920s that home radio became a reality. It all happened in a remarkably brief time and in a totally unforeseen manner. A few manufacturers had experimented with building and marketing home receivers, and several thousand had been purchased by 1920. However, broadcasting was only sporadic; there were no regular "programs" to listen to. In November of that year the presidential election results were beamed through the evening sky to a handful of listeners from an experimental transmitter in Pittsburgh. It was little more than a novelty, but the event captured widespread attention. Soon the demand for sets increased greatly and manufacturers began supplying them to an eager public. Transmitters were operated in several cities by manufacturers who wanted to stimulate sales. It was all great fun and soon people built their own transmitters. They didn't cost very much. There were only a few legal restrictions and no effective control over frequency, use, power, and hours of operation.

Soon, the situation deteriorated; stations operated on the same frequencies and the airwaves became a jumble of sound. New legislation was necessary to control the assignment of frequencies and the power of transmitters so that they did not interfere with each other. Such legislation was finally completed in the form of the Federal Communications Act of 1934.

In revised form this remains the basic legal structure for broadcasting in the United States.

From only a few thousand in 1920, the number of home receivers rose sharply during the next decade. By 1925, four million sets were in use. By 1930 the number of sets had jumped to 13 million. The number of home receivers reached one per household in the United States in 1936, with a total of 30 million sets in the hands of the public. Radio had truly become a mass medium.

Today, Americans own an astonishing number of radio receivers. In the form of automobile, kitchen, bedside, and portable radios, the average is nearly eight sets per household. Thus, radio remains a mass medium in spite of its competition from television. It has a vast daytime and evening audience. There has been a substantial shift from AM broadcasting frequencies to static free FM, which is now the dominant technology.

Radio's most significant period as a major medium was during the twenty years from 1930 to 1950. It had no direct competitor; its technology was sophisticated; live broadcasts could be received from all parts of the world. It provided rapid dissemination of the news, and it was central to the economic institution as an advertising medium; it was also one of the principal forms of home entertainment for millions of citizens. Even though it had to change when television came, radio continues to provide people with information and entertainment at times when attention to other media is inappropriate. With its timely news summaries, local focus, and broad range of music, it appears to have found a stable niche in an increasingly competitive media environment.

Television is a child of radio in many respects. However, the child has grown to dwarf its parent. The earliest television broadcasts outside the laboratory were experimental in nature and took place at various times in the late 1920s. During the 1930s research continued and the technology of the new medium was made more practical. Late in the decade limited scheduled broadcasts to the public began from an experimental station in the Empire State Building. A few thousand people in the New York area had purchased sets and were anticipating the growth of the new phenomenon. However, the fledgling industry was grounded before it got into the air, so to speak. World War II intervened and the electronics manufacturing capacities of the nation were devoted to producing the radio equipment and radar that were desperately needed for defense.

As the war closed, TV began to develop in earnest. In 1946 about 8,000 sets were in the hands of the public. A mere five years later, more than 37 million home receivers were in use! The spread of transmitters matched this spectacular growth. They had been established in all major cities. But the federal government quickly stepped in, in order to avoid the chaos in broadcasting that had taken place during the early years of radio. Frequencies, levels of power, and times of operation needed to be controlled in a master plan for the entire country so that the signal of one station did not block out or interfere with that of another. The Federal Communication Commission placed a four-year freeze (1948–52) on new station licensing while engineers produced the master plan. This work was completed satisfactorily and the rapid pattern of growth resumed during the remainder of the 1950s. By the end of the decade there was slightly more than one television set per household in the United States and a signal reached almost all parts of the country. Today, the figure has reached 1.5 sets per household, and virtually every corner of the country receives network television. Color sets have nearly replaced the older black and white receivers.

Today, television is a highly profitable industry. It inherited its advertising role from radio, along with the free entertainment function. With its penetration into the society, it is currently unmatched as an advertising vehicle for products of wide use. The gross revenues from advertising via the three major American networks are many millions of dollars annually. It can command audiences in the United States of 50 million for a single event (e.g., *Roots*). On a world-wide basis, with the aid of satellites, nearly a billion people can watch a live broadcast (e.g., the wedding of Prince Charles and Lady Diana of Great Britain in 1981).

On the other hand, the future may not be so rosy. Television may be about to face an era of turmoil. Cable systems, independent of the major networks, are rapidly being developed in American cities. For years Congress and the FCC protected the networks against their competition, but now all the barriers have been removed. A cable system can bring far more channels to the viewer than the usual four to six now typical in off-the-air reception. The range of material available across this large number of channels has the capability of dividing up the audience into many smaller ones, compared to the huge ones that now view programs produced by the three major networks. This splintering of the audience took place as magazines moved from huge general circulation periodicals to a large number of specialized audiences. What this will do to the networks financially is anyone's guess. Clearly, there is the possibility that advertisers will turn away from the networks when they can no longer command their huge audiences, and try the more specialized forms of advertising strategies now used in magazines. In any case, the next several years represent an era of transition for the television industries.

Generally, then, in looking at all of the mass media in modern society, it is clear that they are a major feature of social life as we know it. They have a central role in the affairs of the urban–industrial society and bring modernizing influences to the most remote rural community. They have spread through the society, often with startling rapidity, and represent a part of the broader process of industrialization; their growth period covers more than a century. However, their major development as a system of competing media has been used within the last half-century. Today they reach every eye and ear. Children and adults alike spend large proportions of their waking hours with the media in one form or another. They have made us dependent on their information in every sphere of life from economics to religion. It is little wonder that many people are concerned about what they may be doing to us. Great debates have been carried on since the first newspapers appeared to be used by ordinary people. Are the effects of these media evil or good? Do they influence us in ways we do not want? Or do they serve us well by enlarging our consciousness and perspectives?

Such questions and many more have preoccupied the attention of critics, public leaders, scholars, researchers, and intelligent lay persons for many decades. Their curiosity and concerns have led to a number of research studies on various aspects of the media and their effects. However, it was not until the late 1920s that the first large-scale investigation was made. Somewhat predictably, it focused on the influences of motion pictures, a new medium that was growing with great rapidity and had a special appeal for children. The movies were a deep source of concern as millions of youngsters absorbed ideas from them every week. We need to look briefly at the growth in research capability that made it possible to do such a scientific study, and at the theoretical perspectives on mass communication that were a product of the mass society theory outlined earlier.

THE DEVELOPMENT OF RESEARCH TECHNOLOGY

Prior to the 1920s, there was little in the way of systematic investigation of the effects of mass communication within what we would today call a scientific perspective. There was a great deal being written about the media. Most intellectuals of the nineteenth century denounced them at one time or another for their presumed destructive effects on the social order. Such critical claims continued in the twentieth century (and continue still). But these claims were just that—claims. Until well into the present century it was not possible to approach the issue of media influences within a framework of objective, quantitative analysis where conclusions were based on value-free criteria. That is, it was not until scientific methods were available that research findings could replace speculation, accusation, and undocumented conclusions in the discussion of media effects. The development of those scientific methods did not come quickly or easily. They were part of the more general development of the social and behavioral sciences.

The Logical Foundations of Communication Research

Communication research is an extension of the methodology and theory-building strategies of the social and behavioral sciences. These in turn rest heavily upon the underlying logical strategies of the physical and biological sciences. Early in the nineteenth century it became clear to many scholars concerned about human individual and social behavior that the research strategies of the physical sciences offered hope for the future in understanding people. Those research strategies were leading to great success in developing reliable and valid knowledge in such fields as physics, chemistry, and biology. For example, by the time that the first mass newspaper appeared, photography was about to become a reality. People were being vaccinated routinely against at least some serious diseases, and the telegraph had been in existence for five years. The social sciences, by comparison, were still in the age of Plato.

It was not that there was a lack of ideas about the individual or the social order. It was more like an embarrassment of riches. The wisdom of hundreds of philosophers was available. The problem was that they were all saying different things about human nature and society. There was no systematic and objective way to sort out valid conclusions from all the theories that could not be supported by facts. This was not so in the other sciences. Systematic observation, guided by reasoned theoretical perspectives, and careful weighing of numerical evidence, had proved to be enormously successful in reliable and valid generalizations. This procedure had brought Darwin to his historic conclusions about the origins of species; it was leading others to a host of discoveries in medicine, chemistry, astronomy, and physics. Was it not possible, and was it not wise, to try to adapt these strategies and procedures to study human beings in their individual and social activities?

Many scoffed at the idea or found it presumptuous. Some in well-established scientific fields dismissed such an effort as preposterous. Human behavior was too complex, they said, or too erratic and unpredictable. And how on earth could one quantify thoughts and emotions? Human activities did not follow immutable laws, they pointed out, as did the phenomena of the physical and biological world. Thus, the critics concluded, there were no regularities to be discovered by such a science even if the science might be possible. Others proclaimed that the whole idea was wicked. God had given human beings their destiny, and their behavior was the result of His divine plan. To presume that some sort of scientific approach could pry into such matters and see regular predictable patterns of action was little short of blasphemy!

Quantitative Procedures

In spite of the opposition of skeptics and critics, social and psychological pioneers did break away from the undisciplined philosophies of the past. They began to make measurements of limited forms of behavior. By the mid-nineteenth century, the psychologist Weber worked out a mathematically sophisticated system of "psychophysics" to describe patterns in people's perceptions of differences in the intensities of stimuli.[10] Toward the end of the century, the sociologist Durkheim assembled numerical data on deaths by suicide from various countries in Europe and developed an innovative theory concerning that ultimate act. It was not speculation; it was backed by impressive quantitative evidence.[11] Charles Booth used meticulous counting and classification to describe the way of life of London's poor in an early version of the survey.[12] Social psychologist Wilhelm Wundt in Leipzig developed the first laboratory for the precise measurement of human reaction times as early as 1879. He used a number of ingenious brass instruments and experiments.

As the new century began, these pioneering efforts led the way to the future. The social and behavioral sciences were about to become a reality. Still, it was clearly very difficult to use the experimental format or any other quantitative procedure for the study of anything but the most restricted forms of behavior. But new approaches were being developed by mathematicians and other scholars. These were the new techniques for examining the statistical parameters and distributions of numbers—their central tendencies, their scatter, and variability. Laws of probability had already been worked out and these could be used to interpret the likelihood of any given pattern of differences between means. Pearson's new procedure called the "product–moment coefficient of correlation" was another major breakthrough. Its index, r, summarized the tendency of two arrays of numbers to rise and fall jointly.

The beauty of these new statistical techniques was that they were universal in their application to scientific problems. It did not matter whether the numbers used represented observations from agriculture, biology, communication, psychology, sociology, or zoology. These statistical procedures, and the many more that have come since those early times opened the scientific method to the social and behavioral sciences. Communica-

MILESTONES IN MASS COMMUNICATION RESEARCH

tion research followed these traditions and depends on them in the same manner.

By the beginning of the 1920s, the teaching of statistical techniques began in earnest in the social and behavioral sciences. Yet this generated considerable debate. More conservative scholars in the older traditions rejected the radical new procedures, claiming that they were sterile and atheoretical. How could one understand the delicacy and richness of human life, they asked, by looking at a table of numbers or a statistical index? In the end, however, the quantitative procedures found increasing acceptance. With them came the standardized questionnaire as a means of generating numerical data, the random sample that could fit the underlying assumptions of the new statistical procedures, and the probability considerations for deciding whether a given generalization was merely a reflection of chance.

As the movement toward quantification became more sophisticated, additional procedures were devised for probing into areas previously not accessible to scientific approaches. The attitude scales, pioneered by sociologist Emory Bogardus and psychologist L. L. Thurstone, made it possible to reduce people's psychological orientations to numerical scale values. This touched off a tidal wave of attitude studies. The techniques of partial and multiple correlation, the analysis of variance, and nonparametric statistics were added to the tools available for research.

Calculation of large data sets remained a laborious procedure and ways were invented to make this easier. Before there were mechanical calculators and computers, there were Holerith cards with holes punched around their edges so that long wires could be inserted. Those with the holes punched out to the edge of the card would drop out of a pack. The others would remain. This is the same binary principle of the IBM card, and it worked well enough. Calculations from large data sets was also facilitated by grouping the data into class intervals and working with their mid-values. The quantitative procedures of content analysis were developed from this base. These procedures became very important in communication research. The frequency with which specific words, phrases, or themes appeared in a given communication could be counted; statistical relationships between these data and other factors could then be studied. It was a useful procedure for showing trends in the treatment of issues over time, or for comparing the treatment of a given type of content in various media.

It was not until these research tools began to be available that a scientific approach to the study of mass communication could get its start. But numbers alone are not enough: research cannot be done in a theoretical vacuum. The development of statistical procedures, measurement techniques, and research designs can only be effective in advancing a field if at the same time it develops hypotheses and theories that can be guides to what should be studied. For this reason, we need to understand how new frameworks emerged for understanding and explaining the influence of the media.

EMERGING THEORIES OF MEDIA EFFECTS

The ability to do research on the effects of mass communication was of enormous importance in developing theories to explain their role and significance in contemporary society. As investigators made use of increasingly sophisticated techniques and procedures, they began to come up with research findings that required them to modify earlier explanations of how, and to what extent, mass communications had effects on individuals and society. Research within the framework of science and in a large-scale sense began in the late 1920s. These early studies were based on a theory of the effects of mass communication derived directly from the assumptions of the nature of mass society noted earlier. This early theory assumed that the media had great power to influence every individual, more or less uniformly. As we will see, subsequent research increasingly called this idea into question. New theories that assumed more selective and less powerful effects had to be formulated. As research continued, these in turn were called into question as the study of short-term immediate influences of the media revealed a very mixed picture. Eventually, theories and research strategies were to be revised again and again to search for more indirect and long-term effects.

In the present section, we will review several significant theoretical formulations that emerged from research at various points in time over the last half century. Each advanced in some degree our understanding of how mass communication can influence individuals and society. For the most part, none of these theoretical explanations is totally "wrong." Some give more accurate and complete pictures of the effects of mass communication than others. But generally speaking, as research accumulated, increasingly valid and reliable generalizations about the effects of mass communication have emerged.

The Theory of Uniform Influences

It will be recalled that in the assumptions of the nature of mass society, urban–industrial populations were seen as diverse, differentiated, and free from binding social ties. Their members were said to act less on the basis

22

of reason and rationality and more on impulse, sentiment, and emotion. Because of these assumptions modern society was characterized as a "lonely crowd," a society composed of separate individuals not linked to each other but acting on the basis of their own individual psychological forces.[13] Even as early as 1895, Gustave Le Bon, the French social psychologist, characterized modern society as being in "the age of crowds."[14]

If it was indeed true that each individual was uninfluenced by social variables, each had an essentially similar human nature (based on the then current biological models), and each was like all others in terms of emotions and outlook, the mass media could be truly powerful sources of influence. Messages could be sent to every person to be received and understood more or less uniformly. Presumably, such messages would appeal to emotions and sentiments and sway the thinking or actions of each recipient in much the same way. Thus, the mass society concept yielded a theory of mass communication effects in which the media were seen as powerful, and their effects both uniform and direct among the members. Briefly, this theory can be summarized more formally in the following terms:

1. The media present messages to the members of the mass society who perceive them more or less uniformly.
2. Such messages are stimuli that influence the individual's emotions and sentiments strongly.
3. The stimuli lead individuals to respond in a somewhat uniform manner, creating changes in thought and action that are like those changes in other persons.
4. Because individuals are not held back by strong social controls from others, such as shared customs and traditions, the effects of mass communications are powerful, uniform and direct.

This set of ideas has often been called the *magic bullet theory* of media effects. It was the guiding perspective on the process and effects of mass communication prior to the beginnings of scientific research on the media. For example, the theory was current during World War I. Newspapers during the period were used to make people believe that the enemy was immoral and brutal. Atrocity stories played on the fears and other emotions of the masses. The stories described the hideous behavior of the enemy and convinced populations on each side that those whom they opposed were monsters.

After the war, a number of those who had engineered the deceptions were troubled by the part they had played in creating false beliefs. Their revelations, published in numerous books, created deep concern that the media could be used for all kinds of unacceptable purposes in the hands of the unscrupulous. Large-scale efforts were undertaken to educate the public regarding the insidious dangers of propaganda. From the close of World War I well into the present decade, college courses, textbooks, and learned treatises appeared under the general rubric of "propaganda analysis." It was a noble effort, a form of systematic if not scientific analysis clearly based on the beliefs of the magic bullet theory.

Today, little remains of the theory of uniform influences. It does appear in the beliefs of some members of the public who naively assume that the mass media exercise diabolical control over our minds. But, for the most part, the theory of uniform influences is important in that it provided a starting place for early research. As we will see, when reliable research findings began to accumulate, it had to give way to alternative theories of media effects that seemed to fit reality better.

Selective Influence Theories

A major problem of the magic bullet theory was that its underlying assumptions about people were inaccurate. It was soon discovered that people were active rather than passive receivers of information. Psychologists had begun to emphasize individual differences in people's needs, attitudes, values, and other personality variables. These, they said, led people to perceive the world in unique ways and to act on any stimulus in individually distinct ways. Human nature was not uniform but psychologically dissimilar from one person to another because of the selective influence of learning in society. The influence of the environment in shaping human nature began to be emphasized far more than the influence of our rather uniform biological endowment. This led to an emphasis on the selective manner in which people attended to the mass media and to the great variations in the way people could perceive and interpret the mass-mediated message. A new theoretical formulation began to replace the older theory of uniform effects. For the sake of convenience, it can be called the theory of selective influence based on individual differences. Its basic ideas can be summarized as follows:

1. The media present messages to the members of mass society but those messages are received and interpreted selectively.
2. The basis of this selectivity lies in variations in habits of perception among members of the society.
3. Variations in habits of perception occur because each individual has a unique personal organization of beliefs, attitudes, values, needs, and modes of experiencing gratification that has been acquired through learning.

4. Because perception is selective, interpretation, retention and response to media messages are also selective and variable.
5. Thus, the effects of the media are neither uniform, powerful, nor direct. Their influences are selective and limited by individual psychological differences.

As this view of the effects of the media became prominent, a search was undertaken for those psychological factors that operate as perceptual screens, letting some influences in but keeping others out. The idea had important policy implications: if only those magic keys to shaping people's behavior could be found, the media could incorporate them into its messages and could persuade people to buy, vote, donate, or at least think in desired ways. Thus, though the power of the media was less under this view, it was still there in a selective way.

As the selective nature of human perception was being realized by media researchers, another form of selective influence was found. This was what sociologists call *social categories*. People in different positions in the social structure act differently. This includes their mass communication behavior. The poor and the rich, the old and the young, males and females, the educated and the untutored, farmer, merchant, or Indian chief—all represent distinctive categories of people in the complex social system. However, the behavior *within* any category tends to be remarkably similar. Young, affluent females with reasonably high educational level read *Vogue*, *Glamour* and similar magazines. Poor, black, male youths living in the inner city read comic books but not the editorial section of the newspaper. There is, in other words, a very powerful influence on selective mass communication exposure that comes about from such social differentiation. For the sake of convenience we can call this the *theory of selectivity based on social categories*. Its essential propositions can be summarized in the following terms:

1. The media present messages to the members of the mass society but they are received and interpreted selectively.
2. An important basis of this selectivity lies in the location of the individual in the differentiated social structure.
3. That social structure is composed of numerous categories of people, defined by such factors as age, sex, income, education, and occupation.
4. Patterns of media attention and response are shaped by the factors that define these categories, making response to mass communication somewhat similar in each.

5. Thus, the effects of the media are neither uniform, powerful, nor direct, but are selective and limited by social category influences.

As research progressed, systematic efforts were undertaken to identify and measure the influence of these kinds of variables.

Another important discovery was that the audiences of the mass media were not simply isolated individuals, and not simply people who could be grouped into social categories. They remained tied to each other through friends, families, work associates, and membership in larger voluntary associations (e.g., lodges, clubs, political parties, and so on). In a rather dramatic way it was found that these social influences were a critical factor in the individual's exposure to the mass media. These influences produced selective effects that could not be attributed simply to psychological variables or to social categories. Some people were avid in their patterns of exposure to the media. Others attended very lightly, if at all. But through networks of social ties, it was found, some of those who attended heavily were influencing those who attended very little. Again, for the sake of convenience, we will call this set of ideas the *theory of selectivity based on social relationships*. The main ideas can be summarized as follows:

1. The media present messages to members of the mass society but they are received and interpreted selectively.
2. An important basis of this selectivity lies in distinctive patterns of social influences on people from others with whom they have meaningful ties.
3. Such social influences are brought to bear when an individual's decisions regarding behavior toward mass communication are modified by family, friends, acquaintances, or others.
4. Patterns of media attention and response uniquely reflect the networks of meaningful social ties of each individual in the society.
5. Thus, the effects of the media are neither uniform, powerful, nor direct; they are greatly limited and shaped by the person's social interactions with others.

Obviously, this social relationships perspective on media effects represents a substantial movement away from the assumptions of the mass society. It is a product of a more complete understanding of the organizational nature of contemporary society, understandings that were not available at the beginning of the century when it appeared that the three master trends discussed earlier were leading to a rootless, anonymous, differentiated, and alienated social order.

Theories of Indirect Influence

One of the great disappointments of mass communication research as it accumulated was that it seemed to show that the media had only limited influences on their audiences, rather than the powerful influences feared by the critics. One reason why the research findings seemed to indicate this was that investigators had concentrated mainly on studies of specific effects that were supposed to be produced in a short-run sense by specific content in media messages. But as studies went on, this kind of influence was difficult to demonstrate. It was realized that the media could produce long-range and indirect influences, but these were difficult to study. The most popular research strategy was the experiment, modeled after the before–after studies used in the physical sciences. Tracing out indirect and long-term influences was not possible through the use of such an approach.

In later years, new theoretical formulations were developed that did direct research attention on long-range and indirect influences. One of those formulations came from psychology as an adaptation of social learning theory. Another came from sociology and anthropology as an adaptation of theories concerning the nature of symbolic interaction and the influence of language on behavior. The psychological theory is one of both short-term and long-term influences. However, its importance for our present purposes is that it showed how exposure to modeled behavior in mass communication content could provide the individual with a learning source for the adoption of forms of action that could become a more or less permanent part of the person's mode of coping with recurring problems. This formulation has come to be called *modeling theory*. In simplified form, its principal assumptions are as follows:

1. The individual perceives a form of behavior described or portrayed by a character in media content.
2. The individual judges this behavior to be attractive and potentially useful for coping with some personal situation that has arisen or might arise.
3. The portrayed behavior is reproduced by the individual in a relevant personal situation.
4. The reproduced behavior proves useful or effective in coping with the situation, thereby rewarding the individual.
5. With further use, the modeled behavior becomes the person's habitual way of handling that type of situation, unless it is no longer effective and rewarding.

If the individual sees the behavior modeled in media content on numerous occasions, this will probably increase the probability of step 3 above. But the important idea is that the theory does not assume that people see some action in media content and then immediately and uniformly imitate that action. Modeling may come later, and the new behavior may slowly become a part of the person's repertoire, depending upon the frequency of relevant occasions for its use. Thus, in a population, at least some people can be influenced indirectly over a long period of time by behavior forms modeled in media content.

From anthropology came the conclusion that the language used by a given people had a profound influence on the manner in which they perceived, experienced, and acted upon the physical and social worlds around them. Language is a system of labels for aspects of reality, and the way in which we experience that reality depends upon the way we divide it up, establish cultural conventions for meaning, and use those conventions to interpret the world around us. Sociologists have very similar theories that emphasize the meanings attached to symbols by people through shared agreements that shape our interactions with others, the way we think about other people, society as a whole, and ourselves. These theories are very complex and their full range of ideas cannot be expressed in a few sentences. However, the central idea is *meaning*. We respond toward any situation or object in terms of its meaning, as we interpret it. In large part, our personal meanings come to us through participation in our language community. We engage in the process of communication and learn the labels and associated meanings for everything with which we have to cope. The mass media are an important part of those processes of communication in modern society, and they can play a significant role in shaping and stabilizing the meanings we experience for the symbols of our language. Those meanings, in turn, shape our behaviors toward those aspects of the social and physical order that are labeled by our words. We will use the term *meaning theory* to refer to these rather complex ideas. In summary form, the principal propositions of meaning theory are as follows:

1. The individual perceives a situation described or portrayed in media content.
2. That situation is labelled by a standardized symbol or symbols from the shared language.
3. The media content effectively links the label and the portrayed meaning for the individual.
4. By such presentations, the media can establish new meanings, extend older ones to include new elements, substitute alternative meanings for older ones, or stabilize the language conventions concerning the shared meanings for symbols in the language community.

5. Since language (standardized labels and their shared meanings) is a critical factor shaping perception, interpretation, and decisions concerning action, the media can have powerful, indirect and long-term effects.

Thus, a medium like television can show us how to interpret such labels as "women," "black people," "sexual attractiveness," and a host of other terms. It is difficult to assess the influence of the media in this respect within the format of an experiment, a one-shot survey, or even a content analysis of media messages. Nevertheless, it is probably in terms of such indirect and long-term influences that the media exercise their greatest influence.

Generally, then, the accumulation of research on the process and effects of mass communication has led us from the simplistic assumptions of the magic bullet theory through the complexities of the selective influence theories and into theories of long-range and indirect influences. Literally thousands of studies have played a part in this transformation. But among those many investigations only a few stand out as milestones. In the chapters that follow, those studies that have made particularly important contributions have been summarized. Some were experiments; others were done with the survey method; at least one represents a clinical approach. In some cases they were not single studies, but a set of closely related research efforts representing a single program. And, as we pointed out earlier, some contributed to the growth of theory we have outlined; others brought innovative improvements in methodology; still others shaped public thinking about mass communication in significant ways. At least a few did all three.

NOTES AND REFERENCES

1. Melvin L. De Fleur and Everette E. Dennis, *Understanding Mass Communication* (Boston: Houghton Mifflin, 1981), p. 389.
2. Karl Marx, *Capital*, ed. by Friederich Engels (New York: International Publishers, 1967). This is a modern English translation of original 19th-century work.
3. Ferdinand Tönnies, *Community and Society* (Gemeinschaft und Gesellschaft), trans. by Charles P. Loomis (East Lansing: Michigan State University Press, 1957). This is an English translation of the original 19th-century work.
4. J. John Palen, *The Urban World* (New York: McGraw-Hill, 1975), p. 3.
5. Phillip Mauser and Leo Schnore, *The Study of Urbanization* (New York: John Wiley & Sons, 1965), p. 7.

6. Auguste Comte, *The Positive Philosophy,* trans. by Harriet Martineau (London: George Bell and Sons, 1915), p. 293. This is an English translation of the original 19th-century work.

7. Ferdinand Tönnies, op. cit.

8. Daniel Lerner, *The Passing of Traditional Society* (New York: The Free Press, 1958).

9. Melvin L. De Fleur and Sandra Ball-Rokeach, *Theories of Mass Communication,* 4th ed. (New York: Longman Inc., 1982). See Chapter 2, "Society and the Mass Press."

10. E. G. Boring, *A History of Experimental Psychology* (New York: Appleton-Century-Crofts, 1929), p. 279.

11. Emile Durkheim, *Suicide, A Study in Sociology* (Englewood Cliffs, N. J.: Prentice-Hall, 1968). First published in French in 1897.

12. The social survey in its modern sense is usually thought of as beginning with the work of Frederic Le Play, in his *Ouvriers Européens* (1855) or with Charles Booth's 17-volume *Life and Labour of the People of London* (produced between 1891 and 1897). For discussions of both works, see Pitirim Sorokin, *Contemporary Sociological Theories* (New York: Harper and Brothers, 1928).

13. David Riesman, *The Lonely Crowd* (New Haven, Conn.: Yale University Press, 1950).

14. Gustav Le Bon, *The Crowd: A Study of the Popular Mind* (London: Ernest Benn, Ltd., 1896).

2
the payne fund studies: the effects of movies on children

During the 1920s, the motion picture industry suddenly thrust itself into the lives of virtually everyone in the United States. What was this new medium and what influence was it having on those who consumed its products? It was these questions that helped bring into existence one of the largest research projects ever undertaken in an effort to understand the relationship between a medium and a particular audience. Two additional trends taking place in the United States were to play important parts in establishing mass communication research as a field of scientific study. One was the increasing emphasis on the scientific method as a proper strategy for investigation in such fields as sociology, psychology, and education. The other was the extremely rapid rise in concern about the influence of the new motion picture industry. To understand why the first major scientific assessment of the effects of a mass medium was undertaken in the late 1920s, these two trends need to be understood.

One important factor of the times was the maturation of the social sciences. Following World War I, the social sciences began to undergo an important transformation. Increasing attention was being given to the use of quantitative research techniques. The trend was given a boost when procedures were devised for the measurement of aspects of individual human behavior that had previously been thought to be ephemeral. For example, Emory S. Bogardus began the movement to assess racial and ethnic attitudes with his "social distance scale" that was first published in 1924.[1] This was soon followed by the more sophisticated work of Thurstone and Chave with their "equal appearing intervals" scale for measuring almost any kind of attitude.[2]

The 1920s brought statistics to social science research. Important new techniques based on probability had been invented by mathematicians. These were advocated in journals, books, and courses by leading psychologists and sociologists of the period who showed the applications of sampling, measures of central tendency, correlation, and probability to behavioral research problems.[3] Similar transformations had been taking place in educational research in addition to other social sciences.

It was a controversial time and many traditional social scientists resisted the trend. Critics charged that the move toward quantification was merely an attempt to "ape" the physical sciences in a shameless grab for a share in the prestige of those sciences. They pronounced that the emphasis on numbers would "dehumanize" the study of human behavior; it would create mind-boggling accumulations of meaningless facts and it would destroy efforts to build insightful theories. But in spite of these gloomy predictions, the trend continued. By the end of the decade, the scientific perspective, much as we know it today, had taken a strong foothold in both psychology and sociology.

During the same period, American movies took over the world film market. The new medium got its start as the century changed. At first movies were little more than amusing novelties—pictures that appeared to move. By the end of the first decade, nickelodeons were attracting millions of unsophisticated viewers with slapstick films of short duration. By the time of World War I, the movies had become a widely accepted form of family entertainment. It was in the 1920s, however, that motion pictures matured into a major mass medium that was a part of the life of almost every citizen. Hollywood—previously a rather drab village on the suburban fringes of Los Angeles—became the glamour capital of the world. Its film studios ground out a veritable tidal wave of films (hundreds a year) to satisfy the insatiable demands of the public for the new form of entertainment. Its stars represented fantasy success stories that fascinated shop girls and factory workers across the nation. Obscure people were "discovered" by the studios and propelled into instant fame and fortune. Millions were eager to learn of the smallest details of the stars' lives. They became gods and goddesses, adored by publics eager to pay to see their features projected silently on the screen in black-and-white. It was the American Dream in a new form, and it rivalled even the most fanciful rags-to-riches stories of earlier times. By the end of the decade, sound tracks were added, making the movies even more attractive. Theaters had grown larger and more opulent as ticket sales soared.

Going to the movies was a frequent event for most families—they were great fun. Also, there were very few alternatives for inexpensive recreation. Homes had neither radios nor television sets. Some had pianos and wind-up victrolas; a few even had books. But for the majority of families with limited means, taking in a motion picture was an enjoyable and affordable evening out. For those of dating and courting age, movies were made to order: couples in dark theaters could do more than just watch the films. For children, the Saturday matinee was the high point of existence. Many a youngster behaved reasonably well for days in a row on the promise that he or she could go to the show with the other kids on Saturday afternoon.

All of these attractions had caused motion picture attendance to rise dramatically over a very short period of time. Data on movie attendance were not systematically gathered before 1922. During that year, some 40 million tickets were sold every week in the United States. By the end of the decade, the figure had more than doubled to 90 million! Among the movie-goers in 1929 were an estimated 40 million minors, and among those were approximately 17 million children under the age of fourteen.[4]

The content of the motion pictures produced in the 1920s was not much different than the content of movies today. There was less bare skin, sex, and blood, but the themes were very similar. Edgar Dale made an exhaustive study of the content of 1,500 films of the period.[5] As we will note later in greater detail, their content could be grouped into ten major thematic categories. However, a mere three of these categories—love, crime and sex—accounted for nearly three-fourths of the total!

Adults during the period did not quite know what to make of it all. In a single decade, the startling new medium had burgeoned into a national preoccupation. In a society that had barely emerged from the Victorian Age, the love, sex, and crime themes that dominated the films seemed to many to pose troublesome challenges to established moral standards. Above all, their great concern was what the movies were doing to the nation's children. A well-known educator of the time summarized the issues in the following terms:

> Motion pictures are not understood by the present generation of adults. They are new; they make an enormous appeal to children; and they present ideas and situations which parents may not like. Consequently when parents think of the welfare of their children who are exposed to these compelling situations, they wonder about the effects of the pictures upon the ideals and behavior of the children. Do the pictures really influence children in any direction? Are their conduct, ideals and attitudes affected by the movies? Are the scenes which are objectionable to adults understood by children, or at least by very young children? Do children eventually become sophisticated and grow superior to pictures? Are the emotions of children harmfully excited? In short, just what effect do motion pictures have upon children of different ages?[6]

Thus, the situation at the time was not unlike that faced by parents in the 1960s, when television had just emerged as a new national medium with a huge audience of children. The public was deeply concerned about effects and it wanted answers.

By the mid 1920s, pressure began to mount on the motion picture industry. Numerous editorials, sermons, magazine articles, and other forms of public criticism raised questions and made charges that the movies were a negative influence on children. It became increasingly clear that research was needed. Social scientists were seeking opportunities to undertake assessments of the influence of movies on children. In 1928, William H. Short, Executive Director of the Motion Picture Research Council, invited a group of university psychologists, sociologists, and educators to design a series of studies assessing the influence of the movies on children; they responded enthusiastically. There was no government agency to which they could turn to obtain funds for such research, as there would be at a later time. However, a private philanthropic foundation (The Payne Fund) agreed to provide financial support. The end result was a series of thirteen specific studies, done by well-known researchers, on various aspects of the influence of the movies on children. The investigations, known as the Payne Fund Studies, were conducted over a three-year period from 1929 to 1932. They were published in the early 1930s in ten volumes. These classic works have recently been reprinted by the Arno Press and the New York Times (who generously provided a set of the reprints to the authors for purposes of the present book).

In retrospect, then, it was the coming together of two major social changes in the American society—the development of a more precise research capability in the social sciences, and the deepening public concern over the mushrooming growth of the movies—that gave birth to the scientific study of mass communication. As we noted earlier, scholars had long been concerned with the influence of mass communication on individuals and society. However, this was largely in the context of "unmasking" the influence of propaganda, rather than in terms of uncovering cause–effect relationships within the framework of science. The Payne Fund Studies, therefore, represent the first major effort to bring such perspectives, strategies, and techniques to bear on the influence of a major medium on a specific category of people. In the section that follows, we present a brief summary of the individual studies.

OVERVIEW OF THE PAYNE FUND STUDIES

The question of influences of the motion pictures on children was posed in a variety of terms by the researchers who worked on the Payne Fund Studies. Over a dozen major investigations were undertaken simultaneously. Each was of relatively large scale; each had quite different goals. From the perspective of today, the majority of these studies are mainly of historical interest, in the sense that their findings would not be useful for understanding the influence of contemporary movies on modern youth. However, they all played a part in the development of mass communication research as a field of scientific investigation. Several of the studies remain important because they addressed problems that are still under active investigation today. It was these studies that provided a matrix of findings from which simple theoretical perspectives emerged, to be used in subsequent investigations for many years.

From the standpoint of their objectives, the Payne Fund Studies fall into two rather broad categories. In one category the goals are to assess the content of the films and determine the size and composition of their audiences. The second category attempts to assess the effects on those audiences of their exposures to the themes and messages of the motion pictures. There were several kinds of major effects under study. Stated briefly, these were: acquisition of information, change in attitudes, stimulation of emotions, harm to health, erosion of moral standards, and influence on conduct. In the paragraphs that follow, each of the specific investigations is described in very brief terms to give a more complete overview of the goals and scope of this pioneering research series.

The Audience and Content of the Films

No actual records of movie attendance by age-level were available during the period of the studies. To gain an understanding of the size and composition of the youthful audience, Edgar Dale, a well-known educator, used several different strategies and information sources to make estimates. Census data were, of course, available for every state and for the nation as a whole. The problem was to determine what proportion of the population at various age-levels attended the movies, and how often. Dale made studies of actual movie attendance in over fifty Ohio communities in order to estimate the size and composition of their youthful audiences. He then used these data as a basis of projection for the nation as a whole. He found that even children of five to eight years were going to the movies with some frequency. Children of school age attended much more often; in fact, they went more frequently than adults. Boys attended more often than girls. The main finding was that on the average, children in 1929 and 1930 went to the movies once a week.[7] In a society that did not yet understand motion pictures and their potential influences on children, these figures caused considerable concern.

What did these children see? Again, a study by Dale provided clear answers.[8] He reviewed, classified and analyzed 1500 films. Five hundred of these had been produced in 1920, another 500 in 1925, and the remaining 500 in 1930. He was able to classify their content into the following ten categories: crime, sex, love, mystery, war, children, history, travel, comedy, and social propaganda. Not only were the general themes of the stories studied, but their locales or settings; the nature of their heroes or heroines; the actors' clothing styles; their portrayals of how people met, loved and married; how they engaged in crime; used vulgarity; consumed liquor and tobacco; and pursued goals identified as important in the films. In other words, it was a large-scale, systematic and thorough content analysis of motion pictures produced and seen during a decade. The results were scarcely reassuring to critics of the movies. Over three-fourths of the films dealt with only three thematic categories—crime, sex, and love. More wholesome themes, such as travel, children's stories, and history, represented only an insignificant proportion of the total. The use of tobacco and liquor (in a period of prohibition) was openly portrayed.

Acquiring Information

To study the retention of factual information presented in motion pictures, P. W. Holaday and George D. Stoddard conducted a study of over 3,000 children and adults.[9] It took them three years to complete their work. Seventeen full-length motion pictures were used as stimulus material. They tested audiences on details of the plots, and on various kinds of information presented in the films. They found that even eight-year-old children acquired a substantial number of ideas from the movies (about 60 percent of the total learned by adults). In fact, retention of facts by all age-groups was surprisingly high. Subjects were tested six weeks and three months after seeing the films. In some cases, retention was greater than the six month period, suggesting a so-called "sleeper effect" that would be discovered again later (pp. 128; 158). The investigators concluded that movies provided a special learning format that led to unusually high retention of factual material, compared to the acquisition of facts in standard laboratory memory experiments.

Changing Attitudes

One of the more sophisticated investigations of the series was that of Ruth C. Peterson and L. L. Thurstone.[10] Their purpose was to assess the construction of attitude measures. Generally, the attitudes under study were the orientations of children toward selected ethnic groups, racial categories and social issues. Regular commercial motion pictures were used as stimulus material. Children's attitudes were measured before exposure to the film or films and then re-measured with a parallel instrument after seeing the picture material. In many cases, attitude change was found. The details of this study and its implications for the research trends that it stimulated will be discussed more fully in a later section of the present chapter.

Stimulating Emotions

Studies of the capacity of films to arouse children's emotions were conducted by W. S. Dysinger and Christian A. Ruckmick.[11] They used both laboratory techniques and autobiographical case studies to assess the emotional impact of films. Several age categories of children were observed both in a lab setting and in actual theaters while viewing motion pictures. The 150 subjects used were selected to represent "average" intelligence levels. Some adults were also studied for comparison purposes. It was a dramatic form of research for the time. Electrodes and mechanical devices were attached to youthful viewers in order to record their galvanic skin responses and changes in their breathing patterns stimulated by the film content. These neurophysiological changes were used as indices of emotional arousal. Scenes of danger, conflict, or tragedy produced the greatest effects. Romantic and erotic scenes didn't seem to do much for very young children, but they blew the sixteen-year-olds off the graphs! Generally, males and females reacted similarly. By comparison, adults showed little emotional arousal to any of the scenes. The authors concluded that adults had learned to "discount" the films as fantasy, but children experienced substantial emotional arousal.

Harming Health

To study the movies as a potential danger to health, psychologists Samuel Renshaw, Vernon L. Miller, and Dorothy P. Marquis, devised ingenious experiments on children's sleep.[12] A total of 170 boys and girls in an Ohio state institution for juveniles participated in studies of sleep "motility." Special beds and other apparatus were used to measure how much they tossed and turned after seeing various categories of films. First, the researchers studied normal sleep patterns. Then they exposed their young subjects to motion pictures before bed time. A variety of controls and conditions were used to explore different kinds of influences on sleep. Briefly, certain kinds of films did result in disturbed sleep. Such consequences, the authors claimed, could be detrimental to normal health and growth.

Eroding Moral Standards

An elaborate study of the influence of motion pictures on standards of morality was conducted by Charles C. Peters.[13] His point of departure was the sociological theory of William Graham Sumner, whose analyses of folk-ways and mores were published at the beginning of the present century. Sumner's work on the nature and origins of such norms was so thorough that it has never been replicated and still stands as the definitive statement.[14] The goal of Peters' study was to determine whether specific kinds of actions or situations portrayed in the films paralleled or were in conflict with the standards of morality currently prevailing among several categories of subjects. He used written descriptions of movie scenes that included such actions as female aggressiveness in love-making (kissing and caressing in public), the portrayal of democratic practices and attitudes, and different forms of treatment of children by parents. Five categories of people responded to these descriptions in the preliminary standardization of the morality scale. These were college seniors, college faculty members and their wives, socially elite young women, factory working boys, and factory working girls. The result was a scale for "measuring the mores" of different kinds of people. The scale was then used to assess different patterns of approval and disapproval of samples of conduct taken from the films. Peters gathered such responses from seventeen different categories of subjects whose backgrounds ranged from poorly educated workers to upper-status professionals. The general conclusion from this complex study was that many of the depictions presented in the movies, especially in scenes of crime and sex (two of the most frequent themes) were contrary to the mores of the groups under study. Such findings were scarcely comforting to those who feared that the movies were providing unwanted influences on children.

Influencing Conduct

As might be suspected, the issue of motion picture influences on conduct received more attention than any other specific topic. Three separate studies were devoted to the impact of films on various forms of behavior. Each of these deserves separate comment. Two of these investigations will be discussed in some detail following the overviews.

Frank R. Shuttleworth and Mark A. May contrasted children who attended movies frequently ("fans") with a comparison group who seldom or never attended.[15] The study attempted to assess general conduct, deportment in school, and reputation among peers. In all, some 1400 children were studied. For the most part it was a questionnaire study with a variety of paper and pencil questionnaires, rating scales, and other instruments used by both the children and their teachers. The investigators found that movie "fans" were usually rated lower in deportment by their teachers than those children who did not attend the movies frequently. The fans also had less positive reputations; they did worse in their academic work, and they were not as popular with their classmates as the comparison group was.

One of the most interesting of the conduct studies was an investigation by sociologist Herbert Blumer that probed the influences of motion pictures on general day-to-day behavior.[16] In this work he depended primarily on the autobiographical method in which subjects recalled earlier influences of the movies on their lives and on specific activities, such as play, modes of dress, hairstyles, and forms of communication. The autobiographical technique had been worked out to probe specific kinds of influences, including how the films had influenced the subjects' moods, emotions, interpretations of love and romance, ambitions, and temptations to behave in socially disapproved ways. Several hundred college students wrote such autobiographies, as did hundreds of high school youths, factory workers and office personnel. Overall, the accounts seemed to indicate rather clearly that the content of the movies served as substantial influences on children. The subjects reported that they had imitated the movie characters openly in beautification, mannerism, and attempts at love-making.

The movies had also stimulated a great deal of daydreaming and fantasy. In particular, the films had aroused strong emotions in their youthful audiences, including terror, fright, sorrow and pathos. Although this type of research was called "exploratory" by the investigator, and even though it was based on relatively unsophisticated methods, it remains one of the more significant studies of the series. Certainly, its findings reinforced the alarms raised by critics of the movies.

A widely discussed study of conduct was that of Herbert Blumer and another sociologist, Phillip Hauser.[17] Their central focus was on ways in which motion picture content stimulated children to commit acts of delinquency and crime. It was a wide-ranging study that included case histories, questionnaires, essays and life histories of delinquency-prone youngsters. Reports on movie experiences were gathered from reformatory inmates, ex-convicts on parole, female delinquents in a training school, grade school boys and girls in high-delinquency neighborhoods, and several other categories of children and adolescents. Material was also obtained from the heads of penal institutions and other authorities. The methods and strategies used in this study have come under wide criticism from criminologists and specialists in deviant behavior. Nevertheless, at the time, the findings caused considerable concern. According to the authors, motion pictures played a direct role in shaping the delinquent and criminal careers of substantial segments of those studied. Once again, the worst fears of the public were confirmed. Movies appeared to be driving at least some children to a life of crime!

As can be seen from this brief overview, each of the investigations in the Payne Fund Studies was a work of substantial scope. Taken together, they constitute a research effort which would not be matched in size and diversity until forty years later, when the federal government funded the studies of the influence of televised violence of children. The Payne Fund Studies, therefore, remain one of the largest scientific investigations of the influence of mass communication ever undertaken. In order to see in more detail the theoretical assumptions, the methodological strategies and techniques, and some of the major findings, the sections that follow present more detailed summaries of two of the Payne Fund investigations.

STUDIES OF SOCIAL ATTITUDES, GENERAL CONDUCT, AND DELINQUENT BEHAVIOR

While the highlights of the research by Peterson and Thurstone and by Herbert Blumer have been summarized above, these particular studies offer significant lessons regarding the development of both research methods and theory concerning the effects of mass communication. For this reason, the separate investigations are reviewed more fully in the sections that follow.

Motion Pictures and the Social Attitudes of Children

The purpose of the set of experiments by Peterson and Thurstone was to study the degree to which commercial motion pictures could change the attitudes of youthful subjects toward specific topics. Under investigation were attitudes toward people of different nationalities and races, and attitudes toward socially significant topics, such as crime, war, capital punishment, prohibition and the treatment of criminals. The subjects were school children ranging from fourth-graders to college students.

The general strategy was straightforward. An initial measure was achieved by using a paired-comparisons scale developed around the particular attitude under study. The assessment was done in school classrooms in small communities near Chicago, with the cooperation of the authorities. The students participating were then given special tickets to the local movie theater. Since the experiments were done in communities with only one theater, the subjects naturally attended the right movie, using their free tickets. The film seen by the subjects was one that had been specially selected by the experimenters and was being shown by prior arrangement with the local exhibitor.

To obtain suitable films, the investigators had examined more than 600 candidate pictures. Sixteen were selected because they presented particularly favorable or unfavorable views toward one of the attitude topics under investigation. For example, *All Quiet on the Western Front* was an antiwar film. *Birth of a Nation* was (in many respects) anti-Negro. Others were pro-Chinese, pro-Jewish, and so on.

Approximately two weeks after the first attitude assessment and the next day after seeing the film, the attitudes of the subjects were again measured. No direct connection was made between the attitude assessments and the movie experience. Controls were used to ensure that only subjects who had actually seen the film were included in the final determination of attitude change. (It can be noted in passing that no attempt was made to use control groups).

Within this general framework, two dozen experiments were completed. Some studied the effect of a *single* film on changing attitudes. Others studied the *cumulative* effect of two and even three pictures dealing with the same theme. Finally, a number of studies assessed the *persistence* of attitude changes over long periods of time. These periods ranged from two to nineteen months.

The Effect of Single Pictures   In a series of 11 separate experiments, the ability of a single exposure to a motion picture to modify attitudes was assessed. Under study were attitudes toward Germans, war, gambling, prohibition, the Chinese, capital punishment, treatment of criminals, and "the Negro." Each experiment followed the general strategy outlined earlier. The numbers of subjects ranged from 133 in a study of attitudes toward Germans to 522 in an investigation of attitudes toward the punishment of criminals. Because of the number of the experiments it is difficult to discuss the results in a simple way. However, in general, some of the experiments produced substantial attitude change. In others the subjects did not significantly change their orientations.

Two examples illustrate the nature of the results where significant change occurred. In Geneva, Illinois, 182 children in grades 9 through 12 saw a film entitled *Son of the Gods*. It was strongly pro-Chinese. The story concerned Sam Lee, a nice young Chinese-American who had been raised by an older Chinese man. The interpretation of Chinese life and culture was positive, and the characters presented were sympathetic. Figure 1 shows the results. The "before" mean was 6.72 and the "after" mean was 5.50. Statistically, a difference of 1.22 is 17.5 times its probable error. In short, there was a statistically significant attitude change in a favorable direction.

Another experiment showed even more striking results. The film *Birth of a Nation* (updated from its original form with the addition of a sound track) was shown to 434 high school children in Crystal Lake, Illinois. The film portrays Negroes in negative terms and is considered an anti-Negro

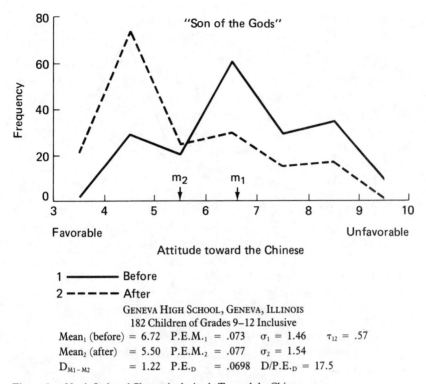

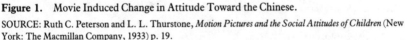

$\text{Mean}_1 \text{ (before)} = 6.72 \quad \text{P.E.M.}_1 = .073 \quad \sigma_1 = 1.46 \quad \tau_{12} = .57$

$\text{Mean}_2 \text{ (after)} = 5.50 \quad \text{P.E.M.}_2 = .077 \quad \sigma_2 = 1.54$

$D_{M1-M2} = 1.22 \quad \text{P.E.}_D = .0698 \quad D/\text{P.E.}_D = 17.5$

Figure 1.   Movie Induced Change in Attitude Toward the Chinese.

SOURCE: Ruth C. Peterson and L. L. Thurstone, *Motion Pictures and the Social Attitudes of Children* (New York: The Macmillan Company, 1933) p. 19.

statement. As it turned out, few of the subjects in the experiment had known or even seen a Negro. Figure 2 shows that at the outset the subjects were relatively favorable, with a mean score of 7.46. The mean after the film had shifted to 5.93, a more negative position. A difference of 1.48 is 25.5 times its probable error. Clearly, this particular movie had a substantial impact on the attitudes of its audience.

Cumulative Effects   A series of experiments were conducted in which subjects viewed two or more pictures dealing with the same issue between their before and after measures. In these studies, 750 children in grades 6–12 were in the various experiments. They were all residents of Mooseheart, a community for children of deceased members of a national organization. Two attitudes were under study. In one set of experiments, the subjects saw two antiwar films—*All Quiet on the Western Front* and *Journey's End*. In another set of experiments, subjects saw three films

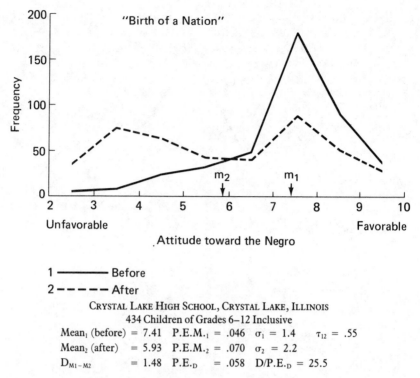

Figure 2. Movie Induced Change in Attitude toward "The Negro." *

SOURCE: Ruth C. Peterson and L. L. Thurstone, *Motion Pictures and the Social Attitudes of Children* (New York: The Macmillan Company, 1933) p. 37.

* Note the reversal of the positions of "Favorable" and "Unfavorable" from those of Figure 1. This was done in the original.

dealing with the punishment of criminals. These were *The Big House, Numbered Men,* and *The Criminal Code.* Each was a relatively sympathetic treatment of the plight of men in prison.

Overall, the results of the cumulative studies were clear. The films shown singly had minor or no effects in terms of attitude change. However, two or three films on the same topic produced significant attitude modification among the subjects under study, toward the view expressed in the films.

The Persistence of Attitude Changes In 11 of the experiments selected from the studies of both single and multiple exposures, follow-ups were conducted at various intervals. In each case, parallel-form attitude scales measured the persistence of the changes achieved in the earlier experiment. The results of these studies can be seen in Table 1. The authors concluded that the effects of motion pictures on the social attitudes of children could persist for considerable periods of time. In one case, 60 percent of the original change was retained a year and a half later! In another case, the attitudes of the subjects had changed even more six months later than they had immediately following exposure to the film (a "sleeper" effect).

The general conclusions reached by Peterson and Thurstone were that the attitudes of children were definitely influenced by some films. These effects tended to be greater for younger children. Seeing two and three

Table 1 The Persistence of Attitude Changes

Place	Film	No. in Exp. Group	Interval	Per Cent of Effect Remaining
Watseka, Illinois	*The Criminal Code*	257	2½ months	87%
Watseka, Illinois	*The Criminal Code*	195	9 months	78%
Geneva, Illinois	*Son of the Gods*	117	5 months	62%
Geneva, Illinois	*Son of the Gods*	76	19 months	60%
Crystal Lake, Illinois	*The Birth of a Nation*	350	5 months	62%
Genoa, Illinois	*Four Sons*	87	6 months	123%
Paxton, Illinois	*All Quiet on the Western Front*	138	8 months	A change in the opposite direction.
Mooseheart, Illinois	*All Quiet on the Western Front* and *Journey's End*	572	2 months	52%
Mooseheart, Illinois	*All Quiet on the Western Front* and *Journey's End*	571	4 months	22%
Mooseheart, Illinois	*The Big House, Numbered Men,* and *The Criminal Code*	559	2 months	100%
Mooseheart, Illinois	*The Big House, Numbered Men,* and *The Criminal Code*	549	4 months	111%

SOURCE: Ruth C. Peterson and L. L. Thurstone, *Motion Pictures and the Social Attitudes of Children* (New York: The Macmillan Company, 1933) p. 63.

pictures treating the same topic in the same general way achieved greater results than was the case with a single film. Finally, attitude changes resulting from exposure to motion pictures can persist for long periods of time.[18]

These attitude change studies were of lasting importance for several reasons. The study of quantitative attitude scales was in its infancy; however, the measurement procedures used by the investigators were based on relatively sophisticated theories derived from the Law of Comparative Judgement. This formulation still remains the underlying rationale for attitude measurement. Thus, the movie studies were a highly visible application of the new technology to a socially significant issue. In addition, the experimental format used in the studies followed the model of science that was being enthusiastically adopted by psychology and sociology. For these reasons, and because the studies showed clear results, the Peterson and Thurstone research made a deep impact, both on the public and the scientific community.

Movies and Conduct

In a very different type of research, Herbert Blumer collected autobiographical accounts from more than 1,800 young men and women, adolescents, and children. The general purpose of the study was to find out how motion pictures had influenced their childhood play, their attempts to imitate various elements of adult behavior, their daydreams, emotional experiences, and general lifestyles. The goals of the research were sweeping. The methodology was *qualitative* rather than quantitative, and the findings can only be regarded as "exploratory" or "suggestive." Yet, in many ways, this is one of the most interesting of all of the Payne Fund Studies because it shows in rich detail the way in which the 1,823 participants in the study thought that the movies had influenced their lives.

The researcher began his investigation with a preliminary study to help design a general format for the personal autobiographies. Students in university classes were "asked merely to write in as natural and truthful a manner, accounts of their prior experiences with movies, as best as these could be recalled."[19] These were extensive documents that required several weeks to prepare. From these accounts, Blumer constructed a set of guidelines for the preparation of autobiographies by the main body of his subjects. These guidelines focused the subject on his or her interest in the movies during childhood. They asked the subject to recall influences on emotions or moods, patterns of imitation of the actors, the subject's remembered interest in love and romantic films, ambitions and temptations which, in recollection, had been aroused by motion pictures.

These accounts were gathered from 634 university students, 481 college and junior college youths, 583 high school students, 67 office workers and 58 factory workers. Considerable care was taken to preserve anonymity, ensure honesty, and encourage full disclosure. The statements were checked for internal consistency and what we would today call "face validity."

To these personal autobiographies the investigator added information obtained in personal interviews with 135 of the subjects. In addition, information was derived from conversations among groups of students as they discussed the movies. Finally, data were obtained from structured questionnaires administered to 1,200 grade school children in the Chicago area.

This mass of material was not reduced to quantitative form. As the author explained it, the general plan of procedure followed in the report was to *let the facts speak for themselves*. This was accomplished by the liberal use of quotations from the autobiographies and general descriptions of the central themes that seemed to emerge from the materials.

Influences on Childhood Play   Nearly all of the subjects studied reported that the movies had been a rich source from which they drew ideas for play. They liberally impersonated screen characters in their games of "Cowboys and Indians" and "Cops and Robbers." Depending upon what they had seen that week they became Robin Hood, Joan of Arc, Rudolph Valentino, a royal knight, a princess in a far-off land, or an African big game hunter. At other times they played at being a daring fighter pilot, Mata Hari, Dracula, Mary Queen of Scots, or the Phantom of the Opera.

> *Male, 19, Jewish, white, college sophomore:* In my childhood it was common for one to imitate consciously heroes of the screen. For instance, I would climb the lone tree that was in the yard of the Catholic school near us and hang by one hand or hammer my chest shouting "Tarzan" and the like. Jumping over fences on a run as did the heroes of the screen was usual in my young life. Fighting with one another, and after conquering him, placing one foot on his chest and raising our arms to the sky as Tarzan did was also common.[20]

Not only had the subjects impersonated actors and their screen roles, but they modeled their games on the plots seen in the pictures. Thus, one day some of the kids would attack a fort with wooden swords and "pretend" shields that were really the tops of wash boilers or garbage cans. The defenders would resist with lances made of sticks and helmets devised from old cooking pots. Auto races could be recreated among makeshift cars devised from apple crates; cavalry charges seen on the screen could be relived on the backs of trusty steeds that were really mops and brooms. Or, daring aviators could duel in the skies over Germany.

A boy of 11 years: The picture I saw was *The Dawn Patrol.* After I came home, we played it. I pretended I was Richard Barthelmess. I pretended I was bombing the German ammunition dumps. Then I went over the airports and bombed the planes and killed the men. Then three German planes came after me. Von Richter, the best German aviator, came up too, and I shot him down and shot his pal also. But the other aviator came from the back and shot me.[21]

Girls of the period pretended to be the pampered darlings of rich parents, with dozens of suitors and fantastic wardrobes. They acted out the part of Juliet, or that of beautiful captives of handsome sheiks. Generally, costumes, weapons, and other artifacts seen in the films were improvised in addition to behavior patterns and social relationships. In short, the movies had a complex set of influences on children's play. The subjects, on the whole, recalled these influences with warmth and pleasure. Whether or not such effects were harmful in any way is not clear. In all likelihood, they were not.

Imitation by Adolescents   Motion picture influences on childhood play were largely in the realm of fantasy and make-believe. Among adolescent movie-goers, however, a somewhat different type of influence was widespread. Forms of conduct such as beautification, personal mannerisms, and social techniques were imitated from movie portrayals and incorporated into the day-to-day behavior patterns of youthful audiences. The styles of dress and hair arrangements used by female stars in the films were a particular source of fascination for female adolescents. In searching for means to bring beauty into their own lives, they experimented enthusiastically with what they had seen on the screen.

Female, 19, Jewish, white, college sophomore: I remember that I got my first striking illumination through the movies of the difference clothes may make in appearance. It was Daddy Long-Legs where Mary Pickford paraded for five scenes, bare-legged, in dark brown cast-offs, pig-tailed, and freckled-faced, good, sweet, but hardly beautiful; and then in the final scene, after a visit from Daddy and a bath in milk, with the curls down, the gangly knees covered, the ankles silk-shod, in pink satin, a pearl-studded dress, a re-born gorgeous queen, she emerged as striking as the caterpillar-butterfly transition. At home that night I tentatively hinted about putting my daily glass of milk to better use, wound my straight black hair in tortuous curl papers, draped myself in red gauze, and compared effects. Since then I have carefully studied, attempted, and compared the effects of these past mistresses of the art of dressing and make-up. They are always first with the latest, my most reliable guide to styles, colors, accessories, combinations, lines, and general effects.[22]

Another important area of influence was in those mannerisms that become identified as attractive or sophisticated in every age. Thus, the movies taught a generation of males how to light a cigarette in a "manly" manner; how to tip one's hat to a lady in a gallant way; or how to offer her one's arm properly. They taught girls how to purse their lips coyly; how to lower their eyelids enticingly; how to sit gracefully; or how to shed a dainty tear for maximum effect.

The films served also to bring some semblance of social polish to upwardly mobile youths who might not have had other role models in their daily lives.

Male, 21, white, college senior: As I got into high school and into my sixteenth and seventeenth year I began to use the movies as a school of etiquette. I began to observe the table manners of the actors in the eating scenes. I watched for the proper way in which to conduct oneself at a night club, because I began to have ideas that way. The fact that the leading man's coat was single-breasted or double-breasted, the number of buttons on it, and the cut of its lapel all influenced me in the choice of my own suits.[23]

The adoption of behavior patterns from adult models is a normal part of the socialization process during childhood and adolescence. The movie stars, however, appeared to be particularly attractive sources from which to obtain modeling influences.

Female, 18, Negro, high-school senior: Movies are the means by which a great many people obtain poise. This is especially true as far as girls are concerned. I am sure I haven't the poise of my movie idols, but I am trying to develop a more ladylike composure as I grow older. My father has caught me several times, as I stood before the mirror trying to tilt my head and hold my arms as the girls on the screen would do. He does not know that I am trying to create that sophisticated manner, which is essential for social success.[24]

Generally, then, the stars and their portrayals were imitated freely by millions of young Americans in the 1920s. In many cases, the forms of beautification, the mannerisms, or the techniques of social adaptation modeled from the movies were but brief experiments that were soon abandoned. In other cases, the people studied felt that these influences had been incorporated more permanently into their daily behavior patterns.

The preoccupation of the films of the period with themes of love and sex has already been noted. Love-making in the movies did not have much attraction for the younger children.

Male, 20, white, college sophomore: Love stories and pictures never held much attraction for me at this time (age 12) . . . Whenever we boys would go to see a love picture and the hero kissed the heroine we would always make a lot of noise and smack our lips very loudly.[25]

Among adolescents, however, the love and romance themes of the movies found an enthusiastic audience. In an era when there were only a limited number of sources from which young people could learn ways of relating to the opposite sex, and especially about techniques of kissing or the meaning of love and romance, the films provided fascinating lessons.

Male, 21, white, college senior: The technique of making love to a girl received considerable of my attention, and it was directly through the movies that I learned to kiss a girl on her ears, neck, and cheeks, as well as on the mouth.[26]

It was, of course, a more innocent time, and "making-love" meant merely kissing and hugging. Nevertheless, the motion pictures were a training vehicle that provided not only models for intimate interpersonal behavior, but media-constructed conceptions of passion, romance, courtship, flirting, and other forms of relationship between males and females.

Daydreaming and Fantasy   The movies were a rich source for adolescent daydreams and fantasies. Two thirds of the autobiographies studied discussed the films as a source of stimulation used during childhood to imagine playing fantastic adult roles: The boys rescued beautiful maidens, danced the tango in smart tuxedos, shot it out with desperados, and drove dog sleds across Alaska. The girls reveled in fabulous wardrobes, toyed with handsome admirers, bedecked themselves with jewels, and succumbed to tall, dark, Latin lovers.

The majority of the audience actually led rather dull lives. It was not unusual, therefore, that the vivid scenes of travel, adventure, glamour, wealth, luxury, success, romance, and heroism depicted in the films would be used in imagination as a basis for Walter Mitty-like constructions of deeply satisfying dreams. Contemporary students of the uses and gratifications provided by media content still pursue this line of inquiry.

Emotional Possession   One of the more pronounced influences of film content of the 1920s on their youthful audiences was termed "emotional possession." The concept refers to a situation where an individual's emotions are aroused so strongly that he or she loses some measure of self-control. Seeing dramatic motion picture portrayals led young audience members to suffer in empathy, cower in horror, or to feel overpowering affection. Such feelings were both strongly stimulated and made manifest in overt behavior (tears, screams, hiding, adulation, and so on) by some forms of communication content.

Powerful responses might be quite difficult to stimulate today among our more media-hardened youthful population. But during the 1920s, being frightened out of one's wits by a movie was a common phenomenon.

Female, 15, white, high-school sophomore: The Phantom of the Opera, with Lon Chaney as the phantom, frightened me more than any other motion picture I have seen. He was made up as the most horrible creature with long teeth, glaring eyes, and a bald head. When he was unmasked by the heroine, I gasped and almost screamed. Although I tried to draw my eyes away from his terrible face, I couldn't; his ugliness was so fascinating. The entire picture was so weird and fantastic that the shivers ran up and down my back. For a long time after that, I dared not go near dark places, particularly the cellar. I did not let anyone else know I was frightened for fear they would call me silly.[27]

Another frequent response to films was to experience grief and sorrow over the plight of a movie character. Two thirds of those who prepared autobiographies recalled such moving emotions vividly. Typical was the following report.

Female, 20, white, college junior: The first picture that I ever cried at was *Uncle Tom's Cabin*, with Marguerite Clarke playing the part of little Eva. I didn't want to cry and tried my best to fight against my emotions, but it was of no use, the tears rolled down just the same. I read the story of *Wings* and in spite of myself I cried over it. When I saw the movie I tried to tell myself that I wouldn't cry as I had already read the book and could have myself steeled against any display of sorrow. It all went well until one of the last scenes and I found myself crying. Most any picture with a touch of pathos to it has me using my handkerchief a great deal.[28]

For some viewers, crying at the movies seemed to have a therapeutic effect. Many reported that they resisted such displays of emotion, but after crying profusely over the agonies portrayed in the plot, they often felt better.

Other Emotional Influences   There were a number of other reported emotional reactions to film content which testified to the strong impact of films on children as they viewed them. Feelings of love and passion were clearly aroused for some. In many cases these emotions were attached to the shadowy figures on the screen as boys and girls fell madly in love with their favorite star. In other cases, the portrayed actions of lovers in the films stimulated strong interpersonal feelings among couples in the audience.

In the gloom of the Fox Theater, I sat with my gang, and I gasped in pleasurable anticipation as the tense moment approached. The hero placed his hands about the heroine's divinely small waist and pulled her half-fiercely toward him. Her beautiful lips parted slightly; he looked into her heavenly eyes with infinite adoration and their kiss was perfect. My response was inevitable. My hand clutched Vera's; we thrilled in ecstasy.[29]

Although the autobiographies do not "contain graphic accounts of physical relationships," the movies clearly stimulated strong desires. Whether or not those pressures led to "the inevitable" is anybody's guess but given the sexual norms of the time, they probably did not. The critics of the movies of the period were sorely concerned that the films were indeed enflaming the "baser passions." The author may have reinforced those concerns when he concluded that "emotional possession induced by passionate love pictures represents an attack on the mores of our contemporary life."[30]

Sheer thrills and generalized excitement were also a part of children's emotional response patterns to the movies. They shouted their relief when the hero escaped from danger; they groaned when things went badly. During the Saturday matinee, with audiences composed almost exclusively of children, whistles, screaming, laughter, cheers, shouts, and big sighs of relief were a normal part of the viewing experience. Nails were bitten, seats were clutched, eyes were covered, and caps were wrung into shreds.

Perhaps the most significant aspect of "emotional possession" in all its forms (according to Blumer) was that it often provided frameworks for perception and behavior choice long after the film had been seen. A familiar example is the reluctance of many children to enter dark rooms or to pass by graveyards at night, after seeing horror films and spook shows. Another familiar example was the young female who derived definitions of romance and courtship mainly from the films. Carrying these conceptualizations into real-life relationships with suitors sometimes led to disappointments. It was this type of long-term and indirect influence that was of concern to the researcher—although it could clearly not be established in an experimental design.

Long-term Influences　In the final sections of his report, Blumer tried to pull together in a general way the long-term and overall influences on children provided by their motion picture viewing. In so doing, he anticipated two theories of mass communication influence which have become more systematically developed in recent years. One is the "meaning" theory of media portrayals advanced by De Fleur and his associates.[31] The other is the modeling theory of Albert Bandura.[32]

Blumer did not have these formulations available at the time. However, in commenting on the role of media portrayals in providing socially constructed meanings for various aspects of reality, he anticipated the central thesis of meaning theory.

> One would expect that movies would be effective in shaping the images which people form of their world and in giving form to the schemes of conduct which they come to develop. Motion pictures depict types of life which are unfamiliar to many people and consequently shape their conceptions of such a life.[33]

In terms of modeling, the author noted that the films "show situations and various forms of conduct in very attractive ways." Because of that attractive quality, social relationships, patterns of behavior, or attitudes and values depicted in the movies provide clear lessons for children to copy—models for imitation and incorporation into one's own lifestyle.

Blumer found evidence in his autobiographies that motion pictures had indeed shaped modes of thinking and interpretation of many aspects of his subjects' worlds. These modes included stereotypes of ethnic and racial groups; of villains and heroes; of rich and poor; of wrongdoers and the righteous, and many other social categories. The movies provided conceptions of war, family life, work, sexual mores, romantic behavior, religious belief, the roles of men and women, parent-child relationships, college life, and hundreds of other social activities and arrangements. These depictions not only served as bases for belief and interpretation regarding activities removed from the lives of the subjects, but as guidelines for daily conduct as subjects actually participated in real-life versions of what had been modeled on the screen.

Overall, then, Blumer's work *The Movies and Conduct* emerges as perhaps the most significant of all of the Payne Fund Studies, in view of its early concern with two processes that have recently become the focus of both theory and research. Both meaning theory and modeling theory are now central to the analysis of the *long-term* influences of the media content on human behavior. We can also note that Blumer's work delved into other aspects of the effects of mass communication. For example, in the context of the motion pictures of the era, he made a very detailed analysis of the uses and gratifications provided by movie content for his youthful subjects. Movies were used in play, as a source of daydreams, as guides to etiquette, dress, mannerisms, and beautification.

The limitations of the research are many by the standards of experimentation and quantification that came to dominate media research in the decades that followed. Yet, those strategies—with their emphasis on stimulus–response conceptions, short-term effects, and point-by-point correspondence between components of a message and specific forms of response —are themselves being seriously questioned today. There is a real possibility that the detailed, subjective, and analytical procedures used by Blumer in his "exploratory study" revealed a greater richness and insight into the effects of the films than the "scientific" studies that were done at the same time.

CONCLUSIONS AND IMPLICATIONS

What can we learn from this fascinating series of studies done when the movies were young? First, we can gain a profound respect for the imagination and diligence of the researchers who designed, conducted, and reported on the individual investigations. These were truly massive research efforts, involving (in total) tens of thousands of subjects. The investigators made use of the best research procedures, strategies, and techniques available at the time. Those strategies ranged from laboratory-type efforts (e.g., those of Dysinger and Ruckmick) with elaborate controls and apparatus, to content analyses, surveys, field experiments, and the autobiographical approach of Blumer.

Interpreting the findings of this massive effort presents a very difficult picture. At the time they seemed relatively clear! The movies did seem to bring new ideas to children; to influence their attitudes; stimulate their emotions; present moral standards different from those of many adults; disturb sleep; and influence interpretations of the world and day-to-day conduct.

These conclusions may well have been quite correct at the time. America was not a media society except in a limited sense during the 1920s. The only mature medium was the newspaper. Radio was only a toy. The movies came with a rush—almost overnight—to delight, frighten, thrill, and fascinate an audience of millions of children who had never seen anything like them. The idea that this new medium, suddenly thrust upon a society just emerging from the Victorian Age, could have profound and visible effects upon such an audience does not seem far-fetched.

This does not mean that the findings of the Payne Fund Studies provide useful guides for understanding media influences on children today. Contemporary society bears only a faint resemblance, in terms of media presence, to the simpler times of the 1920s. Today's children and adolescents are surrounded by media content to a degree unimaginable fifty years ago.

The importance of the Payne Fund Studies lies elsewhere. Clearly, they were the great pioneering effort that established media research as a serious scientific field. They brought together in one extraordinary group of studies a major problem of public concern and the perspectives of young sciences. The fact that various disciplines participated in the research was a harbinger of things to come; the fact that a broad range of topics was studied with many different techniques was also an indicator of future directions.

When the findings of the Payne Fund Studies were published they confirmed the worst fears of the critics of the medium and the movie industry. W. W. Charters, who wrote a volume summarizing the main findings, concluded that "the commercial movies are an unsavory mess," and that "the producers ought to have heart" over their bad influences on children.[34]

Such conclusions played a part in reinforcing the *legacy of fear* that had been kept alive by strident denunciations of the evils of propaganda during the same decade and by the widely held beliefs about the horrors of newspaper influence current during the late-nineteenth century. This legacy of fear was the key factor in bringing public pressure to bear on the movies to "clean up their act." By the early 1930s, the motion picture industry strengthened its Production Code and began enforcing it more rigidly through its Hays Office. After establishing such self-censorship, in which all the major producers cooperated, the movies of the mid and late 1930s altered greatly the degree to which they portrayed socially controversial scenes. The Payne Fund Studies were part of the effort by which this change was achieved.

In summary, the Payne Fund Studies undoubtedly presented a reasonably valid picture of the influences of the movies of the 1920s on the youth of that period. The films were an influence on attitudes; they provided models for behavior; they shaped interpretations of life. They probably had as many prosocial influences (or at least harmless influences) as those that disturbed adults of the time. The Payne Fund Studies were clearly the pioneer studies that established the field of media research within the perspectives of science. They anticipated contemporary interest in meaning theory and the influence of models, and focused the new field on such topics as attitude change, the sleeper effect, uses and gratifications, content analysis, modeling influences, and the social construction of reality. They placed an emphasis on quantitative, experimental, and survey methodologies, but they still made use of more qualitative approaches. Above all, the studies shifted the long-standing pattern of concern on the part of communication scholars with propaganda criticism that represented an earlier rhetorical form of analysis. In these senses, the Payne Fund Studies will remain one of the most significant milestones in the development of mass communication as a scientific field of study.

NOTES AND REFERENCES

1. For a full description of the history of this concept and its measurement, see Emory S. Bogardus, *Social Distance* (Yellow Springs, Ohio: Antioch Press, 1959).

2. L. L. Thurstone and E. J. Chave, *The Measurement of Attitude* (Chicago: The University of Chicago Press, 1929).
3. Basing their ideas on the work of such pioneers as G. Udny Yule and R. A. Fisher, sociologists and psychologists were transforming their fields by advocating quantitative approaches to the study of human behavior. See F. Stuart Chapin, *Field Work and Social Statistics* (New York: The Century Company, 1920); Robert R. Burgess, *Introduction to the Mathematics of Statistics* (Boston: Houghton Mifflin, 1927); Louis L. Thurstone, *The Fundamentals of Statistics* (New York: The Macmillan Company, 1925).
4. Edgar Dale, *Children's Attendance at Motion Pictures* (New York: The Macmillan Company, 1935), pp. 71–72.
5. Edgar Dale, *The Content of Motion Pictures* (New York: The Macmillan Company, 1935), p. 8.
6. W. W. Charters, *Motion Pictures and Youth: A Summary* (New York: The Macmillan Company, 1933), p. v.
7. Edgar Dale, *Children's Attendance at Motion Pictures* (New York: The Macmillan Company, 1935), pp. 30–73. See also Henry James Forman, *Our Movie Made Children* (New York: The Macmillan Company, 1935), pp. 12–27.
8. Edgar Dale, *The Content of Motion Pictures* (New York: The Macmillan Company, 1935). Note especially Table 2, p. 17.
9. P. W. Holaday and George D. Stoddard, *Getting Ideas From the Movies* (New York: The Macmillan Company, 1933), pp. 65–66.
10. Ruth C. Peterson and L. L. Thurstone, *Motion Pictures and the Social Attitudes of Children* (New York: The Macmillan Company, 1933).
11. W. S. Dysinger and Christian A. Ruckmick, *The Emotional Responses of Children to the Motion Picture Situation* (New York: The Macmillan Company, 1933), pp. 110–119.
12. Samuel Renshaw, Vernon L. Miller, and Dorothy P. Marquis, *Children's Sleep* (New York: The Macmillan Company, 1939), pp. 153–155 and 183–186.
13. Charles C. Peters, *Motion Pictures and Standards of Morality* (New York: The Macmillan Company, 1933).
14. William Graham Sumner, *Folkways* (London: Ginn and Company, 1906).
15. Frank K. Shuttleworth and Mark A. May, *The Social Conduct and Attitudes of Movie Fans* (New York: The Macmillan Company, 1933).
16. Herbert Blumer, *The Movies and Conduct* (New York: The Macmillan Company, 1933).
17. Herbert Blumer and Philip M. Hauser, *Movies, Delinquency, and Crime* (New York: The Macmillan Company, 1933).
18. Ruth C. Peterson and L. L. Thurstone, op. cit., pp. 64–66.
19. Herbert Blumer, op. cit., pp. 3–12.
20. Ibid., p. 22.
21. Ibid., p. 23.
22. Ibid., p. 31
23. Ibid., pp. 38–39.
24. Ibid., p. 40.

25. Ibid., p. 45.
26. Ibid., p. 47
27. Ibid., p. 88.
28. Ibid., p. 96.
29. Ibid., p. 105.
30. Ibid., p. 116.
31. Melvin L. De Fleur and Everette E. Dennis, *Understanding Mass Communication* (Boston: Houghton Mifflin, 1981).
32. Albert Bandura, *Social Learning Theory* (Englewood Cliffs, N.J.: Prentice-Hall, 1977).
33. Ibid., p. 141.
34. W. W. Charters, *Motion Pictures and Youth: A Summary* (New York: The Macmillan Company, 1933), p. 54.

3

the invasion from mars: radio panics america

On October 30, 1938, the United States was at war—invaded by monstrous creatures from Mars. At least that was the firm belief of a large segment of the 6 million people who were listening that night to CBS' "Mercury Theatre on the Air." What they heard was, of course, a radio drama—a chilling adaptation of H. G. Wells's science fiction masterpiece, *War of the Worlds*. Because the dramatization was presented in a clever newscast style, many listeners believed that the Martians were actually taking over. Others were driven to mindless panic because the invasion seemed a direct threat to their lives. Many thought their world was ending; terrified people cried, hid, prayed, or fled into the countryside. The panic was, of course, an accident; there was no intent to frighten anyone. Nevertheless, what occurred that October night was one of the most remarkable media events of all time. If nothing else was proved that night, it was demonstrated to many people that radio could have a powerful impact on its audience. The broadcast also provided a unique opportunity for social scientists to study panic behavior triggered by a mass communication event. Before we begin a discussion of that research, it is important to take note of two features of the times which probably had a significant impact on the effect of the broadcast: (1) the popularity of radio, and (2) the contemporary world situation (i.e., the historical setting).

Much to the dismay of newspapermen, radio had become the primary mode of mass communication and entertainment in the late 1930s and the popularity of newspapers had begun to fade. It was estimated that of the 32 million families in the United States in 1938, 27 million had radios. Thus, a greater proportion of the population at that time had radios than had telephones, automobiles, plumbing, electricity, newspapers or magazines.[1] The ownership of radios had been increasing dramatically; the number of radio sets owned by Americans doubled almost every five years.[2]

Overall, radio had a deeply established role in the lives of Americans. It provided entertainment and brought the news of the world to the public almost as it happened. British Prime Minister Chamberlain explained the Munich concessions; President Roosevelt instilled confidence in the American population with his "fireside chats" in which he seemed to be speaking to each American personally. Radio made Edgar Bergen and "Charlie McCarthy" stars, popularized the music of the big bands and stars like Benny Goodman, and introduced millions of Americans to performers and performances of classical music. Thus, radio brought drama, soap operas, sports broadcasts, and music into the American home, but it also brought rapid and dramatic coverage of news events in a very tense and troubled time—the last was perhaps its most significant service.

The misery of the worst years of the Depression in the early 1930s was still vivid in people's minds in 1938. Many Americans had experienced the loss of their jobs or their farms or businesses. Many had seen their families hungry and even homeless; banks had foreclosed mortgages on a vast scale. For many, the solid rock upon which our social structure had been built turned out to be shifting sand. Although conditions had begun to improve by 1938, many people still wondered whether or not they would ever regain any sense of economic security. The complexity of modern finance and government, and the disagreements in the economic and political proposals of the various "experts" created an environment which the average American was unable to interpret.

The ominous and growing shadow of war added to these economic anxieties. On October 30, 1938, the Munich Crisis was still fresh in the memories of most Americans. The rise of Hitler and his transformation of Germany created anxiety for many. And if the threat of Fascism were not enough, there was also Communism. Both of these rising philosophies of government and politics were alien to the beliefs of most Americans. Indeed, at the time of the *War of the Worlds* broadcast, the American people had been hanging on the words of the radio broadcasts for weeks. They eagerly sought the most current international news. To facilitate the dissemination of this news, the broadcast industry had developed a new technique—"on the spot" reporting. Radio played a crucial role in keeping a nervous and news-hungry populace informed. Thus, it is no mere coincidence that the Halloween eve panic was created by a radio broadcast.

THE MERCURY THEATRE AND
THE WAR OF THE WORLDS

"Mercury Theatre on the Air," sponsored by CBS, had been broadcasting since June of 1938. (The program lacked a commercial sponsor until the week following the *War of the Worlds* broadcast, when it obtained a lucrative contract with Campbell Soups). The program was aired on Sunday evenings between 8 and 9 P.M. Eastern Standard Time. The dramatic programs were built around the name and talents of Orson Welles, co-founder, with John Houseman, of Mercury Theatre. Welles and Houseman selected the shows; Howard Koch wrote the dramatic scripts.

Interestingly, the panic broadcast almost did not come off. On the Tuesday preceding the broadcast, Howard Koch had not yet finished the show. He was having problems adapting Wells' novel into a dramatic format. A particularly troublesome problem was the novel's setting (England); in addition, it was written in narrative style. Koch recalled:

> I realized that I could use practically nothing but the author's idea of a Martian invasion and his description of their appearance and their machines. In short, I was being asked to do an almost original hour-length play in six days.[3]

At the time, Koch felt that under no circumstances could the story be made "interesting or in any way credible to modern American ears."[4] Koch pleaded with Houseman to have his assignment changed to another play. This might have been done if an interesting alternative project had been available. Houseman recalled that the "only possible alternative for that week was a dreary one—*Lorna Doone.*[5] At the first rehearsal of the show, on Thursday, all involved agreed that the show was extremely dull. They thought that the only chance of success for the show would be to emphasize its newscast style—its simultaneous, eyewitness quality. Koch went back to work on the script, spicing up the newscast style with circumstantial allusions and authentic detail.

The revised script was rehearsed Saturday afternoon with sound effects but without its star. Welles did telephone later to find out how things were going. During that call, a CBS employee told him that it was "frankly not one of our better shows." Confidentially, according to this man, "it just didn't come off."[6] Twenty-seven hours later, many CBS executives would have been a good deal happier had that evaluation turned out to be accurate.

The Broadcast

The Mercury Theatre always began with its theme. As 8 P.M. approached, Welles finished drinking his pineapple juice in the studio and poised himself, amid the debris of the frenzied preparation, to throw the cue to begin the theme. He signaled and Tchaikovsky's *Piano Concerto #1 in B Flat Minor* began; when the music faded, routine introductions were made. Then an announcer indicated that a dramatization of H. G. Wells' *War of the Worlds* would be performed. About one minute into the hour—intoning as only he could—Welles began his narration:

We know now that in the early years of the twentieth century, this world was being watched closely by intelligences greater than man's and yet as mortal as his own. We know now that as human beings busied themselves about their various concerns they were scrutinized and studied, perhaps almost as narrowly as a man with a microscope might scrutinize the transient creatures that swarm and multiply in a drop of water. With infinite complacence people went to and fro over the earth about their little affairs, serene in the assurance of their dominion over this small spinning fragment of solar driftwood which by chance or design man has inherited out of the dark mystery of Time and Space. Yet across an immense ethereal gulf minds that are to our minds as ours are to the beasts in the jungle, intellects vast, cool, and unsympathetic regarded this earth with envious eyes and slowly and surely drew their plans against us. In the thirty-ninth year of the twentieth century came the great disillusionment.

It was near the end of October. Business was better. The war scare was over. More men were back at work. Sales were picking up. On this particular evening, October 30, the Crossley service estimated that thirty-two million people were listening to their radios.[7]

Then, very smoothly, without perceptible transition, an anonymous announcer followed him on the air delivering a very routine bulletin:

> . . . for the next twenty-four hours not much change in temperature. A slight atmospheric disturbance of undetermined origin is reported over Nova Scotia, causing a low pressure area to move down rather rapidly over the northeastern states, bringing a forecast of rain, accompanied by winds of light gale force. Maximum temperature 66; minimum 48. This weather report comes to you from the Government Weather Bureau. . . . We now take you to the Meridian Room in the Hotel Park Plaza in downtown New York, where you will be entertained by the music of Ramon Raquello and his orchestra.

The audience then heard a CBS house orchestra playing the tango, *La Cumparsita*.

It is evident that the first few minutes of the broadcast were strictly realistic in regard to time-frame and were perfectly credible, although somewhat boring. The adapted script of *War of the Worlds* started very slowly and continued to move at a snail's pace. There were some meteorological and astronomical bulletins, alternating with musical interludes and a rather dull scientific interview. These first few minutes were *intended* to bore or lull the listener into a false sense of security and furnish a solid base of real time from which to accelerate later into dramatic time. Some 12 minutes into the show, there was a news flash that "a huge, flaming object, believed to be a meteorite, fell on a farm in the neighborhood of Grover's Mill, New Jersey, twenty-two miles from Trenton."[8]

Musical interludes were then alternated with interviews with people on the scene. A few minutes later, the Martians reared their ugly heads and the scene was set. The dramatic action picked up speed after the audience had been significantly conditioned to additional scientific observations interspersed with a program of dance music. The program suddenly shifted from real time to the condensed and telescoped time required of dramatic presentations. The transition to dramatic time was outstanding, executed with such technical and dramatic skill that it was all but imperceptible.

Perhaps the skill of the transition helps to explain why much of the audience accepted a large number of events contained in a single broadcast as real, events which would have taken days, weeks, or longer to have occurred in fact. Within a span of 45 minutes, the Martians had blasted off their planet, set up their destructive machines, defeated our armies, disrupted our communications, demoralized the population, and occupied whole sections of the country! In addition, the United States had mobilized large bodies of troops; reporters had traveled great distances; government cabinet meetings were held; and savage battles were fought on land and in the air. Yet, it is estimated that approximately one million people believed all this to have taken place!

Because the actions of the Martians and the defenders of the country were compressed in time, it seemed unlikely that most people would mistake the broadcast for an actual occurrence—especially if they had heard the program introduction which clearly stated that a dramatization of the Wells novel would follow. The entire "hoax" could easily have been recognized in these early minutes—except that few people were listening. Instead, they were being entertained by Charlie McCarthy and Edgar Bergen, then at the height of their popularity, on another network. The Crossley survey of listeners taken the week before the broadcast gave 34.7 percent of the listening audience to "The Edgar Bergen Show" and only 3.6 percent to the "Mercury Theatre." The critical factor here was the American listener's habit of *dial-twisting*. That particular evening Edgar Bergen had an unpopular guest who went on at approximately 8:12 P.M.; listeners began changing stations. By that time, the mysterious meteorite had already fallen on Grover's Mill, New Jersey; shortly thereafter, the Martians had shown their foul, leathery heads and the New Jersey police authorities had rushed to the scene.

What made things more credible to the newly tuned listeners was the genuine-sounding appeal by the Secretary of the Interior around 8:31, at the height of the crisis:

> Citizens of the nation: I shall not try to conceal the gravity of the situation that confronts the country, nor the concern of your Government in protecting

the lives and property of its people. However, I wish to impress upon you—private citizens and public officials, all of you—the urgent need of calm and resourceful action. Fortunately, this formidable enemy is still confined to a comparatively small area, and we may place our faith in the military forces to keep them there. In the meantime placing our trust in God, we must continue the performance of our duties, each and every one of us, so that we may confront this destructive adversary with a nation united, courageous, and consecrated to the preservation of human supremacy on this earth. I thank you.

Davidson Taylor, CBS' supervisor of the broadcast, was summoned from the control room near the end of the Secretary's appeal. A few minutes later, when he returned, he appeared shaken. By now the Martians had swept all opposition aside as they advanced upon New York. Those participating in the broadcast thought it was going well. Taylor, however, had just learned how well. The CBS switchboards were uselessly swamped; a madness was sweeping the country because of the broadcast. Rumors had reached the network of panic injuries, deaths and suicides. Taylor had been requested to interrupt the show immediately—to issue an announcement by the station about the broadcast.

The broadcast was less than a minute from the station break. The Martians were blanketing New York with poison gas. The music swirled, the "last announcer," Ray Collins, died heroically on the roof of the Broadcasting Building, and the boats in the harbor whistled until all who manned them were dead. As all these sounds died away, an amateur radio operator was heard, reaching weakly into the dark night to an empty world.

> 2X2L calling CQ
> 2X2L calling CQ
> 2X2L calling CQ
> Isn't there anyone on the air?
> Isn't there anyone?

There followed complete silence. Five seconds later, the network announcer broke the spell, shattering the "reality" of the end of the world:

> You are listening to the CBS presentation of Orson Welles and the Mercury Theatre on the Air in an original dramatization of *The War of the Worlds*, by H. G. Wells. The performance will continue after a brief intermission.

According to Houseman, the remainder of the show was well written and sensitively played.

In the last part of the broadcast, the play was clearly identified as a fantasy. The problem was that almost no one heard it. It described the adventures of a lone survivor and his observations on human society. The Martians finally died, but not by man's action. All his defenses had failed. What finally destroyed them was bacteria. The microorganisms of the earth overpowered the conquerors. Finally came the hope of rebuilding a new world.

The broadcast ended with an informal speech by Welles:

> This is Orson Welles, ladies and gentlemen, out of character to assure you that the *War of the Worlds* has no further significance than as the holiday offering it was intended to be. The Mercury Theatre's own radio version of dressing up in a sheet and jumping out of a bush and saying BOO! Starting now, we couldn't soap all your windows and steal all your garden gates, by tomorrow night. . . . so we did the next best thing. We annihilated the world before your very ears, and utterly destroyed the Columbia Broadcasting System. You will be relieved, I hope, to learn that we didn't mean it, and that both institutions are still open for business. So good-bye everybody and remember, please, for the next day or so, the terrible lesson you learned tonight. That grinning, glowing globular invader of your living room is an inhabitant of the pumpkin patch, and if your doorbell rings and nobody's there, that was NO Martian . . . it's Halloween.

Also identifying the presentation as fantasy were additional announcements made by CBS immediately following the broadcast. For example, one such announcement was aired right away:

> For those listeners who tuned in to Orson Welles's Mercury Theatre on the air broadcast from 8:00 to 9:00 P.M. Eastern Standard Time tonight and did not realize that the program was merely a modernized adaptation of H. G. Wells' famous novel *War of the Worlds*, we are repeating the fact which was made clear four times on the program, that, while the names of some American cities were used, as in all novels and dramatizations, the entire story and all of its incidents were fictitious.

The four announcements CBS referred to occurred (1) at the beginning of the broadcast (when most people were not listening), (2) before the station break, about 8:35 (by this time, most of those who panicked were no longer listening, but fleeing), (3) right after the station break, and (4) at the end of the broadcast. Moreover, the most terrifying part of the broadcast, it should be remembered, came *before* the station break. Those listeners who failed to hear the original announcement therefore had ample opportunity to become frightened.

The Panic   The panic began well before the broadcast had ended. Terrified people all over America prayed and tried frantically, in one way or another, to escape death from the Martians. The reaction was strongest in the New Jersey area (in a single block, more than 20 families rushed out of their houses with wet handkerchiefs and towels over their faces) but people were affected in all sections of the country. Some examples: [9]

New York—Hundreds of people fled their homes. Bus terminals were crowded. One woman telephoned Dixie Bus Terminal for information and spoke impatiently, "hurry please, the world is coming to an end and I have a lot to do."

Rhode Island—Hysterical people swamped the switchboard of the *Providence Journal* for details of the Martian invasion. Officials of the electric company reported that they received many calls urging them to turn off all lights so that the city would be safe from the enemy.

Boston—The *Boston Globe* was swamped with calls from frightened individuals. One woman said she could see the smoke and the fire brought about by the Martian invasion.

Pittsburgh—A man came home in the middle of the broadcast and found his wife in the bathroom with a bottle of poison in her hand and screaming, "I'd rather die this way than that."

Birmingham, Alabama—Many people gathered in churches and prayed. On the campus of a southeastern college—"The girls in the sorority houses and dormitories huddled around their radios trembling and weeping in each other's arms. They separated themselves from their friends only to take their turn at the telephone to make long distance calls to their parents, saying goodbye for what they thought might be the last time."

Kansas City, Missouri—One telephone informant said that he had loaded all his children into his car, filled it with gasoline, and was going somewhere. "Where is it safe?" he wanted to know. The Kansas City Bureau of the Associated Press received queries on the "meteors" from Los Angeles, Salt Lake City, Beaumont, Texas and St. Joseph, Missouri.

Concrete, Washington—The town experienced a power failure at the very moment the Martians were supposed to have been interrupting communications across the nation and disrupting the nation's power sources. This created mass hysteria because it appeared to confirm the broadcast.

Newspapers carried stories relating the shock and terror of many citizens for weeks after the broadcast. Around the world, newspaper accounts tried to recreate the atmosphere of terror that spread throughout America that October night.

As we shall show in a later section, several million people heard the broadcast. It has been estimated that about one million of these were frightened. Many of them engaged in panic behavior, a reaction that brought wide criticism to the producers of the show. Welles bore the brunt of most of the initial criticism. Reporters hounded him; outraged citizens threatened him. But the focus eventually shifted to CBS and Mercury Theatre. Legal actions were filed against both seeking compensation for injuries and damages totalling millions of dollars. None of these suits ever went to trial, however; there was no legal precedent for such claims. CBS did choose to settle one claim. A man living in Massachusetts wrote:

> I thought the best thing to do was to go away. So I took three dollars twenty-five cents out of my savings and bought a ticket. After I had gone sixty miles I knew it was a play. Now I don't have money left for the shoes I was saving up for. Will you please have someone send me a pair of black shoes size 9B![10]

Against the advice of its lawyers, CBS sent the shoes.

The casualties turned out to be neither as numerous nor as serious as first thought. One young woman had broken her arm when she fell while running down stairs. The Federal Communications Commission held hearings on the broadcast and adopted a resolution prohibiting the use of "on the spot" news stories in dramatic broadcasts. CBS issued a public apology and promised no more Halloween scares. The incident was then officially closed.

THE RESEARCH

The Office of Radio Research of Princeton University hastily organized a research study following the panic. The group had been formed a year earlier when the Rockefeller Foundation provided the University with funds to assess the influence of radio on listeners in the United States. The occurrence of the great panic suddenly presented it with a rare opportunity. Social scientists could study, for the first time, panic behavior triggered by a mass communication event. Funds for the special investigation were provided through a special grant from the General Education Board.

Although the scope of the investigation was limited in many ways, and the research had a number of methodological problems, the study became one of the classics of mass communication research. The results were reported in *The Invasion From Mars* by Hadley Cantril, written with the assistance of Hazel Gaudet and Herta Herzog. The purpose of the study was to discover the psychological conditions and the situational circumstances that led people to believe that the broadcast drama was real. The result was a sensitive study of the feelings and reactions of people who were badly frightened by the believed arrival of the Martians.

The researchers were trying to answer three basic questions: (1) What was the extent of the panic (i.e., how many listened and how many panicked); (2) Why did this broadcast frighten some people when other fantastic broadcasts did not; and (3) Why did this broadcast frighten some people but not others?

Methods

Because the research questions were so complex and complicated, several approaches were employed to seek out the answers. The results obtained by one method could thus be compared with those obtained by another. Such a pluralistic approach to the research was desirable because the phenomena under investigation were of so transient a nature. The following techniques were used: personal interviews, scientific surveys, analysis of newspaper accounts, and an examination of volume of mail. We shall discuss each of these in turn, in the order of their importance for the study.

Personal Interviews   Much of the information contained in Cantril's book was derived from in-depth personal interviews with persons who listened to the broadcast. These interviews began one week after the broadcast and were completed by the time four weeks had elapsed. A total of 135 individuals were interviewed. Of these, 107 were selected because the broadcast had badly frightened them; an additional 28 listeners who had not been frightened by the broadcast were interviewed to provide a basis for comparison.

The interviews were limited to the New Jersey vicinity (Princeton's locale) for two reasons: (1) funds were limited, and (2) the researchers wanted to insure that there was proper supervision of this aspect of the research program. According to Cantril:

> Every attempt was made to keep the group representative of the population at large. However, no pretense is made that the group is a proper example of the total population.[11]

In addition, the respondents who had been frightened were identified almost entirely through the personal initiative and inquiry *of the interviewers.*

Many more persons were identified than could possibly have been interviewed, given the funding limitations.

Surveys The results of several different surveys were included in the study. The most significant were: (1) a special survey conducted by CBS the week after the broadcast in which the interviews were taken throughout the country from 920 persons who had listened to the broadcast; and (2) a nationwide survey of several thousand adults conducted by the American Institute of Public Opinion (AIPO) about six weeks after the broadcast. Although the delay was unfortunate, it was also unavoidable. It took that long to obtain sufficient funding to conduct it. The results obtained, however, are extremely valuable because the Institute reached many small communities and homes without telephones that were not regularly sampled by the radio research organizations.

Newspaper Accounts and Mail Twelve thousand five hundred newspaper clippings which appeared in papers throughout the country for three weeks following the broadcast were analyzed in the study. Analysis indicated continued interest in the broadcast, although the number of articles diminished somewhat at the end of the three weeks.

In addition, analysis of the volume of mail to CBS stations, The Mercury Theatre itself, and to the Federal Communications Commission (FCC) was also undertaken. It was not surprising that huge increases in the volume of mail were reported. Interestingly, most of the letters to the Mercury Theatre in particular and to CBS stations in general were favorable, even congratulatory. However, letters to the FCC, the "watchdog of broadcasting," were generally unfavorable. It seemed that those who wanted their protests taken seriously did not hesitate to communicate with the proper authorities, while those who appreciated good drama gave praise where praise was due.

It is clear that even with the study's multifaceted approach, it had many methodological problems. For example, there was almost a haphazard aspect to the selection of subjects for personal interviews. This aspect of the research program was almost totally lacking in rigor. Moreover, the delays of up to four weeks in obtaining the interviews was unfortunate. One of the major scientific surveys also shared this shortcoming.

There was also a validity problem. Many people may have been reluctant to confess their gullibility in an interview after having read newspaper accounts, such as one by Dorothy Thompson, in which she claimed that nothing about the broadcast was in the least credible. Nevertheless, the authors freely admitted the shortcomings of their data-gathering procedures and qualified many of their findings. On the other hand, we must remember that no one anticipated that a panic would occur and the delays in the research were therefore unavoidable. Although the findings may have limitations, they give us insight and understanding of the reasons why a radio broadcast caused more than a million people to panic.

The Findings

The findings have several dimensions. As we noted earlier, the study sought to determine the size of the audience (including how many were frightened), the unique aspects of the broadcast as a trigger for panic behavior, and why some listeners were frightened while others were not.

The Size of the Audience   The best evidence regarding "who listened" came from the American Institute of Public Opinion poll. It was estimated from their sample that nine million adults heard the broadcast. If children were included, the number would increase to 12 million. The AIPO estimate was, however, much *higher* than that yielded by any other known audience measure. This may be due to the fact that its sample, unlike those of other surveys, included small communities and homes without telephones. Because of the wide discrepancy, Cantril pooled the results of the AIPO poll with the findings of C. E. Hooper, Inc., a commercial research organization which made continuous checks on program popularity. The Hooper figures indicated a listening audience of about four million for the Mercury Theatre broadcast on October 30, 1938. The pooled results yielded a final estimate of six million listeners—admittedly conservative.

How Many Were Frightened   The AIPO survey asked "At the time you were listening, did you think the broadcast was a play or a real news report?" Twenty-eight percent of the respondents thought that it was news, and 70 percent of those who thought it was a news report were frightened or disturbed. Thus, AIPO estimated that 1.7 million listeners thought the broadcast was a news bulletin and 1.2 million were excited by the news. Even more conservative estimates place the number of people frightened at one million or more. Had the program enjoyed greater popularity, the panic might have been even more widespread, depending upon whether or not they heard the introductory announcements.

Unique Aspects of the Broadcast   What was there about this broadcast that caused it to frighten some people when other fantastic broadcasts did not? Cantril's research indicated that the following five factors were important in distinguishing *War of the Worlds* from other "frightening" programs.

1. The sheer dramatic excellence of the program was an important factor, Dorothy Thompson's remark about its credibility notwithstanding. No one reading the script can deny that the broadcast was so realistic for the first few minutes that it was almost credible, even to relatively sophisticated and well-informed listeners.

2. Radio was an accepted vehicle for important announcements. A large proportion of listeners, particularly those in the lower income and educational groups, had learned to rely more on radio for the news than on newspapers. Almost all of the listeners who had been frightened and were interviewed mentioned somewhere during the course of the interview the great confidence they had in radio. They expected that it would be used for such an important announcement. Listeners had learned to expect that dramas, musical programs, and the like would be interrupted or even cut off in an emergency in order to inform the public. A few examples of the respondents' comments indicate their attitudes toward and reliance on radio.

> We have so much *faith in broadcasting*. In a crisis it has to reach all people. That's what radio is here for.

> I always feel that the *commentators bring the best possible news*. Even after this I still will believe what I hear on the radio.

> It didn't sound like a play the *way it interrupted the music when it started*.

3. The use of the "expert" in the broadcast gave it credibility. In many situations where events and/or ideas are too complicated, or too far removed from one's immediate experience, then only the expert is expected to understand them. The rest of the people must rely on the expert's interpretations. The logical "expert" in the panic broadcast was the astronomer, "Professor Richard Pierson," the chief character in the drama (played by Orson Welles). Other fictitious astronomers were also mentioned: "Professor Farrell of the Mount Jennings Observatory of Chicago," "Professor Morse of MacMillan University in Toronto," and "Professor Indellkoffer of the California Astronomical Society."

   When the dramatic situation changed, other experts were introduced. "Gen. Montgomery Smith of the State Militia" provided expertise for organized defense. "Mr. Harry McDonald" of the Red

Cross, "Capt. Lansing" of the Signal Corps, and the "Secretary of the Interior" all described the terrible conditions and gave orders to evacuate or attack. This technique appeared to have a powerful effect on the listeners.

I believed the broadcast as soon *as I heard the Professor from Princeton* and the officials in Washington.

I knew it was an awfully dangerous situation *when all those military men were there and the Secretary of State spoke.*

If so many of these astronomers saw the explosions they must have been real. *They ought to know.*

4. The *use of real places* added a familiar frame of reference to the broadcast. The use of actual towns, city streets and highways, and so on in the broadcast were crucial cues for many people. For example, mention of places well known to them was particularly frightening to listeners in New Jersey and Manhattan. The towns of Grover's Mill, Princeton, and Trenton, New Jersey were all mentioned early in the broadcast. Other familiar places such as Watchung Mountains, Bayonne, the Hutchison River Parkway, Newark, the Palisades, Times Square, the Pulaski Skyway and the Holland Tunnel were all familiar to residents of the New York/New Jersey area. Even listeners in other areas of the country recognized many of the names as real.

When he said, "Ladies and Gentlemen, do not use *route number 23*," that made me sure.

I was most inclined to believe the broadcast *when they mentioned places like South Street and the Pulaski Highway.*

If they had mentioned any other places but streets right around here, I would not have been so ready to believe.

5. Tuning in late was a major factor in leading people to believe that the broadcast was real. It seems highly unlikely that a listener would take the broadcast seriously if the opening announcements had been heard. Indeed, data from two separate surveys (CBS, AIPO) indicated that the time a person tuned in was a major factor in determining whether or not the person was frightened by the broadcast. For example, among the questions asked as part of the CBS study were: "At what part of the program did you tune in?" and "Did you realize it was a play or did you think it was a real news broadcast?"

Forty-two percent indicated that they had tuned in late. As Table 2 shows, there was a very pronounced tendency for those who tuned in late to accept the broadcast as news, and for those who tuned in at the beginning to take it as a play. Only 20 percent of the persons interviewed who listened from the beginning thought they were hearing a news report.

Why did such a large percentage of the listeners tune in late? We mentioned earlier that Mercury Theatre was competing with the most popular program on the air, Edgar Bergen and Charlie McCarthy. Most listeners heard their first routine and changed the station when an unpopular singer came on the show. Another reason people tuned in late was the contagion that the excitement of the show created. Many who were frightened called friends and relatives who then tuned in. In the AIPO survey, the respondents who tuned in late were asked: "Did someone suggest that you tune in after the program had begun?" Twenty-one percent responded that someone had. In the CBS survey the figure was 19 percent.

Still, there *were* those who tuned in from the beginning yet believed the clearly introduced play to be a news broadcast. Analysis of the data revealed two main reasons such a misinterpretation came about. First, many people who had tuned in to hear the Mercury Theatre play thought that it had been interrupted for special news bulletins. They were familiar with this kind of interruption and had experience with it in the war crisis earlier that October. It was easier to accept the news interruption as irrelevant to the expected play than to infer that it was a part of the play. In the CBS survey, 20 percent listened from the beginning and thought it was a newscast. Of these nearly two-thirds (61 percent) thought the interruption was authentic. Their comments make this apparent.

Table 2   Time of Tuning in and Interpretation (CBS Survey)

| | Tuned in | | |
Interpretation	From the Beginning (percent)	After Beginning (percent)	Total Number
News	20	63	175
Play	80	37	285
Total percent	100	100	—
Total numbers	269	191	460

SOURCE: Hadley Cantril, *The Invasion from Mars* (Princeton: Princeton University Press, 1940) p. 78.

I have heard other programs interrupted in the same way for news broadcasts.

I believed Welles' statement that he was interrupting the program for a news flash.

The second major reason for the misunderstanding was that many people simply did not pay attention to the opening announcements. Some people kept their radios turned on and paid attention to them only when something of interest caught their attention. Since the beginning announcements frequently contained station identifications and commercials, many people were probably inattentive. For example, ten percent of those people who heard it from the beginning said that they had not paid any attention to the announcements.

My radio had been tuned to the station several hours. I heard loud talking and excitement and became interested.

My radio was tuned to the station but I wasn't paying attention to it.

We had company at home and were playing cards while the radio was turned on. I heard a news commentator interrupt the program but at first did not pay much attention to him.

I started to listen only when the farmer began giving a description of the landing of the tube.

Tuning in late, however, was a much more important factor in determining whether the listener would follow the program as a play or as a news report than was ignoring or misunderstanding the beginning of the show.

Why Some Were Frightened and Some Were Not   In spite of the fact that many persons tuned in to the *War of the Worlds* broadcast late, certainly not all of them believed the show to be news. Even among those who believed the invasion to be real, the patterns of behavior differed significantly. To understand better the varying behavior demonstrated, Cantril and his associates placed the listeners into four categories, identifying why some were frightened while others were not (assuming that all persons at first thought the broadcast was a news report):

1.   *Those who checked the internal evidence of the broadcast. (They made successful internal checks.)*

The persons in this category did *not* remain frightened throughout the entire broadcast because they were able to discern that the program was fictitious. Some realized that the reports must be false because they sounded so much like science fiction literature.

At first I was very interested in the fall of the meteor. It isn't often they find a big one just when it falls. But when it started to unscrew and monsters came out, I said to myself, "They've taken one of those amazing stories and are acting it out. It just couldn't be real. It was just like some of the stories I read in *Amazing Stories* but it was even more exciting."

Other persons in this category initially believed the broadcast to be news but could not believe the subsequent description of events.

It all sounded perfectly real until people began hopping around too fast. . . . when people moved 20 miles in a couple of minutes I put my tongue in my cheek and figured it was just about the smartest play I'd ever heard.

I kept translating the unbelievable parts into something I could believe until finally I reached the breaking point—I mean my mind just couldn't twist things any more, and somehow I knew it couldn't be true literally, so I just stopped believing and knew it must be a play.

2. *Those who checked the broadcast against other information and learned that it was a play. (They made a successful external check.)*

Like the listeners in the first category, these were suspicious of the "news" they were getting. Some thought the reports too incredible to believe; others realized things were moving too quickly. Some listeners checked simply because they thought it was a reasonable thing to do. Mostly, they compared the news on the program with some other information. Many checked to see if other stations were reporting the invasion. Some even looked up the program in the paper.

I tuned in and heard that a meteor had fallen. Then when they talked about monsters, I thought something was the matter. So I looked in the newspaper to see what program was supposed to be on and discovered it was only a play.

3. *Those who tried to check the program against other information but who, for various reasons, continued to believe the broadcast was an authentic news report. (They made unsuccessful external checks.)*

These people differed from those in category 2 (those who made successful external checks) in two ways. First, it was difficult to determine why they even wanted to check; they were not seeking evidence to test the authenticity of the reports. They appeared to be frightened individuals who wanted to find out if they were yet in any personal danger. Second, they used ineffective and unreliable checks. For example, the most frequent method of checking was to look out the window or go outdoors. Some telephoned their friends or ran to consult with their neighbors. Whatever "new" information they obtained tended to be used to verify their existing beliefs.

> I looked out of the window and everything looked the same as usual so I thought it hadn't reached our section yet.

> We looked out of the window and Wyoming Avenue was black with cars. People are rushing away, I figured.

> No cars came down my street. "Traffic is jammed on account of the roads being destroyed," I thought.

> My husband tried to calm me and said, "If this were really so, it would be on all stations" and he turned to one of the other stations and there was music. I retorted, "Nero fiddled while Rome burned."

> We tuned in to another station and heard some church music. I was sure a lot of people were worshipping God while waiting for their death.

4. *Those who made no attempt to check the broadcast or the event.*

Many of these people were so frightened they stopped listening, became frenzied, or paralyzed with fear. Cantril subdivided them according to the apparent reasons for their actions.

a. Persons so frightened they never thought of checking.

> We were so intent upon listening that we didn't have enough sense to try other hook-ups—we were just so frightened.

b. Persons who adopted an attitude of complete resignation. To them, any attempt to check the broadcast appeared senseless.

> I didn't do anything. I just kept listening. I thought if this is the real thing you only die once—why get excited?

> The lady from the next floor rushed downstairs, yelling to turn on the radio. I heard the explosion, people from Mars, end of the world. I was very scared and everybody in the room was scared stiff too. There was nothing else to do for everything would be destroyed very soon. If I had had a little bottle of whiskey, I would have had a drink and said, "let it go."

c. Persons who felt that, in light of the crisis situation, immediate action was required.

I couldn't stand it so I turned it off. I don't remember when, but everything was coming closer. My husband wanted to put it back on but I told him we'd better do something instead of just listen, so we started to pack.

d. Listeners who interpreted the situation in such a way that they were not interested in making a check-up.

In some cases the individuals tuned in so late that they missed the most incredible parts of the broadcast and were only aware that some type of conflict was in progress.

I was in my drugstore and my brother phoned and said, "Turn the radio on, a meteor has just fallen." We did and heard gas was coming up South Street. There were a few customers and we all began wondering where it could come from. I was worried about the gas, it was spreading so rapidly but I was puzzled as to what was actually happening, when I heard aeroplanes I thought another country was attacking us.

I knew it was some Germans trying to gas all of us. When the announcer kept calling them people from Mars I just thought he was ignorant and didn't know yet that Hitler had sent them all.

For other listeners, the events described did not appear to involve *immediate* personal danger.

I was at a party, somebody was fooling around with the radio, and we heard a voice, the Secretary of Interior was talking. We thought it was a normal bulletin because of the conditions abroad. Then the local militia was called so we decided to listen. It sounded real but not like anything to get panicky about. This riot or whatever it was was still a couple of miles away.

Both the personal interviews and the CBS survey indicated that those individuals who were able to make successful checks (either by internal or external tests) remained fairly calm. Those who checked unsuccessfully or not at all tended to become either excited or paralyzed. Thus, there was a very strong relationship between feelings, beliefs and subsequent behavior.

The researchers found that those people who were frightened by the broadcast were *highly suggestible;* they believed what they heard without making sufficient checks to see if the information was accurate. But some people did not jump to conclusions but instead scrutinized what they heard and then rejected it as news. These people were said to possess *critical ability*. Cantril defined it in the following manner:

By this we mean that they had a capacity to evaluate the stimulus in such a way that they were able to understand its inherent characteristics so they could judge and act appropriately.[12]

Thus, individuals possessing critical ability were able to assess the credibility of the events in the radio play against their knowledge of the world. And there were just too many events in the play that did not conform to their conception of reality.

Unfortunately, although the concept of critical ability was the single most promising "psychological tool" for examining the data, there was no way to measure it directly. However, the researchers hypothesized that it was related to the amount of formal education a person possessed. Education "instills a readiness to examine interpretations before accepting them," they argued.[13] Indeed, such a relationship between education and orientation toward the broadcast was found, as shown in Table 3. While college graduates were not immune to panic behavior, the response to the broadcast varied in proportion to the amount of education an individual possessed.

Religious Beliefs and Personality Factors   Religiosity was also an important variable in determining how an individual would react to the broadcast. Those with strong religious beliefs were likely to think that the invasion was actually an act of God and that the end of the world was near.

We just sat and listened. You see we're good Christians and a Providence will take care of us. We're not afraid to die because we're prepared for it.

At first I didn't think it was the end of the world because I read in the Bible, in Revelations, that the end of the world was coming by fire and I didn't think this was a fire. I thought buildings were being struck and falling down. But then I realized that eventually they might catch on fire so I thought the end was coming.

Table 3   Education and Interpretation as News (CBS Survey)

Education	Percent Who Thought Program Was News Report	Total Number of Cases
College	28	69
High School	36	257
Grammar School	46	132

SOURCE: Hadley Cantril, *The Invasion from Mars* (Princeton University Press, 1940) p. 112.

The Bible says that the first time the end of the world was by flood and next time it will be by fire and that went through my mind.

Other individuals were found to be particularly susceptible to the broadcast because of personality factors such as (1) emotional insecurity, (2) phobic personality, (3) lack of self-confidence, and (4) fatalism. A person who believes that his life is in the control of somewhat mysterious powers is obviously capable of rationalizing *any* experience as preordained.

I believe what is to be will be. I didn't pray during the broadcast.

I just kept listening. I thought if this is the real thing you only die once—why get excited. When the time comes you go and there is no way getting away from it.

Finally, it was discovered in addition that the characteristics of the listening situation could also influence an individual's susceptibility to the broadcast. For example, a person who was told to tune in by a frightened friend would listen under different conditions than someone who tuned in for other reasons. If the person who called or informed the listener was someone in whom he had confidence, the listener would be particularly susceptible to accepting that person's opinion.

I had just gone to the store to get some last-minute things for my daughter's party. When I came in my son said, "Mother, something has come down from Mars and the world is coming to an end." I said, "Don't be silly." Then my husband said, "It is true." So I started to listen. And really, I heard forty people were killed and there was gas and everybody was choking.

Moreover, the sight and sound of other people (even strangers) who were frightened might increase the emotional tension of an otherwise calm individual and thus reduce that person's critical ability.

I don't think we would have gotten so excited if those couples hadn't come rushing in the way they did. We were both very calm people, especially my husband, and if we had tuned in ourselves I am sure we would have checked up on the program but they led me to believe it was any station.

When I came out of the telephone booth, the store was filled with people in a rather high state of hysteria. . . . This hysterical group convinced me that something was wrong.

In short, the researchers found that "critical ability" was the most important factor in distinguishing those who panicked from those who did not. However, other factors such as religiosity and personality factors were also important. In fact, critical ability alone, as measured by the amount of formal education, was not a sure preventive of panic behavior. The authors concluded that critical ability may be overpowered by either an individual's own susceptible personality or by emotions generated in a person by an unusual listening situation.

Causal Factors in Extreme Behavior   Recognizing that some people believed the broadcast to be true, why did they become so hysterical? Why did they pray, telephone relatives, drive at dangerous speeds, cry, awaken sleeping children and flee? Of all the possible modes of reaction they may have followed, why did these particular patterns emerge? The obvious answer is that this was a serious affair. As in all other panics, the well-being of individuals, their safety, or their lives were at stake. The situation was perceived as a real threat.

Social scientists generally agree that a panic occurs when some commonly accepted values are threatened and when no possible elimination of that threat is in sight. The invasion by the Martians was a direct threat to life, one's own as well as that of loved ones. Indeed, it was a threat to all other cherished values. Frustration resulted when no directed behavior seemed possible. One could either resign oneself to complete annihilation or attempt to escape. One could flee, call upon a higher authority for protection, or seek out someone stronger to destroy the enemy.

If listeners assumed the destruction was inevitable, their choices were limited. They could accept their fate in a number of ways: crying, prayer, gathering the family together. Or they could run. If they believed something could still be done to stop the enemy, they could appeal to stronger powers (e.g., God). But none of these alternatives attacked the problem directly. Nothing was done to remove the cause of the crisis. Panic behavior is characteristically undirected; it is, in terms of the situation, nonfunctional.

In short, the extreme behavior evoked by the broadcast was due to the threat to values that the situation created and the complete inability of the individual to alleviate or control the consequences of the invasion. People could not choose one value over another and thus preserve some; all stood to be lost. All their loved ones, their country, and indeed their world, would be ruined physically, financially and socially. Believing total ruin imminent, panic was inescapable.

CONCLUSIONS AND IMPLICATIONS

Overall, what were the principal findings and the major conclusions of the Cantril study? What was their importance from the point of view of developing mass communication theory and methodology? Finally, how did this broadcast, its aftermath, and the research project influence the public's perceptions of radio as a medium?

Summary of the Findings

First, at least six million people listened to the program and, of those, at least one million were severely frightened or panicked. Second, there were several important reasons why this particular broadcast frightened many listeners while other such "fantastic" broadcasts did not. Among these reasons are:

1. The confidence that the American public had developed in radio. It had become their primary source of news and the public expected that radio would be used to present important announcements.
2. The historical timing. The broadcast came at a time when Americans had endured years of economic insecurity and were facing the imminent threat of another war.
3. The sheer technical brilliance of the show—especially the innovative use of the "on-the-spot reporting" technique and the interviewing of "experts."
4. Tuning in late. Missing the announcement that the broadcast was a dramatic adaptation of the *War of the Worlds* was an important factor.

A third conclusion was that there were many reasons why some individuals panicked while others did not.

1. Those who possessed critical ability were most likely to discover that the broadcast was a play, rather than news.
2. Those with strong religious beliefs were likely to believe that the invasion was real.
3. Personality factors such as emotional insecurity, phobic personality, lack of self-confidence, and fatalism were also important. Those manifesting such traits were more likely to believe that an invasion was taking place.
4. An individual's susceptibility to the broadcast could also be influenced by an unusual listening situation. For example, someone encouraged to tune in by frightened friends would listen under different conditions (expectations) than someone who tuned in the broadcast for other reasons.

Subsequent events made it evident that the social and psychological factors which contributed to the panic were not confined to the United States. A few years later, similar broadcasts of the *War of the Worlds* in Spanish induced panics in two Latin American countries—Chile and Peru. The idea for the Chilean program came from William Steele, a former writer for Mutual Broadcasting's "The Shadow" series, who was then writing for a station in Santiago. Steele set the scene for his adaptation in Puente Alto, fifteen miles south of Santiago. Like Koch, he depicted horrible Martians overrunning the country. "News flashes" reported the Civic Center in Santiago destroyed, the armed forces defeated, and the roads flooded with fleeing refugees. Thousands of people all over Chile were panic stricken.

At least one death was verified (an electric company employee, Jose Villarroel, died from a heart attack believed to have been brought on by his terrified state of mind). Ample warning had been given the public for this *War of the Worlds* broadcast during the week preceding it, by both radio and the press. It was said to be "all in fun." Announcements were repeated twice during the broadcast warning that it was only a play. Again, as in the United States, many people failed to notice the message. In the aftermath of the broadcast, the indignant Chilean people pressured the station to close and they sought to have Steele suspended. However, no official action was taken.[14]

In Lima, Peru, another similar broadcast also created a panic, although on a much smaller scale because there were fewer radios within the station's broadcast range. However, the aftermath was even more devastating. When the Peruvians discovered they had been tricked and the world was not coming to an end, they decided to put an end to the offending station. They burned it to the ground. Since that time, because broadcasts of *War of the Worlds* have demonstrated such power, there has been a conscious effort to keep the "Martian genie" from escaping its bottle. A broadcaster opens it at his own peril.[15]

The Significance of the Study

The Cantril study has remained important in the history of mass communication for a number of reasons. It was the first (and only, to date) study of panic behavior triggered by a mass medium. However, it has theoretical significance beyond that particular focus. The researchers were not trying to develop a theory about the effects of mass communication; they were more narrowly interested in the psychological and sociological factors associated with panic behavior. In retrospect, however, their framework for research in addition to their findings played a part in the evolution of contemporary media theory.

Looking back, it is clear that Cantril shaped his study around what we have called the selective influence perspective based upon individual differences. This perspective is obvious in one of Cantril's major research objectives—determining why some people were frightened or panicked while others were not. The answers to that question were found in the differences in critical ability which led to selective forms of response to the broadcast. Certain personality factors also played a role (emotional insecurity, phobic personality, lack of self-confidence, and fatalism). Social categories were found to be important. Factors such as religion and education influenced the probability of perceiving the broadcast as news or as a play. Finally, in retrospect, a review of the findings reveals that social relationships were significant influences on the patterns of behavior people selected to cope with the invasion. The activities and perceptions of family, friends, and even strangers contributed to the meaning that the subjects attributed to the broadcast. Thus, although it was by no means clear at the time, the panic study was one of the first challenges to the magic bullet theory. It opened the way to theories stressing selective influences.

Methodologically, no innovative techniques were used in the study. In fact, the techniques that were used were not particularly impressive; indeed, more rigor should have been applied. Yet, given the unexpected nature of the event, and the constraints of time and money, it is remarkable that the research was performed at all with any degree of precision. The logistics of planning and obtaining funding for such a study require enormous investments of time. As a matter of fact, the bureaucracy of research which has developed in the intervening years would probably preclude such an "instant" research effort should another similar event occur.

Perhaps the real significance of the study was the way in which it confirmed public thinking about the effects of the mass media. In short, it reinforced the legacy of fear. October 30, 1938, continues to be remembered as the night American panicked. For many people, the powerful influence of radio had been proven in a most unorthodox manner. Contrary to the unnamed CBS employee's pre-broadcast evaluation, the show did "come off." Of that, there can be no doubt.

NOTES AND REFERENCES

1. Hadley Cantril, *The Invasion From Mars: A Study in the Psychology of Panic* (Princeton, N.J.: Princeton University Press, 1940), p. x.

2. Melvin L. De Fleur and Sandra Ball-Rokeach, *Theories of Mass Communication*, 3rd ed. (New York: Longman Inc., 1975), p. 93.

3. Howard Koch, *The Panic Broadcast: Portrait of an Event* (Boston: Little, Brown and Co., 1970), p. 13.

4. John Houseman, "The Men From Mars," *Harper's*, 168:76, 1948.

5. Ibid., p. 76.

6. Ibid., p. 76.

7. This quotation and those that follow (from the original radio script) are presented in full in Hadley Cantril, op. cit., pp. 4–43.

8. Hadley Cantril, op. cit., pp. 10–11.

9. John Houseman, op. cit., pp. 76–77.

10. John Houseman, op. cit., p. 82.

11. Hadley Cantril, op. cit., p. xi.

12. Ibid., pp. 111–112.

13. Ibid., p. 112.

14. "The Men From Mars," *Newsweek*, November 27, 1944, p. 89.

15. Howard Koch, op. cit.

4

the people's choice: the media in a political campaign

The year 1940 was a fateful one for the United States. It represented the end of one era and the beginning of another. It was the last year during which the principal concerns of Americans were the issues associated with the Great Depression of the 1930s, and also the last peace-time year before the United States was plunged into war. The selection of a national leader in 1940, then, was a matter of far graver concern than any of the voters could imagine as the spring approached and the media campaign for the presidency slowly began to gear up. The incumbent was Franklin Roosevelt; the challenger, Wendell Willkie, an almost unknown candidate without prior political experience. Franklin Delano Roosevelt was a very popular president. First elected in 1932, he inherited a country nearly paralyzed by the worst financial crisis in its history. The stock market had crashed late in 1929, and by 1932 banks were on the thin edge of failure all over the country. Unemployment soared as factories closed because people had no money to buy things. Farmers couldn't even give their crops away. People were going hungry, but food was rotting in the fields. It was a democratic depression; the previously well-to-do suffered along with ordinary people who worked with their hands in mines, mills, and farms. Bread lines were long in the cities and rural people were driven from their farms when their mortgages were foreclosed.

Into this situation came the calm and cultured voice of Franklin Roosevelt, soothing people via the radio, telling them that "all we have to fear is fear itself." He was elected in a landslide, and in his first weeks in office he surrounded himself by a "brain trust" of liberal university professors who helped him design and set into motion a set of sweeping changes and social programs that were labeled the "New Deal" for the American people. These included the Social Security Act of 1935, still our basic welfare legislation; it provided a number of welfare measures, funded on a national basis for the first time in the history of the nation. Many other economic policies, governmental controls, and social programs were added. The country shifted jarringly away from the earlier reliance on unfettered free enterprise and a limited role for government to a profusion of social programs and policies funded by a progressive income tax and policed by a large bureaucracy in Washington.

These changes received great approval from the common people, from whom Roosevelt drew his political strength. The business community deplored them to the point where many people would not even use Roosevelt's name, but simply referred to him disgustedly as "that man in the White House." Nevertheless, he was reelected in 1936 in another landslide. He overwhelmed the hapless Republican candidate, Governor Alfred M. Landon of Kansas, and solidly swept 46 of the (then) 48 states.

But as Roosevelt entered his second term, he began to have serious political difficulties. For one thing, he tried to gain control of the U.S. Supreme Court (which had blocked some of his New Deal measures) by enlarging it considerably with appointees loyal to his administration. It didn't work. In fact, it backfired and his "court-packing" attempt was a total humiliation. Undaunted, he pressed on with his enlargement of the role of the federal government in regulating and controlling the economy. He succeeded in "ramming through" legislation that provided for public housing, agricultural support programs, and an expansion of the power of organized labor. These were important additions to the earlier New Deal measures.

One major problem of the New Deal changes as a means of restoring prosperity to the country was that they didn't work very well. By 1938, it became clear that the country was sliding back into a recession. Roosevelt responded by initiating what he called "pump priming." He persuaded Congress to spend huge sums for relief programs and public works that would put the unemployed on the payroll. These measures put federal dollars into the pockets of working people and some recovery resulted, even though the measures were very costly to the taxpayers. The country borrowed to pay its bills—a trend that continues even today.

In consequence, the Republicans began to realize what the limitations to Roosevelt's economic programs were. They began to smell just a hint of the possibility of defeating the Democrats in the next election in 1940. After all, they reasoned, Roosevelt had already been elected twice, and they would face a new candidate. Little did they know that shortly before the Democratic Convention in the summer of 1940, Roosevelt would decide to run for an unprecedented third term! Not suspecting this, the Republicans began to seek a candidate with just the right characteristics that would be needed to rout the Democrats, or at least give them a run for their money.

A new area of intense debate emerged during that time, one that would have great significance for the future. It concerned the role of the United States with respect to the war that had broken out in 1939 in Europe. One large bloc of Americans—mainly conservative Republicans—were "isolationists." They demanded that the country remain completely neutral. In fact, in 1937 they succeeded in getting passed a National Neutrality Act. Roosevelt had signed the measure with misgivings. Later, as the European war intensified and Britain was threatened, he tried various ways to get around this Act, with Lend-Lease programs and other efforts aimed at helping the British while avoiding formal hostilities with Germany. Those who sympathized with the idea of gearing up America's defenses because the country might be drawn into the war were advocates of "preparedness." The division between these two points of view was substantial, and to a considerable degree paralleled party lines.

The Republicans started with a number of contenders but eventually narrowed their field to three serious candidates for the nomination. One was Thomas Dewey, a young and aggressive District Attorney from New York. He had gained the national spotlight because of his "racket-busting" activities and was acknowledged as an excellent speaker and a shrewd politician. His major shortcomings as a presidential nominee were his lack of experience in an important national office and his youth. At 37 he was so young as a possible president that Harold Ickes, the sharp-tongued Secretary of the Interior, ridiculed his candidacy by declaring that Dewey had "thrown his diaper into the ring." [1]

A formidable candidate was Ohio Senator Robert A. Taft, the son of former President William Howard Taft. He was a bitter opponent of the New Deal and an ardent isolationist. Taft's problem was his somewhat narrow political constituency. He represented the "Old Guard" among Republicans and was an outspoken advocate of a return to the "good old days" of a very limited role for government and a free-enterprise economy unbounded by the measures of the Roosevelt administration.

The "dark horse" was Wendell L. Willkie, a former Indiana farm boy who had risen in the world of business to head a giant public utilities corporation. Curiously, he had never been elected to public office or been appointed to high political position. Yet, it was clear that he was an extraordinarily capable administrator, and a man of considerable intelligence and personal charm. To try to gain the nomination he had mounted a very well-financed and energetic campaign among his fellow Republicans. Willkie captured the nomination largely because the Republicans could not agree on anyone else. What finally convinced the delegates was that he had a background that would make him attractive to a broad spectrum of voters. He was not a moss-backed conservative and he did not take a strong isolationist position. In fact, he was actually a former Democrat and something of a liberal! This caused a great deal of concern among Old Guard Republicans. In fact, it led conservative Senator Jim Watson to tell Willkie as he pushed for the nomination as the Republican presidential candidate, "Well, Wendell, you know that back home in Indiana it's alright if the town whore joins the church, but they don't let her lead the choir the first night."[2] Nevertheless, Willkie finally captured the nomination in the convention on the sixth ballot and went on to confront the mighty Roosevelt.

In many ways it was a David and Goliath battle. Roosevelt had won his party's nomination overwhelmingly on the first ballot and he had no serious opposition. Roosevelt was deeply entrenched; his name was known and respected throughout the nation; he was a skilled orator who made effective use of radio as a new medium of national politics; and he was a consummate politician who had crushed every previous opponent.

Willkie, on the other hand, was a brilliant and engaging man with a rather touseled and rumpled "down home" look. He often wrote his own speeches and delivered them somewhat awkwardly at times. But he was a tireless campaigner who hammered skillfully at the significant issues where Roosevelt was weakest. In a short time he developed a considerable national following, considering the nature of his opponent.

In the end, of course, Roosevelt won decisively. He gained 449 electoral votes to Willkie's 82. The popular vote gave Roosevelt a large margin of nearly 5 million. Willkie conceded defeat graciously and made a national plea for an end to the internal differences in the nation that had arisen during the campaign. Roosevelt admired him greatly and gave him significant roles and missions that Willkie performed in the national interest. Roosevelt even explored with him the prospects of a joint ticket in 1944. All in all, it was a great election.

THE RESEARCH PROCEDURES

The small book in which the research project on this election was reported is entitled *The People's Choice*, by Lazarsfeld, Berelson, and Gaudet. It has the subtitle, *How the Voter Makes Up His Mind in a Presidential Election.* That subtitle rather succinctly summarizes the main focus of the investigation. More generally, the authors stated their objectives in the following terms:

> We are interested here in all those conditions which determine the political behavior of people. Briefly, our problem is this: to discover how and why people decided to vote as they did.[3]

The investigators choose the survey method to find answers to their research question. In fact, the study represents one of the most imaginative uses of survey designs and techniques in the history of social science.

The methodology and techniques of survey research have proven to be one of the most significant contributions of the social sciences to the study of human behavior in the twentieth century. The use of this research tool began with the primitive surveys among mining families in France during the last century and early in the new century with Charles Booth's exhaustive studies of London's poor. However, it was during the 1920s that the basic techniques of modern survey research were finally put together. Sampling theory and applied procedures had been developed by statisticians and had come into use by scientists in many fields. The idea of sampling was combined with systematic interviewing procedures and adopted for use in many kinds of sociological studies. This new approach to social research was so effective that it was quickly adopted by public opinion pollsters, market researchers, and many other professionals interested in assessing the characteristics, behavior, or ideas of large aggregates of people. Combined with procedures for statistical analysis and control, it came to rival the experiment as a major tool of social and behavioral science.

By the time of the election of 1940, the survey method had been highly refined and was little different from what it is today. Its major pitfalls and limitations had become increasingly understood, along with its numerous advantages. As we noted, the study of mass communication and political behavior that was conducted during the presidential election by Paul F. Lazarsfeld and his associates, using the survey method, represents a remarkable appreciation of this research strategy. Their sophisticated study still stands as a monument to good survey research, and represents a high point of innovation and precision in the study of the effects of mass communication during a presidential political campaign. The investigators were able to probe deeply into the influence of political propaganda presented by the media as voters pondered their choice of a candidate.

The study was funded by the Rockefeller Foundation, Columbia University's Office of Radio Research, *Life* Magazine, and Elmo Roper, the public opinion analyst. The investigation was on a large scale. It made use of a professional field staff and 15 locally hired but carefully trained interviewers. Some 3,000 households were initially contacted to gain data that would be used in designing the study. Later, repeated interviews would be held with samples of these people. In an era before computers were available, organizing, processing and interpreting the mass of statistical data assembled from thousands of detailed interviews was a formidable task. The first version of the results was not available in published form for four years.

Erie County, Ohio

The researchers had to select a site for their investigation. They reviewed many possibilities and finally settled on a small county in Ohio. In 1940,

Erie County had a culturally homogeneous population of about 43,000. Its population size had been stable for about 40 years; its inhabitants were almost all white and almost evenly divided between farming people and those involved in the industrial labor force.

Erie County is located in the northern part of the state on the lake of the same name. It is about halfway between Cleveland and Toledo. The main city, Sandusky, with its population at that time of 25,000, was both the county seat and principal industrial center. There were three newspapers in Sandusky, but many people read the *Cleveland Plain Dealer*. Radio stations from Cleveland and Toledo were received clearly, and all major networks were represented.

Erie County had one additional characteristic that intrigued the investigators considerably. *In every presidential election in the twentieth century, the county had deviated very little from the national voting patterns.* The authors of *The People's Choice* disclaimed this as one of their main reasons for selecting Erie County as the site of their research. However, the county's representative voting patterns were certainly a plus in using the results of the study to interpret the relationship between the media and political behavior on a wider basis. The researchers maintained that Erie County was finally chosen because it was small enough to permit effective supervision of interviewers; free from sectional peculiarities; not dominated by a large urban center; and diverse enough in terms of its rural–urban split to make meaningful comparisons possible.

The Panel Design

In May of 1940, every fourth house in Erie County was visited by an interviewer. The results of these initial contacts permitted the investigators to select some 3,000 persons in such a way that they were representative of the county as a whole. The key variables in this determination were age, sex, rural–urban residence, education, nativity, telephone ownership and automobile ownership.

From these 3,000 individuals, four separate stratified samples of 600 persons were drawn. Each of these samples was matched in such a way that all four were like each other and representative of the county as a whole. The four samples were called "panels" because they were used to construct an innovative *panel design*. The purpose of this special research design was to provide effective controls to assess the effects of repeated interviewing. It must be kept in mind that the purpose of the research was to study the formation of voting decisions *over time*. In more specific terms, this meant observing respondents repeatedly between May, at the start of the campaign, through early November, the time of the actual election.

The procedure used to make such repeated observations was a monthly survey, in which the same individuals were interviewed as the campaign progressed. It was an excellent idea because each subject could be interviewed before making a decision for whom to vote, again at the time of that decision, and after the decision had been made. The role of the mass-communicated political propaganda could be related to political behavior at each of these stages. The only problem with repeated observations is that they might be an influence on the very process under study. Perhaps, it was hypothesized, the voter who was interviewed repeatedly over a seven-month span would reach different decisions and see the issues differently than one who was not interviewed, or interviewed only once.

The panel design was an ingenious method for discovering whether, and to what extent, such repeated interviews did influence decisions about the election. The general idea was to use one sample of 600 subjects as the "main panel" to be interviewed every month, from May to November. However, another panel of 600 (Control A) was to be interviewed during the third month (July). The results of a number of key variables could then be compared to see if the main panel differed, and to what degree, from the main control panel.

As is shown in Figure 3, the same thing was done during the fourth month (August) using Control B. Finally, in October, Control C was interviewed along with the main panel. Overall, then, 600 people were under

	May	June	July	August	September	October	November
Time Table			REP. CONVEN.	DEM. CONVEN.		ELECTION	
Interview Number	1	2	3	4	5	6	7
Group	Total	Main Panel 600	Main Panel 600	Main Panel 600	Main Panel 600	Main Panel 600	Main Panel 600
	Poll						
Interviewed	(3000)		Control A 600	Control B 600		Control C 600	

Figure 3. Outline of the Panel Design and Schedule of Interviews.

SOURCE: Paul F. Lazarsfeld, Bernard Berelson and Hazel Gaudet, *The People's Choice* (New York: Columbia University Press, 1948) p. 4.

MILESTONES IN MASS COMMUNICATION RESEARCH

repeated monthly observation with seven interviews between May and November. Three other panels of 600 each were interviewed as controls in July, August, and October, respectively. The final interview with the main panel was just after the election in November.

As it turned out, the interviews with the matched control panels showed few differences from the results obtained with the main panels. In other words, the repeated interviews did not seem to have any notable influence on the behavior of the voters who were studied month after month.[4] This finding laid to rest any suspicions that the interviewing itself changed the decisions or the behavior of the main panel. Although it was an expensive procedure, the additional interviewing with the controls did provide larger numbers of cases on which to base conclusions on many of the issues under study.

The most significant aspect of the panel technique was that a given individual could be followed longitudinally over the time period of the election as he or she became interested in the election, began to pay attention to the media campaign, was influenced by others, reached a decision, possibly wavered or changed sides, and finally voted. The usual one-shot survey cannot provide such data over time. The same is true of an experiment, which is particularly difficult to repeat with the same subjects. As the authors put it, the panel design was an effective method for studying a whole list of questions:

> What is the effect of social status upon vote? How are people influenced by the party conventions and the nominations? What role does formal propaganda play? How about the press and radio? What of the influence of family and friends? Where do issues come in, and how? Why do some people settle their vote early and some late? In short, how do votes develop? Why do people vote as they do?[5]

Neither the research report of the investigators nor the summary of their work in the present chapter provides full and complete answers to all of these questions. Nevertheless, a number of important insights into many of these questions can be summarized.

THE RESULTS

Generally, the findings obtained in this large-scale study can be divided into two broad categories: those that help us in understanding the voters themselves and the forces that influenced their political ideas and behavior, and the role of the mass media political propaganda in helping to shape their voting decisions. The sections that follow present the highlights of what the results revealed.

Assessing Participation in the Election

Political life in the United States was more predictable before World War II than it has been since. Generally, the country had been dominated by the Republican party until Roosevelt won in 1932. After Wilson left the White House, a series of Republican presidents—McKinley, Harding, Coolidge, and Hoover—were all more or less firmly committed to the idea that "the business of America is business." In other words, the route to national prosperity and a more abundant society was held to be through the fostering of private enterprise, limiting the role of government, and avoiding participation in the troubles of foreign nations. It was a conservative philosophy, but for decades it had seemed to work. Until the crash of 1929, the country had experienced rather steady growth.

When the Great Depression shattered the economy, Franklin Roosevelt put together a broad coalition of organized labor, northern Blacks, liberal Jews, and a huge base of poor people who had not previously been politically active. With the country reeling from hard times it had not been difficult to pin the blame on Hoover and the Republicans and to formulate and implement his New Deal. He sharply elevated the role of government in regulating business, gave increasing power to organized labor, brought considerable change to the federal income tax structure, and developed a national welfare system. These moves polarized the two parties. Later, his strong sentiments and policies concerning national defense preparedness and sympathy toward aiding Britain further split the two groups. These clear differences in the ideologies and composition of the two parties led the researchers to look for social characteristics of voters that would predispose them to lean toward one candidate or the other.

Social Categories and Voting Predispositions   Following the lead that the social composition of the two parties differed, the hypothesis was formulated that those who intended to vote as Republicans or Democrats would differ in *socioeconomic status,* and that such SES differences would predispose them to vote in one way or the other regardless of who the candidates were. *Religion* provided another such variable. Republicans and those inclined toward their views were more likely to be Protestant, while Catholics were more likely to favor the Democrats. Other variables that would predispose voters in this way were thought to be *rural–urban residence* (with farmers more likely to vote Republican), *occupation* (with blue-collar laborers more likely to be sympathetic toward the Democratic candidate), and *age* (with older people more conservative generally and more likely to lean toward the Republican candidate). Each of these possibilities was examined with care to see how it correlated with claimed party affiliation and an intended vote for the Democratic or Republican candidate.

Generally, the variables were interrelated in a number of complex ways, but the following summary provides an overview of the general picture:

1. Those high in socioeconomic level (SES) were more likely to intend to vote Republican than Democratic.
2. Fewer laborers than white collar workers intended to vote Republican. (However, if SES level was held constant, occupation seemed to make little difference).
3. Self-identification made a difference. If a person felt that he or she belonged to "the business class" they generally intended to vote Republican. If the self-identification was with "the laboring class" the intention was more likely to be Democratic (regardless of the actual occupation of the person).
4. Religious category was a strong influence on voting intention. At all levels of SES and among all occupations, Catholics leaned toward a Democratic vote and Protestants toward the Republicans.
5. Age was very significant as a predictor of intended voting patterns. Among both Protestants and Catholics, younger people leaned toward the Democrats and the older toward the Republicans.

These complex relationships were painstakingly sorted out and illustrated with bar charts based on simple percentage comparisons. Armed with today's linear models for multivariate analysis, and a computer to do the "slave labor" of computation, a far more efficient analysis would be possible. Nevertheless, the overall finding that emerged was expressed elegantly enough: "Different social characteristics, different votes."[6]

An Index of Political Predisposition   The predisposing factors noted above made it possible to develop for each subject an index of the likelihood of a Democratic or a Republican vote. This was done before knowing how the person actually voted in November, basing the predictions on the hypothesis that the variables would be predictive. Later, three of the factors were found to have provided the greatest predictive value. These were SES, religion, and rural–urban residence. For each person, the researchers constructed an index of political predisposition (IPP) and used this in studying the way in which the subjects reached their voting decisions. The index classified the voters into six categories: (1) Strongly Republican, (2) Moderately Republican, (3) Slightly Republican, (4) Slightly Democratic, (5) Moderately Democratic, and (6) Strongly Democratic. For example, a person was classified in category (1) if he was a rich, Protestant, farmer. At the other end, a person was in category (6) if he was a Catholic laborer living in Sandusky. (Category 7 was combined with 6.) Others were in the intermediate categories, depending on their SES level and their mix of the other critical factors.

This IPP proved to be remarkably well correlated with vote intention. Figure 4 shows the relationship. Clearly, the social composition of the public made a considerable difference. Later, the way in which these predispositions led people to attend and respond to media propaganda in different patterns will be brought out.

The concept of political predisposition based on social categories was to prove valuable in understanding the process by which people initially formed and then solidified their vote intention, even if they did not know themselves what they were going to do initially. The simple fact is that most eventually went in the direction predicted by their IPP category.

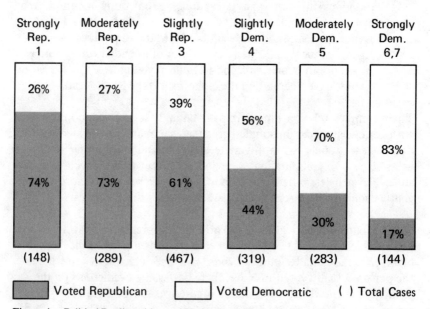

Figure 4. Political Predisposition and Voting Pattern.

SOURCE: Paul F. Lazarsfeld, Bernard Berelson and Hazel Gaudet, *The People's Choice* (New York: Columbia University Press, 1948) p. 26.

Their social categories led them to be selective in their exposure to media propaganda and selective in influences from other people. This was clearest for people toward the ends of the scale, but considerably less clear for those subjected to conflicting forces if they were somewhere in the middle categories.

Democratic and Republican Ideas about Public Affairs   Not all voters are aware of the critical issues confronting their nation, even during a presidential election when the issues are receiving heavy attention in the campaign. However, thinking about the issues does make a difference in voting intentions and behavior. Those leaning toward the Republicans or the Democrats had different ideas about social and economic matters in 1940 and the researchers tried to probe these differences in awareness and thinking carefully to see how they influenced vote intention. For example, on such issues as "unemployment," "relief" (welfare), and the "WPA" (a make-work program using federal funds to reduce unemployment), members of both parties conceded a Roosevelt victory to the poor, who after all were the recipients of such measures. However, the Republicans did not feel that these were the kinds of people who should be helped by federal expenditures. Republicans wanted a more favorable climate for business, rather than increased expenditures on social benefits for the needy. On the other hand, more than half of the Democrats felt that a Willkie victory would benefit only business groups and the relatively well-to-do. Republicans tended to deny this and maintain that stimulating business would provide more jobs and consequently a more prosperous nation. In short, both groups tended to see Willkie as a businessman's candidate and Roosevelt as a working man's candidate. Thus, the rich man versus poor man theme was salient during the entire campaign.

The war in Europe also provided ample grounds for political differences. We noted earlier that one large segment of the society was "isolationist" and wanted to stay completely clear of the "mess in Europe." Another part of the population felt that Hitler's and Mussolini's totalitarianism was threatening to overwhelm democracy in Europe and that it was only a matter of time until America would have to become involved. With these isolationist versus interventionist views in the background, Republicans generally opposed the recently passed conscription (draft) bill, and were against increases in military aid to Britain. Democrats, on the other hand, were behind various measures related to "national preparedness" and efforts to aid Britain. Military participation in the war, however, was not thought by either party to be likely in the near future.

In addition to the domestic economy and national defense, there was a host of other issues on which Democrats and Republicans found themselves on different sides. Roosevelt's third term was one. Farm issues, and policies toward labor were others. The strikingly different personalities of the candidates appealed to different types of voters. Willkie's lack of experience in foreign affairs troubled some; his strong business background attracted others. Roosevelt's boldness in reshaping American government put some people off; his imaginative leadership made a great deal of sense to others.

These were the kinds of issues around which the media campaign was organized. Each of these topics provided the basis for newspaper editorials, radio commentaries, magazine articles, movie newsreels, political speeches, and arguments between friends. They were debated in every setting from dingy barrooms to lofty mansions. And it was these issues that provided the grounds upon which people formed their opinions, reached a decision concerning their vote, decided to remain aloof, shifted from one candidate to another or remained firm in their resolve.

Before the media campaign could interact with predispositions of the voters, however, their interest in the election had to be stimulated sufficiently so that they would attend. Not everyone was equally interested at the outset. In fact, interest in the election was a function of a number of variables.

Variables Related to Interest in the Election The social composition of the parties and their opinions about the issues are not the only significant factors that shape a presidential election. The level of interest in the election and the campaign is also critical. Throughout the interviewing program data were collected to try to assess what variables, what categories of people or their personal characteristics, would provide the best index of their interest in the election. As it turned out, the best predictor was the simplest of all: the respondent's self-rating of his or her level of interest. During the interviews the respondents were asked to classify themselves according to their level of interest. In other words, people were asked to indicate whether they had (1) a great deal, (2) moderate, (3) mild, or (4) no interest in the election. These four were later reduced to three by combining moderate and mild. This provided only a crude ordinal measure of level of interest, but the researchers justified the procedure by their findings. Those who claimed the highest level of interest were more familiar with the issues and had clearer opinions than those who claimed less interest. The most interested also participated more in election events, were more likely to attend to political communications and discuss them with others.

Interest was also related to some of the social categories discussed earlier. For example, both a higher SES and educational level were positively correlated with interest. The least interested respondents tended to be the poor and the relatively uneducated. Urban versus rural residence was not a predictor of level of interest, but age certainly was. Regardless of educational level and nearly everything else, it was the older respondents who had the highest level of interest in the election. Finally, men were more interested than women.

Level of interest was a good predictor of actual participation in the voting. As might be suspected, the greatest proportion of nonvoters was found at the lowest level of interest. Figure 5 shows the dramatic impact of this variable. It can be added that nonvoting tended to be deliberate rather than accidental or unwitting. In two out of every three cases of nonvoting, the respondents had indicated their intention not to vote early in the campaign. There were, in 1940, factors operating to produce alienation among at least some citizens.

Factors Influencing Voters at the Time of Final Decision

A respondent's level of interest in the campaign was a good indicator of how *early* or *late* he or she reached a final decision concerning which candidate to vote for. Another strong factor at the time of final decision was the degree to which the person was caught in *cross pressures*, or, in other words, conflicts and inconsistencies among the variables that influence vote decision.

Early versus Late Decisions   The more interested people were in the election, the earlier they reached a decision as to how they would vote. This

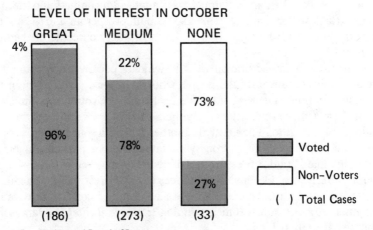

Figure 5.   Voting and Level of Interest.

SOURCE: Paul F. Lazarfeld, Bernard Berelson and Hazel Gaudet, *The People's Choice* (New York: Columbia University Press, 1948) p. 46.

held true regardless of party affiliation or other factors. Nearly two-thirds of the respondents with a "great deal" of interest in the election had already made up their minds by May when the interviewing began (even though the nominees had not yet been selected in their respective conventions). Only one-eighth of such respondents waited until late in the campaign to make their choice. As we will note later, this closing of the mind early in the campaign was an important condition, because it had a strong influence on their mass communication behavior, with respect to selecting political propaganda from the media.

On the other side of the coin, those with less interest decided on their candidates much later. This posed some interesting problems for those in charge of the media campaigns. How could these people whose minds remained open be attracted to a particular candidate? One difficulty was that even though they were uncommitted, they were also uninterested. This meant that they paid little attention to political propaganda. At the same time, in a close election their votes could spell the difference between victory and defeat.

Toward the end of the campaign, the pool of such uninterested and undecided potential voters grew smaller and smaller. Campaign managers had to exert their greatest efforts to interest such people in supporting their candidate.

The Problem of Cross Pressures Earlier, three specific variables were discussed that most sharply differentiated Republicans and Democrats. These were SES, religion, and rural–urban residence. These three factors were the basis of the index of political predisposition (IPP). But what happened when an individual was caught in a conflicting pattern of these variables? For example, if a person is both prosperous and a Catholic, or both poor and a farmer, what is the most likely outcome of the vote decision?

There are many additional ways in which a person can be caught in cross pressures. For example, people who voted for a given party in the previous election have a considerable probability of voting the same way again. Yet, if they are disaffected by their party's new candidate, they are under cross pressure. The family is another potential source of cross pressure. If a person's family is strongly affiliated with one party or the other, the individual is under pressure to vote with them, even if he or she has another preference. Other similar sources of cross pressures are friends or even work associates. All of these together make up a considerable web of potential cross pressures, some stemming from social categories and some from social relationships.

But whatever the source of such cross pressures, one effect was clear. Cross pressures *delayed* the voter's final decision. Among the various sources of cross pressures, the most influential in causing delays was the family. The reluctance of many voters to commit themselves to a particular candidate was often traceable to exactly this kind of difference with family members.

Cross pressures and their associated delays have implications for the media campaign of political propaganda. Voters under cross pressures delay their vote hoping that some event will occur to resolve their indecision. This indecision makes these voters fair game for political managers, who hope to get into their propaganda just the right message to break the indecision and attract the person to their candidate. Toward the end of the campaign, efforts are intensified to attract undecided voters, and these efforts can pay off. Thus, both the potential voter with low interest in the campaign and those under cross pressures become targets of special efforts as the media campaign begins to come to an end.

The overall effects of low interest and cross pressures were very different for different kinds of voters. In other words, the process of delay did not work in the same way for all people. Some remained undecided until the last moment. Others moved tentatively to one candidate but then shifted later to the other. Still others reached a decision, fell back into doubt, went over to the other side, and eventually shifted back to the earlier choice. For the most part, there were three main patterns of changes that described such voters. Some 28 percent were *crystallizers*. They simply delayed reaching a decision until the last minute. These were evenly divided between the parties. Another 15 percent were *waverers*. They started out in May with a clear vote intention. Later in the campaign they slid back into indecision, but later returned to their original choice. Finally, a smaller proportion (eight percent) were *party changers*. They started out with a clear vote intention but eventually deserted to the other candidate. The simplest generalization that emerged from all of this data was that individuals who leave their party and fall into indecision usually return to their first choice. Those who change from one party to another, however, seldom return.

Major Effects of the Media Campaign

One of the main results of the study was to identify three clear patterns of influence of the mass-mediated campaign of political propaganda. These patterns describe the way in which mass-mediated information can play key roles in leading voters to form voting decisions, given their existing pattern of political predispositions. In other words, there is a considerable amount of interaction between the predisposing social characteristics of voters, what they select and use from the political propaganda presented by the media, and their ultimate voting choice. These complex relationships can best be understood by examining three concepts that identify the patterns of influence of the mediated propaganda. These are *activation, reinforcement,* and *conversion.*

Activation   Political communications activate latent predispositions. They do so by presenting effective arguments to people who selectively attend to them because they are consistent with their predisposing orientations. This is true both for formal propaganda presented by mass-mediated campaigns and more personal persuasion presented by family members or friends.

Activation refers to the process of making something manifest or observable. In the case of a voter, it refers to bringing the individual to a conscious decision that is consistent with the kinds of predisposing variables identified earlier as making up the IPP. Since about half of the voters had already made up their minds in May, and some never did reach a decision, activation took place only among a limited number of voters. The best estimate places it at about 14 percent among the people studied.

The activation of political predispositions is a process that takes place in stages or steps. These steps identify the relationship between the voter's latent predispositions and political persuasion presented as either media propaganda or personal influences:

1. *Propaganda arouses interest.* We showed earlier that interest was a key variable in reaching a decision to vote. Thus, a rising level of propaganda gets attention and begins to increase interest.
2. *Increased interest brings increased exposure.* This is a circular effect. The more people pay attention, the more interesting the campaign becomes and this increases their interest even more.
3. *Increased attention causes voter to select information.* As interest and attention increase, the more likely it is that the voter will select information consistent with his or her underlying predispositions. Thus, selective attention reinforces predispositions, which in turn increases selectivity.
4. *Votes crystallize.* The latent becomes manifest. The voter is now aware of the candidate and the candidate's position on the issues. This awareness is highly selective but it leads to the forming of a decision based on a body of information.

The process of activation is somewhat inconsistent with the concept of the "rational" voter, supposedly the ideal in a democratic society. Such ideal voters would review carefully the issues and the candidates and make a decision on the basis of enlightened self-interest only after learning and assessing all of the facts. Activation, on the other hand, takes place because voters already are strongly predisposed to one party or the other and they crystallize their vote to support that party's candidate. It is hardly a rational model, because the opposition is given little systematic consideration. Nevertheless, activation is one of the principal effects that results from the flow of information during a political campaign.

Reinforcement   More than half of the voters had already consciously selected their candidate before the interviewing began in May. They were not certain who their party would select in the convention, but they intended to vote for him in any case. For those people the propaganda campaign served quite another purpose. Campaign managers have to supply such already-decided voters with a continuing flow of arguments and justifications for remaining right where they are. This is a very important function of the media campaign. We noted that about half of the people interviewed already knew in May for whom they would vote. If such partisans are not kept in line, they could become waverers, or even worse, party changers. As the researchers put it:

> Party propaganda—from his own party—provides an arsenal of political arguments which serve to allay the partisan's doubts and to refute the opposition arguments which he encounters in exposure to media and friends—in short, to secure and stabilize and solidify his vote intention and translate it into an actual vote. A continuing flow of partisan arguments enables him to reinterpret otherwise unsettling events and counter-arguments so that they do not leave him in an uncomfortable state of mental indecision or inconsistency.[7]

Generally, then, reinforcement is far less dramatic than the process of persuading voters to desert their party for the other camp. However, because such a large proportion of the voters are involved, it is far more important. A failure to understand the reinforcement effects of political propaganda could easily cost a candidate the election.

Conversion   When ordinary people think of the influence of political propaganda, they usually have conversion in mind. Through the clever use of words, emotional appeals, or even rational arguments, it is assumed, individuals can be persuaded to desert their candidate and switch sides. But does it really happen? The answer is a highly qualified "yes" but only in a few cases and in particular circumstances. In Erie County there were people who were converted, but they were few indeed. Only about eight percent of the voters made a switch.

There are a number of reasons why it is unrealistic to look for large numbers of conversions. For one thing, fully half of the voters never wavered from their early decisions, making them unavailable for conversion attempts. Clear-cut political predispositions anchor another large proportion of voters in their party, even though they remain undecided and undergo the process of activation and eventually reach a decision that is entirely consistent with those predispositions: These voters are not open to conversion. Only those who remained less interested and who were under strong cross pressures were the prospects for conversion when they did reach a tentative decision. In such decisions, their commitments were weak, unsupported by strong interest, ties to a party, or a consistent network of social pressures. The numbers of such people grew smaller and smaller as activation and reinforcement took place, as interest grew stronger, and as cross pressures were resolved. In the final stages, only a handful could be persuaded to switch from an earlier tentative vote decision. For the most part, the authors concluded, the completely open-minded voter who remains undecided until the end, or who switches from one candidate to another because of compelling logic in the discussion of issues, exists only in textbooks on civics.

Overall Effects   The speeches, newspaper editorials, magazine articles, radio talks, and all of the rest making up the presidential campaign had three principal effects. They activated the indifferent voter who was predisposed; reinforced the partisan; and converted a few of the doubtful. For Erie County as a whole, the Republicans made gains over their pattern of support in the election that had been held four years earlier. The 1936 election had been a considerable victory for Roosevelt in the county. Basically, his modifications of the American economic and governmental institutions made during his first term were well-received by the electorate. But events since 1936 had, to a degree, dimmed that enthusiasm. The issues of the third term, the slow recovery from the Depression, the war clouds in Europe, and the unknowns of the new welfare state troubled many people in Erie County. For these reasons they had returned in the direction of their basically conservative orientations of the past. Nationwide, of course, the election went overwhelmingly to Roosevelt. However, the conservatives of Erie County decided that their day would come at a later time.

Patterns of Attention to Campaign Propaganda

Those who design and manage presidential campaigns devise detailed, comprehensive, and sophisticated strategies in their efforts to attract the votes of the electorate to their candidate. This was as true in 1940 as it is now. At that time, of course, television was only an experimental device being studied in laboratories and test sites. The media of the campaign were radio, newspapers, and magazines. And, in the case of magazines, the country was still in the era of the general, huge circulation periodical, such as the *Saturday Evening Post*. Some specialty magazines, such as the *Farm Journal*, also played a role.

Whatever the medium, the purpose of political propaganda is to capture the attention, whet the interest, and shape the decisions of voters. As the authors of *The People's Choice* put it, political messages are designed

> . . . to corral the timid, lead the willing, and convince the reluctant. Partisan leaders of opinion—the newspaper editor, the columnist, the free lance writer, the syndicated cartoonist, the radio commentator, and the local sage—all edge into the campaign by placing the weight of their authority behind the cause of their favorite candidate. Propaganda is let loose upon the land to control or inform, to constrain or tease potential voters into the appropriate decision.[8]

In other words, an enormous amount of political information is transmitted by the media at election time. However, the big question is not how much was printed, broadcast, or said, but how many in the audience attended and understood that information. The big question also includes another issue. Was the media exposure more or less evenly spread through the population, or was it concentrated more among some kinds of people?

This last issue is one with considerable theoretical relevance. Early thinking about propaganda was that, like magic bullets, it struck all members of the mass audience equally and created uniform effects among them in a very direct way. This idea was, as we have seen, under considerable question by the time the present research was undertaken. However, the research strategy of *The People's Choice*—in particular the repeated interviewing—permitted the researchers to address fairly directly the question of who attended to a particular medium, and with what outcome. It was an opportunity, in other words, to test the major propositions of the magic bullet theory. To be historically accurate, *The People's Choice* researchers did not actually pose their investigation of patterns of media attention in those terms. They simply wanted to know whether every voter received a more or less equal exposure to the media, or whether attention to the campaign was concentrated among a few. And, if the latter were the case, who were they, and what did the exposure do to them? Yet, in retrospect, their study *did* test the magic bullet theory, even if the authors did not specifically set out to do so at the time.

An associated issue under investigation in 1940 was the question of the relative importance of the three major media. Did people attend to radio, the newspapers, or magazines in an equal manner, or was one a dominant source of political information for certain kinds of people? Answers to these several questions were provided as the analysis examined the formation of decisions about choosing a candidate in relation to patterns of attention to mediated propaganda.

The Concentration of Exposure Who listened and who read? Those were critical questions concerning the outpouring of political information during the election. The answer was that close attention was given to the media propaganda by some but certainly not all. The pattern was dependent upon what medium, what candidate, what issues, and what voters were under consideration. Patterns of attention, in other words, were very *selective*. They were by no means spread evenly among the electorate. For example, during the last 12 days of the campaign, 54 percent of the respondents had attended to at least one political talk on radio; another 51 percent had read at least one front page campaign story in a newspaper; and 26 percent had read a campaign-related article in a magazine. Earlier in the campaign, such material had been ignored by one-half to three-fourths of the population interviewed. But even in the last days of the campaign, only part of the voters attended to any of the material, and a very large proportion ignored the media campaign altogether. In other words, as the campaign moved into its last days, a flood of political material was directed at the voters. But, as the authors put it, "far from drowning any of these people, it did not even get their feet wet." [9]

Who were the people who did attend to the messages? Actually, with remarkable consistency, political propaganda presented by the various media reached the *same* segment of the population. In other words, those who listened to material about the campaign on the radio also tended to read about the same issues in the newspapers and follow the treatments of the topics in magazine stories. Thus, there was a segment of the population that was heavily exposed to the campaign propaganda while the remainder gave the same material only little if any attention.

Who were these people who received multiple exposure? The answers to that question have already been suggested in previous analyses of the process by which people arrive at their voting decision. Those who attended most to the media were the highly *interested* voters, those who had *already decided*, and those of *higher SES*. In particular among those categories, it was the more affluent, well-educated, and older males who lived in urban areas.

There are a number of possible explanations for this pattern of concentration of attention among particular kinds of voters. The researchers suggested that such people probably believe that they have an especially large stake in the outcome of the election. Certainly, they tend to be more politically aware, and they have a deeper understanding of the issues. But whatever the explanation of this particular pattern of concentration, it was clear that the propositions of the magic bullet theory concerning uniform patterns of attention and influence from the media were not consistent with the findings. So much for the magic bullet theory!

Radio versus Print   The study of the presidential election provided one of the first large-scale investigations of what was, in 1940, still a relatively new medium of mass communication. Radio was compared with newspapers (and magazines) in terms of their comparative roles in the campaign. No one really understood radio as an instrument of politics. Ten years earlier, only about 40 percent of American homes had radio ownership. By 1940, that figure had risen so rapidly that virtually everyone had a receiver. In fact, the figure in that year was 1.4 sets per household, on the average, in the United States. In a decade, radio had become a giant and had saturated the American population.

But how did this new medium compare with the venerable newspaper? After all, the mass newspaper had been around for a century. Its role in politics was virtually undisputed. In 1940, newspapers were still close to their all-time peak of popularity in American society. Only a decade earlier, Americans had subscribed to daily newspapers at near-record levels of 1.32 per household. In the highest year, 1910, the figure had been 1.36 subscriptions per household; in 1940, the figure was still high at 1.18. This compares to a mere .82 subscriptions per household in 1980.

Some had begun to claim that radio was the medium of the future in politics, and that even in 1940 it was more meaningful than print in the campaign because the audiences could hear the speeches of the candidates and get a feeling for their personal qualities far more than from reading about them. Others felt that the printed word still retained its authority, and that a mere gadget like radio could never replace the newspaper as a medium for the serious presentation and exchange of political ideas.

The researchers decided to sort out this question—to try to find out to what media people had attended and how much they had been influenced by these media. They proceeded by getting people to identify in very specific terms exactly what newspaper editorials, news stories, or speeches they had read, and how this exposure had influenced their thinking about the issues. They probed into what magazine stories the voters had read, what kinds of information they had learned from such sources, and how this had helped shape their political views. They also had their respondents indicate what particular program they had listened to on the radio—what speeches they had heard, what commentaries, and so forth. By such detailed assessment of the exposure patterns for each medium among various categories of voters, the relative role and comparative significance of newspapers, magazines and radio could be determined.

As it turned out, radio had played a larger role in the campaign than anyone had suspected. When respondents were asked which media were "helpful" as they were making their decisions, about two-thirds mentioned both radio and newspapers about equally. However, when the voters were asked to indicate which of the media was the "most important" source for political information which played a part in their decisions, radio clearly led (by roughly a 50 percent margin).

Radio was also more heavily used by the Democrats. In both 1936 and 1940, the majority of the nation's newspapers openly supported the Republicans. Presumably this was because of the close ties newspapers had to the business community. Meanwhile, Democrats had turned to radio as an alternative. Roosevelt, in particular, used the medium masterfully as a political tool. He often went on the air to explain his programs to the nation. He held periodic "fireside chats" via radio, in which he spoke informally concerning the issues of the day. Because of these "fireside chats," his voice was well known to almost everyone. Willkie, on the other hand, was not an effective radio personality and this hurt him in the election.

In the final analysis, radio emerged as a medium favored by the Democrats and newspapers were favored by the Republicans. But in spite of the overwhelming support given by newspapers to the Republican candidate, he lost badly. Radio emerged as a politically potent medium with considerably greater significance than the printed page. It was the beginning of an era in which the personal qualities of the candidates could come under the close scrutiny of the electorate via a medium of telecommunication, bringing the personality of the presidential hopeful to a level of significance not known in earlier times.

It can be added that magazines played a minor role in the election. Some 15 to 25 percent of the respondents obtained political information from magazines. For those individuals, magazines did play a part in shaping their political views and decisions, along with exposure to political propaganda from the other media. In other words, few voters, if any, relied solely on magazines for their information. They used them to supplement information obtained from newspapers and radio.

Personal Influence and the Two-Step Flow

As the interviewing progressed month after month in Erie County, it became increasingly apparent that there were sources of influence on people's political decisions that had not been given sufficient attention when planning the study. The interviewers were discovering that people received a great deal of their information and influence directly from other people! Whenever the respondents were asked to report on their recent exposure to political communications, they mentioned discussions about politics with friends, relatives, or acquaintances much more frequently than exposure to radio or print. Face-to-face discussions were a more important source of political influence than the researchers had anticipated.

The significance of personal influence was not realized until the study was well under way. It was a serendipitous finding that simply emerged as the research was in progress. For that reason, no formal hypotheses had been built into the study to assess this phenomenon. However, once the investigators realized that people were talking to each other extensively about the election, and that these interpersonal exchanges played a key role in leading the voters to their decisions, they quickly revised what they were doing and gathered as much data concerning this interpersonal flow of information and influence as they could.

The hypothesis the investigators developed would have a significant impact on the direction of mass communication research for many years. They called it the "two-step flow of communication." After examining their data they concluded that some individuals among the people they had studied were serving as "opinion leaders." These were people who were heavily exposed to the political campaign, and to whom others, who had lower levels of exposure, knowledge, and interest, would turn for information and advice. The opinion leaders would pass on to these others information that they had received from first-hand exposure to the media, along with their own special interpretations of what it all meant. Thus, the heavy involvement of people in political discussions led the researchers to suggest that: "ideas often flow *from* radio and print *to* the opinion leaders and *from* them to the less active sections of the population." [10] This was their formal statement of the two-step flow hypothesis.

There were a number of reasons, the researchers pointed out, why personal influence would be particularly effective in helping shape people's decisions—in many cases much more effective than persuasive information presented in more formal media. For example, personal influence from opinion leaders was more likely to reach the undecided and the uninterested voter, both of whom were all but impervious to the political campaign presented via the media. The opinion leaders were also likely to be trusted as nonpurposive sources of information and interpretation. Political propaganda presented by radio and print, on the other hand, is clearly designed to persuade and is therefore not trustworthy. There is also the factor of flexibility. In a casual discussion setting, the person giving another his or her views can be very flexible and counter resistance that might occur—a fact well known by all effective sales people. The factor of reward can be added. When one agrees with or accepts the views or interpretations of another who is trying to "set us straight" a considerable amount of social approval is likely to be forthcoming. It is rewarding to accept personal influence; yet this factor is absent in more formal media presentations. Finally, one seldom mistrusts an intimate source. This may be largely because those who exercise personal influence do it unwittingly. And those whose views are modified may not even realize that this is happening to them. Generally, then, as information moves from the media to the opinion leaders and from them to the less active, the idea that they are engaging in political persuasion or are accepting political influence may never cross their minds.

CONCLUSIONS AND IMPLICATIONS

The People's Choice was one of the most important studies in the history of mass communication research for several reasons. First, it showed how an innovative survey design could be used in longitudinal research. Many important forms of social behavior are processes that take place over time. Typically, researchers study subjects with an experiment or a survey at only one point in that time. Sometimes, to try and get around that limitation, they will study different samples of people representing cohorts at different stages in the process, but this has many pitfalls. The panel design used in *The People's Choice* got around those limitations and pitfalls by following the same subjects through the entire process. The design effectively answered the question of which influences were introduced by the repeated assessments. The answer in this case was none. Although there is no guarantee that repeated interviewing will never influence subjects, the panel design continues to be a major procedure used in longitudinal research.

A second major contribution of the research was its insights into the role of political propaganda presented by the media during the campaign. The findings showed clearly that such propaganda activated those with latent predispositions based on social category membership; reinforced those whose decisions were already firmly anchored by the constraints of those category memberships; and even swayed a few to move from one side to the other. The conversion process, however, was shown to be very limited. It occurred mainly among voters who had made a tentative earlier choice to which they were only weakly tied. Such individuals were not much interested in the campaign and they were under confusing cross pressures from their social category memberships.

These findings on selective influences based on social categories were to prove to be theoretically significant in ways that the researchers of the time could not appreciate. Activation and reinforcement—the principal media effects according to the study—are really quite limited by comparison with the kinds of effects of the media envisioned by the critics of World War I propaganda. The legacy of fear had people believing that clever politicians could use newspapers, or even the new medium of radio, to sway and control the political behavior of the masses at will. The specter that alarmed critics the most was that of clever manipulators controlling the mass society in such a way that democratic nations could be converted to fascism, or even worse, to communism. *The People's Choice,* however, showed that conversion on this scale was extremely unlikely. The effects were not all-powerful, swaying helpless audiences uniformly and directly. They were limited effects linked to the demographic characteristics of the audiences in highly selective ways. Opinion leaders, a small category, were selectively influenced by the media. However, the majority of the people remained little touched by the propaganda from the media. As it turned out, interpersonal channels brought them more influence than the media.

Above all, it was the issue of the "two-step flow" that caught the imagination of a new generation of researchers. The edition of *The People's Choice* that became widely available to the scientific community did not appear until 1948. Following that, research on the interpersonal processes linked to mass communication burgeoned. The two-step flow hypothesis, in other words, opened up a new theoretical vista. Social relationships between people had definitely *not* been thought to be significant in the process of mass communication. Mass society theory, and its mass communication derivative, the magic bullet conceptualization, had stressed a *lack* of social ties between people. Yet, here were research findings from a large-scale study showing that ties between people were one of the most important parts of the mass communication process.

The two-step flow hypothesis emerged serendipitously from the research. But in many ways the hypothesis seems, in retrospect, the study's most important contribution. It certainly called into question most of the assumptions of the magic bullet theory and it did little to vindicate continued belief in the legacy of fear. But in spite of this, both ideas remained in force among the beliefs of the public regarding the influence of mass communication on people.

Overall, *The People's Choice* remains one of the most sophisticated survey research studies in the history of social science. Its place in the development of mass communication theory is undisputed. It forced communication theorists to reconsider the mass society concept, the powerful influences idea, the role of social category membership, and the significance of interpersonal ties. Few studies in the history of mass communication research have had such an impact.

NOTES AND REFERENCES

1. Arthur M. Schlesinger, Jr., Fred L. Israel, and William P. Hanson, eds., *History of American Presidential Elections, Vol. IV* (New York: Chelsea House Publishers, 1971). See Chapter 1 by Robert E. Burke, "Election of 1940," p. 2923.
2. Ibid., p. 2925.
3. Paul F. Lazarsfeld, Bernard Berelson, and Hazel Gaudet, *The People's Choice* (New York: Columbia University Press, 1948).
4. Ibid., p. 159 (footnote 2).
5. Ibid., pp. 6–7.
6. Ibid., p. 21.
7. Ibid., p. 88.
8. Ibid., p. 120.
9. Ibid., p. 121.
10. Ibid., p. 151.

5

experiments on mass communication: persuading the american soldier in world war II

On Sunday, December 7, 1941, Americans, in near disbelief, heard from their radios that Japanese aircraft had without warning attacked U. S. naval and other military forces at Pearl Harbor. The heavy loss of life and disastrous destruction of ships, aircraft, and Army bases left the nation reeling. Nearly a quarter of a century of peacetime had come to a sudden end.

How could it be? Who were these strange people who came from nowhere to commit such a dastardly deed? The Japanese, in the minds of most Americans—if they thought of them at all—were a rather pathetic little nation of slant-eyed people who made cheap imitations of products developed by more advanced countries. It simply did not seem possible that such people could dare to assault the might of the United States of America! Nevertheless, the forces of the Empire of Japan had blasted most of the U. S. Pacific Fleet to ruined hulks, and had humiliated the armed forces of what Americans regarded as the finest nation on earth.

The next day, President Franklin D. Roosevelt in a special joint session of the Congress addressed the country by radio to declare that a state of war existed between the United States and the Empire of Japan. The President called December 7 "a day that will live in infamy." The state of war was extended to include all of the Axis Powers who were allied with Japan.

In the days that followed, Japan's victories at Pearl Harbor were to be repeated in other areas of vital significance to the United States. The Philippines were quickly overrun, and their American defenders were subjected to a terrible "death march" on the Bataan peninsula. The Japanese overran virtually the whole Southwest Pacific, threatening Australia and New Zealand. They even landed on remote parts of Alaska. For the first time the United States was called upon to fight for its very existence against the hostile forces of a foreign enemy.

THE NATION AT WAR

World War II was a conflict with a clear-cut moral purpose. The Axis Powers (Germany, Japan and Italy) vowed to subdue the world with military might and to dominate it with their various brands of dictatorship and fascism. The Allied Forces, made up of the United States, what was left of the British Empire, and the remnants of various armed forces from countries that had been overrun by the early victories of the enemy, vowed to fight back to an eventual "unconditional surrender" of the Axis nations.

From the point of view of the United States, it was a war with the highest possible justification—a very different situation from more recent conflicts. The Japanese had "stabbed America in the back." In the minds of most citizens the Japanese were sneaky, cruel, and virtually subhuman. The Germans had overrun helpless people in Europe and violated every treaty that had been forged at the end of World War I. They were widely held to be ruthless, cunning, and brutal. The Italians, on the other hand, were regarded with low esteem—a joke as soldiers, but a bother nevertheless.

All of these attitudes and beliefs were quickly taken up and reinforced by the mass media, by thousands of political speeches, cartoons, posters, and barroom exchanges. Hollywood epics and newspaper editorials portrayed the Germans as "pretty tough," but the Japanese as monkey-like people who should not be taken seriously. Some people maintained that the enemy would be easily defeated and the war brought to an end within a year. But as many a soldier, sailor, and marine found out later in combat, crude stereotypes obscured the fact that the enemy was tough, determined, and thoroughly courageous.

Turning Citizens into Soldiers

For a few weeks after Pearl Harbor, volunteers lined up at the recruiting offices and even scuffled with each other to be among the earliest to enlist. But the rush to get into the fight soon waned and the less enthusiastic had to be brought in by the Selective Service System—the draft. Actually there was little resistance; to be a "draft dodger" during World War II was considered a disgrace. Even those classified as 4-F (not suitable for military service because of health or occupation essential to the war effort) were all but accused of being cowards. By the war's end, some 15 million Americans, mostly males but a few females, had donned uniforms.

The sheer logistics of locating, sorting, classifying, training, and assigning 15 million people to military duties staggers the imagination. Nevertheless, it was done. Young men and women from every walk of civilian life were transformed from their roles and statuses as bank clerks, secretaries, truck drivers, farmers, and so on, into riflemen, artillerymen, bosuns, sergeants, cooks, signalmen, pilots, navigators, and all of the other specialists that were required by the military services. What is more, it was done in a very short time.

Camps were set up in all parts of the nation and recruits were quickly brought in for training. Their hair was cut short and they exchanged their civilian clothes for uniforms. Awkward at first, they soon settled into the routines of training—close order drill, how to use weapons, the intricacies of military life, and the inevitable specialized training required in the complex division of labor of a modern army or navy.

Teaching a recruit such matters as wearing a uniform, how to salute, march, and use weapons is the less difficult part of military training. Beyond that lies the more complex task of shaping his motivation and morale. He has to be taught to hate the enemy and love his country, to be intensely dedicated to his military unit, and to place its survival and welfare above his own. In other words, in developing an effective fighting force it is essential to instill attitudes and loyalties that can provide critical psychological and social supports which sustain the combat soldier when the going gets tough. As a matter of fact, the vast majority of those so trained never saw combat. Nevertheless, they had to be taught to place military goals above their personal convenience and comfort even when the job was boring, seemingly endless, and obviously insignificant. For those who would see combat, indoctrination was needed to prepare them psychologically to confront and defeat a very determined and dangerous enemy. There was simply no other choice.

Turning millions of young civilians into effective teams of military personnel was no easy task. The training was made more difficult by the sheer diversity of American society. Draftees were called into service from every corner of the country. They came from ethnic communities in urban centers, small towns in the midwest, farms in the rural south, and cattle ranches in the far west. Not only were they diverse in regional origin, but they varied greatly in every other respect. They differed in education, income, occupation, religion, political affiliation, and so on. This diversity in social origins meant that the recruits also represented a broad range of individual differences in intelligence, aptitudes, values, skills, and other psychological factors. It was not easy to assess their differences and to assign these human resources to military tasks that they were capable of performing. To do so the Army (and other services) made use of psychologists, sociologists, and other social scientists who developed tests to measure intelligence and other attributes so that the proverbial "square pegs" among the recruits would not wind up in the "round holes" among the tasks that needed to be performed.

The Lessons to be Learned: The *Why We Fight* Films

Another serious problem was the sheer ignorance of the majority of the draftees concerning public affairs. Few of the recruits had any real grasp of the complex international events that had led up to the entry of the United States into the war. They knew well enough that "the Japs were the dirty guys" because they had bombed Pearl Harbor in a sneaky way. They also knew that "the Germans were mean guys" because they had overrun some of the countries of Europe and wanted to take over the world. That was about it! Beyond those simple ideas the majority had very little knowledge of the political history of the period between the two world wars, the existence or substance of the negotiations between the United States and Japan before Pearl Harbor, or the sequences of events that led to the rise of totalitarian governments in Europe, or the strategies of those governments for world conquest.

Why were they so ignorant of international events? In large part, the United States was isolated from world problems, by both by its physical location in the new world and by its preoccupation with its own internal affairs. Since the end of World War I, Americans had been focusing their attention on such domestic matters as Prohibition, the Great Depression, the Dust Bowl, and the New Deal. The troubles in Europe and Asia were beyond the interest and comprehension of all but a few of the draftees. Yet, it was essential that the recruits have a good understanding of these events.

The Army was painfully aware of the need to inform its recruits, but how it could be done was another matter. Army leaders saw immediately that they needed a rapid and effective means of teaching soldiers about the nature of the enemy, their allies, and why it was necessary to be there training for war. The use of a series of training films to do the task quickly and for large numbers of trainees seemed a sensible way to get the job done. However, there were no such films and they would have to be prepared very quickly.

Early in 1942, General George C. Marshall, newly appointed Chief of Staff of the Army, turned to Hollywood to assist in the preparation of the necessary orientation films. Specifically, he sought the aid of Frank Capra, a well-known director. His proposal was simple:

> Now Capra, I want to nail down with you a plan to make a series of documentary, factual information films—the first in our history—that will explain to our boys why we are fighting and the principles for which we are fighting.[1]

Capra wanted to help, but he wasn't certain that he was the right person to do the job. He explained to General Marshall that he lacked the right kind of experience. He had never made documentary films before. General Marshall had a simple answer:

> Capra, I have never been Chief of Staff before. Thousands of young Americans have never had their legs shot off before. Boys are commanding ships today who a year ago had never seen the ocean.[2]

Capra was convinced and began work immediately. In a very short time he had produced seven 50-minute documentary films and the Army started making them a part of the training program for its recruits.

> The style of the films was for the most part objective and documentary, with direct quotations, reference to official sources, animated diagrams, cuts from domestic newsreels, and cuts from foreign newsreels and propaganda films. The visual presentation was drawn together by a running narration which told the story of the war and explained the scenes. While the general tenor of the films was "let the facts speak for themselves," they were not dryly factual. Foreign speech was frequently translated into English with a "foreign accent," "production" shots using actors were employed to tie the documentary material together, the films were scored throughout with background music, and montages and trick photography were used in trying to achieve vivid and dramatic presentation.[3]

Generally, these seven films traced the history of World War II from the rise of fascism in Italy and Germany, and the Japanese in Manchuria in 1931, through America's mobilization for war and participation in the conflict following Pearl Harbor.[4] The title of the series was *Why We Fight*, and the films were seen by hundreds of thousands of Americans as they trained for war. However, only four of these films were used in the research described in the present chapter. The content of these four films can be summarized briefly.

Prelude to War. This first film in the series described the rise of Mussolini and fascism in Italy, the rise of Hitler and Nazism in Germany, and the manner in which a military clique gained control in Japan. It showed the Japanese attack on Manchuria in 1931 and the military conquest of Ethiopia in 1935. In contrast the film showed how the United States had followed a noninterventionist policy and had not prepared for global war. It made clear how the Axis countries had emphasized the growth of aggressive militarism and the massing of armed might. The major theme of the film was that the three Axis countries had joined in a plan to conquer the world and to divide it up to suit themselves. There was no way for the United States to ignore the war and it had to defend itself; this defense was all the more difficult because of the lack of preparedness.

The Nazis Strike. This film presented a summary of the past military conquests of Germany under Bismarck and Kaiser Wilhelm, indicating that Hitler's aggressions were repeat performances of such behavior. The way in which Hitler had built up his war forces was described and his first acquisitions of territory were shown (the Austrian *Anschluss,* and other actions in which Britain tried to appease Hitler by agreeing to his activities). The straw that broke the camel's back was Hitler's attack on Poland, which brought a declaration of war by Britain and France. The Polish campaign was shown in great detail to illustrate the ruthlessness, brutality, and efficiency of the German forces. The major theme of the film was that Hitler could not be appeased and that the Allies had to stop him by declaring war.

Divide and Conquer. This was a sequel to *The Nazis Strike.* It continued to show the strategy of the Nazis. It explained how they overran Denmark and Norway to the north. They were aided in this activity by traitors among the local populations (called quislings, after Vidkun Quisling, a Norwegian Nazi collaborator) and by the failure of Allied efforts to help the Norwegians. To the South, the Nazis invaded the Low Countries (Holland and Belgium) and broke through the French defensive fortresses, which permitted the Germans to move through France and catch Britain in a kind of pincers from both North and South. The theme of the film was that the early defensive strategies relied upon by the Allies were unsuccessful in the face of the strategy and tactics used by the Germans.

The Battle of Britain. This film dealt with Hitler's plan for world conquest, which had succeeded thus far as his forces defeated France and forced the British to evacuate their armies from the beaches at Dunkirk. The next step was to conquer Britain itself. If Hitler had taken over the British Isles and neutralized the British fleet, the United States would have found itself in a very dangerous situation. The film showed how Hitler failed to conquer England because of the tough resistance of the British, both in the air and on the ground. The Royal Air Force stopped the Luftwaffe cold, even after weeks of the latter's relentless bombing and fighter attacks; the British were bombed severely but they continued their war effort in spite of the attacks. Thus, winning the "Battle of Britain" gave the United States precious time to prepare.

Overview of the Research Mission

Generally, two basic assumptions were made by the War Department concerning the *Why We Fight* films. First, it was assumed that they would do an effective job of teaching the recruits *factual knowledge* about the war, the enemy, and the Allies. Second, it was assumed that such factual knowledge

would shape *interpretations* and *opinions* in ways needed to improve acceptance of military roles and the sacrifices necessary to achieve victory.

In more detail, the orientation program using these films had a number
of specific objectives that were spelled out in a directive from the office of
the Chief of Staff to the Information and Education Division, which was in
charge of the orientation program. According to this directive, the films
were intended to foster:

1. A firm belief in the right of the cause for which we fight.
2. A realization that we are up against a tough job.
3. A determined confidence in our own ability and the abilities of our
   comrades and leaders to do the job that has to be done.
4. A feeling of confidence, insofar as is possible under the circumstances, in the integrity and fighting ability of our Allies.
5. A resentment, based on knowledge of the facts, against our enemies
   who have made it necessary to fight.
6. A belief that through military victory, the political achievement of
   a better world order is possible.

Each of the films had been designed to achieve these objectives, although
every one of the seven "Why We Fight" films told only a part of the story.

The big question, of course, is did the films work? The films seemed
great, and common sense implied that showing them to the recruits as part
of their training would not only teach them the factual information, but
would raise their commitment and morale. Yet, common sense is not always an adequate basis for reaching reliable conclusions. A systematic and
objective evaluation was needed to see if these films were in fact reaching
their goals. To accomplish this assessment, the task of designing and conducting evaluation studies of the orientation program was assigned to a
special unit within the War Department's Information and Education Division.

Early in the war, the Army had taken the precaution of bringing a
number of distinguished social and behavioral scientists into the service.
These scientists, in consultation with civilian colleagues, assisted the armed
services with a variety of problems involving psychological measurement,
evaluation of programs, surveys of many kinds, and studies of "morale."
Within the Information and Education Division, the Research Branch was
composed of the Experimental Section and the Survey Section. These units
often cooperated with the Military Training Division of the Army Service
Forces. Indeed, the present research represents just such a cooperative
venture between the Experimental Section and Training Division.

While there were a number of psychologists and social psychologists involved in the evaluation of the *Why We Fight* series, the main team that planned and conducted the studies for the Army consisted of Frances J. Anderson, John L. Finan, Carl I. Hovland, Irving L. Janis, Arthur A. Lumsdaine, Nathan Macoby, Fred D. Sheffield, and M. Brewster Smith. The report on which the present summary chapter is based was prepared as Volume III in the "American Soldier Series," which was published several years after the war. The authors of the report were Carl I. Hovland, Arthur A. Lumsdaine, and Fred D. Sheffield. Like the others in the longer list above, each went on after the war to become an internationally known psychologist. The remaining sections of the present chapter are devoted to a presentation of the highlights of *Experiments on Mass Communication*, which brought together the results of the film evaluation studies and a number of additional experiments on communication issues. The work touched off a considerable interest, as we will note later, in the experimental study of the persuasion process.[5]

THE FILM EVALUATION STUDIES

A series of experiments were carried out, aimed at assessing the degree to which exposure to the films described above resulted in changes in their audiences. These changes were, broadly speaking, the acquisition of factual information about various aspects of the war and modification in the recruits' interpretations and opinions concerning the six objectives listed earlier.

In designing this research, the experimenters had advantages that had seldom before existed regarding control over their subjects. They could choose where, when, and how many subjects would see a particular film. They did not have to rely on voluntary cooperation in the completion of the questionnaires. They were already in possession of a substantial amount of background information on each subject from Army records, to which they had complete access. The population they were studying had limited variation in terms of age, sex, race, and current residential circumstances. And finally, the costs of the research were not really a consideration. For contemporary scholars struggling with the realities of research among today's populations, such conditions seem close to ideal.

Assessment of *The Battle of Britain*

Somewhat parallel experiments were completed on each of the four films described earlier. The main difference between them was that the research on *The Battle of Britain* assessed the impact of a single film, while the remaining experiments studied the cumulative impact of two or more films or made use of alternative research designs.

Objectives   *The Battle of Britain* presented a considerable amount of factual material but in the list of the Army's six objectives to be achieved it emphasized number four (a feeling of confidence in our allies). The overall purpose of the research itself was to measure both knowledge and opinion orientations among the subjects before they saw the film, to expose them to the film, and then to assess any *change* in knowledge and opinions that had been created by seeing the moving picture.

Various procedures and strategies were used to minimize the influence of other sources of information about topics covered in the movie so that whatever change took place could realistically be regarded as due to exposure to the film. The situation of the subjects, relatively isolated from civilian life, was an aid to the researchers in this respect.

Experimental Procedures   The research was organized around (1) the use of an *experimental group* of subjects that actually saw the film, and a *control* group of very similar subjects who did not see the film, and (2) the administration of anonymous checklist questionnaires to both groups *before* and *after* the time when the experimental group viewed the film. While such procedures are now common in research, at the time this was a relatively new research strategy in communication studies. This way of conducting such an experiment is called a "before–after design with control group." However, an additional study was done with an "after-only" design, where no "before" measure was used and the control and experimental groups were simply compared after the film was shown to the experimental group.

The measuring instruments for the experiment were constructed with great care, and each item that finally became a part of the questionnaires was carefully pretested to make certain that it could be understood by the subjects and that it gathered the exact information that was needed by the researchers. Such pretesting, item by item, is a hallmark of careful research procedures today. The items finally used in the checklist questionnaires were of two types. These were (1) *fact-quiz* questions, such as those found on a multiple choice test, where the subject selects the correct answer from a list of alternatives, and (2) *opinion* items, either in a multiple choice style, expressing varying opinion positions from which the subject could select that closest to his own, or agree–disagree statements that the subject could endorse or reject as consistent with his own opinions. Some of these opinion items were highly related to the factual information and were quite specific.

Other items dealt with broader and more general issues less tied to the facts. The questionnaires also included several personal history items (education, age, and so on) that could be used, along with handwriting, to match the before and after questionnaires of each subject. Finally, there was a need to direct the attention of the subjects away from the idea that they were simply being tested to see what they had obtained from the film. The study was portrayed to the soldiers as a sort of "general opinion survey." For this reason, the questionnaire contained a number of "camouflage" items intended to distract the subjects from perceiving its actual purpose. (Ethical considerations today might raise questions about deception, but it was not a problem for the Army at the time.)

Two such questionnaires were prepared around the content of *The Battle of Britain*. They were intended to be parallel and to cover the same items in essentially the same way. This permitted a "before" and "after" measure to be taken on each subject without using the same measuring instrument, which could have confused the results.

The time interval between seeing the film and responding to the "after" questionnaire was one week. (One segment of the group of subjects was measured nine weeks later to study long-term effects. This will be discussed later.) At one camp, 2,100 subjects (half of whom saw the film) were studied in the "before–after with control group" design. In another camp an additional 900 were studied in the same way. Finally, the "after-only with control group" design was used for the study of another 1,200 subjects. Overall, this added up to an impressive 4,200 subjects, all of whom responded to the questionnaire at least once, and half of whom saw the experimental film.

The sampling was done in a practical way by selecting company units rather than individuals. However, considerable effort was made to equate or "match" the experimental groups and the controls. Various background variables on the soldiers were studied well beforehand and those companies most alike in their distributions of such variables as age, region of birth, and scores on Army tests were paired.

As was mentioned, the questionnaires were presented to the men as a "general opinion survey" to find out "how soldiers felt about various subjects connected with the war." The subjects were assembled in platoon groups (of about 50 men) to fill out the questionnaires in their mess halls under the watchful eyes of trained personnel. Anonymity was assured and no officers were present.

To distract the men from wondering why they had to respond to the questionnaire twice (in the before–after design) it was explained that "the questionnaire had been revised" on the basis of the earlier results, and it was being studied again. In fact, the second version had REVISED printed in large type at the top. A number of other precautions were taken to avoid suspicion that some other purpose was at stake.

Results The outcome of the evaluations of the *Battle of Britain* can best be understood by contrasting the responses of the control and experimental, or as we will call it, the "film" group. We noted that various objectives were built into the content of the film, and these were assessed by items in the questionnaire. Simple percentage comparisons show the influence of the film in reaching those objectives. A difference of six percent between the control and the film group constitutes a statistically significant result, ruling out chance and implying that the film did have an effect on those who saw it.

Generally, it is convenient to review the findings around four major issues. These define broadly the kinds of effects that the makers of the film hoped to achieve. These effects concern the following questions:

1. Was the film effective in improving *factual knowledge* about military events?
2. Did the content of the film alter the *opinions and interpretations* of viewers regarding several major themes presented in the film?
3. How much did the film improve the *general attitudes* of the soldiers toward their British allies?
4. Was the film a significant factor in improving *overall motivation* among the recruits to fight a tough war?

Each of the above was a complex issue, and only the highlights of the results of the experiment can be presented. Nevertheless, the findings were relatively clear.

First, the film did have a major effect on the acquisition of factual knowledge. Differences between the control and the film groups were consistently large. For example, the questionnaire asked why the Germans "were not successful at bombing British planes on the ground?" The answer given in the film was "because the British kept their planes scattered at the edges of the field." Only 21 percent of the control group checked this answer while 78 percent of the film group got it right. Similarly, other factual items were consistently answered correctly by much larger proportions of the film group.

The effects of the film on opinions and interpretations were also in the direction desired by the designers of the film, but the differences between the control and film groups were not as great as with the factual material. There were four major content themes present in the film about which opinions or interpretations could be altered. Each can be discussed briefly.

One major content theme was that the actual battle of Britain was a major defeat for the Nazis. Many of the soldiers had not previously interpreted the German bombings of England early in the war in this light. The film increased the percent of soldiers who concluded that the German raids were part of a preparation for invasion and that the Nazis suffered a defeat. For example, one questionnaire item stated that "The heavy bombing attacks on Britain were an attempt by the Nazis to . . ." The key answer provided by the content of the film was "to invade and conquer England." Only 43 percent of the control group checked this, while 58 percent of the film group selected this answer. Several similar items showed parallel patterns.

A second content theme in the film was that the British resisted heroically. Items in the questionnaire probed the degree to which the control and film groups differed in their opinions on this issue. A typical item asked "What do you think is the real reason why the Nazis did not invade and conquer Britain after the fall of France?" Only 48 percent of the control group checked the answer provided by the film, "the Nazis tried and would have succeeded except for the determined resistance by the British." By contrast, this answer was selected by 70 percent of those who saw the film.

Two additional content themes in the film produced similar results. More of the film group agreed that the Royal Air Force did a magnificent job than did the control group. And finally, the belief that the British resistance provided other nations time to prepare (the fourth content theme) was held by more of the film group than the control group. Generally, then, the experience of seeing the film did alter the opinions and interpretations of its viewers regarding these four content themes.

The film had less effect on the general attitudes of the soldiers toward the British. In contrast to the clear influence on learning factual information about military events, and in changing opinions concerning the content themes of the film, the viewing experience did not improve general attitudes toward the British allies. This was found in a variety of items where the differences between the control and film groups were consistently negligible. For example, the questionnaire posed the following item: "Do you feel that the British are doing all they can to help win the war?" The difference between the control and the film group in terms of those who answered positively was only seven percent. A number of other items designed to measure general attitudes toward the British showed even smaller differences between the two groups. On several of these items two and three percentage points of difference were found. In other words, it could not be concluded that the film had improved attitudes toward the British.

The film was also clearly ineffective in strengthening the overall motivation and morale of its viewers. Major objectives of the film were to increase willingness to serve, encourage attitudes toward demanding unconditional surrender, and deepen resentment of the enemy. To put it simply, the film had no effect at all on these issues. On such items as whether or not the trainees would prefer military duty in the United States, or would like to join the fighting overseas, only 38 percent of the control group wanted to go fight. For the film group—supposedly fired up by the film—the comparable figure was 41 percent, not a significant difference. Similarly, about the same percent of the control group and the film group thought unconditional surrender was important (control group, 60 percent; film group, 62 percent). Finally, resentment of the enemy, measured by several items, showed differences that ranged from one to four percent between the two groups. It was not possible to conclude that the film improved motivation or morale. These were very important findings. Their significance to mass communication theory will be made clear.

There were many additional issues probed by analyzing data from the questionnaire. Mainly these issues pertained to checks on whether or not one set of ideas in the film might have adversely affected reactions to some other set of ideas to create a kind of "boomerang" effect. Generally, no significant effects of this were located.

The research design used with *The Battle of Britain* was also used with the other three orientation movies that were part of the overall film evaluation studies: *Prelude to War, The Nazis Strike,* and *Divide and Conquer*. However the last two films were shown to the men in combination to test for cumulative effects. Two days were allowed between these showings and then the combined effects were measured by the questionnaire in the usual way.

The findings of these additional studies need not be presented in detail because they parallel on almost every point those obtained from the evaluation of *The Battle of Britain*. Instead, the implications of the findings from the research on all of these films can be discussed together because of their close similarity.

Implications   The film evaluation studies made use of research procedures such as sampling, control groups, matching, pretesting, and measurement, that were the equal of some of the best social science research conducted today. There are few grounds, if any at all, to reject the findings of these experiments as misleading because of methodological or procedural flaws.

The films themselves were produced by the best talent in the nation at the time and no expense was spared in their production. Even by today's criteria, nearly a half-century later, these films offer a powerful message, in which totalitarian and militaristic forces make brutal war on neighboring nations that had done little to provoke such a conflict. The films portray, in short, a very convincing argument. There are few features of these films, other than color photography, that could be used to improve their technical, dramatic, or persuasive quality.

Given these qualities of the stimulus material and of the assessments of their impact, what can be said about the overall results? Clearly, these films did well in achieving some kinds of results but poorly at gaining other objectives. The authors of *Experiments on Mass Communication* summarized the findings of the film evaluation studies as follows:

1. The *Why We Fight* films had marked effects on the men's knowledge of factual material concerning the events leading up to the war. The fact that the upper limit of effects was so large—as for example in the cases where the correct answer was learned well enough to be remembered a week later by the *majority* of the men—indicates that highly effective presentation methods are possible with this type of film.
2. The films also had some marked effects on opinions where the film specifically covered the factors involved in the particular interpretation, that is, where the opinion item was prepared on the basis of film-content analysis and anticipated opinion change from such analysis. Such opinion changes were, however, less frequent and in general less marked than changes in factual knowledge.
3. The films had only very few effects on opinion items of a more general nature that had been prepared independently of film content but which were considered the criteria for determining the effectiveness of the films in achieving their orientation objectives.
4. The films had no effects on the items prepared for the purpose of measuring effects on the men's motivation to serve as soldiers, which was considered the ultimate objective of the orientation program.[6]

An important issue is *why* these films were so ineffective in achieving their major objectives. As noted above, neither attitudes nor motivations were influenced. Hovland and his colleagues had a number of possible explanations that they explored as best they could. For example, they speculated that information from the civilian mass media about many of the topics and themes treated in the films had reached the recruits before they were drafted (after all, material was used in the films from earlier newsreels). This could have reduced the differences found between control and film groups because a substantial number in each case already had positive attitudes toward the British, and at least some motivation to serve.

By contrast, neither the control nor the film groups had the factual type of knowledge presented to any great degree, so larger effects could be predicted.

Moreover, motivation to serve and fight in the armed forces is a very complex phenomenon with many dimensions: pressures from one's family, general social norms, fear of death or injury, or prior feelings about the combatants. All could have been factors in the dynamics of change when trying to modify such motivation through the use of persuasive films. There are a number of additional issues about which one can speculate, the amount of time between film and measurement being one of those issues. For example, there may be a "sleeper" effect. That is, even though little change had taken place in the viewers by the time the measurements were made after seeing the film, perhaps much later the film's influences could have been found. Finally, there is the question of the entire configuration of a given subject's values, system of beliefs, and personality traits. These can interact in a dynamic way with new stimulus material to produce one kind of effect or another. However, in spite of rather sophisticated attempts to address some of these issues, no clear answers were obtained as to why these films achieved clear effects in the area of factual knowledge, but failed to do so with respect to attitudes and motivations.

Other Film Studies

In using a film to try to change knowledge, opinions, attitudes, or motivations, it is important to know how the audience itself evaluates the film. That is, do they like the film, find it interesting and objective, or do they dislike it, become bored by it, or believe it to be a biased presentation? Such perceptions on the part of the audience may be closely related to whether or not a given film can achieve the objectives for which it was designed.

The Army researchers made extensive studies of the reactions of the men to various aspects of the orientation films. They were concerned about their level of interest and whether the viewers saw it as "propaganda" designed to manipulate them. The researchers were also concerned as to whether the soldiers saw the movies as Hollywood products, staged with actors and props, or as films of actual events as they happened.

Another significant question about films as media for training or orientation is, how do they compare to the available alternatives? Films like the "Why We Fight" series are obviously very expensive to produce and the process takes a long time. In contrast, a recorded radio-type program with a lecture, or even film strips (which are like projected slides) can be used with narration and are both inexpensive and rapid to produce. Finally, if a film *is* used for training or orientation, what are some ways by which retention of the material presented can be enhanced? For example, having the audience engage in discussion of the content in small groups is one way; having a speaker lead them in a simple review is another. All of these questions and issues were under study, and the "Why We Fight" films provided convenient vehicles for trying to find answers. As we will note, however, other kinds of films were also used in these parts of the research program.

Audience Evaluation of Films　Both questionnaires and group interviews were used to try to understand how the recruits themselves evaluated the "Why We Fight" films at the time they saw them. The questionnaires were aimed at three basic issues: Did the men *like* the films? What did they think was the *purpose* of the films? And did they believe that the films gave a *true picture* of the events depicted? For the most part, the men studied were those involved in the film evaluation studies, who had seen the film. However, as we will indicate, some additional subjects were involved.

In general, the men liked the "Why We Fight" films. They liked some more than others, but fewer than 10 percent gave a negative appraisal on any film (or could give no answer). Those who did not like the films tended to be less educated, or to have foreign-born parents from Axis countries.

The *Battle of Britain* study provided more information about the perceived purpose of the film than some of the other films under study. The majority of the men questioned simply saw it as an effort to teach them the facts of the war in an interesting way. Few thought that they were being used as "guinea pigs" or manipulated in some way. A sizeable number did connect the film with its real objective. For example, 27 percent on the questionnaire studies wrote in on the space provided for comments that its purpose was "to raise our morale," "to improve the fighting spirit," or even "to make us want to kill those sons of bitches." Even with this recognition of its manipulative intent, they still tended to like the film.

The majority of those involved in the study saw the *Battle of Britain* as a true picture of what had happened during those days when Britain stood alone (some 65 percent gave such an evaluation). Another 33 percent believed that it gave essentially a true picture even though it was "one-sided" at times. Only a handful (two percent) said that it did not give a true or honest picture. Similar assessments of the film, *The Nazis Strike* yielded results with even larger numbers believing that the film was truthful (some 81 percent), a smaller number feeling that it was basically truthful, if one-sided (18 percent), and only one percent who felt that it was "mostly untrue or one-sided."

These audience evaluations are important in trying to sort out the overall effects of the films. The evaluations indicate that there were no glaring problems with the films themselves: By and large the soldiers liked them; they did not see them as untruthful propaganda, and they did not feel improperly manipulated. The reasons for the films' failure to achieve their objectives in the areas of attitudes and morale lie elsewhere.

Group interviews were conducted with 150 men selected so as to be a representative cross section of the recruits under training. These men were not part of the film evaluation experiments discussed earlier but a completely different group. The interviews were conducted in an informal setting after the subjects had seen the film; each interview group discussed the film and an effort was made to put together a picture of how the men evaluated the film.

About the only additional insights obtained from this approach were that some of the men thought the films had some poor features. For example, in the air combat footage, the same German plane was shown being shot down several times. Some of the men thought that shots of Hitler and his staff planning the assault on England were Hollywood actors (they were not; the footage was genuine). Generally, however, the findings from these group interviews supported those obtained from the questionnaire studies.

A second series of studies of audience evaluation of films did not focus on the *Why We Fight* series, but another separate and rather different series. These were short features, similar to newsreels, shown in conjunction with regular feature films at the base theater. Attendance at these regular entertainment movies was, of course, voluntary. However, those who went to the movies saw a different short feature each week called *The War* as part of the regular program. Each of these short features was made up of five episodes, with the content of each varied every week. However, the same titles for these episodes were used in each issue of *The War*. For example, Issue 5 of *The War* had the following five episodes:

Episode a: *Finishing School*. This showed training of amphibious (Ranger) troops in invasion tactics such as embarking and disembarking and advancing under live ammunition.

Episode b: *Back Home*. This showed machine tools being produced by a small family shop in Connecticut which was awarded the Navy "E" for contribution to war production.

Episode c: *I Was There*. This featured an Army nurse's eye-witness account of the bombing of Manila and the fall of Corregidor, with action shots to illustrate part of her commentary. The whole story was told in the nurse's voice and was introduced and concluded by shots of the nurse telling her story.

Episode d: *First Birthday*. This documentary reviewed the founding and first year's activities of the Women's Army Corps and depicted the training and duties of WACs.

Episode e: *Snafu*. This was an animated cartoon showing the adventures of a comic character called "Private Snafu," whose complaints about Army routine and duties led to his magically being put in charge of the camp, with disastrous consequences.[7]

Two means of studying evaluations of this type of film were used. Questionnaires filled out by men who had seen the film were used, and a special recording device (called the "program analyzer") was used in the theater itself. This device consisted of a small box for every viewer with two clearly marked buttons. As the viewer watched the film, he pushed down the "like" button if he found the material interesting. If not, he pushed down the "dislike" button. There was no neutral button, but the viewer could refrain from pushing either the like or dislike buttons.

The results from these two approaches show similar patterns. Figure 6 summarizes the questionnaire data and Figure 7 shows a typical pattern obtained from the use of the program analyzer. The findings are not definitive because of the limitations on sampling. But, along with supplemental information obtained from written comments on the questionnaires, and after pulling together findings from studying four separate issues of *The War*, the following generalizations seemed to apply:

1. Where the film simply showed someone talking, interest tended to be low.
2. Where real shots of military action were shown, interest was high.
3. Where shots of action were shown with voice-over narration, interest remained high.
4. Repetition of shots seen earlier in the film (as in seeing the same plane shot down) was not well received.
5. Highly realistic material, as opposed to Hollywood versions acted out with props, was much preferred.

Again, these were tentative conclusions pertaining only to the films studied and should not be regarded as guides to audience evaluations of all kinds of films. Yet, they offer useful hypotheses for studying other types of training films for military personnel.

Alternative Presentations The relative effectiveness of various media for accomplishing a given objective still merits much research atten-

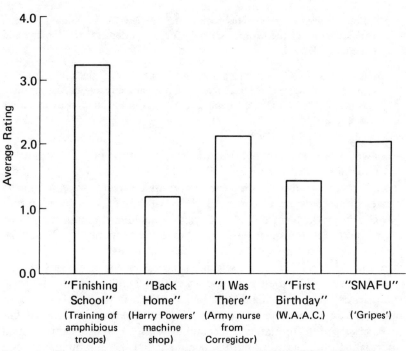

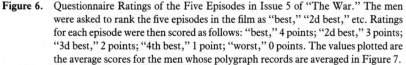

Figure 6. Questionnaire Ratings of the Five Episodes in Issue 5 of "The War." The men were asked to rank the five episodes in the film as "best," "2d best," etc. Ratings for each episode were then scored as follows: "best," 4 points; "2d best," 3 points; "3d best," 2 points; "4th best," 1 point; "worst," 0 points. The values plotted are the average scores for the men whose polygraph records are averaged in Figure 7.

SOURCE: Carl I. Hovland, Arthur A. Lumsdaine and Fred D. Sheffield, *Experiments on Mass Communication* (Princeton, N.J.: Princeton University Press, 1949) p. 110.

tion. The Army researchers made attempts to probe this issue. They were quite aware that this is a very difficult question to answer, being based on assumptions that the medium may have special properties that themselves can influence change in the audience (i.e., that the "medium is the message" in its own right). However, in spite of the difficulties, the investigators saw such research as possible beginning analyses of any factors that might underly the use of various media for instructional or persuasive purposes.

Among the studies completed, three still appear to be important. One compared a motion picture versus a film strip presentation of the same subject; a second compared two types of radio program styles (a "commentator" versus a dramatized "documentary"); and the third compared the technique of having an introductory lecture to a film before seeing it to a

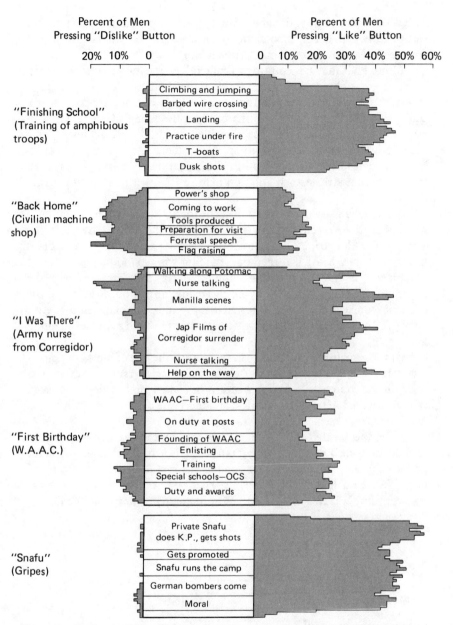

20% 10%   0   0   10% 20% 30% 40% 50% 60%

"Finishing School"
(Training of amphibious
troops)

Climbing and jumping
Barbed wire crossing
Landing
Practice under fire
T-boats
Dusk shots

"Back Home"
(Civilian machine
shop)

Power's shop
Coming to work
Tools produced
Preparation for visit
Forrestal speech
Flag raising

"I Was There"
(Army nurse
from Corregidor)

Walking along Potomac
Nurse talking
Manilla scenes
Jap Films of
Corregidor surrender
Nurse talking
Help on the way

"First Birthday"
(W.A.A.C.)

WAAC—First birthday
On duty at posts
Founding of WAAC
Enlisting
Training
Special schools—OCS
Duty and awards

"Snafu"
(Gripes)

Private Snafu
does K.P., gets shots
Gets promoted
Snafu runs the camp
German bombers come
Moral

Figure 7. Continuous Polygraph Records of the Group "Likes" and "Dislikes" During
Showing of Issue 5 of "The War."

SOURCE: Carl I. Hovland, Arthur A. Lumsdaine and Fred D. Sheffield, *Experiments on Mass Communication* (Princeton, N.J.: Princeton University Press, 1949) p. 111.

133

review summary of what its salient points were after seeing it. The purpose was to see whether the introduction or the review was the best means of enhancing learning from an instructional film.

Although it may be tempting to conclude that a motion picture with a sound track is obviously a better training device than a film strip supplemented with a verbal presentation, the findings did not support such a conclusion. Six companies were matched on the Army's General Classification Test (AGCT) and the educational level that they had achieved. Two were designated as the control group. Two others saw a 43-minute sound film designed to teach map reading. The remaining two companies saw a 50-minute film strip presentation on map reading with an accompanying lecture.

After viewing these presentations, the soldiers (plus the control group) responded to a 39-item multiple choice test on the topics covered in the film and the film strip. The comparative effectiveness of the two media is shown in Figure 8. As it turned out, the film with sound had no inherent advantage over the still pictures of the film strip (supplemented with the lecture). The experiment was by no means definitive, but it points to the need for empirical checks on untested assumptions that one medium (e.g., television) automatically has some "greater power" than a simpler medium in all cases.

Of the remaining two studies in this series, the one of most contemporary interest is the comparison of the introductory versus the review lectures on the content of a film as a means of enhancing learning. Films are still widely used in teaching settings, and this issue has not been fully tested in more recent times.

More specifically, the question addressed by the research was the following: In using a film for training purposes, is it better that an instructor provide a preliminary commentary on the major points that will be covered in the film, or is it better to review its salient points after the audience has seen the film? Which approach will most increase learning from the film?

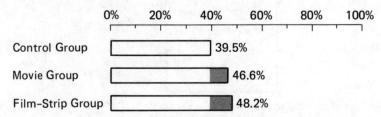

Figure 8. Average Test Scores Received by Men in Each Group (N = 253 in each group).

SOURCE: Carl I. Hovland, Arthur A. Lumsdaine and Fred D. Sheffield, *Experiments on Mass Communication* (Princeton, N.J.: Princeton University Press, 1949) p. 126.

In the Army studies on this issue, four platoons of soldiers were shown the 43-minute film on mapreading after receiving a 20-minute lecture on its main ideas. Another four platoons saw the film first and then had a 20-minute review of its salient points. Care was taken that the persons doing the reviews and preliminary lectures were not greatly different from each other in terms of style or ability. The trainees did not know that they were part of a research effort.

After these presentations, each soldier took a 15-item quiz about the major topics that had been covered in the film. The results of this testing are summarized in Figure 9. As can be seen, viewing the movie by itself (as did the control group) improved performance rather considerably. However, both the introductory lecture and the review increased learning even more. The former seemed to have a slight advantage, but the difference was not significant. Results such as these indicate that just "showing a movie" is not the most effective practice in using film as a teaching device. Supplementing the film with an oral presentation before or after the film enhances learning effects.

Films and Intellectual Ability

A complex question concerning the film evaluation research described earlier (the *Why We Fight* series) concerns the degree to which different patterns of effects were observed among different categories of viewers. In the Army studies, the influence of such demographic variables as education, religious affiliation, marital status, intellectual level and other social categories on the learning of factual material and opinion change was studied wherever possible. Among all of these variables, the one most often related to differences in the results was the intellectual ability of the viewer. A brief summary of some of the main findings relating intellectual ability

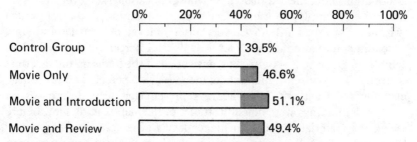

Figure 9. Average Test Scores for Each Group (N = 253 in each group).

SOURCE: Carl I. Hovland, Arthur A. Lumsdaine and Fred D. Sheffield, *Experiments on Mass Communication* (Princeton, N.J.: Princeton University Press, 1949) p. 143.

to learning factual material and to opinion change will demonstrate the major points.

Measurement   It was not possible to give the soldiers who saw the *Why We Fight* films, or who served in the control groups, an IQ test. This not only would have been difficult, but would have violated the assurances of anonymity involved in the research. Fortunately, it was not necessary to do this. Two indices of general intellectual ability were readily available. One was the individual's score on the AGCT. A considerable accumulation of research had established that these scores were highly correlated with intelligence test scores. An even simpler index was the level of educational attainment of the soldier. Research had also established the high correlation between amount of schooling completed and IQ test scores. Educational attainment was also, logically enough, highly correlated with AGCT scores. For this reason, the researchers felt confident that they could categorize the men in terms of simple classifications of educational attainment (such as completion of grade school, high school or college) and use this as a reliable measure of intellectual ability. And, since all subjects in the film evaluation studies had been asked to give their level of educational attainment, the data were already a part of their questionnaire responses.

To determine if seeing a film such as the *Battle of Britain* had different effects on men in these three educational levels, the control and the film groups from the evaluation studies were contrasted. Simple comparisons of the percents in each group who had learned factual information, or whose opinions had been changed, were sufficient, and for the most part, the results showed clear patterns.

Learning Factual Material   It was found, first of all, that even before seeing the films the men with the most education already knew more factual information about the war than those whose educational achievements were lower. For example, on a brief fact quiz, the men in the control groups (who never saw the film) showed very different levels of factual knowledge, depending on their educational level. Only 21.1 percent of those who had completed grade school only could answer all of the items on the fact quiz correctly. The figure for high school men was 28.6 percent and for college men it was 41.8 percent. These figures represent significant differences.

Similar findings were noted in studies of the map-reading film. Before seeing the material, those with higher levels of education *already* knew larger percents of the answers to the multiple choice test on map-reading than those in lower categories (grade school, 26.1 percent; high school,

28.9 percent; and college, 37.1 percent). In other words, intellectual ability, as measured, was a significant indicator of the initial level of factual knowledge commanded by the men, even before they saw any of the films.

But even though those with higher levels of intellectual ability already knew more, they also learned more from the film. A 29-item factual information test was prepared on the *Why We Fight* films. Comparisons were then made of the percents of these items learned, on the average, by the men in each of the three intellectual levels. Substantial differences were found. For example, the grade school men averaged only 16.3 percent on this test after seeing the films. The high school men averaged 36.6 percent, and the college men had 54.2 percent correct. These differences in levels of performance were even more pronounced when only the items of greatest difficulty were taken into account. Clearly, intellectual ability was the key factor in accounting for how much an individual learned from the films.

Opinion Changes   The relationship between intellectual attainment and opinion change presents a more complex picture. A trend was noted for the effects of the films on opinion change to increase with higher intellectual ability. However, in some opinion items, the opposite was found. But another situation was noted in the data that helped to explain what had happened. The more factual material that had to be grasped, especially more difficult material, the more opinion change was seen only among the men of higher intellectual level. The authors considered such changes as "informed opinion." On the other hand, the men of lower intellectual levels often changed their opinion position on the basis of a minimal number of facts or those easier to grasp. This was considered "uninformed opinion." To make matters even more interesting, the findings showed that men of lower intellectual ability were prone to change their opinion on the basis of facts that men of higher intellectual level did not regard as particularly valid.

Implications   Higher learning ability (intellectual level) led to increased levels of initial knowledge. However, it also led to learning more factual material from the film. On opinion change, the more complex the issue and facts concerning it, the more likely that opinion change would be primarily among the more intelligent men. Those of lower ability tended to change their opinions on issues of lesser complexity, less well supported by the facts, and on issues that more intelligent men found difficult to accept. While, as the authors note, these are tentative conclusions based on this research only, it would appear that the less educated are easier to sway with propaganda.

ADDITIONAL EXPERIMENTAL STUDIES

The research findings on films summarized above were obtained for the most part from evaluation studies where the film had been prepared by persons other than the experimenters, and it was introduced in its entirety as the experimental treatment. In these studies, the dependent variable was one or more of the objectives set by the War Department for the film series. Extraneous variables were controlled by a variety of techniques, methodologies and designs.

Another type of research on the effects of communication on opinion change employs variations in some specific aspect of the message, some characteristic of the audience, or some factor in the communication setting. Generally, such research seeks to find those conditions of the persuasive message, the communicator, the mode of presentation, etc., that will lead to a maximum degree of opinion change. The underlying assumption is that changes in opinion (or attitude, value, belief, and so on) are *keys to changing overt behavior*. After all, mere changes in opinion mean relatively little unless they are linked to changes in action.

The remainder of the present chapter summarizes briefly the results of two (from a set of three) experiments that sought such keys to opinion change. One experiment attempted to see whether opinion change after seeing a persuasive communication was a short-term effect or if it had stable long-term effects. The second experiment assessed a persuasive message that was structured in one of two ways. One structure was one-sided, and presented only arguments in favor of an opinion change under study. The other was essentially the same persuasive message, but some points on the opposite side were also presented in an effort to make the message seem more objective. The goal, of course, was to see which provided a better key to changing opinions in the direction desired by the communicator.

Short-Term versus Long-Term Effects

A significant question in the search for ways to change people's opinions through the use of persuasive communications is whether the effects achieved, if any, will disappear rapidly or persist over a long period. Studies of remembering and forgetting have been made by psychologists for decades. Such research has established that there is a "curve of forgetting," of factual information learned by a subject. The greatest amount of forgetting takes place rather quickly, and then the curve levels off after a few days to decline more slowly. Since opinion changes are based on factual information, the Army researchers hypothesized that opinion changes would follow a somewhat similar pattern. That is, they expected changes of opinion achieved through persuasive communications to have a relatively short life, with the subject regressing over time to his earlier position.

The study of short-term versus long-term effects was carried out with one of the orientation films—*The Battle of Britain*—because the film was clearly capable of producing effects on both factual knowledge and opinion change. The sample used for this study had already been given their "before" measures as part of the film evaluation studies. In those studies, the subjects took their "after" measures a week after seeing the film. All that was needed was a group of subjects who had seen the film and whose opinions could be measured a relatively long time after seeing the film. It was also necessary, of course, to match the various groups so that any differences in effects could be assigned to the time variable, rather than to differences of some other kind between the two sets of subjects.

The "before–after with control group" design was used for both the short-time subjects and the long-time group. The long-time group was treated in the same manner as the short-time subjects, except that they received their "after" questionnaire *nine weeks* after seeing the film (rather than one week). Table 4 shows the general plan.

A clear pattern of forgetting factual material was found. On a ten-item fact quiz based on *The Battle of Britain*, there was a substantial decrement in recalling facts when comparing the short-time and the long-time experi-

Table 4 General Research Design for Comparing Short-time and Long-time Effects of Seeing an Orientation Film

| | Short-time Groups | | Long-time Groups | |
	Experimental (3 Companies)	*Control* (3 Companies)	*Experimental* (2 Companies)	*Control* (2 Companies)
First week:	"Before" questionnaire	"Before" questionnaire	"Before" questionnaire	"Before" questionnaire
Second week:	Film showing	———	———	———
Third week:	"After" questionnaire	"After" questionnaire	———	———
Eleventh week:	———	———	"After" questionnaire	"After" questionnaire
No. of subjects	450	450	250	250

SOURCE: Carl I. Hovland, Arthur A. Lumsdaine, and Fred D. Sheffield, *Experiments on Mass Communication* (Princeton, N.J.: Princeton University Press, 1949) p. 183.

mental groups. Over the nine weeks, the long-time groups retained only about 50 percent as many of the fact items as had the short-time group at the end of the first week after seeing the film.

But the main question was the influence of time on opinions. To assess opinion shifts caused by the film, and to compare the long- and short-time subjects, a 15-item opinion measuring instrument was prepared and used. The results of the comparison revealed some unexpected findings. On approximately a third of the opinion issues the long-time group showed less change than the short-time group. This was the pattern to be expected from the "curve of forgetting." After all, the underlying factual material had shown a clear pattern of being forgotten. However, on more than half of the 15 opinion issues under study, the long-time group showed a *greater* change than the short-time group. This was not expected. The researchers referred to this kind of outcome as a "sleeper effect." It was difficult to explain, but what had happened was that the subjects had forgotten some of the facts in the film on which their opinions had originally been changed to some degree. Then, freed from the factual basis, the opinions changed even more.

In an attempt to understand this phenomenon better a number of rather complex analyses of the data were made. The analyses were not particularly enlightening except in one case. There was a high probability of being influenced by the film on a long-time basis if one was *initially predisposed* toward a given opinion change (on a particular topic). Finally, the authors noted that changes in opinion of a general rather than specific nature may show increasing effects with lapse of time. Such general opinions are less firmly anchored to specific facts.

The sleeper effect raises many difficult psychological problems, and the investigators felt that they could not answer them within the context of the data of their studies. The effects of time on opinion change following persuasive communication remains a significant issue around which much research was organized in the years following the Army studies. The problem of initial position on an issue, however, was to prove a valuable key to understanding some of the effects in the next study to be discussed.

Effects of Presenting One versus Both Sides of an Argument

When attempting to change opinions on a controversial topic, is it more effective to present only the materials and arguments supporting the position of the communicator ("one side")? Or is it better to introduce at least some of the opposing arguments ("both sides") to make the persuasive communication look like a balanced treatment of the issues? These were the main questions for a study of the influence of a persuasive message that was used in 1945, toward the end of the war. New draftees were still being trained even though the European war was clearly about to end. The grim facts were that the war in the Pacific was seen likely to continue for two years or more. Although American forces had defeated the Japanese in a number of bitterly fought assaults on island bases, the main body of the Japanese Army had remained at home, anticipating a major invasion attempt. It was estimated that if this were to take place, the Americans would probably suffer hundreds of thousands of casualties. In fact, the war could drag on for years. The Japanese had reserved supplies at home in spite of the heavy bombings of major cities. Each island was a fortress. And there was the vast Pacific to cross: the Americans would have to bring troops and supplies over thousands of miles of ocean. Even the high-level planners in the War Department did not know of the atom bomb that made the assault on Japan unnecessary. This closely guarded secret weapon was known only to a handful at Los Alamos, to the President and his staff, and to a few select people in the military. Thus, the War Department issued directives to begin preparing *all* troops to anticipate a long war. A factor complicating this need was that, with Italy out of the war and Germany clearly about to collapse, the majority of the soldiers felt that the war was about to end. This posed a potential morale problem of serious proportions. The troops *had* to be made to understand and believe that there were still tough years ahead and that there was no choice but to carry on.

Under the new directives, the social scientists of the Experimental Section set about to study the most effective ways to persuade trainees that it would be a long and difficult war in the Pacific. The keys to such persuasion were badly needed. For this reason, the social scientists moved away from films made in Hollywood and prepared their own persuasive messages so that they could build in various message factors in a search for those keys. Fortunately for hundreds of thousands of American young men, the atom bomb *was* used and the war came to a speedy end. This aspect of the bomb's use tends to be overlooked today. In any case, if it had not been used, it is likely that this phase of the research program would have been greatly extended.

Included in the routines of the training camp was a weekly "orientation hour" that had been used for soldiers to see films, fill out questionnaires, participate in discussions, and so on. This tradition made it possible to use the same general approach for the new research program as had been used earlier with the "Why We Fight" film evaluations.

Since there was no time to prepare films, the more rapid and flexible medium of radio was used. The Armed Forces Radio Service prepared recorded materials according to the specifications of the researchers. The new research program began with a study organized around the issue posed at the beginning of the present section. Would a one-sided radio talk be more effective in changing the opinions of the soldiers concerning the probable length of the war in the Pacific, or would it be more effective to use a radio talk that presented at least some of the arguments on both sides (with the weight of arguments still on the side of a long war)?

Some careful preliminary work was done before designing the two radio programs. Interviews were held with 200 men to see how long they thought that the Pacific war would last, and why they felt the way they did. What, in other words, were the counterarguments to the position that the war would be lengthy? This preliminary work paid off, because those counterarguments could be carefully rebutted by material included in the radio messages.

The two transcripts were prepared as a commentator's analysis of the Pacific war. The one-side presentation (about 15 minutes in length) marshalled all the factual information and arguments supporting the conclusion that the war would last at least two more years. The both-sides presentation had essentially the same material, but an additional four minutes of arguments on the other side were included early in the message. These were then carefully rebutted. Overall, the program as a whole supported the conclusion that the war would last at least two more years.

The "before–after with control group" design was used to assess the results. Considerable effort was made to obscure the idea that there was an experiment going on, or that the men were being tested in some way. The before and after measurements took place in very different locations for very different announced purposes. Furthermore, in each case the central items were embedded in larger questionnaires addressed to different purposes. This camouflaging of the experiment within other important activities appears to have been entirely successful.

As in previous experiments, the subjects were selected in group units. A total of 24 platoons were used in all; 625 men were involved, with 214 in each of the two experimental groups and 197 in the control group. The after measures were made one week after the men in the experimental groups heard the radio programs. Once again, anonymity was assured, but it was possible to match the before and after questionnaires with the use of background data and handwriting.

When the results were first reviewed it appeared that the two forms of the persuasive message had not achieved different results. The opinions on the length of the war were compared for both experimental groups (one side versus both sides) by calculating the percent of men from each treatment who thought that the war would last more than a year and a half. These differences could then be compared to those found for the two measures of the control group. The results are shown in Table 5. Thus, it appeared that both programs were capable of changing the opinions of the men concerning the length of the war.

A different pattern of results became evident when the initial opinions of the men were taken into account. For those who were initially *opposed* to the conclusion that it would be a lengthy war, the one-side program had some effect (36 percent extended their estimates). But for such men the both-sides program had a much greater effect (48 percent extended their estimate). This is a difference of 12 percent. On the opposite side, the effects were even more striking. For those who initially *favored* the opinion that the war would be longer 52 percent extended their estimates after hearing the one-side radio commentary. But when these initially favorable men heard the both-sides program only 23 percent extended their estimate. This is a difference of 19 percent and in the opposite direction! Clearly, initial position on the issue seemed to be one of the keys concerning the effectiveness of a persuasive message.

Intellectual ability proved to be another important key to the results. A striking set of differences was found when comparing men of different educational attainment levels (used as an index of intellectual ability). Briefly summarized, the two-sides program was more effective with those of at least high school level (49 percent changed to a long war estimate). The one-side program produced a change of 35 percent in this category. Exactly the opposite was found for men with limited schooling. For those with only grade school or less, the one-side program persuaded 46 percent

---

Table 5 Overall Effects of the Two Programs on Distribution of Estimated Length of War

| | Percentage Estimating a War of More Than One-And-One-Half Years | | |
| | Experimental groups | | |
	Program I "One Side"	Program II "Both Sides"	Control Group
Before	37%	38%	36%
After	59	59	34
Difference	22%	21%	− 2%
Probability	<.01	<.01	

SOURCE: Carl I. Hovland, Arthur A. Lumsdaine, and Fred D. Sheffield, *Experiments on Mass Communication* (Princeton, N.J.: Princeton University Press, 1949) p. 210.

xtend their estimates. The two-sides program brought only 31 percent
his category to make such an opinion change.

When both initial position and intellectual level were considered, even
_eater differences were noted. For example, among those of lower educa-
tion who initially favored a longer estimate, the one-side program brought
an increased estimate of the war's length among 64 percent. This result can
be compared to the effects of the both-sides program on the same type of
men. Here, estimates of the length of the war actually *decreased!* It appears
that the two-sides program confused these poorly educated men and created an effect in the opposite direction from that desired by the communicator. For other combinations of initial position and intellectual ability, the
differences were not dramatic.

CONCLUSIONS AND IMPLICATIONS

The various research programs described in *Experiments on Mass Communication* constitute a remarkable effort to bring the research expertise of the
social psychologist and other social scientists to the practical problems
imposed by the urgencies of a national crisis. The researchers, drawn into
the war effort from the academic world, were able to make a significant
contribution to the practical problems of designing and testing orientation,
teaching, and persuasive communication. But perhaps their most significant contribution was that they uncovered significant issues that would be
explored by communication researchers in the decades that followed the
war.

The film evaluation studies showed that this form of communication
could teach factual material effectively to large numbers of people in a short
time. The studies also showed that it was possible to alter opinions and
interpretations of those facts, and that at least some of these opinions would
remain stable through time. Yet, it was clear that the films did not create
more general effects on broader attitudes and motivations. In other words,
the effects of the films were *clearly limited*. Such communications were not
the all-powerful shapers of the psychic structures of their audiences that
had been assumed by the magic bullet theory of prior decades. The findings
from *Experiments on Mass Communication* led clearly toward a "limited
effects" hypothesis concerning the short-term influences of a single communication on its audiences, rather than a "powerful effects" interpretation.

From the standpoint of research methods, the film evaluation studies
and the other research programs reported set new standards for communication research. The "before–after with control group" design was not new

to social science, but it had not been used so effectively before in communication research. It became a standard. The meticulous care taken in studying the "Why We Fight" films posed other models for later researchers. The investigators carefully analyzed the content of each film and developed their questionnaires around their findings. They took numerous precautions to pretest and fine-tune their instruments. They carefully disguised what they were doing so that their subjects would not modify their behavior according to some conception of the demands of the experiment. They matched groups, used controls, and camouflaged their tests and assessments in larger survey instruments. Finally, they carefully sorted through every set of results so that they understood as fully as possible what they had found and why. Of course their lack of concern over costs and their almost complete control over their subjects made this an almost unique situation that would be hard to duplicate in civilian life.

The results of their experiments supported the perspective that the effects of mass communication are strongly influenced by *individual differences* among the members of the audience. Individual differences led to selective perception, interpretation, and change. Such factors as the initial position of the subject were found to be very important in understanding the results. Similarly, there were differential influences that were related to the *social categories* (e.g., educational attainment) of the audience. Curiously, however, the researchers did not look into the *social relationships* that prevailed among their subjects as a source of influences on their results. Research on the role of the mass media in an election campaign was uncovering such influences, but the results of that work were not available to the Army researchers at the time.

Perhaps most of all, the Army research on how to persuade the American soldier represents a significant turning point in the study of mass communication. It can be seen in retrospect as the end of an era when the assumptions of the magic bullet theory were still thought to be viable. In its place, and in many ways as a result of these experiments, a new search began—a search for the "magic keys" of persuasion. The basic assumptions of the magic keys theory of persuasive communication are closely related to what DeFleur has referred to as the "psychodynamic approach" to persuasion.[8] It is assumed that there is some set of characteristics that can be built into the message that will modify the structure or functioning of the cognitive/emotional processes within the individual. These in turn will lead to changes in decisions and subsequent patterns of overt action, if all goes well, in the direction desired by the communicator. Thus, it is important to discover whether a one-side or a two-side form of a communication will alter opinions more effectively. If opinion is altered, it can be assumed that some form of action will then be altered. The authors of

Experiments on Mass Communication fully believed that there was a regular relationship between attitude and opinion states and forms of overt action —a set of assumptions that does not seem so attractive today.[9]

But at the time, when researchers were undisturbed by the thought that opinions and attitudes might *not* be related to overt behavior, the magic keys approach to communication research appeared to hold great promise. In fact, it became the dominant perspective on research on persuasive communication for many years to follow:

> Untold numbers of studies have tried to identify ways in which we can persuade people to view some perceptual object differently—and thereby cause them to act toward that object in modified ways. If only the right combination of words, message structure, emotional appeals, type of communicator, or mode of presentation can be found (so the vision goes) then people's subjective orientations can be reshaped and their patterns of overt behavior can be influenced.[10]

So the search for the magic keys began in earnest. It was the ultimate idea of pragmatic application of social and behavioral science. Find the ways to persuade people to buy, vote, give, accept military training cheerfully, and so on, and the world will beat a pathway to the door of social science. Unfortunately, as will be seen in later chapters, the search for the magic keys, like the search for the Philosopher's Stone, has had less than spectacular results.

NOTES AND REFERENCES

1. Frank Capra, *The Name Above the Title: An Autobiography* (New York: The Macmillan Company, 1971), p. 327.
2. Ibid., p. 237.
3. Carl I. Hovland, Arthur A. Lumsdaine, and Fred D. Sheffield, *Experiments on Mass Communication* (Princeton, N. J.: Princeton University Press, 1949), p. 22.
4. For a detailed analysis of the films' techniques and content, see Paul Rotha, *The Film Till Now* (New York: Funk and Wagnalls, 1949), p. 462.
5. Carl I. Hovland, et al., op. cit.
6. Ibid., pp. 64–65.
7. Ibid., p. 215.
8. Melvin L. De Fleur, *Theories of Mass Communication* (New York: David McKay, 1970), p. 141; see also 4th edition, 1982, p. 218.
9. Melvin L. De Fleur, op. cit., pp. 247–248; see also H. Schuman and P. Johnson, "Attitudes and Behavior" in A. Inkeles, J. Coleman, and N. Smelser,

eds., *Annual Review of Sociology,* (Palo Alto, Calif.: Annual Review, Inc., 1976).

10. Timothy G. Plax and Melvin L. De Fleur, "Communication, Attitudes, and Behavior: An Axiomatic Theory with Implications for Persuasion Research," paper presented at the annual meeting of the Western Speech Communication Association, Portland, Oregon, 1980.

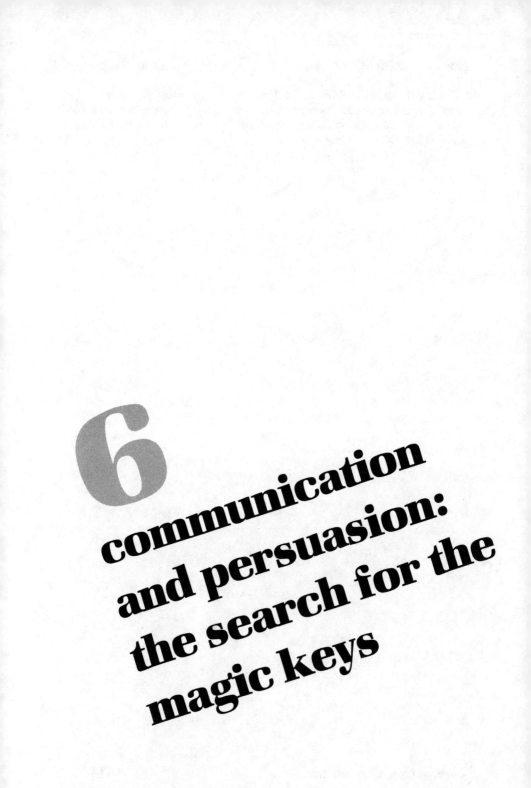

6

communication
and persuasion:
the search for the
magic keys

World War II was finally over. Through that brutal struggle the world—and America—was changed forever. Before the war, the nation had remained somewhat isolated; its concerns had been mainly with its own affairs. However, by the end of the war it had been thrust into global responsibilities for which its people were ill-prepared. Yet they responded both ideologically and militarily; the nation rose to the challenge and prevailed against formidable odds. The United States had become the most powerful nation on the earth and the unquestioned leader of the "Free World."

The war years also had a profound impact on the American national consciousness. Americans had come to nurture an almost boundless faith in their ability to solve the world's problems. Beginning as a marked underdog, they had martialed their industrial and military might to crush the powerful forces of fascism. Once that was accomplished, and the war over, the United States set out to solve the problems of its former enemies. It helped them to rebuild their ravaged countries and economies, an act of generosity unprecedented in the world's history.

Perhaps the greatest victory of the war was America's conquest of the atom. It was an amazing feat; science won the battle by splitting the atom. This accomplishment brought the role of science a new significance in modern life. Although atomic power had been developed for use as a weapon, many thoughtful people saw in it a bright vision for the future—unlimited power for peaceful purposes.

Thus, it was science that emerged from the war as the great hope of mankind. And science dedicated to basic research seemed the most important kind. Once new principles were uncovered, they could then be used by pragmatic, innovative Americans to make a better world for everyone. That post-war dream fired the imagination of all scientists—and social scientists were no exception.

There was much work to be done by social and behavioral scientists. The world was still filled with prejudice, discrimination, and bigotry. And now that nuclear weapons were a reality, the task of improving relationships between peoples seemed more urgent than ever. Badly needed, for example, was a better understanding of how people's beliefs, attitudes and behavior could be modified in socially approved ways through carefully designed persuasive communication. If basic research into the "laws" of persuasion could be successful, then such knowledge could be used to achieve many prosocial goals. It seemed clear enough from earlier research on communication, such as that done by the Army researchers in training camps during the war, that there were underlying regularities waiting to be discovered by careful scientific research. Once those keys to the communication–persuasion relationship were available, they could be used to unlock the mysteries of how opinions and attitudes could be modified. Then it would be possible to change overt behavior patterns in socially desirable ways. Thus, such keys were critical in order to improve the human condition.

This mission held great appeal to social psychologists such as Carl Hovland, who had been one of the principal researchers in the Army's investigations of the persuasive use of films. Prior to the war, Hovland had been a "rising star" in experimental psychology at Yale, but the demands of the war altered the direction of his career. While the Army research involved the investigation of "practical" problems, Hovland could see the implications of that research for building a systematic theory of persuasion. Thus, the seeds of a new program of scientific research were planted and took root in Hovland's wartime experience. During the war, he had worked with an outstanding group of social scientists, including Irvin Janis, Arthur Lumsdaine, Fred Sheffield, Nathan Macoby, and M. Brewster Smith. When he returned to Yale at the end of the war, he took Janis, Lumsdaine, and Sheffield with him. Together they founded a broad-based research program drawing on scholars and theories from several disciplines.

THE RESEARCH PROGRAM

Between 1946 and 1961, the Yale Program of Research on Communication and Attitude Change conducted more than 50 experiments that produced a considerable body of published results. Hovland remained the driving force behind the research during the entire period. The theoretical bases as well as the framework for the program's experiments were outlined in *Communication and Persuasion* (1953), the first major book to emerge from the research program.[1] *Communication and Persuasion* reports the results of a number of investigations of the ways in which opinions and beliefs are modified by persuasive communications. Funded by the Rockefeller Foundation, the work involved the efforts of some 30 social scientists—mainly psychologists, but including sociologists, anthropologists and political scientists.

It should be noted that the Yale Program did not actually study mass communication or actual media campaigns. It made use of experiments in a variety of settings. The research dealt with more intimate, interpersonal channels of communication, such as live speeches and illustrated lectures. A few of the studies did use recorded speeches and written passages, but they were not used to stimulate mass communication situations. Nevertheless, many scholars of the time felt that the laws of persuasion would operate similarly in both the experimental and real-life situations, and that uncovering the keys to the process in the laboratory would also lead to an understanding of their operation in mass communication persuasion.

The project focused on several areas thought to be important to the persuasion process. These areas were generated by the researchers' definition of communication. They defined communication in terms of stimuli that create changes in the responses of people. More specifically, they defined communication as "the process by which an individual (the communicator) transmits stimuli (usually verbal) to modify the behavior of other individuals (the audience)." [2] This stimulus-response definition was characteristic of the way in which the process of communication was viewed at the time. Harold D. Lasswell had formulated a well-known statement that indicated that the proper study of the act of communication was to look at *who* said *what* to *whom* over what *channel* with what *effect*. [3] Thus, the main categories of analysis were: (1) the communicator, (2) the content of the communication, (3) the audience, and (4) the actual responses made by the audience. Selected topics, such as communicator credibility and group conformity effects, were then studied in each of these categories.

There are several reasons why most of the research reported in *Communication and Persuasion* was conducted in controlled experimental settings. For one, most of the researchers had backgrounds in experimental psychology. They were therefore familiar with and had confidence in experimental methods. More importantly, the researchers were searching for causal regularities—the "laws" of persuasion. They believed that in this search it was necessary to use methods which they thought would allow for causal interpretations of their data.

The nature of the experimental situation was basically the same throughout the various studies. Messages were constructed for the project, then tested under specially defined circumstances where the effects of various factors influencing persuasion could be isolated. The communication was one-way. No verbal interaction was allowed between the audience and the communicator; in addition, interaction was restricted among audience members during the experimental sessions. Moreover, the subjects were part of a "captive" audience (i.e., they were not allowed to leave the sessions once they had begun). The topics presented in the studies were carefully chosen: they were selected on the basis of their relative neutrality, in other words, "to arouse little motivation for either suppression or distortion."[4] Finally, standard methodological precautions were taken throughout the studies. These precautions included careful attention to questionnaire construction; independent test administrators; assurances of anonymity, and so on. In general, the research techniques used in the project were rigorous and attention to detail appeared complete.

Assumptions About the Nature of Opinion and Attitude Change

Hovland and his associates measured persuasion in terms of the amount of attitude and opinion change. They viewed attitudes and opinions as intimately related, yet analytically distinct. The term "opinion" was used in a very general sense by the authors. It referred to "interpretations, expectations, and evaluations." For example, this term included beliefs about the intentions of others, anticipations of future events, or appraisals of the consequences of alternate courses of action. While *opinion* was used to refer to a broad class of anticipations, *attitude* was more exclusive; it was reserved only for explicit responses approaching or avoiding some object, person, group, or symbol. In other words, attitudes possessed "drive value."

Another factor which distinguished an attitude from an opinion was that opinions could always be verbalized and attitudes need not be: an attitude might be unconscious. However, the researchers' formulation includes a high degree of interaction between attitudes and opinions. A change in general approach and avoidance orientations (attitudes) might affect a person's expectations (opinions) on a number of related issues. A more important aspect of this interaction for the research reported in *Communication and Persuasion* was that change in a person's general attitude might result from changes in opinion. Hovland, Janis, and Kelley assumed that attitudes were mediated by verbal beliefs, expectations, and judgments, and that one of the primary ways in which communications could change attitudes was to change those verbal responses (opinions).

Some important methodological problems arose out of this conceptualization of opinions and attitudes. When the authors said that opinions could be verbalized and were "implicit responses" they meant that they were the verbal answers a person gives in inner speech. They were thus to be distinguished from overt verbal responses, the answers to those questions as expressed to others. Typically, the overt and covert answers are identical, but they need not be—especially if external constraints (e.g., social pressure) hinder their free expression. Thus, the methodological problem in the context of this research was: How do you observe changes in the implicit responses? Hovland, Janis, and Kelley resolved this problem by assuming that under certain conditions (which they tried to arrange) the overt verbalizations approximated the implicit verbal responses. Thus, they elicited verbal responses to questionnaire items, where the questions they used were designed and administered to minimize distorted responses to the items.

Another methodological problem which confronted the authors was whether they were measuring real opinion change rather than simply change in response to the question items. They handled this problem by using a series of items which approached the subject matter from a number of points of view. In addition, they used stimuli (e.g., language) similar to those found in everyday situations. The ultimate justification for the questionnaires, in their eyes, was their utility. The questionnaires allowed the investigators to observe consistent relationships between communicated stimuli and changes in verbal responses. The researchers checked the validity of these relationships by comparing them with observations from other studies. In addition, they also checked the relationships by examining behavioral data concerning changes in voting, buying products, and contributing to charities.

The Theoretical Model

The researchers assumed that attitudes and opinions were enduring. That is, they assumed that a particular attitude or opinion would persist unless the individual underwent some new learning experience. And, in fact, the theoretical framework presented by Hovland, Janis, and Kelley was a learning model—in essence, a stimulus–response model.

In the learning of new attitudes, Hovland and his associates believed that three variables were important: attention, comprehension, and acceptance. The first of these factors, *attention*, recognizes the fact that not all message stimuli that a person encounters are noticed. Driving down a highway littered with billboards, for example, you may notice only a fraction of the persuasive messages that you pass. Lacking your attention, the attempted persuasion will not be successful. But even when an appeal is noticed, it might not be effective. The second factor posited by Hovland and his colleagues, *comprehension*, recognizes the fact that some messages may be too complex and too ambiguous for their intended audience to understand. Thus, a highly complex treatise on the balance-of-payments deficit, for example, may be totally ineffective in persuading the economic novice to vote for or against the passage of a particular bill. Finally, a person must decide to accept the communication before any real attitude change takes place. The degree of *acceptance* is largely related to the incentives that are offered. The message may provide arguments or reasons for accepting the advocated point of view, or it may engender expectations of rewards or other pleasant experiences. For example, a billboard on the highway may tell you that a nationally known restaurant is only minutes off the highway, thus promising you something better than you had planned at the next truck stop. Stimulus–response theories regard this assumption as basic— attitudes are changed only if the incentives for making a new response are greater than the incentives for making the old response. In short, the theoretical model of Hovland and his associates suggests the following steps in the process of changing attitudes or opinions:

1. A recommended opinion (the stimulus) is presented.
2. Assuming that the subjects have paid attention to and understood the message, the audience responds or reacts. That is, they think about their initial opinions and also about the recommended opinion.
3. The subjects will change their attitudes if incentives (rewards) for making a new response are greater than the incentives for making the old response.

Overall, the research discussed in *Communication and Persuasion* could be described in terms of three of its principal characteristics. First, it was primarily concerned with theoretical issues and basic research; its main purpose was to discover the "laws" of persuasion. Second, the principal theoretical approach used was a version of stimulus–response learning theory in which it was assumed that attitudes (and opinions) could be changed *only if* the incentives for change are greater than the incentive for stability. Third, the methodological emphasis was on controlled experimental research.

THE EXPERIMENTS AND THEIR FINDINGS

Both the experiments and their findings were numerous, complex, and were discussed in detail by the authors. There were far too many studies to review each separately. For the sake of simplicity, only the major ideas in each of the four categories (communicator, content, audience, response) will be discussed. A representative study in each category will also be presented.

Characteristics of the Communicator

The first area discussed in *Communication and Persuasion* was that of the communicator's credibility. It was assumed by the researchers that the effectiveness of a communication depended to a considerable extent upon who delivered it. Government agencies, for example, take great pains to have their statements to Congress presented by the most acceptable advocate. Even backyard gossips liberally sprinkle the names of respectable sources throughout their rumors. How often, for example, have you heard "it came from a good source" attached to a rumor?

Hovland and his associates were particularly interested in how differences in the credibility of the communicator would affect: (1) the way in which the presentation and the content of the presentation would be perceived and evaluated by members of the audience, and (2) the degree to which the attitudes and opinions of the audience members would be modified. The researchers limited their investigation to the influence of the following two factors: (1) "expertness" or "the extent to which the communicator is perceived to be a source of valid assertions"[5] and (2) "trustworthiness" or "the degree of confidence in the communicator's intent to communicate the assertions he considers most valid."[6] It would appear to be obvious that "expertness" of the sources is an important factor. For example, previous research had found that the credibility of an advertisement appears to be related to some extent to the reputation of the particular magazine in which it appeared. As an example of this, consider your own reaction when you read a sensational news story. Does it make any difference to you whether the story appeared in *The New York Times* or in *The National Enquirer?*

Trustworthiness also appeared to be an important factor from previous research. For example, in Chapter 5, it was indicated that men who viewed the film *The Battle of Britain* and thought it was "propaganda" showed less opinion change in the direction advocated by the film than did those who viewed the film and thought it simply "information." Again, in everyday life we often wonder about people's "ulterior motives." If we perceive a person as having a definite *intention* to persuade us, the likelihood is increased that this source will be perceived as an individual with something to gain by our persuasion; therefore, that person is less worthy of trust.

To test the effects of variations in expertness and trustworthiness, Hovland and Weiss designed an experiment which consisted of presenting an identical communication to two groups. Four different topics were used. Table 6 lists the topics of the articles and the sources to whom they were attributed. In one group, the articles were attributed to *high-credibility* sources and in the other they were attributed to *low-credibility* sources.

Table 6   The Topics of Four Persuasive Communications and the Sources to Whom They Were Attributed.

	High Credibility Source	Low Credibility Source
A. *Antihistamine Drugs:* Should the antihistamine drugs continue to be sold without a doctor's prescription?	*New England Journal of Biology and Medicine*	Magazine A (A mass circulation monthly pictorial magazine)
B. *Atomic Submarines:* Can a practicable atomic-powered submarine be built at the present time?	Robert J. Oppenheimer	*Pravda*
C. *The Steel Shortage:* Is the steel industry to blame for the current shortage of steel?	*Bulletin of National Resources Planning Board*	Writer A (An antilabor, anti-New Deal, "rightist" newspaper columnist)
D. *The Future of Movie Theaters:* As a result of TV, will there be a decrease in the number of movie theaters in operation by 1955?	*Fortune* magazine	Writer B (A woman movie-gossip columnist)

SOURCE: Carl I. Hovland, Irving L. Janis, and Harold H. Kelly, *Communication and Persuasion* (New Haven, Conn.: Yale University Press, 1953) p. 28

Both affirmative and negative versions of each topic were employed. Opinion questionnaires were administered before, immediately after, and a month after the communication. In the questionnaire given before the communication, college students were asked to judge the trustworthiness of a long list of sources, including those used in the study. Analysis of these judgments showed that the sources which the researchers felt had high credibility did, in fact, have high credibility; that is, they were judged so by the subjects. The same was true for the low-credibility sources: they were judged by the students to be low in trustworthiness. The subjects were then given the articles to read. Each student received a booklet containing one article on each of the four topics; the name of the source was given at the end of each article. Then, another questionnaire was administered immediately following this reading, asking for their opinions and evaluations of the article.

The results of the experiment showed that differences in initial attitude toward the source influenced evaluation of the presentations. Even though the communications judged were identical in content, the presentations were considered to be "less fair" and the conclusions "less justified" when the source was of low credibility. (See Table 7).

Table 8 displays the effects of source credibility on opinion change in these subjects, taken immediately after the exposure. Opinion change in the direction advocated by the communication occurred significantly more often when the communication originated from a high-credibility source than when it originated from a low-credibility source. More specifically, the expected difference was obtained on three of the four topics, the exception being the one which discussed the future of movies.

However, the researchers obtained additional data on these opinion changes four weeks later and the differences between the effectiveness of the high-credibility and low-credibility sources had disappeared. This resulted from both (1) a decreased acceptance of the point of view advocated by the high-credibility source, and (2) an increased acceptance of the posi-

---

Table 7   The Effects of High and Low Credibility Sources on Evaluations of Fairness and Justifiability of Identical Communications.

A. *Percent considering author "fair" in his presentation*

Topic	High Credibility Source		Low Credibility Source	
	N*	Percent	N	Percent
Antihistamines	31	64.5	27	59.3
Atomic Submarines	25	96.0	36	69.4
Steel Shortage	37	24.3	26	19.2
Future of Movies	29	93.1	33	63.7
Mean		65.6		54.9

B. *Percent considering author's conclusion "justified" by the facts*

Topic	High Credibility Source		Low Credibility Source	
	N	Percent	N	Percent
Antihistamines	31	67.7	27	51.8
Atomic Submarines	25	80.0	36	44.4
Steel Shortage	37	32.4	26	26.9
Future of Movies	29	58.6	33	42.4
Mean		58.2		41.8

* N = number of cases used.

SOURCE: Carl I. Hovland, Irving L. Janis, and Harold H. Kelly, *Communication and Persuasion* (New Haven, Conn.: Yale University Press, 1953) p. 29.

Table 8   Net Changes of Opinion in Direction of Communication for Sources Classified by Experimenters as High or Low Credibility.*

Topic	High Credibility Sources N	Percent	Low Credibility Sources N	Percent
	Net Percentage of Cases in Which Subjects Changed Opinion in Direction of Communication			
Antihistamines	31	22.6	30	13.3
Atomic Submarines	25	36.0	36	0.0
Steel Shortage	35	22.9	26	−3.8
Future of Movies	31	12.9	30	16.7
Mean		23.0		6.6
Difference		16.4		
p		<.01		

* Net changes = positive changes *minus* negative changes. Cf. [18] pp. 302–305 for a discussion of the use of this measure.

SOURCE: Carl I. Hovland, Irving L. Janis, and Harold H. Kelley, *Communication and Persuasion* (New Haven, Conn.: Yale University Press, 1953) p. 30.

tion advocated by the low-credibility sources. Of course, the first could be attributed to forgetting the content. However, the second suggested that the negative effects of the untrustworthy source wore off and permitted the arguments presented in the communication to produce a delayed positive effect, known as the "sleeper effect" (discussed in Chapters 2 and 5). Thus, the researchers concluded that the effect of the source is maximal at the time of communication but decreases with the passage of time more rapidly than the effects of the content.

Based upon this evidence and the results derived from follow-up studies, the researchers concluded:

1. When a communication was attributed to a low-credibility source it was considered to be more biased and unfair in its presentation than when it was attributed to a high-credibility source.
2. High-credibility sources had a considerably greater immediate effect on audience opinion than did low-credibility sources. However, after a few weeks the positive effects of high-credibility sources and the negative effects of low-credibility sources tended to disappear. There were no differences between the two sources in either subject evaluations of the presentation or in their acceptance of the conclusions which each source advocated.

3. The immediate effects on opinion were not the result of differences in either the amount of attention the audience paid to the communicator or of the audience's comprehension of the presentation. Tests taken of the amount of information retained by the audience revealed that the audience learned what was said equally well, no matter what the perceived credibility of the communication. Variations in source credibility thus influence primarily the motivation of the audience to accept the conclusions which were advocated.

The Content and Structure of the Message

The study of the effects of the content in a communication on persuasion was broken down into two areas: (1) motivating appeals, and (2) the organization of persuasive arguments. Motivating appeals were defined as "stimuli which operate as appeals that arouse motives to accept recommended opinions."[7] Hovland, Janis, and Kelley discuss three major classes of such incentives: (1) substantiating arguments, (2) positive appeals, and (3) negative appeals. Substantiating arguments tend to lead the audience to believe that the conclusion advocated in the presentation is true or correct. Positive appeals emphasize the rewards of accepting those conclusions, whereas negative appeals (including fear-arousing content) depict the unpleasant consequences of not accepting that conclusion. The researchers present evidence involving only negative, fear-arousing appeals.

Fear Appeals Research into fear-arousing appeals was designed to investigate factors which determine the degree to which threat appeals are effective or ineffective in producing opinion change. Research in this area focused on two problems: (1) identifying content stimuli that were effective in arousing fear or threat, and then (2) determining how they facilitated or interfered with the overall effectiveness of the communication.

The researchers assumed that any intensely disturbing emotion, such as fear, guilt, anger, and so on, has the functional properties of a drive. In other words, these emotions provide motivation for some kind of behavior. A successful fear appeal arouses, then relieves, emotional tension. The tension is removed through the presentation of new opinions for acceptance which provide solutions to the problem. Specifically, the actual persuasion process using fear appeals involves the following steps:

1. The individual is first exposed to relatively neutral content which defines the topic of communication.

2. Threat statements follow, which are interpreted as referring to a genuine danger and which evoke anticipations such as "This might happen to me."
3. As these anticipations are mentally rehearsed, the individual experiences a marked increase in emotional tension.
4. While in a state of high emotional tension, the individual is exposed to other statements in the communication which make assertions about ways of averting the threat. That is, the threat can or should be avoided by performing the recommended action or by adopting the recommended attitude.
5. As the reassuring recommendation is mentally rehearsed, emotional tension subsides.
6. The reduction of emotional tension operates as a reinforcement of the reassuring recommendation and thus this new response will tend to occur on subsequent occasions, when similar stimuli are present.

As part of the research program, Janis and Feshbach tested the above model of fear-arousing communication. Using the entire senior class of a large Connecticut high school as subjects, they presented a 15-minute lecture to four randomly assigned groups. Three of those groups saw lectures concerning dental hygiene; each of the lectures contained essentially the same information about the causes and prevention of tooth decay. However, each group was given a separate form of lecture containing a different amount of threat or fear-arousing material. Form 1 contained a "strong" appeal, emphasizing the painful consequences of tooth decay and gum disease. Cancer and blindness were even mentioned as possible consequences of such dental neglect. Form 2 presented a "moderate" appeal in which dangers were described in a milder, more factual manner. This appeal, at its worst, emphasized mouth infections, sore swollen gums, and tooth decay. Form 3, on the other hand, presented a "minimal" appeal which contained few references to the consequences of tooth neglect, although "cavities" were mentioned several times as were "decayed teeth." The fourth group, the control group, was given a non-threatening lecture on the human eye. Measures were taken before and after the lectures. These included: (1) a measure of each subject's feelings about the possibilities of tooth decay, taken before and after the lecture; (2) a measure of emotional arousal taken immediately after the lecture; and (3) a measure of each subject's conformity with prescribed dental practices, taken one week before and one week after the lecture.

Overall, the lectures did elicit the anxiety that was predicted. As Table 9 indicates, all three forms of the presentation produced different amounts

Table 9 **Percent of Subjects Reporting Feelings of Worry or Concern Evoked during the Dental Hygiene Communication.**

	Experimental Groups		
Questionnaire Responses	Exposed to Strong Appeal (N = 50)	Exposed to Moderate Appeal (N = 50)	Exposed to Minimal Appeal (N = 50)
1. Felt worried—a "few times" or "many times"—about own mouth condition	74	60	48
2. Felt "somewhat" or "very" worried about improper care of own teeth	66	36	34
3. Thought about condition of own teeth "most of the time"	42	34	22

SOURCE: Carl I. Hovland, Irving L. Janis, and Harold H. Kelley, *Communication and Persuasion* (New Haven, Conn.: Yale University Press, 1953) p. 70.

of emotional arousal, with the amount of arousal positively correlated with the amount of threat presented. Specifically, the strong appeal produced greater emotional tension than did the moderate appeal, which in turn, produced greater tension than did the minimal appeal. Additionally, there was a marked increase in worrying about the possibility of tooth decay after the lecture, which again correlated positively with the amount of threat. This led Janis and Feshbach to conclude that content factors which increase the meaningfulness of a threat (i.e., elaborating on the consequences and relating them to the audience) tend to increase the level of emotional arousal.

Furthermore, it was found that fear-appeals did increase conformity with recommended practices. However, the results were surprising, to say the least. It was the minimal appeal (not the strongest appeal) which produced the greatest changes in conformity with the communicator's recommendations! (See Table 10.) In fact, the group exposed to the strong threat failed to differ significantly from the control group. Overall, Hovland, Janis and Kelley concluded that a minimal amount of fear-appeal is the most effective in terms of persuasion. Moderate and strong appeals may be effective in arousing interest and a high degree of emotional tension, but decrease the overall effectiveness of the presentation by evoking some form of interference. For example, when a communication arouses intense feelings of anxiety, individuals will sometimes fail to pay attention to what is

| Type of Change | Group | | | |
	Strong (N = 50)	Moderate (N = 50)	Minimal (N = 50)	Control (N = 50)
Increased conformity	28%	44%	50%	22%
Decreased conformity	20	22	14	22
No change	52	34	36	56
Total	100	100	100	100
Net change in conformity	+8%	+22%	+36%	0%

Reliability of Differences	Critical Ratio	Probability Value
Control vs. minimal	2.54	<.01
Control vs. moderate	1.50	.07
Control vs. strong	0.59	.28
Strong vs. moderate	0.95	.17
Strong vs. minimal	1.96	.03
Moderate vs. minimal	0.93	.18

SOURCE: Carl I. Hovland, Irving L. Janis, and Harold H. Kelley, *Communication and Persuasion* (New Haven, Conn.: Yale University Press, 1953) p. 80.

being said and miss the intended message. Other individuals, when ex-posed to anxiety-producing communications may react to the unpleasant experience by becoming aggressive toward the communicator and rejecting his/her statements. In short, high levels of anxiety can interfere with the person attending to, comprehending or accepting the communication.

Message Organization   Whether or not a persuasive communication is effective depends not only on the nature of the motivating appeals used, but also upon the organization of the arguments used in support of the position advocated. Typical problems discussed under this topic include: (1) whether or not a conclusion should be explicitly stated, (2) whether or not both sides of an argument should be presented, and (3) if both sides are to be presented, which one should be presented first.

Overall, the results of the studies on these topics were rather predict-able and in line with the findings of earlier research. For example, Hovland and Mandell performed a study to test the relative effectiveness of either explicitly drawing a conclusion or leaving it implicit. The topic used was

"Devaluation of Currency." The communication was tape-recorded and presented as a transcription from a radio program called "Education for Americans." All subjects (college students) heard the identical communication, but for half of them the part containing the explicit conclusion drawn was omitted. It was found that much more opinion change occurred when the conclusion was explicitly drawn by the communicator. However, the researchers cautioned that the intelligence and the degree of sophistication of the members of the audience, in terms of the issue being presented, are important factors in the relative effectiveness of other methods of presentation. Thus, with a sophisticated audience, it might be more effective to leave the conclusion implicit.

Another issue that relates to the organization of persuasive messages is the question of one-sided communications versus two-sided communications. For example, if you are arguing in favor of reduced television time for children, should you present only arguments that are favorable to your position, or should you acknowledge and attempt to refute an opposing viewpoint? The issue, of course, had been dealt with in the film research discussed in Chapter 5. In that work, Hovland, Lumsdaine and Sheffield argued that, on the whole, there was no difference between a one-sided and a two-sided presentation in terms of opinion change. However, few answers are "all or none" and Hovland et al. did find some differences when special conditions were considered (see Chapter 5).

One study in this present research program which provided some interesting results was one conducted by Lumsdaine and Janis. They considered the effectiveness of a one-sided message versus a two-sided message. Their special interest, however, was which of these two types of messages would be most likely to prepare an audience to resist influences of subsequent counterpropaganda. Their subjects were high school students with whom they used two different versions of a recorded radio program. In both versions, the commentator presented the view that the U.S.S.R. would not be able to produce A-bombs in quantity for at least five years. One group, however, received a one-sided version and were presented only arguments which supported the speaker's position. (They were told, for example, that Soviet scientists had not yet discovered all the crucial secrets and that even after acquiring all the know-how, the U.S.S.R. still did not have sufficient industrial potential to produce the bombs in quantity.)

The second group received a two-sided version that contained all of the arguments in the first group's presentation, reached the same conclusion, but also discussed the main arguments on the other side of the question. (For example, they were given the additional information that the U.S.S.R. had many first-rate atomic scientists and that Soviet industries had made a tremendous recovery since the war.) A week later, half of the subjects in each group were given a second communication in which another speaker advocated a position opposite the one presented in the original communication. That is, he argued that the U.S.S.R. had probably already developed the A-bomb and that within two years would be producing it in large quantities. The main question used to measure the effects of the communication was: "About how long from now do you think it will be before the Russians are really producing *large numbers* of atomic bombs?"[8] Questionnaires were filled out several weeks before the presentations and after the presentations. The results showed that when there was no subsequent exposure to counterpropaganda the two versions were equally effective in changing opinions. However, when there *was* subsequent exposure to counterpropaganda the two-sided version was more effective in producing sustained opinion change. The researchers concluded that when the two-sided presentation was used, the listeners were led to accept the recommended opinion; they had already taken into account the opposing arguments, and thus had a basis for either ignoring or discounting contradictory arguments. This process of inducing resistance to later persuasive attempts was labelled "innoculation." (This became an important concept in the study of attitude change.)

The last major issue considered in message organization was the old "primacy versus recency" debate. In other words, when there are occasions in which it is most effective to present both sides of an argument, which side should be presented first for maximum impact? Will the side presented first or the side presented last be the more persuasive? After reviewing the existing research, Hovland et al. concluded: "It is doubtful it will ever be meaning(ful) to postulate a Law of Primacy in social psychology."[9] This issue, in other words, was one which Hovland thought best laid to rest. In short, then, the most effective message is one in which a conclusion is explicitly drawn and both sides of the argument presented; the order of presentation does not really make a difference.

The Audience

The audience was first studied in two ways. The researchers examined the effects of group membership and group conformity on the acceptance of persuasive communications. In addition, personality factors and their effects upon persuasibility were examined.

Effects of Group Membership   Hovland, et al. argued that individuals' conforming tendencies stem from membership in groups. These tendencies are based upon knowledge of what behavior is expected of them by other members and upon the individual's motivation to live up to those expectations. Thus, group norms often interfere with the effectiveness of persuasive communications because they tend to make the individual resist change. The researchers were therefore particularly interested in "counter-norm communications," that is, in messages which argue in direct opposition to group norms.

Previous research had shown that the more highly a person valued his membership in a group, the more closely his attitudes and opinion conformed to the consensus within that group. From this, Kelley and Volkhart hypothesized that individuals who highly value their membership in a group will be less influenced by communications contrary to the group's norms than will those who do not value membership as much. That is, opinion change will be inversely related to the degree to which the person values group membership.

In testing this hypothesis, they experimented with twelve troops of Boy Scouts from a large New England industrial community. The boys filled out a questionnaire in which they were asked how highly they valued their membership in the troop and what their attitudes toward woodcraft were. These attitudes were compared with attitudes about other, more urban activities. A week later, the boys were presented with a speech in which a non-Scout adult criticized woodcraft activities and suggested that the Scouts would be better off learning about the city. Finally, each group was divided in half and everyone filled out the questionnaire again. Half of each group was told that their answers would be kept secret (private condition), while the other half was told that their responses would probably be made known to the rest of the group (public condition).

The results of this experiment at least partially confirmed Kelley and Volkart's hypothesis. That is, when the opinions were expressed privately, the boys who most valued their scout membership were the least influenced by the communication. However, in the public condition the results were inconsistent and no definite pattern could be identified. Overall, however, the authors argued that the findings did support the general hypothesis that persons who were strongly motivated to remain members of the group would be the most resistant to communications which presented recommendations contrary to the standards of the group.

Personality Factors in Persuasibility   The authors argued that the effects of a communication are partly dependent upon the characteristics of individual members of the audience. Thus, taking account of personality characteristics should improve predictions concerning the way in which a given type of audience (or a given individual within the audience) will respond. Therefore, the researchers believed that investigations of personality factors were necessary if they were to discover the elusive "laws" and thus be able to predict the degree to which a persuasive communication will succeed in changing beliefs and attitudes.

Hovland and his associates discussed two general types of personality factors: intellectual abilities and "motive factors." Intellectual abilities are significant because they determine the way an individual attends to, interprets, and assimilates the many communications to which a person is constantly exposed. However, Hovland and his associates believed that for those individuals who possess "at least a certain minimum of essential intellectual abilities," "motive factors" are probably more important determinants of individual differences in persuasibility. Motive factors are said to involve "predominant personality needs, emotional disturbances, defense mechanisms, frustration tolerance, thresholds of excitability, etc., which may facilitate or interfere with a person's responsiveness to many different types of persuasive communications."

The authors concluded, in regard to the relation between intellectual ability and persuasibility, that it was a complex matter. On the one hand, it is *easier* to persuade individuals with high intelligence than those low in intellectual ability. This is because the former have more ability to draw valid inferences when exposed to persuasive communications which rely primarily on impressive logical arguments. At the same time, those with high intellectual ability are also more likely to be critical of the arguments presented. They will therefore be *less likely* to be influenced than those with low intellectual ability when they are exposed to persuasive communications which rely primarily on unsupported generalities or upon false, illogical, irrelevant argumentation. The researchers hypothesized that there would be an interplay between intellectual factors and motive factors. Mental ability alone would be insufficient data when predicting the influence of individual differences on persuasibility. Some individuals, the researchers hypothesized, had personality needs which inclined them to be highly gullible. What motive factors, then, do make for indiscriminate acceptance of persuasive communications? Janis attempted to link personality characteristics to susceptibility to persuasion. The experiment measured opinion change in 78 male college students. Each student was exposed to the same set of three persuasive communications. In addition, the researchers obtained information about the personality characteristics of the subjects. Thus, it was possible to examine the relationship between opinion changes and personality factors.

The students were given a series of written communications similar to magazine articles or news commentaries or editorials. These materials provided a series of factual statements in an attempt to convince the audience that a particular belief or expectation was the correct one. Because the communications were in simple language, it is probable that all of the student subjects had the minimal skills necessary for absorbing the message.

Each subject was exposed to the communications in a standard way. The subject had to read all three communications; in addition, he had to present one of them orally, then listen to oral presentations of the other two. The subjects' initial opinions on these issues were obtained through an opinion questionnaire administered approximately four weeks earlier. The key items in the questionnaire for this study focused directly on the issues dealt with in the communications. These were: (1) the number of movie theaters in business in three years, (2) the amount of meat available to the population of the United States in two years, and (3) the length of time before a cure for the common cold is discovered. No one in this original survey gave estimates which were anywhere as low as the ones advocated by the communication. After exposure to the communications, questionnaires containing these three items were administered to each subject again. Approximately two-thirds of the subjects lowered their estimates; they changed in the direction advocated by the communication to which they had been exposed.

Janis then divided the subjects into categories on the basis of the degree of change they exhibited: high, moderate, and low persuasibility. The "high" category contained 32 cases; all of these individuals had been influenced by all three communications. Another 21 cases were classified as "moderate"; they were influenced by two of the communications. The "low" category was composed of the 25 cases in which the individuals were influenced by one or none of the persuasive communications. The three groups were then compared with respect to personality characteristics.

Personality data were obtained from two independent sources. Janis obtained detailed clinical reports for 16 of the subjects who had received psychiatric counseling. In addition, he administered a personality inventory to all 78 subjects at the time they completed the precommunication questionnaire. Both sets of data indicated that there were marked differences between the men who were highly influenced and those who were relatively uninfluenced by the persuasive communications. Those who were highly influenced possessed low levels of self-esteem. They expressed feelings of social inadequacy; for example, they showed concern about feelings of shyness, lack of confidence in their conversational abilities, high concern about the possibility that friends may have a low opinion of them, and uneasiness at social gatherings. Moreover, this group was also described as "aggressively inhibited." In other words, they rarely criticized others, rarely felt angry toward anyone, rarely felt like resisting the demands of others, and felt a lack of resentment when deceived by others. In addition, the group was also highly characterized by depression. They often reported feeling "blue," "unhappy," and "discouraged." In short, then, the study found that high persuasibility was associated with feelings of social inadequacy, inhibition of aggression, and depression, in addition to general levels of low self-esteem.

Up to this point, we have been discussing personality factors associated with persons who are relatively easy to persuade. The researchers did, however, discover three distinct personality traits associated with those who are difficult to persuade. These traits were: persistent aggressiveness toward others, social withdrawal tendencies, and acute psychoneurotic complaints. Persons who openly expressed hostility and displayed overt aggression toward others in everyday life were found to be relatively unaffected by persuasive communications. Moreover, socially withdrawn persons, those extremely indifferent toward others, were typically resistant to change. This was also true of persons displaying acute psychoneurotic symptoms—notably, obsessional ideas, hypochondriacal complaints, insomnia, and work inhibitions. The author hypothesized that these symptoms interfere with the person's attention, comprehension and acceptance, thereby explaining why such individuals are difficult to influence.

While in this chapter we have categorized the research presented in *Communication and Persuasion* as focusing on the communicator, the communication, and the audience, all of the studies in Hovland et al.'s book examined the *effects* of communications. Thus, all of the studies were implicitly concerned with the responses of the audience. Some, however, examined special aspects of the audience's response to communications.

Audience Response Patterns

The two issues which the Yale Program focused upon in its analysis of response factors were: active versus passive participation by the subject, and the duration of the effects of the communication. More specifically, does active participation by individuals have any effect on attitude or opinion acquisition or change? Is attitude or opinion change brought about by persuasive communications typically long-term or short-term change?

Active versus Passive Participation   In everyday life, most people occupy several roles, such as mother, wife, lawyer, community leader. When fulfilling some of the behavior required by these roles, some individuals may find themselves expected to express ideas that are not necessarily in accord with their private beliefs. What happens to an individual's private opinion when this person is induced to assert what has been said in a communication as though it represented his/her own opinion? This is a question that the researchers sought to answer. Janis and King compared the opinion change of two groups: "active participants" and "passive controls." In one group, subjects were induced to play a role which required them to deliver a persuasive communication to others; in the other group, the subjects were required only to read and listen to the same communication. The experiment was conducted in a series of small group meetings involving male college students. Each student was given an "oral speaking test." In the process, they were exposed to three different communications. The purpose of the study was supposed to be to assess their ability to speak effectively in a group conference. At the end of the session, ratings were obtained from each subject on each speaker's performance. In addition, the subjects answered a series of questions concerning their interest in, and their opinions on the various topics covered. The subjects were told that this information was necessary in order to study agreement among different judges. The researchers compared each subject's post-communication answers with those he had given in a general opinion survey approximately four weeks earlier. They were thus able to detect opinion changes produced by the communications.

Subjects were asked to give an informal talk in each of the experimental sessions. The talk was based upon a prepared outline provided by the researchers. Each active participant was instructed to play the role of a sincere advocate of the point of view he was presenting. The others listened to this talk and read the outline as he spoke. Each subject delivered a talk in turn, while the other two were passively exposed to the communication. None of the subjects knew which topic he would speak on in advance, in order to prevent selective attention effects.

In each communication the speaker talked about a controversial issue involving future events. In all cases the communication took an extreme position. While the arguments were highly relevant, they were also highly biased; they emphasized evidence that supported only one side of the issue. Communication A predicted that two out of three movie theaters would be forced out of business in the next three years because of the intense competition of television and other recent events. The essence of Communication B was that within the next two years the availability of meat to the civilian population of the United States would decline to 50 percent of its present level. Communication C argued that a completely effective cure for the common cold was very close to development; it would probably be available in the next year or so.

The results indicated that active participation (in the experiment role playing) was a much more effective way of changing opinions than passive participation (merely listening to and reading the outline). Additional studies of this topic in the research program yielded similar results. All confirmed the importance of active participation in bringing about opinion change.

Duration of Opinion Change   All of the studies in the Yale Program focused to some degree on the duration of opinion change, many issues relevant to this topic have already been discussed. The researchers raised two questions when they addressed this topic: (1) What are the factors dealing with learning and remembering the content of a communication, and (2) What are the factors dealing with the persistence of acceptance of the communicator's conclusions?

Research on the learning and retention of content delineated several important factors. In general, it was found that the meaningfulness of the content will influence retention. That is, the more vivid and the more emotional the material, the better the retention. Also, the more completely the material is initially learned, the longer it will be remembered. Moreover, the type of retention required was found to be an important factor. Specifically, the rate of forgetting depended upon the criteria used to evaluate retention. For example, simple recognition was easier than total recall. Finally, it was found that the motivation of the audience will influence both the quality and quantity of retention. That is, "unpleasant" material tended to be forgotten more rapidly than "pleasant" material.

In terms of the retention of opinion change, or acceptance of the communicator's conclusions, the researchers reviewed a previous study that provided insight. Hovland and Weiss, in a study described earlier, found that a "high credibility" source was initially more successful in producing opinion change than was a "low credibility" source. However, after four weeks, differences between the sources' respective success ratios had disappeared. This was due to increased acceptance of the low credibility source and decreased acceptance of the high credibility source (the sleeper effect). While forgetting could account for the decreased acceptance of the high credibility source, it could not explain the delayed opinion change in a positive direction. The researchers hypothesized that a dissociation between the communication and the communicator might be producing the sleeper effect. In other words, arguments and conclusions were being recalled without associating them with the source.

Kelman and Hovland therefore conducted a study to find out what would happen if the subjects were reminded of the source at a later testing. They used a total of 330 high school seniors as subjects during regular class periods. The subjects were asked to listen to a recording of an educational radio program and judge its educational value. During the program, a guest speaker gave a talk favoring extreme leniency in the treatment of juvenile delinquents. Three different versions of the introduction to the speaker were used in the experiment. In the positive version, he was identified as a juvenile court judge—well-trained and well-informed. In a neutral version, he was identified as a member of the studio audience, chosen at random. No additional information was given concerning him. In the negative version, he was again presented as coming from the studio audience, but it was also divulged that he had been delinquent in his youth and that he was presently free on bail after an arrest for peddling dope.

After hearing the speech, each group completed an opinion questionnaire concerning juvenile delinquency. Three weeks later all three groups completed the same questionnaire, except that *half* of each group heard the same introduction again (a "reinstatement of the source"). Initially, the positive communicator had the greatest effect and the negative communicator the smallest effect. When the source was not reinstated, there was a decline in agreement with the positive speaker and an increase in agreement with the negative speaker, just as in the Hovland and Weiss study. When the source was reinstated, however, the extent of agreement with the positive communicator increased and agreement with the negative source decreased. The effects produced by the reinstated sources were approximately equal to those which were produced by the original communication. Kelman and Hovland concluded that overall, with the passage of time, the content of a statement is less likely to be associated spontaneously with the source. That is, people often remember *what* was said without recalling *who* said it.

In general, the two most common results concerning retention effects were: (1) An individual may be exposed to a communication and accept the communicator's point of view (at the time), but after a period of time revert to his/her previously held attitude. (2) An individual may at first reject the communicator's point of view but after a time "come around" to the communicator's position. Of the two, the first was the more common.

CONCLUSIONS AND IMPLICATIONS

Overall, what were the principal findings and the major conclusions of the *Communication and Persuasion* studies? Moreover, what was their importance from the point of view of developing the theory and the methodology of mass communication? Finally, what did the researchers find regarding the "magic keys" to persuasion? Do we know, from their work, the right combination of words, message structure, emotional appeals, type of communicator, and so on, to change people's attitudes and opinions? These questions need careful review.

In summary, the many separate but related studies of the Yale Communication Research Program can be categorized as focusing on the communicator, the message, the audience, and the audience's responses to persuasive communications. In terms of the communicator, the program found that source credibility was an important factor in obtaining immediate opinion change. Low-credibility sources were seen as more biased and more unfair than were high-credibility sources. The researchers also found that the effects of the communicator's credibility diminish over time, because members of the audience tend to dissociate the message from the communicator. However, these credibility effects can be reinstated simply by reminding the audience *who* said *what*. Overall, however, most of the opinion change obtained was short term rather than long term. Thus, while it is not difficult to change opinion *immediately* after a persuasive communication, when the change is measured a month later, the audience often has "reverted" to its original opinion.

The content and structure of the message were also found to have important effects. Threatening or fear-arousing materials were shown to arouse emotional tension and to produce opinion change, if used in the proper amounts. It was necessary to be careful not to evoke so much fear that high levels of anxiety resulted, since such intense feelings of anxiety can interfere with the individual's acceptance of the communication. In terms of structure, communications should generally state their conclusions explicitly, unless the audience is intelligent and sophisticated. Moreover, both sides of an issue should be included if it is likely that the audience will be exposed to subsequent counterpropaganda.

The studies of the audience provided some interesting, if not always conclusive, results. For example, the studies found that people who value their membership in groups highly will be least affected by communications which advocate positions counter to the norms of the group. Personality factors were also examined and it was discovered that persons who have low self-esteem are easily influenced. In addition, people who are aggressive toward others and who have psychoneurotic tendencies are very difficult to influence.

Finally, the research into response factors indicated that active participation in the communication, such as having to deliver a speech and argue one side of a question, changes opinions in the direction argued more effectively than does passive participation such as reading the speech or listening to it.

There are several reasons why *Communication and Persuasion* is an important study in the history of communication research. Even though the research did not focus on mass media, it led to a greater understanding of the process of persuasion—a truly significant issue in mass communication. Its studies led to a better understanding of the many facets of persuasion such as the nature of credibility, "innoculation" against propaganda, the nature of fear appeals, group allegiance, the "sleeper effect," and audience participation. And this new understanding was just a beginning; media researchers have followed these leads ever since. It does not matter that the findings reported in *Communication and Persuasion* did not always hold up in subsequent studies. These studies were the seeds from which sprouted a veritable garden of research, sinking its roots in the firm soil prepared by Hovland and his associates. The (inverse relationship) results obtained with the fear appeals, for example, have not always been confirmed in later studies. Indeed, it has been found that the greater the fear, the greater the opinion change.[10] That is, there is often greater attitude/opinion change following high-intensity fear appeals. Moreover, advertising and public service agencies have been influenced in the content of their commercials and public service announcements by this work. For example, recall the last American Cancer Society TV "spot" announcement you saw.

The Yale Program studies were innovative methodologically. They introduced many refinements in the use of the methods of experimental psychology applied to the study of the effects of communications. The project provided for experiments with "strategic variations" to test for and isolate the effects of relevant variables. Some researchers, however, have questioned the use of experimental methodology by itself to study persuasion. They have raised the often repeated objection: Can research conducted under artificial conditions be generalized to more natural conditions? The researchers in the Yale Program obviously felt that this could be done. As mentioned earlier, they felt that experimental research was essential to the formulation of a theory in which basic "laws" could be postulated. These "laws" would then allow social scientists to make valid predictions about future events. This, they thought, was the real goal of any kind of research. Thus, they argued that not only was the experimental method a valid one in this context, but that it was also basic to understanding. It is important for us to remember, however, that the results obtained in any experiment are not, in and of themselves, conclusive. They should not be taken as "the answer." Their potential validity lies in replication and in the integration of the findings with data from other sources (e.g., survey generalizations, field observations, etc.). Even Carl Hovland, in later years, came to recognize the importance of survey data:

> I should like to stress . . . the mutual importance of the two approaches to the problem of communication effectiveness. Neither is a royal road to wisdom,

but each represents an important emphasis. The challenge of future work is one of fruitfully combining their virtues so that we may develop a social psychology of communication with the conceptual breadth provided by correlational study of process and with the rigorous but more delimited methodology of the experiment.

However, in spite of its drawbacks, the use of the experimental design has had profound and lasting influence on the conduct of communication research. That influence continues today.

The theoretical model used in this study was a version of learning theory which assumed that attitudes and opinions could be changed by persuasive communications only if the incentives for change were greater than the incentives for stability. However, before an individual could be influenced by a persuasive communication, he or she must first attend to it and accept it. The researchers were looking for the "keys" to this process. What kind of communicator was most effective? What was the best way to design and structure a message? And what role did personality factors and group allegiances play? Obviously, the general theoretical approach was that of *selective influence*, based upon individual differences. Other theories of selective influence, such as those based upon social categories and social relationships were not pertinent to this research program. The subjects, for the most part, fell into one major social category: students. Most were college students, but some were high school students. In addition, the researchers did not look into the *social* relationships that prevailed among their subjects as a source of influence.

The researchers began with the hope of discovering basic "laws" of persuasion. The idea was that once those keys to the communication–persuasion process were available, they could unlock the mysteries of many social doors. With the possession of these magic keys, we would be able to modify opinions, attitudes, and, theoretically, behavior; we could then reduce prejudice and discrimination, and improve relationships among human beings. In light of the advancement of the "hard" sciences, obtaining this knowledge seemed urgent.

But did these researchers find the magic keys? Not really! Certainly, new findings resulted from the experiments. We remain uncertain whether experiments portray the "real world," but we gained information about the characteristics of an effective communicator; we learned how to "innoculate" subjects from later propaganda; we learned that active participation is more effective than passive. Overall, we learned a great deal concerning immediate or *short-term* opinion change. But we did not learn how to modify opinions and attitudes permanently, or even for as long as three or four weeks. How could we accomplish some of our real world goals—such as reduction of prejudice—when opinions and attitudes apparently tend to revert to the *status quo ante?* Certainly, the new information seemed useful to some people, such as advertising consultants. Armed with it, they may have persuaded more of us to buy products that we ordinarily would not have purchased and didn't know we needed. But this information did not dramatically improve our social world—not as we had hoped. However, Hovland and the other researchers at the Yale Communication Program did not give up on the search for the magic keys. *Communication and Persuasion* was only a start. For years to come, the search would continue. Carl Hovland led the way; a host of others followed.

NOTES AND REFERENCES

1. Two other books, *The Order of Presentation in Persuasion* (1957) and *Personality and Persuasibility* (1959), refined and extended some of the findings presented in *Communication and Persuasion.*
2. Carl Hovland, Irving Janis, and Harold H. Kelley, *Communication and Persuasion* (New Haven: Yale University Press, 1953), p. 12.
3. Harold D. Lasswell, "The Structure and Function of Communication in Society," in *The Communication of Ideas*, ed. by Lyman Bryson (New York: Harper & Brothers, 1948), pp. 37–51.
4. Carl Hovland et al, op. cit., p. 9.
5. Ibid., p. 21.
6. Ibid., p. 21.
7. Ibid., p. 56.
8. Ibid., p. 109.
9. Ibid., p. 9.
10. See, for example, K. L. Higbee, "Fifteen years of fear arousal: Research on threat appeals: 1953–1968, *Psychological Bulletin*, 1969, 72, pp. 426–444. See also H. Leventhal, "Findings and theory in the study of fear communications." In L. Berkowitz, ed., *Advances in Experimental Social Psychology* (Vol. 5), (New York: Academic Press, 1970), pp. 119–186.

7

personal influence: the two-step flow of communication

The decade following World War II was an extraordinarily active period for research on the effects of mass communication. Carl Hovland and his associates followed up the Army studies by conducting experiments on communication issues. The Erie County study of the 1940 presidential campaign had uncovered the possible significance of social ties among members of the audience in the second stage of the "two-step" flow. Other researchers were turning their attention to other media, such as airborne leaflets and comic books (to be discussed in chapters to follow). All of these studies were pressing forward vigorously the task of discovering the principles, processes, and influences of mass communication. This enthusiastic curiosity was aided by a growth in sophistication of the research methods available to social scientists. Although the computer was not yet at hand for academic researchers, statistical procedures were highly developed and the electric calculating machines of the day permitted the analysis of relatively large data sets.

Controversies raged in both academic and political circles regarding the implications of our society's expanding ability to communicate on a mass scale with its citizens. For some, the escalating technology of the media seemed to hold high promise for improving both society and the human condition. Mass communication could save democracy, some said, because the media had the capacity to create informed public opinion. The media could become a kind of mass society version of the "town meeting," where citizens would have increasing access to accurate and complete accounts of the events, issues, and problems that required their attention and decisions. The growing power of the mass media to enlighten people, in other words, would make possible that expansion of the human consciousness forecast by Charles Horton Cooley at the beginning of the century.[1] Although newspapers were the only mass medium of his time, he felt that the huge increase in access to information that they provided for ordinary people had brought mankind to the dawn of a new era of enlightenment.

For others, the media continued to loom as menacing agents that threatened the destruction of democracy. The expansion of the media from print, to film, to broadcasting, seemed only to make it easier to shape and control the ideas of people who were becoming increasingly defenseless against media suggestions. In a society thought to be characterized by increasing urbanization, industrialization, and modernization, the original magic bullet theory, linked with the related conception of mass societal organization (Chapter 1), seemed to provide a clear basis for concern about the effects of the media. The legacy of fear, in other words, appeared to many citizens to be increasingly justified as the media continued to expand.

As research on mass communication intensified, however, communication scholars were forced to reassess their thinking. The problem was that the powerful effects that had been attributed to the media—both good and bad—simply did not seem to be there. The earliest large-scale research, such as the Payne Fund studies (Chapter 2) and the investigation of the "War of the Worlds" broadcast (Chapter 3) had seemed to support the conclusion that the media had immediate, powerful, and direct influences on their audiences. But subsequent studies, with more careful research designs, controls, and measurements, showed far less dramatic effects. The idea that the media controlled people's beliefs, attitudes, and behavior was not being supported by the accumulating evidence. This was not only true of the large-scale studies reviewed in the present book, but of the hundreds of smaller efforts that were increasingly appearing in the research journals.

In his well-known book summarizing the findings in the entire field of mass communication studies that had accumulated up until about 1958, Joseph Klapper maintained that the main conclusions were approximately the following: [2]

1. The media appear to have *less* power than the average citizen has assumed (then or now). No case can be made for simple cause–effect relationships between a person's paying attention to some message conveyed by the mass media and his or her beliefs, attitudes, or behavior.
2. Many studies have found that the messages conveyed by the media do have effects on their audiences, but these effects are relatively *minor*.
3. The conditions under which these messages have effects on their audiences are far *more complex* than had been suspected by social scientists who first studied the media.

Replacing the hypothesis of powerful and immediate effects was not an easy matter, or one that took place overnight. For one thing, the public was deeply committed to the kind of thinking represented by the magic bullet theory. And, as we will show in Chapter 9, a very popular book by a well-known psychiatrist, who claimed that he had clearly demonstrated the powerful influences of one medium (comic books), strongly reinforced among the public the old idea that mass communication could achieve dreadful effects. Thus, by the early 1950s the study of mass communication was proceeding with vigor, but for social scientists the findings seemed to demand new approaches to further investigation of the mass communication process.

Increasingly, research became designed not to demonstrate the awesome power of mass communication but to trace more subtle and complex patterns of its influence. The research community, if not the public, was clearly aware that a hypothesis of minimal effects was closer to reality. To some communication scientists this was a source of disappointment and frustration. One prominent researcher even decided that studying the media was no longer worthwhile and declared the field to be dead.[3] Many others, however, remained excited by media research and designed numerous innovative studies of the more subtle and indirect influences of mass communication.

One important large-scale study of indirect influences of the mass media was actually a follow-up of the research reported in Chapter 4, on the impact of a mass-communicated presidential campaign. The new effort probed into the nature of opinion leaders and the kinds of influences they had on their followers. It focused on, in other words, those who were involved in the second stage of the two-step flow of communication. The research was actually planned in 1944, and its field work was started in 1945. However, its data analyses and final report were not completed for a decade. Its findings were finally published in 1955 by Elihu Katz and Paul F. Lazarsfeld, in their book *Personal Influence: The Part Played by People in the Flow of Mass Communication*. It is with this research that the present chapter is principally concerned. The book was much more than simply a research report; it was an effort to interpret the authors' research within a framework of conceptual schemes, theoretical issues, and research findings drawn broadly from the scientific study of small groups.

THE PART PLAYED BY PEOPLE:
THE NEED FOR A NEW APPROACH

With the recognition that the process of mass communication was far more complex than anyone had previously thought, researchers from several disciplines sought to find the many factors that played a part in shaping what happened between media and mass. The Hovland team of social psychologists was convinced that the keys were in such factors as message structure, which could interact with individual differences in personality factors, including attitudes, emotions, credibility or other variables that influenced perception, remembering, or motivation to respond. The sociologists who had uncovered the two-step flow process felt that a more promising focus of research would be on the close personal groups that Cooley, at the beginning of the century, had labeled *primary groups*.[4] Katz and Lazarsfeld reviewed this concept in some detail.

Actually, the idea that primary groups might play an important role in the process of mass communication was an almost radical departure from earlier thinking about the media. We showed in Chapter 1 that the first rather simplistic stimulus–response theories dealing with the influences of mass communication in modern life were premised on assumptions about "mass" society, with its emphasis on individuality, loss of meaningful interpersonal ties, and a reduction of informal social controls. Yet, at the heart of the two-step flow idea is the assumption that very opposite kinds of variables might be important. The two-step flow concept presumed a movement of information through interpersonal networks, from the media to people and from there to other people, rather than directly from media to mass.

It seemed to follow, then, that a member of the audience of mass communication was not an impersonal individual without effective social ties to others. More likely, the audience member was in some way *influenced* by his or her ties with others in the interpretation of mass media messages and in making decisions whether to act one way or another on the basis of such messages.

Preliminary evidence from Paul Lazarsfeld et al.'s *The People's Choice* clearly suggested that it was one's family and peers that were the most important in the secondary stage of the two-step flow. In other words, the primary group was an obvious and logical focus for research aimed at better understanding the movement of messages from media to audiences via the two-step flow.

The "Rediscovery" of the Primary Group

As soon as it became apparent that close social ties played a part in the flow of information from media to mass, it seemed in retrospect that communication researchers should have started with such a model in the first place. The problem was that the theory of mass society led inevitably to assumptions that people in modern social life were isolated and individualistic. But as research on contemporary populations and social systems progressed, it had become increasingly apparent that the theory of mass society was not a very accurate model. Over and over, the important role of close personal ties in modern life was being uncovered in major research studies on social behavior.

The primary group, in other words, was *rediscovered* in modern urban society. The term "rediscovery" is appropriate because the concept became important shortly after the turn of the century with the work of social psychologists who were concerned with the process of socialization. The primary group was seen as a very important source from which people derived their "human nature." This was at a time when the famous *nature* versus *nurture* debates sought to settle whether personality was mainly a product of inherited factors or was heavily influenced by learning in social settings. The result of those debates was that older theories of human nature based on such biological factors as "instinct" became increasingly obsolete to many social scientists. The influence of learning from social and cultural sources became correspondingly more predominant in theories of human socialization.

But while students of socialization had given primary group interaction a central place in their thinking, this idea did not carry over into the accounts of those who were examining other kinds of social processes. Mass society thinking, in other words, continued to dominate the conceptual formulations of most social scientists. Then, starting in the early 1930s, a series of studies, one after the other, began to find that primary social relationships were a significant factor in the way people behaved. A very brief summary of several of these "rediscoveries" of the primary group will place the issue in perspective. Such a perspective is important in understanding the new directions in mass communication research represented by the *Personal Influence* project.

The classic rediscovery of the primary group as a set of influences that helps us understand life in modern society emerged as a central theme in the work of Rothlisberger and Dixon.[5] Theirs was a study of worker productivity in a factory that made parts for the Western Electric Company. Called the Hawthorne studies (after the name of the plant), the research showed that the so-called "piece rate" system for motivating greater worker productivity was often ineffective because workers had strong personal ties to each other. They did not act in an individualistic manner to maximize their own rewards but regulated their output in conjunction with the norms and expectations of their fellow workers with whom they had close personal ties.

In the late 1930s, social scientists studying the patterning of social relationships in American communities found that clique structures (e.g., primary groups) played a key role in placing people socially in one level or another.[6] In fact, in determining patterns of social stratification, cliques turned out to be second only to the family in importance.

Finally, during World War II, research on American soldiers and their willingness to fight revealed that combat motivation was associated with attachment to a close personal group.[7] Primary groups, in other words, emerged within the framework of a large, formally organized social structure (the Army) and determined to a considerable degree the willingness of individuals to carry out their roles in an effective manner. Soldiers would fight tenaciously if it meant protecting the lives of their buddies. Such factors as hatred of the enemy or broad ideological values counted for relatively little on the actual field of battle.

The Contribution of Small Groups Research

What did all of this mean for the investigation being summarized in the present chapter? One implication was that the development of theories about the nature of mass communication needed to rest upon the assumption that small intimate groups have a profound influence on nearly every aspect of social life—including the activities engaged in by people involved in the flow of information from media to mass. Once this assumption was made, it opened much broader vistas for conceptualizing the *process* of mass communication. It meant that the accumulated findings of social and behavioral science research concerning the nature and functioning of small groups became a fertile source for insights into how people could be expected to act in a mass communication setting. The research findings provided concepts and generalizations about how people could be expected to act and interact as they perceived messages from the media, told those messages to others, received influences from others whom they trusted, and eventually made some form of response to media content.

By the time the Katz and Lazarsfeld study of opinion leaders and their influences was first begun, small-groups research was off to a good start. By the time the research report was written a decade later the accumulated findings of the social sciences regarding the nature and functioning of small groups was impressive indeed. In *Personal Influence*, the authors presented a detailed summary of the relationship between their study of opinion leaders and a host of factors to which their research objectives were related. For the most part, this work was an *ex post facto* analysis. Such an "after the fact" strategy is often criticized because the research is conducted first without the organizing framework of a strong conceptual basis, which comes later when the theoretical implications are sorted out against the findings of previous studies or interpretations. Nevertheless, the authors' analyses did illustrate the broader base of evidence, regarding the primary group and the functioning of close interpersonal ties, that needs to be taken into account in the study of the two-step flow of communication. The authors discussed how opinions and attitudes within such groups tend to be shared. Dozens of studies were summarized to show that people tend to conform to the norms and expectations of such groups, and that numerous benefits result from such conformity.

Small Groups and Meaning Theory   As an illustration of the significance of the study of small groups in general to the development of theory in mass communication, the authors pointed to the functions of such groups in providing *meanings* for their members regarding ambiguous situations for which individuals do not have an adequate or standard interpretive framework. During the 1940s, Kurt Lewin, a well-known social psychologist, and his followers studied the processes by which a "social reality" is created in small group settings:

> Experiments dealing with memory and group pressure on the individual show that what exists as "reality" for the individual is to a high degree determined by what is socially accepted as reality. This holds even in the field of physical fact: to the South Sea Islanders the world may be flat; to the European it is round. "Reality," therefore, is not an absolute. It differs with the group to which the individual belongs.[8]

It is through social processes that we develop meanings for the words and labels that make up our language. Few people can have, or even want to have, personal and direct experience with every aspect of reality for which we have a label (e.g., "death in the electric chair"). Nevertheless, we collectively construct a socially derived reality that we share and use to provide meaning to such labels.

Although these authors did not extend their ideas to the mass media, it has become clear today that the mass media, as well as small groups, are an important part of the social processes of communication by which we collectively develop social constructions of reality. This idea is at the heart of what is now called the *meaning theory* of the effects of the mass media.[9]

The significance of the social reality function of small groups for Katz's and Lazarsfeld's research on personal influence was explained by them: In a presidential election the media provide confusing and often contradictory facts about the issues and candidates; yet, the individual must choose between one or the other, even in this ambiguous situation. He or she can turn to members of the primary group for interpretations, which then become "reality."

Values and the Reference Function The values shared in small groups are another source that draws people to the groups as sources of influence and interpretation. Research had shown that people with similar values tended to be drawn toward each other and to form close-knit groups. When people are in a system of close and interdependent interaction with one another, they tend to demand a high degree of conformity of each other. Thus, the primary group becomes a "reference group" to whom its members turn for interpretations, advice, and influences as they shape their responses to the external world. An important part of that external world is what they encounter, or think that they encounter, in mass communication.

Many other aspects and functions of small groups in daily life are discussed in *The People's Choice.* Indeed, the first half of the work is a rich source of ideas of how mass communication behavior is linked to other important social processes and activities:

> The whole moral of these chapters is that knowledge of an individual's inter-
> personal environment is basic to an understanding of his exposure and reac-
> tions to the mass media. Thus, planning for future research on the short-run
> influencing effects of the mass media must build, first, on the systematic inves-
> tigation of the everyday processes which influence people and, secondly, on
> the study of the points of contact between those everyday influences and the
> mass media.[10]

To this, most researchers even today would say "amen." Unfortunately, too few have chosen to follow the path pointed out by Katz and Lazarsfeld nearly thirty years ago.

THE DECATUR STUDY OF OPINION LEADERS

Leadership comes in many forms. Most visible are official leaders that head formally organized groups—corporations, labor unions, schools, govern-ment, clubs, banks, and so on. The leaders are easily identified in any community by their official positions of power and authority. The decisions of these leaders can clearly have an impact on the ebb and flow of the vital social and economic political processes of community life.

But another kind of leadership is far less visible. It is informal and often unwitting. It takes place when people turn to others at their same social level whom they know and trust. They do this because they need advice or interpretations to try to make sense out of some complex situation confronting them. They need to understand the dimensions of the reality before them, so that they can make sensible decisions and act in their own best interests. The others they select as leaders in this process are people like themselves but whom they feel command some special expertise, or possess some special wisdom, regarding the topic about which a decision must be made. When ordinary people make decisions on such matters as to what to believe, purchase, join, avoid, support, like, or dislike, they turn to *opinion leaders* for advice. Often, the opinion leaders' personal influence is both given and received without either party consciously recognizing it as such.

It is this type of informal personal influence that was under investigation in what has come to be called the Decatur Study (after the community in which it was done). As we noted earlier, the research was designed to follow up more systematically the idea of the two-step flow of communication, first noted in the study of the 1940 presidential election in Erie County, Ohio. The research was conducted under the auspices of the Bureau of Applied Social Research of Columbia University. Financial support for the project was supplied by Mcfadden Publications, Inc. (presumably because of its potential implications for advertisers) and the Roper polling organization (presumably because of its implications for understanding the process of opinion formation).

The study focused on the role of opinion leaders as they influenced others in four areas of decision-making in day-to-day life. These were (1) *marketing* (where choices must be made regarding foods, household products, and small consumer items), (2) the world of *fashion* (where choices must be made concerning clothing, hair styles, and cosmetics), (3) *public affairs* (a potentially confusing arena of political and social issues in the news, civic activities, and national and local events), and (4) the selection of *movies* to see (again, a multiplicity of choices). In other words, the problem was to determine who influenced whom in these areas where decisions often have to be made, but where there are many potential choices and few clear definitions of objective reality.

The Research Procedures

To locate instances of personal influence regarding these four topics, the research procedures included selecting a suitable community to study, drawing a sample of people to interview (on two separate occasions, once in June and once in August), identifying leaders and followers, and studying the characteristics of each. A fairly unique feature of the research plan was the intention to trace out who had, in a face-to-face manner, influenced whom. In other words the researchers wanted to study opinion leaders who were in actual contact with recipients of their influence on a day-to-day basis. It was not their intention to study persons who might be influential by virtue of their prominent position in the social, political, or business life of the city.

Selecting the Research Site   The financial resources available for the investigation played a key role in dictating the size of the community to be studied. The plan was to maintain a ratio of no fewer than one interview to every twenty homes in the city. Since 800 interviews were anticipated, this indicated a community with a population of approximately 60,000. The Middle West was chosen as a region within which to locate such a community, on the grounds that this part of the country was generally less characterized by sectional peculiarities. The problem, therefore, was to locate the most "typical" communities in the Middle West which were of the required population size.

First, all cities in the range 50,000 to 80,000 located in Ohio, Michigan, Indiana, Illinois, Wisconsin, Iowa, and Kansas were listed for detailed demographic, social, and economic analysis. This search yielded 28 cities. From these, all that were suburban communities dominated by a large city were eliminated. This left 18 potential sites. For each of these, data were assembled on 36 indices relevant to the problem under study. These indices provided key information on population composition, economic status, commercial activities, mass communication usage patterns, and the general quality of community life.

With all of this information at hand it was possible to reduce the list to three cities that deviated the least from the central tendencies (Decatur, Illinois; Terre Haute, Indiana; and Springfield, Indiana). Of the three, Decatur was judged to be the most consistently typical in the clusters of variables thought to be potentially significant to the research goals. As such it was chosen as the site for the research.[11]

The Sample   The authors of *Personal Influence* provide relatively little information about the actual procedures used to develop their original sample. In fact, they provide only the following paragraph:

> Within Decatur, the sample to be interviewed was drawn according to usual probability methods and nothing special need be said about it. Within each household, women residents (not domestic help) age 16 and over were

interviewed alternating on successive interviews between older and younger women whenever more than two women occupied the same household.[12]

Elsewhere (p. 335) they indicate that a sample size of 800 was dictated by their financial resources. It is not clear, however, whether this sample size was actually achieved in their first round of interviews (in June) or not. However, it should be kept in mind that the final assembly of data was not simply a compilation of results from a single social survey. As will be made clear, the researchers sought to apply *sociometric* methods to their research by tracing out who claimed to have influenced whom concerning the four topics discussed above.

The Problem of Defining and Locating Personal Influence

This was a pioneering study into a largely unknown territory. Very little was known at the time about what kinds of people influenced others on an informal basis. Therefore, no clear guidelines were available *a priori* concerning the best means to identify informal influentials or to gather quantitative information on instances of opinion leadership. Consequently, several approaches were tried.

Alternative Approaches   Four different strategies were tried to locate opinion leaders and instances of personal influence. One technique was an attempt to identify "generally influential" people who gave advice or interpretations to others on a range of topics. The question was whether opinion leadership was *specific* to a particular topic, or whether people turned to the same individuals more generally. There was some limited evidence that there were general influentials. For example, in the initial interviews, respondents were asked if they regularly turned to a particular person for advice concerning public affairs (a rather general topic). Specifically, the question was asked: "Do you know anyone around here who keeps up with the news and whom you can trust to let you know what is really going on?" About half of the women studied could identify such a person. This varied considerably with age and education. Older, better educated women were more able to identify such a generally influential person. Younger women with less education often could not. Even so, the "generally influential" individuals were for the most part the *husbands* for the married women, *male parents* for the unmarried, and *male friends* for the once married. In fact, women of all categories tended strongly to nominate males as individuals of general competence in public affairs rather than females (about two to one). In any case, this particular strategy was not judged to be especially fruitful for the study of opinion leaders.

Another strategy for defining and locating opinion leaders focused on "specific influentials." This procedure was based on information provided by the two separate interviews with the 800 respondents, in June and again in August. Again using the area of public affairs as an illustration, the women's opinions on nine specific topics of current interest were recorded during the first interview. On the second interview, any *changes* in those opinions were noted. Once these changes had been verified, careful probing was undertaken to determine with whom the respondents had discussed these issues, and if those discussions had been influential in modifying their opinions. This proved to be a fruitful strategy and some 619 verified opinion changes were identified. The "specific influentials" who had played a key role in each change were nominated by the respondents, providing both empirical instances of personal influence and the names of the opinion leaders. Again, family relationships were paramount and males played a predominant role.

The third technique tried for studying opinion leadership was a somewhat less complicated effort to identify the "everyday contacts" of the respondents—people with whom they usually talked things over, regardless of the direction of influence. This approach was not particularly fruitful because only about half of the women could identify someone with whom they usually talked things over. Those that did usually nominated a member of their family.

The final technique tried for identifying opinion leaders was *self-designation*. This procedure was the one actually used to generate the main body of data that made up the research report. Self-designation means that the women interviewed were asked whether they had recently been influential to others. This line of questioning was used in both the first and second interviews. For example, the following question was posed for each respondent: "Have you recently been asked for your advice about (one of the four main topics: marketing, fashions, movies, or public affairs)?" If the respondent answered "yes," detailed information was collected regarding who asked for advice, about what, and so forth. In other words, the respondent was asked to identify the exact individual, by name and address, with whom the interaction took place. In this way, instances of opinion leadership were identified both in terms of the persons involved, the direction of the process, and the topic of influence.

The obvious problem with self-designation as a means of identifying and studying opinion leaders and their influence is that it views the process from only one end. There is, in other words, a problem of *validity*. If a person claims to have talked to and influenced another, how can such a claim be verified? Because the researchers had asked their respondents for the names and addresses of those whom they claimed to have influenced, one possible means of verification was to go to those designated and ask for confirmation. In fact, the investigators did obtain some 1,549 designations of persons who had sought advice from 693 of their 800 respondents. The intention was to contact all of those designated in order to view the influence process from their end. Unfortunately, many were unavailable during the study period (out of town, and so on). However, some 634 were contacted. Of these, two-thirds confirmed the contact and the topic of the conversation. A fourth could not recall the claimed contact. Between nine and ten percent denied that the conversation ever took place! Overall, then, the question of validity was never answered in a rigorous manner, but at least some confirmations were made and the researchers were satisfied that self-designation was a realistic strategy for the study of personal influence. The main subjects for the analysis, then, were the 693 "self-detected" opinion leaders.

After looking at all of the types mentioned—the generally influential, specific influentials, everyday contacts, and self-designations, the researchers narrowed their conceptualization of opinion leadership and personal influence. Opinion leaders are people recognized by their peers as having some special competence in a particular subject. People turn to opinion leaders for advice about a specific topic, but usually do not seek them out for their opinions on a range of issues. Personal influence, then, takes place between people in face-to-face settings and concerning rather specific topics.

Opinion Leadership versus Other Influences   A major difficulty in studying the impact of opinion leadership on decisions is to sort it out from other sources of influence. For example, we are all influenced to an unknown degree by mass media advertising in our purchasing consumer goods, household products, or even food at the supermarket. For women, salespeople may play an influential role in the purchase of cosmetics or fashionable clothing. Newspaper ads for movies may be a factor for all of us in selecting a film to attend. In other words, opinion leadership is only one influence in a context of many. Identifying which influence played a predominant role in any particular decision may not always be possible, even for the person who made the choice.

Still, most people can recall whether or not they talked to someone else about a new brand of household cleaner, a new nail polish, or the merits of a particular movie before attending it. They can also assess to a reasonably accurate degree the extent to which these contacts influenced them to adopt the product in question.

The researchers made an extensive study of the comparative impact on such decisions by personal contacts versus media advertising and salespeople. In the area of marketing, for example, personal contacts with opinion leaders were substantially more effective in prompting marketing shifts than were advertisements in newspapers, radio, or magazines. Salespeople played an even smaller role. But for selecting a motion picture, newspaper ads had a much greater effect than personal contacts. In the world of fashion, by contrast, personal influence played an especially powerful role, although salespeople and magazine ads were also important.

Generally, in the areas of marketing, fashions, and movie selection, the impact of personal influence on people's decisions to change patterns of use, or to adopt something new, was greater than that of the formal media. There were many exceptions to this generalization, and there are undoubtedly many reasons why this tendency was found. Also, opinion leadership does not occur in a vacuum. A person may be exposed to media advertising, the blandishments of salespeople, *and* personal influence from a trusted source. Nevertheless, the data clearly supported the conclusion that opinion leaders were one of the more powerful influences on people's decisions in the marketplace of either consumer products and services, or of ideas.

The Characteristics of Opinion Leaders

Who were these 693 "self-detected" opinion leaders?[13] That is, how did they fit into the social life of Decatur? The researchers identified three significant dimensions in the lives of their respondents that were related to the opinion leader role. These factors played a central part in determining *if* a woman was likely to influence others, and if so, with respect to *what*. These dimensions were: (1) position in the "life cycle," (2) position on the community's socioeconomic ladder, and (3) the extent of the individual's social contacts. These three factors provided a convenient framework within which to describe and analyze the flow of interpersonal influence concerning the four topics under study.

Position in the Life Cycle   The classifications used to describe this dimension identify clusters of variables that change as the individual moves from one position to another. For example, younger, unmarried women have greater knowledge concerning fashionable clothing, hairstyles, and cosmetics than those whose lives are more centered on homemaking and raising children. By contrast with both groups, older women, whose children have grown, and who have a wide circle of contacts within the community, can be expected to know more of public affairs and community issues. Position in the life cycle, in other words, raises the probability of being knowledgeable about some topics but not others. Familiarity with a topic, and possession of the skills to deal with it effectively, are the foundations of the capacity to exercise personal leadership and be perceived as an effective opinion leader.

The investigators identified four life cycle classifications into which they could categorize the opinion leaders identified in their sample (see Table 11).

Socioeconomic Status People at distinctive levels in a community are characterized by differences in education, prestige, and income. These may be important factors in determining whether or not they will be sought out as sources for interpretation and advice. An important question for this research on opinion leaders was whether personal influence travels up, down, or laterally among such community social strata. To address this issue, the researchers divided their sample into three categories—high, middle, and low status—with about one-third in each. This was done on the basis of years of education, and amount of rent paid (as an indicator of economic level).[14]

Social Contacts The woman with limited social contacts has few opportunities to exercise personal influence. The one who regularly interacts with many people will have more opportunities to serve as an opinion leader. To test this idea, the researchers constructed a simple index of *gregariousness*. It was based on: (1) the number of persons in the community the subject claimed to be "friendly with and talk with fairly often," and (2) the number of organizations and clubs to which she belonged.[15]

Information on these kinds of social contacts provided a relatively simple classification pattern. A subject who claimed seven or more friends

---

Table 11   Distribution of Life Cycle Types in the Sample

Girls (single women, under 35)	12%
Small Family Wives (married, under 45, with one or no children)	26
Large Family Wives (married, under 45, with two or more children)	25
Matrons (married, over 45, most of whose children are older than 15)	37
	100%
	N = 693

SOURCE: Elihu Katz and Paul F. Lazarsfeld, *Personal Influence* (Glencoe, Ill.: The Free Press of Glencoe, 1955) p. 225.

---

and belonged to at least one organization was placed in the high category. At the other end, a subject with no organization memberships and few friends were placed in the low category. These subjects were then cross-classified into the four categories shown in Table 12.

These three factors, life cycle, socioeconomic status, and gregariousness, were found to be related in many complex ways among the women in the sample. Summarized briefly, the more important of these relationships were as follows:

1. High gregariousness increases with life cycle progression.
2. Girls (as defined) tend to score medium in gregariousness. They belong to fewer organizations but have many friends.
3. Lower socioeconomic status women tend to be low in gregariousness.

The significance of these three factors appears to lie in their power, either singly or in combination, to shape a woman's interest in certain life areas. They place her at different points in the social structure and limit or expand her contact with others in the community.

THE FINDINGS

The four topics of personal influence chosen for study were everyday concerns in the life of Decatur: what to buy for the family, how to select from the world of fashions, what movie choices to make, and what to believe or decide regarding public events and issues. The three characteristics discussed in the previous section were used as a framework to follow the flow of personal influence from different types of opinion leaders to those who sought their advice and interpretation on these four topics.

Table 12 Distribution of Sample by Social Activity

		Number of Friendships	
		high	low
Number of organizations	high	27%	14%
	low	31%	28%

SOURCE: Elihu Katz and Paul F. Lazarsfeld, *Personal Influence* (Glencoe, Ill.: The Free Press of Glencoe, 1955) p. 228.

Marketing Leaders

The researchers found that the women in their sample often consulted each other for opinions about new products, the quality of different brands, and shopping economies. In fact, about half of the respondents interviewed in the June and August efforts reported making some kind of change from a product or brand that they had regularly used to something new. Opportunities for personal influence in this area were abundant. The task was to study how this influence flowed from one type of person to another. The analysis of who influenced whom in marketing decisions was made in terms of social status, life cycle, and gregariousness, in that order.

The Horizontal Flow of Marketing Leadership   There was little reason to assume that higher social status women were more skilled at marketing. A "trickle down" effect was a possibility, with higher prestige making advice seem more significant. However, an examination of the proportion of the women at each status level who claimed to have provided marketing advice did not support the trickle down concept. Marketing opinion leaders were found more or less equally at all status levels: Among the high social status women, some 27 percent claimed to have given marketing advice. The figures for middle and low social status respondents were 24 and 21 percent respectively (differences not statistically significant). In other words, high status did not seem to increase a woman's chances to serve as an opinion leader in any significant way. Generally, according to the authors, the flow of marketing influence was *horizontal*. They explained it in the following terms:

> . . . it is more reasonable to expect that marketing influence is confined within the boundaries of each of the several social strata than it is [to assume] a random exchange conducted without regard for status differences. Seeking out a woman of like status for advice means seeking out a woman with similar budgetary problems and limitations. That is one major reason why we may expect that traffic in marketing is a status-bound activity. Secondly, since stores and shopping centers are likely to cater somewhat more to women of one status than another—by design or because of location or the like—women are more likely to encounter status peers during their marketing activities than to encounter status unequals.[16]

This generalization was confirmed in some degree by comparing the status levels of both the giver of advice and the receiver in those cases where both could be established. Unfortunately, such information was available for less than half of the cases where follow-up interviews were attempted to verify the self-designations of opinion leaders (see p. 188). Although these data have many limitations, they appear to show that "influencees turn to influentials of their own status level much more often than they turn to those of other statuses." [17] Where cross-overs in status levels did occur, they were just as likely to go up as down. In short, personal influence in marketing appears to take place horizontally, in other words, between people at the same general status level.

Life Cycle and Marketing Leadership The researchers anticipated that position in the life cycle would be an especially important factor in marketing leadership. Unmarried, younger women with no children would be unlikely sources for consultation about products related to family meal preparation, child rearing, or household domestic tasks. Older women, most of whose children had grown, might have had years of experience in marketing. However, their current responsibilities are more limited. Therefore, they were not expected to be the dominant category. The category with the heaviest current responsibilities and daily experience in marketing matters would be *large family wives*, and the data strongly supported the speculation that they would be most sought for advice. In fact, 38 percent of the large family wives claimed that they had served as marketing opinion leaders. The comparable figures were 23 percent for small family wives, 20 percent for girls, and 16 percent for matrons.

A second question is whether these large family wives mainly influenced each other, or whether their personal influence flowed disproportionately to the other categories. The study provided only limited data on this issue. The authors were able to conclude only that women of age 25–44 seemed to influence women somewhat younger or somewhat older than themselves. This included both small and large family wives. While not conclusive by any means, such information offers minor support for the conclusion that active homemakers offered marketing influence disproportionately to younger single women and older matrons.

Gregariousness and Marketing Here the findings were very clear. At all status levels and in all life cycle positions, the women with more social contacts were the most influential in marketing. Among those classified as high in gregariousness, 33 percent had offered marketing advice. The corresponding figures for the other categories were 25 percent for those of medium gregariousness and 13 percent for those classified as low. These are statistically significant differences and they imply a clear positive relationship between gregariousness and marketing leadership.

Fashion Leaders

Fashion is an area of constant change. Keeping up with change in just the right sequence is the essence of being fashionable. Some two-thirds of the women in the sample had made some sort of change in fashion between their two major interviews. The problem was to discover what the role of opinion leaders of various kinds had been in influencing those changes.

Fashions and the Life Cycle Position   The factor that proved to be most important in fashions was life cycle position, the same factor that had played a central role in marketing. In fashions, however, it was the "girls" who provided the greatest amount of influence. In terms of the four life cycle categories, there were considerable differences in the proportions who claimed to have offered advice to others on fashions (see Table 13). Clearly, fashion leadership declined with each step in the life cycle. The authors explained this progression in terms of a rather traditional interpretation of womens' roles:

> According to this view, marriage, as the realization of one goal of fashion participation, would be associated with a decrease in fashion activities and leadership; motherhood, as a competing interest and activity, would also be accompanied by a further decrease in such fashion leadership; and matronhood, which for most women involves a withdrawal from youth-oriented competitiveness, should be associated with least fashion advice giving.[18]

In other words, the authors saw attention to fashion as a means of catching a man. Once a male was landed, however, women were likely to increasingly forget fashion matters and concentrate more on their children. Later, they would lose even the little interest they might have left. This is obviously a very old-fashioned view by today's standards.

Whatever the reasons, the younger single women were the most active as opinion leaders in the area of fashion. The "girls" were well ahead of the others in such matters as cosmetics, hairstyles, and fashionable clothing.

Table 13   Percent Who Offered Fashion Influence by Life Cycle Position

Girls	48%
Small Family Wives	31
Large Family Wives	18
Matrons	14

SOURCE: Elihu Katz and Paul F. Lazarsfeld, *Personal Influence* (Glencoe, Ill.: The Free Press of Glencoe, 1955) p. 248.

They had made more purchases and showed a considerably greater propensity to change. They were also the greatest "exporters" of fashion advice. That is, they not only talked to each other about fashion matters but were the strongest influences on the other categories of women.

Gregariousness and Fashion Leadership As was the case in marketing, gregariousness was an important factor in fashion leadership. In fact, there was a very similar pattern of positive association between gregariousness and influence. For the high category on gregariousness, 29 percent claimed to have offered fashion advice. The corresponding figures for the medium and low categories were 23 percent and 15 percent respectively. These different rates appear to have occurred for much the same reason in fashions as they did in marketing: The socially active have more opportunities to offer advice to a broader range of recipients. Also, gregarious women at all social levels and in all life cycle positions were more *interested* in fashion matters than their more reclusive counterparts. Presumably, then, there is a link between more intensive social activity and more intensive interest in fashion, leading to offering more advice, regardless of other life circumstances.

Status and Fashions Most people assume a relationship between being fashionable and being high in socioeconomic status. The stereotype of the wealthy and glamorous woman is well established in our culture. This, however, was not what the investigators had in mind when they probed into a possible link between social status in Decatur and serving as a source of advice on fashions. They anticipated that there would be a positive relationship between the two variables, but not a concentration of leadership at the top.

What they discovered was that there was no such concentration. There were as many fashion leaders among the women of middle status as among those at the high level. On the other hand, women low in status played a much more minor role in distributing fashion advice. For example, among those in the high category, 26 percent claimed to have served as sources for influence on fashions. The middle category claimed the same figure, 26 percent. Only 16 percent of those in the low category claimed to have offered personal influence on fashions.

To summarize the flow of fashion influence, it is dependent most of all on life cycle position. The younger, single women were much more active as fashion opinion leaders. Gregariousness was also important. Status made little difference, unless one was low in this factor. It was the young, socially active women with high status that had the most influence. Older women who were less active socially and of low status had virtually no influence on fashion at all.

Public Affairs Leaders

Katz and Lazarsfeld made their analysis of public affairs opinion leaders on the basis of several assumptions about the role of women in such matters:

> Without endangering their self-respect or the respect of others, women can, to a greater extent than men, get through life without participating in, or having opinions about, public affairs. Much more often than men, women express ignorance about current national and local events and issues; they talk less about these matters, and, when asked directly about their interest in politics and specific political events, they claim less interest than men.[19]

In other words, women of the time tended to be seen but not heard! Obviously, times have changed, but these conditions appear to have been present in Decatur at the time of the study in the immediate postwar years. Thus, findings in this area need to be interpreted within such a framework. In any case, the three factors—social status, gregariousness, and life cycle position—once again provided the principal framework for analysis.

Status and Public Affairs Leadership The investigators reasoned that the factors that would lead their subjects to participate actively in the arena of public affairs would be contacts with politically active people (mainly males), level of education, and enough leisure time to pursue extra-household activities. These are obviously associated with high social status in a community like Decatur. For this reason, the researchers hypothesized that there would be a positive association between socioeconomic status and opinion leadership in the area of public affairs.

Their prediction was clearly supported. First, there were fewer women who were opinion leaders in public affairs than in the other areas studied, and those women tended to be concentrated in the high social status level. Among high status women, 19 percent claimed to have provided personal influence on some aspect of public affairs. For the middle and low status categories, the figures were 12 percent and six percent, respectively.

Following up their assumption that women were generally inactive in public affairs, the authors asked women who had been influenced to identify their sources of influence. Generally, the answer that they received was *men:*

Unlike marketing and fashions, the public affairs arena is one in which men play an important role in influencing opinions and attitudes. Almost two-thirds of the persons named by the respondents as having influenced their opinion changes were men.[20]

These influences from men were likely to come from members of the family. In other words, husbands and fathers were the principal public affairs influentials for these subjects, rather than other women.

Gregariousness and Public Affairs Leadership   There is little doubt that women who have numerous social contacts offer more advice on public affairs than those who are less gregarious. Among those classified as high on this factor, 20 percent claimed to have offered personal influence on some aspect of public affairs. Among the medium category, the figure was 11 percent, and among those low in gregariousness, only four percent claimed to have been influential.

Gregariousness and status level were found to be associated, and both were factors in predicting opinion leadership. However, statistically controlling for gregariousness in the analysis did not account for the variations in the proportion of public affairs leadership at each status level. In other words, gregariousness and status were independent variables, but gregariousness was the more important.

Life Cycle Position and Public Affairs   The authors noted that women who are busy with housekeeping and child rearing may not be active in public affairs. This would suggest a dominant role for the "girls." On the other hand, younger people generally take less interest in public affairs than those who are more mature. This meant that there were contradictory factors at work, making prediction difficult.

The data showed a rather weak association between life cycle stage and public affairs leadership. The proportion who claimed to have influenced others on public issues declined somewhat with each stage: For girls, the figure was 17 percent; small family wives, 13 percent; large family wives, ten percent; and matrons, eight percent. Such a trend suggests an inverse relationship between age (and life cycle stage) and informal influence in public affairs.

In summarizing the flow of influence on public affairs, the authors noted the following: The public affairs leaders among these women were different from those who were influential in marketing or fashions. Life cycle was somewhat less important. On the other hand, social status, which is almost unimportant in marketing leadership, and which is only marginally related to fashions, is a key factor here. Gregariousness is also related to being influential. Generally, the most influential women were the better educated and more affluent, who had many social contacts in the community. Even so, most personal influence on public affairs issues came from men.

Movie Selection Leaders

At the time the data were gathered, Americans went to the movies far more often than they do now. Television had not yet entered every home. Some 60 percent of the respondents said that they went to the movies at least once a month. The analysis of personal influence on movie selections was confined to this segment of the total sample.

From their earliest days, movies have had a special appeal to youth. This was certainly true in Decatur: Among the youngest category of subjects, those under 25, two-thirds went to the movies once a week or more! About half of those 25–34 went to the movies once a week or more. For those 35–44 the figure was about one-third. Among those 45 or older, less than a fifth went that often. In other words, movie-going was clearly related to age and it was far more popular than it is now.

These data led the investigators to anticipate that it would be the younger women in their sample, the girls, who would be highest in opinion leadership in movie selection. We will see that this was clearly the case. However, gregariousness and socioeconomic status offered further guides to understanding the findings.

The "Youth Culture" and Movie Leadership   The influence of life cycle position on this form of opinion leadership was especially clear. This reflects the central role of motion pictures in the lives of the young people of the time. Among the girls, 58 percent claimed to have influenced others on movie choices, a very high figure. For small family wives the figure was 23 percent; large family wives, 27 percent; and for matrons, 16 percent. For the single women, then, movies with friends were an important form of recreation and dating.

Movie Leadership and Gregariousness   Here, a pattern emerged that was rather distinct from those of other areas. It was not those with the largest number of social contacts that were most influential. There was no clear relationship between gregariousness and personal influence on movie choices. Those subjects classified as medium in gregariousness claimed to have provided the most opinion leadership (32 percent) on movie selections. Those who were high and low were quite similar, with 26 percent and 24 percent, respectively.

The investigators tried to interpret these findings by noting that going to the movies is an activity that is almost always shared by others. People go to the movies with friends and members of their families but seldom alone. The selection of a movie takes place within a complex social process involving other people, namely family and friends. Whether one belongs to clubs and has a wide circle of acquaintances may make little difference on how a motion picture is selected.

Socioeconomic Status and Movie Influence   As in the case of gregariousness, status did not seem to be a factor in providing personal influence on movie selection. This was probably the case because people at all levels in Decatur went to the movies rather frequently. About 25 percent of the women at each level claimed that they had offered advice to others regarding a movie. Within each of the status levels, however, it was the young unmarried women who played the dominant role.

In summary, movie-going in Decatur was an important part of the youth culture. At all status levels and among shy as well as socially active people it was the young single women who gave the most advice.

CONCLUSIONS AND IMPLICATIONS

The two-step flow hypothesis, first identified as a result of the study of the 1940 presidential election, provided an important turning point in the development of theory and research in mass communication. The hypothesis as first formulated said merely that "ideas often flow *from* radio and print *to* opinion leaders and *from* them to less active sections of the population."[21] In retrospect this seems like a simple idea; yet it was overlooked for decades. However, when attention was finally focused on this secondary movement of information and influence through interpersonal networks among members of the audience, it changed thinking about the process of mass communication forever. No longer could mass communication be thought of solely in terms of a stimulus–response framework in which the media were on one side and members of the audience on the other, with little in between.

This new way of thinking was badly needed at the time. The accumulated findings of mass communication research at the time of the Decatur study were not providing support for the idea of simple, immediate, and direct effects that were produced by stimulation from mass-communicated messages. It was time to look for more indirect effects that were produced over a longer span of time by more complex processes. It was *Personal Influence* that opened up this avenue of research. It tried to explore "the part played by people" in the social flow of information and influence from media to mass.

The Decatur study can be faulted on many grounds if the standards of contemporary research are imposed. Its measurements, statistical analyses, sampling techniques, and verification procedures have clear limitations, to say the least. In addition, the goals of the research were never made clear from a conceptual point of view. For example, although much was made of the "flow" idea, the study did not trace the actual movement of ideas from the media to those who were identified as opinion leaders and on to the individuals that they influenced. The authors appear to have set out to do this but they had to give up (mainly for lack of resources). Thus, when one woman in their sample claimed to have influenced another about nail polish, canned soup, or an issue in the community, it is not at all clear that this actually represented some type of flow from a mass medium to an audience. The strategy of interviewing in April, then returning some months later to look for changes, was not adequate to the task. The researchers should have focused on specific media content (e.g., advertising messages or public affairs presentations) and then traced them from opinion leaders through interpersonal networks to study the two-step flow as it actually took place.

In spite of these criticisms, based on 20/20 hindsight, the Decatur study is one of the milestones in mass communication research. Earlier research had concentrated on individual differences characterizing the people who made up the audiences for mass communication and how those differences shaped their psychological and overt responses to the media. A little later, there was a shift to the study of social category memberships among members of the audience, and how these influenced patterns of attention and response. *Personal Influence* represented the first clear and intensive focus on social relationships and their role in the mass communication process. The ties between people were seen as the most important factors, rather than the structure of the message stimulus, the perceived characteristics of the communicator, or the psychological make-up of the receiver, in significantly shaping the mass communication process.

We noted earlier that in its analysis of the findings from small-groups research of the time, the research report clearly identified the meaning functions of primary groups, an idea which is an important part of the meaning theory of mass media portrayals (Chapter 1) that has only recently moved to center stage in thinking about media effects.[22] More important, the Decatur Study, and the two-step flow idea generally, set off significant new directions of research in the adoption of innovation, the diffusion of the news, and the study of distortions in interpersonal communication.

Perhaps most important of all, the influences of the media studied in *Personal Influence* seem a far cry from the powerful effects feared by those who saw the media as the ultimate agents of evil—or for that matter the powerful effects of those who thought the media would be the means of salvation of modern democracy. The influences investigated were minor, difficult to detect, and completely nonthreatening. The study not only failed to confirm the validity of the legacy of fear, it went a long way toward making the idea look quite unrealistic.

NOTES AND REFERENCES

1. Charles Horton Cooley, *Social Organization* (New York: Charles Scribners and Sons, 1909), pp. 80–90.
2. Joseph T. Klapper, *The Effects of the Mass Media* (Glencoe, Ill.: The Free Press of Glencoe, 1960).
3. Bernard Berelson, "The State of Communication Research," *Public Opinion Quarterly*, 1, 23, Spring 1959, pp. 1–17.
4. Charles Horton Cooley, op. cit., pp. 23–31.
5. Fritz J. Rothlisberger and William J. Dickson, *Management and the Worker* (Cambridge, Mass.: Harvard University Press, 1939). See also: Elton Mayo, *Human Problems in an Industrial Civilization* (New York: The Viking Press, 1966); first published in 1933.
6. W. Lloyd Warner and Paul S. Lunt, *The Social Life of a Modern Community*, Vol. I, Yankee City Series (New Haven: Yale University Press, 1941).
7. Samuel A. Stauffer et al., *The American Soldier: Studies in Social Psychology in World War Two*, Vols. I and II (Princeton, N.J.: Princeton University Press, 1948).
8. Kurt Lewin and Paul Grabbe, "Conduct, Knowledge, and Acceptance of New Values," *Journal of Social Issues*, Vol. 1, No. 3, 1948, pp. 53–64.
9. Melvin L. De Fleur and Everette E. Dennis, *Understanding Mass Communication* (Boston: Houghton Mifflin, 1981).
10. Elihu Katz and Paul F. Lazarsfeld, *Personal Influence: The Part Played by People in the Flow of Mass Communication* (Glencoe, Ill.: The Free Press of Glencoe, 1955), p. 133.
11. Ibid., p. 137.
12. Ibid., pp. 335–338.
13. The exact number of the original interviewees who served as opinion leaders is a bit difficult to pin down. The figure 693 is the largest N of any of the tables appearing in the analysis (p. 225). In other places different and smaller Ns are given.
14. No indication was given as to how home owners, who pay no rent, were handled.
15. Ibid., p. 227.
16. Ibid., p. 236.

17. Ibid.
18. Ibid., p. 248.
19. Ibid., p. 271.
20. Ibid., p. 276.
21. Paul F. Lazarsfeld, Bernard Berelson, and Hazel Gaudet, *The People's Choice* (New York: Columbia University Press, 1948), p. 151. This is an earlier report than the one cited in Chapter 4.
22. Katz and Lazarsfeld, op cit., pp. 53–56.

8

project revere:
the quality and
pathways of
message diffusion

As the 1950s began, it became increasingly clear that World War II had not resolved the major political differences among the powerful nations of the world. If anything, the defeat of Germany and Japan had simply moved forward in time the point at which the political philosophies of the Soviet Union and China would confront those of the United States and its allies in a global struggle for power, even though they had all fought together to defeat the Axis powers. In the end it led to the cold war, and the possibility of nuclear holocaust. Thus, the first half of the twentieth century ended with an uneasy confrontation between democracy, communism, and the remnants of fascism. But for the ordinary people in the United States there was no such global perspective—only a frustrated feeling of *déja vu* as once more American soldiers battled an Asian enemy.

The Korean conflict was very different from World War II in a number of respects. It had not caught the nation off guard and unprepared militarily. The United States had a large fleet left over from the earlier war. It had an adequate number of well-trained combat divisions equipped with modern weapons. Above all, it had a large and aggressive Air Force. The country had emerged from the second world war as the most powerful nation on earth, and it took on a peacekeeping mission that was worldwide in scope. Its so-called containment policy, forged by John Foster Dulles, was to keep the Soviet Union and China, as well as their satellite countries, surrounded by coalitions of allied forces. Therefore, when North Korea invaded South Korea and challenged that policy, President Truman felt that intervention was essential.

But whatever their causes or labels, wars are not won by force of arms alone. In every war, ancient or modern, the beliefs, attitudes, and loyalties of the participants—whether military or civilian—have had a critical role in the outcome. Such factors have strong influences on motivations, decisions, and actions that can sometimes shape victory or defeat. Military leaders understand these issues very well and they try to use whatever persuasive communications they can to shape people's behavior to the best advantage. The use of propaganda in wartime can be clumsy and a waste of time. However, if on occasion propaganda can reduce the efficiency of the enemy by only a fraction of one percent, it can be effective. Under the right circumstances, the right message delivered to the right people at the right time can profoundly alter the course of a conflict.

It was for these reasons that the American forces in Korea were highly interested in communicating with civilian as well as military groups in enemy territory. In fact, they used every opportunity to deliver a great variety of messages to North Korean communities, military units, and rural populations. Most of these messages were designed to bring to a target population information that could serve as the basis for changes in beliefs, modifications of opinions and attitudes, reductions in motivations, and a weakening of loyalties.

Most of the time it didn't work! For one thing, when one is trying to communicate on a large scale with an enemy population, there are a limited number of ways to do so. Obviously, one has no access to the usual mass media. Under such closed conditions, one alternative is to broadcast to the relevant population from the outside and hope that someone is listening. But this can be very ineffective where people have few receivers, where those receivers that exist must be operated clandestinely, or where there is little motivation on the part of potential listeners to tune in. All of these conditions prevailed in North Korea. About the only medium left under such circumstances is the airborne leaflet.

LEAFLETS AS A MEDIUM OF LAST RESORT

Leaflets are pieces of paper containing print, photographs, or drawings. They are a primitive device for communicating to people, but if they can be delivered in large numbers with messages that can be readily understood by the recipients, they can provide a significant channel for communication. Leaflets have been used ever since the printing press has been around. They have a long history in politics as well as in war. They remain a significant medium in countries which control their media as a means of limiting dissent, and they are being used every day in countries around the world for a variety of reasons and causes, especially where power and authority are being challenged.

American forces distributed about three million leaflets during World War I. This figure rose to about three *billion* during World War II. Additional billions were used during the Korean conflict. They have been used in all subsequent military operations. One of their more effective uses in wartime settings has been in the form of "surrender passes" for enemy troops who want to give up but are afraid of being killed. The official-looking "passes" delivered over enemy areas in large numbers can be effective, on occasion, in triggering surrenders. Leaflets have had other successes. In 1945, airborne leaflets delivered on a massive scale to the Japanese population, in conjunction with both conventional and atomic bombing, probably shortened that war somewhat by convincing people that further resistance was unrealistic. In spite of their occasional successes, leaflets have clear limitations. If other more usual ways of communicating are available, almost any other medium would probably be more efficient. Still, when other channels are *not* available, as in wartime or during periods of political repression, this primitive device may be the only means by which information can be delivered to large numbers of people.

A major problem with leaflets as a medium is that their limitations and capacities are poorly understood. Almost no scientific research has been done on their effectiveness as a communication medium. Controlled studies of communication to hostile populations are not possible during wartime. Impressions of their effectiveness can sometimes be gained by interviewing prisoners who have seen propaganda leaflets, or who have used surrender passes. However, these impressions are limited at best. What is needed is more systematic information about who will pick up leaflets, under what conditions, who will read them, pass on their messages to others, or comply with requests for action. These questions need to be answered not only for war, but under more peaceful conditions. Generalizations are needed about how leaflets can be used to provide vital information in *any* situation where the normal channels of communication are not available.

With this lack of knowledge in mind, the U.S. Air Force made a decision to learn more about the communication efficiency of airborne leaflets as a mass medium. It sought a research contractor who would design and conduct investigations into the use of airborne leaflets as a means of communicating simple messages to civilian populations: a contractor who would not necessarily answer all possible questions about leaflets when used under all possible circumstances, but who would at least provide a beginning point, seeking basic generalizations about the advantages, capacities, and limitations of leaflets when studied under controlled conditions.

Responding to this challenge was a group of sociologists at the University of Washington under the leadership of Stuart C. Dodd. This group agreed to make the studies over a three-year period. The overall program was called *Project Revere* (after the well-known American patriot). It is a series of studies conducted between 1951 and 1953. The series had the common purpose of investigating some aspect of the problem of disseminating information by airborne leaflets, including the spread of information from these printed sources by word-of-mouth to other segments of the population who did not directly see them first hand.

PROJECT REVERE

The climate of opinion on American campuses during the early 1950s concerning the merits of the military establishment, and the wisdom of responding to its research needs, was far different from the case during the Vietnam years. In the early 1950s, large numbers of World War II veterans were in school because of the G.I. Bill. Many were working on graduate degrees. These young scholars respected the military services, thought that they were important, and felt it was patriotic to assist them. It was in this climate of opinion that Project Revere was designed and conducted. Those responsible for specific studies in the series had all seen active service in the Navy, Army, or Marines. The military-related research appeared to them an opportunity to conduct studies on complex communication issues and to help their country at the same time.

The Air Force laid down few restrictions on what should be done and their emphasis was on basic research rather than practical problems or wartime applications. The fact is, the Air Force left it to the research team to formulate the problem, design the means of addressing it, and sort out the implications of the findings. The only requirement was that the researchers try to find out more about leaflets as a device for communication. In an era before large-scale federal government grants became widely available, the third of a million (1950s) dollars allocated to the research provided an almost unprecedented opportunity. The researchers noted this at the time:

> To social scientists characteristically working on meager budgets it seems somewhat incredible that a group of researchers would have placed at its disposal almost unlimited funds for the purpose of deliberately conducting research into basic problems of communication without the insistence that practical problems were of importance. Yet, this is the context within which the present research was carried out. The United States Air Force felt that a truly practical research program into communication problems would be one that had long range aims. They recognized that the development of a full understanding of communication procedures requires first of all a good understanding of fundamentals.[1]

The research program was complex and included many separate studies. These investigations were completed in settings that included towns, grade schools, universities, colleges, large urban centers, housing projects, boys' camps, small groups, and communities struck by disaster. The central objective in these wide-ranging investigations was to gain knowledge about the leaflet as a medium of communication.

Leaflets can be delivered in a number of ways, openly or clandestinely, depending on the situation of the area. Most frequently in modern times large-scale leaflet operations have depended upon distribution from aircraft. Airborne delivery is, of course, a chancy proposition at best. In addition to the vagaries of the elements—wind, weather, terrain—it is difficult to predict who will pick up a leaflet and what they will do with it once they have it. With luck, the leaflet will arrive at the relevant site in good condition, be picked up by a member of the intended audience, read, and passed on to other appropriate individuals. With even more luck, this will stimulate some form of desired action.

Sometimes the process works; usually it does not. In some respects, this is a problem with all mass-communicated messages. Newspapers, magazines, film producers and broadcasting stations have only limited control over their intended audiences. Exactly who will receive what and how this will influence them remain questions for every attempt at communication, no matter what the medium. The unknowns, however, seem far greater for leaflets than for other kinds of media.

The only advantages that leaflets have over other media were noted earlier. They can be distributed to target populations under circumstances where other media do not exist, are inoperative, or are forbidden. And in spite of their small size, they do provide a permanent record that can be read or reviewed in secret and at the reader's own pace. With the use of pictures, maps, cartoons, diagrams, or symbols of authority, a leaflet can deliver both verbal and nonverbal messages in a relatively straightforward manner.

Under some circumstances, leaflets can stimulate significant action. For example, under wartime conditions leaflets have been used to warn civilian populations of forthcoming heavy bombing raids on particular targets. This has sometimes resulted in mass evacuations, with consequent disruption of the enemy's transportation routes and production facilities. In non-war settings, leaflets can be used as an emergency medium to warn people of hazards, provide directions, indicate safe evacuation routes, or indicate that help is on the way. In a situation of political repression or occupation by hostile forces, even crudely printed leaflets delivered by any means possible can provide a last-resort medium of communication. In spite of their simplicity, then, leaflets can be a significant mass medium under certain conditions.

The use of leaflets in Project Revere was in the context of civilian populations and their role in emergency conditions. No attempt was made to use leaflets to communicate propaganda messages in the usual meaning of that term, or to use them under the stress of wartime, or during politically disruptive conditions.

The Coffee Slogan Experiment

The investigators quickly became aware that research on the spread of a message through a population via leaflets involved the study of two distinct processes. The first was getting the message designed, printed, and delivered into the hands of at least some segment of the intended audience. The delivery would presumably ensure that at least some part of the relevant population had read and understood the message. The second process was to get the initial receivers not only to read the message but to give leaflets to others, or at least to *tell* others what they had learned: to get the initial receivers, in other words, to pass on the message by word-of-mouth. Broadly speaking, these two processes can be thought of as *message delivery* (to the target population) and *interpersonal message diffusion* (through the target population).

To provide initial information on message delivery, 55,000 airborne leaflets were dropped on Salt Lake City, Utah. Both face-to-face and telephone interviews were conducted in the drop zones to determine what kinds of people and how many had received a leaflet and if they had understood its message. A mail-back postcard questionnaire was attached to each leaflet. The purpose was to try out the mail-back request to see how compliance was related to a list of social and demographic factors. A similar but much larger study was then conducted in Birmingham, Alabama, where 326,000 airborne leaflets were dropped. The purpose here was to study the mail-back procedure more closely and to try to gain further information on what kinds of people would learn the message, pass on a leaflet to others, or mail back a completed postcard questionnaire.

While much was learned in these preliminary studies about dropping leaflets and assessing the degree to which people obtained information from them, it became increasingly apparent that getting subjects to pass on messages by word-of-mouth was entirely another matter. Generally, it appeared, people would do so only under rather special circumstances that provided adequate motivation. In fact, it became increasingly vexing and frustrating for the researchers as attempt after attempt failed to get people to pass on oral messages.

After a number of abortive attempts to stimulate spontaneous oral message transmission through several different kinds of groups, it was realized that special efforts would be needed to get some sort of message started through an actual community so that its routes by word-of-mouth could be traced. To achieve this objective, and to generate the data needed to identify and study the problems and dimensions of person-to-person message diffusion in a natural (community) setting, a rather elaborate experiment was conceived. The purpose of this unusual experiment was to stimulate a high level of social transmission of a simple message through a community, strongly motivating its residents to pass it on. This would make it possible to study the message's speed, accuracy, and extent of penetration as it spread through the community's word-of-mouth networks.

Stimulating Interpersonal Diffusion　A small and relatively isolated rural community in western Washington State was chosen as the research site. It was a town of just over 1,000 inhabitants, with 249 dwellings included in its city limits and immediate environs. The community was carefully mapped, with the location of every dwelling and place of business plotted. The immediate goals were to start a short message with a sample of the residents, to motivate them strongly to pass the message on to others, and to encourage those who did *not* know the message to learn it. The research team planned to return several days later and interview every household in town. The long-range goal was a detailed study of the social routing through which the message had travelled as it diffused through the community. In other words, the experiment would permit a study of the extent, speed, accuracy, and directions taken by a message started with a limited number of people and spread solely via interpersonal diffusion.[2]

A major problem was to design a simple message that could easily be spread and that could later be traced as it moved from person to person. Another problem was to provide some sort of "cover" for the experiment so that the community residents would see what they were doing as natural and not as part of some study of "human guinea pigs." There was also the problem of motivation; an effective reward had to be attached to the acts of learning the message and passing it on to others.

A happy, if unusual, solution was found to this set of problems. A wholesale coffee distributing company was located that wanted to promote its house brand, called *Gold Shield Coffee*. The company was intrigued with the idea of working with the researchers on the message experiment. Its directors agreed to donate several hundred pounds of their product as rewards in exchange for the advertising exposure they would receive. The researchers and company officials made up a simple six-word slogan: "Gold Shield Coffee; Good as Gold!" This was the message to be passed along.

To stimulate people to learn this message and pass it on to others, the investigators and their interviewer team posed as representatives of the coffee company. They called upon a carefully selected sample of the households in the community, representing 17 percent of the dwellings. Each subject interviewed at these households was given a free pound of coffee and was informed that the company was "trying out a new advertising slogan to see how it would catch on." Each recipient of the coffee read the six-word slogan from a printed card and then repeated it back. These respondents were to serve as "starters" of the message. They were told that the "advertising team" would return in three days with additional coffee to call on *every household in town*. Those that knew the slogan, the interviewers made clear, would receive a free pound of coffee. This would include the starters who were originally taught the slogan, provided that they could remember it three days later.

The coffee reward and the advertising cover turned out to be fortuitous selections. The price of the product had risen sharply about a month before the experiment, and many people in the area were deploring the situation. The free pound of coffee was gratefully received and the prospect of an additional gift three days later was keenly anticipated. This advertising venture seemed to make sense to the subjects. They had long since become accustomed to both free samples and the sometimes curious antics of the advertising world. The entire community seemed eager to spread the slogan. (Indeed, in many cases while the interviewer was departing the front door of a dwelling the householder could be seen running out the back door to spread the word to a neighbor.)

Nevertheless, the investigators were determined to use every means to get people to pass on the message to others and accordingly they had prepared an additional way of stimulating interest and providing motivation to spread the message. Late in the day of the first interview, 30,000 airborne leaflets were distributed evenly over the community by a low-flying light plane (with official clearance). These leaflets informed the members of the community about the slogan-spreading venture (but did not reveal the slogan itself). They pointed out that "one out of every five housewives in town already knew the message." The reader was informed that the "advertisers" would return in three days to every household, and that a free pound of coffee would be awarded at each dwelling where the slogan was known. (It should be noted that the news media serving this community had agreed to avoid mentioning the study until after it was completed. This cooperation was excellent.)

With these steps completed, the community was left to its own devices for a three-day period. During this time the people of the town became very active in spreading the message. The leaflets were widely picked up and distributed, raising curiosity about the mysterious message. The starters were in a position to reward others by passing on the slogan, and they did so with enthusiasm. When the researchers returned three days after the initial contacts they found an eager community waiting to tell them the message and get their reward. Often, the interviewer was confronted in the street before he or she could even call on the householder. After it was over, it was found that some 84 percent of those interviewed had a recognizable version of the original slogan. A number of others reported incorrect or badly garbled slogans, but they received coffee in any case. In fact, several hundred pounds were given away. The householders were pleased with their rewards; the coffee company was delighted with the relatively inexpensive product exposure; and the Project Revere researchers obtained their badly-needed data.

   Tracing the Social Pathways   The interpersonal networks through which the slogan spread were carefully traced. This was possible, if laborious, through the use of the aerial photographs, the maps of the dwelling places, the questionnaire data, and the addresses of the respondents. A person who received the message from a starter was identified as being in the *first remove* (from the starter); one who was two stages away from a starter was in the second remove, and so forth. By this means a total of 92 interpersonal networks were reconstructed. (There were 64 two-stage networks; 18 had three stages; there were five with four stages; two with five stages; and finally, one complex network involved 18 people and six stages.) These networks represented first tellings only; many people in town told the slogan to people who already knew. Overall, during the three-day period the message travelled repeatedly through the social structure—up, down, and sideways. The only people who *didn't* know the message were social recluses, people who had been out of town, and a few who were retarded, senile, or too ill to be involved.

The Patterns of Message Distortion

It should be emphasized that a major reason for choosing a simple six-word slogan with most words of one syllable was to minimize distortion as the message moved from person to person. One goal in studying the data was to reconstruct the curve showing the proportion of the population which knew the slogan at different points in time. Thus, it was anticipated that distortion of the message would pose few problems, and people who knew the message could easily be distinguished from those who did not.

   In spite of these hopes, many inaccuracies crept into the message as it moved along the interpersonal networks of the community. In fact, it soon became apparent that message distortion was a major problem and that the emerging patterns of distortion resembled closely those that had been identified by students of the "rumor" process, for instance, by Bartlett in the 1930s and Allport and Postman in the 1940s.[3] In other words, as the number of stages or removes through which the information passed became greater, the message became less and less like the original. It became noticeably shorter; extraneous words crept in; new ideas replaced the original content; and contents from the surrounding culture of the subjects were incorporated. These changes constitute the *embedding pattern* that has been widely found in laboratory-type studies of serial message retelling.[4] The key concepts in these studies are *leveling, sharpening,* and *assimilation*. These patterns described the distortions that occurred in the slogan unusually well.

Leveling The six-word slogan was frequently shortened as it passed from person to person. Figure 10 shows that a fairly high degree of accuracy was retained through the first two removes from the starter. After that, the message deteriorated; the number of words declined sharply. These results raised serious doubts about the accuracy of interpersonal networks as communication channels. Due to the short message which the starters received, and the fact that they were carefully taught its content, the pattern of leveling in this community experiment was not as dramatic as those obtained from laboratory experiments which provide the starters with a wealth of detail, a long message taxing the memory, and freedom to construct the meaning as the individual starter sees fit. Even so, the simple message was leveled to a considerable degree.

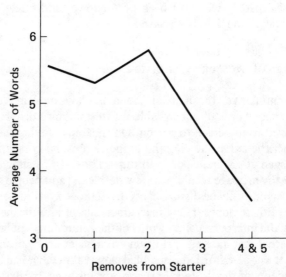

Figure 10. Leveling: Average Number of Words from Original Slogan Reported by Each Remove from the Starters.

SOURCE: Melvin L. DeFleur, "Mass Communication and the Study of Rumor," *Sociological Inquiry* 32, 1, Winter 1962, p. 63.

Sharpening Sharpening in rumor experiments occurs when certain details of a message are retained and emphasized as the message is passed along. These details then become the central core of the surviving message in serial retelling. Two somewhat different types of sharpening were noted in the respondents' versions of the six-word slogan. The first can be called *sharpening by selection*. This pattern of message distortion is what Allport and Postman referred to when they defined sharpening as "the selective perception, retention and reporting of a limited number of details from a larger context."[5] In the present situation it means that certain words in the original slogan were retained to become its central ideas while others were selectively dropped out as the message moved from person to person. Specifically, the last three words of the slogan, "Good as Gold," tended to survive the retelling process better than the first three. The words "Gold Shield Coffee" frequently dropped out during the leveling process as the number of removes increased. In addition, another form of sharpening identified as selective emphasis was given to certain parts of the message. This was termed *sharpening by intensification*. It is illustrated by the fact that some respondents in their enthusiasm intensified the basic idea of the slogan and reported that (the coffee) was "better than gold," "finer than gold," "pure gold," or even a "pot of gold."

The sharpening pattern, then, was one where the last half of the slogan tended to survive, and in some instances to become intensified by exaggeration as the message diffused through the interpersonal networks. The brand name of the product, and the word "coffee" itself, were both essential to the original idea of the slogan. Nevertheless, they were frequently omitted as the message moved along its social pathways.

Assimilation Investigators of rumors in laboratory settings have uniformly noted that messages undergoing serial retelling tend to become distorted in accord with the interests, attitudes, cultural norms, or stereotyped expectations of the subjects. Collectively, such forms of distortion are referred to as "assimilation." In other words, extraneous meanings or content are assimilated into the message as it is passed along. The instances of assimilation that occurred in the slogan study were essentially of three types. First, many respondents introduced a word or two into their version of the slogan to make it conform more closely to their verbal habits or to common modes of English speech. Thus, words such as "is as," "it's as," or "is just as" were variants of this practice of adding words to the middle of the slogan. This type of *linguistic* assimilation is frequently found in laboratory studies of serial retelling. For the most part, the proportion of respondents distorting the message in this minor way increased during the first two removes and declined sharply when the slogan became much shorter in the later removes (where such extra words were not relevant).

A second, and more important, type of assimilation is illustrated by respondents who altered the slogan conceptually by substituting or incorporating ideas which they obtained from the culture around them. For example, one person reported that the message was "The coffee that is good to the last drop" (the slogan of another brand). Another individual reported that the message was "The coffee that is *so* good" (an advertising claim of yet another brand). Another form of such *conceptual* assimilation occurred when respondents incorporated into their versions of the slogan ideas commonly associated with the word "gold." Such words as "pot," and "pure" are frequently used in connection with the term "gold" and were thus assimilated to the concept. This type of distortion appeared to be more frequent in later removes.

Finally, another source of distortion was called *assimilation to logical source*. While not strictly a change in message content, it is illustrated by respondents who claimed to have obtained the slogan via the regular mass media, or from some other source. Several persons claimed to have heard it on the radio. Others mentioned newspapers or television. One person reported reading it on a can of coffee. These claims were, of course, without foundation. The only possible source for learning the slogan was other people in the community.

What did these findings imply for the study of leaflets as a means of communicating to large numbers of people? While the results were in no way definitive, they indicated that even a very brief message, diffused under motivational conditions stressing accuracy, became substantially distorted as it moved from person to person. The resulting embedding pattern included leveling, sharpening, and assimilation in a manner closely resembling results obtained from typical laboratory research on rumoring. If the results of this community diffusion experiment can be interpreted as a reasonable guide to what can be expected to happen to information as it moves through the interpersonal networks involved in the "two-step flow" of communication (from a mass medium to a secondary audience) then several implications follow. Those people who are informed by others, as opposed to those who receive direct exposure to the medium, are likely to be poorly informed indeed. The farther they are removed from the person who had direct contact with the medium, the more inaccurate the information they receive is likely to be. The individual at the end of a chain of tellers and retellers is likely to receive a version of the message that is substantially shorter, and which has been selectively edited and distorted in accord with prevailing verbal habits, cultural themes and stereotypes.

When mass communication depends heavily upon word-of-mouth diffusion to extend its range of contact, a low degree of fidelity to the original content is likely to prevail. These truncated or highly distorted messages are likely to be of limited utility in attempts to achieve propaganda goals or even to transmit simple instructions in times of emergency. What this social diffusion experiment told the researchers of Project Revere was that *first-hand contact with the medium itself is essential in achieving accurate communication*. It was for this reason that further experiments were deemed necessary to find the most effective way to get leaflets directly into the hands of their intended recipients. In other words, interpersonal message diffusion was undoubtedly important, but direct message delivery—getting a leaflet to its intended audience member was even more important.

THE REPETITION EXPERIMENT

A major experiment was designed to try to determine how to use leaflets efficiently. Stated simply, how many leaflets per person in the intended audience does it take to insure that the message will be learned by a given percent of the recipients? Obviously, using too few would not result in a satisfactory level of communication. On the other hand, oversaturation might have various negative effects and achieve less in getting the message across than an optimum number. Although in the Project Revere studies this issue was studied in the context of airborne leaflets, it is clearly a problem with many kinds of communications. For example, how often should an advertising message be repeated in order to maximize its influence on a given category of consumers? How often should a charity appeal be presented; or how frequently should an idea be presented in an educational setting? There are obviously a host of other considerations in these questions; the personality characteristics of the receivers, their cultural milieux, and the relationship between the factors and the content of the message remain paramount. But no message, no matter how closely related to the interests, values, and motivations of its audience, can achieve its effect if it is not perceived accurately and fully by the largest proportion of its intended recipients.

Instead of proceeding by trial and error blindly to study the question of message repetition versus level of response, the Project Revere researchers felt that it would be better to develop a *formal theory*. It was hoped that a formal theory would predict the relationship between the frequency of message presentation and the proportion of the intended audience who would learn its content.

The basis for a formal theory was found in the much-studied relationships between stimulus intensity and response from the field of classical psychophysics. Work on this problem began during the mid-nineteenth century. The purpose was to understand the relationship between the external world of stimuli and the internal or subjective world of sensations. For the purposes of developing the needed theory, it was postulated that any message transmitted over any medium can be regarded as a *stimulus* intended to elicit some form of desired *response*. This stimulation can be presented to a responding audience in varying intensities, either by presenting it more frequently or in greater volume. In the case of leaflets, increasing the sheer number dropped on a given group can be regarded as one method of increasing the intensity of stimulation toward the desired response of knowing the message or taking some action proposed by it. The development of an equation, a formally derived hypothesis, stating this relationship between communication stimulus intensity and amount of group response was the next step.

Stimulus Intensity versus Response

There had been little systematic investigation dealing with quantitative stimulus–response relationships in leaflet communication. Herz had summarized problems of measuring response to propaganda leaflets during wartime, but this literature was of little help.[6] A review of literature for the twenty-five years prior to Project Revere revealed a few studies of other media where variations in stimulus intensity were studied in relation to response, but most of these dealt with advertising messages and were characterized by contradictory findings.[7] In other words, it was necessary to begin from scratch.

Any discussion of stimulus intensity and response automatically brings to mind the sensory psychology studies of the last century, which resulted in the much-tested Weber's Law. A voluminous literature was available on this generalization concerning variations in sensations which result from quantitative alterations in the intensity of stimulation. Weber's Law is an equation (actually developed by Fechner) relating magnitudes of response —used as an index of sensation—to various magnitudes of stimulus intensity. Fechner wrote the *fundamentalformal,* the basic equation, after integration, in the following form:

$$R = a \log_e S + b$$

The equation can be explained rather simply: S is the level of stimulus intensity, while a and b are constants of proportionality and integration respectively. Even if one is not familiar with mathematical representations, the idea is not very complex. The equation describes a *curve* showing that when stimulus intensity (S) is increased by a given amount, the response of the subject (R) will also increase by a regular and predictable amount. The pattern of the curve is one of *diminishing returns* and this shape is set by the other terms in the equation. What it all boils down to is that doubling the intensity of a stimulus will not double the sensation felt by the subject (measured by some form of response). In fact, as stimulus intensity is increased, it takes larger and larger increases to elicit increasingly smaller increments of sensation (response). This relationship has been supported by numerous experimental studies conducted over many decades.

This psychophysical formulation was used as a basis for developing a parallel "law" (actually a formal hypothesis) to describe the relationship between stimulus intensity and response in leaflet communication. In other words, the more leaflets that are dropped on a community, the greater will be the response of learning the message. However, this was expected to occur in a pattern of diminishing returns. In other words, the increments in response, when one increased the number of leaflets per person in the target population, were expected to become smaller and smaller as ever larger numbers of leaflets were used for each inhabitant. This general idea was tested in a preliminary study that used varying ratios of leaflets per person.

The Pilot Study   An investigation was conducted to test the diminishing returns idea and to train the research team. Four small communities were used (populations ranged between 969 and 1,175). These communities were carefully selected for their similarity. All had the same type of economic base, none were satellites of an urban area, and all had similar population compositions. A ratio of one leaflet per person was used on one community, four per person on two others, and sixteen to one on the other community. This provided three points along a possible curve, showing what proportion of the population in each community had learned the message.

The experiment was carried out in cooperation with the Washington State Office of Civil Defense, and the leaflets stated that "One visit from an enemy bomber could send evacuees pouring into your town!" It went on to ask recipients to consider, if such a disaster occurred, "how many refugees they could take into their home." The leaflet was signed by the State Civil Defense Director, and it indicated that a Civil Defense representative would soon call at each home in the community to get their answers. The "representatives" were, of course, interviewers from the Project Revere team. Careful preparations had been made with aerial photographs and maps for each community, and interviews were conducted at every household. Once again, local media cooperated by refraining from mentioning the leaflet drop. The study was a training exercise for the larger experiment to come, but a considerable amount of useful data were obtained on inter-personal diffusion, time-growth patterns of the message, and other issues.

The civil defense theme provided an excellent cover for the experiment. The civil defense authorities were delighted with the information the researchers provided and the townspeople found it to be a realistic issue, much on the minds of people during the time.

The data showed that using one leaflet per person resulted in 18 percent of the residents learning the message by the end of the first day. A four-fold increase of the ratio of leaflets per person (four for each inhabitant) nearly doubled the proportion who learned the message: 32 percent. Another four-fold increase, 16 leaflets per person, resulted in 55 percent of the population learning the message. When plotted on a simple graph these three figures imply a curve of diminishing returns. Clearly, however, three points are insufficient to test the idea that this regularity will hold over a large number of cases. Nevertheless, the results of this pilot study were most encouraging and the investigators decided to plan and conduct a more definitive test of the diminishing returns relationship. The first task in planning the study was to develop the hypothesis into a statement of greater precision.

Formalizing the Hypothesis   In the discussion below, the manner in which the formalized diminishing returns hypothesis was derived in equation form is explained. For the reader who is not familiar with this type of mathematics, it is not essential to follow the formal derivation to understand the experiment and its results. The present section provides a verbal explanation of what the formal hypothesis was about. The mathematical derivation is presented in the section that follows. In nonmathematical terms, then, the general idea was to come up with an equation that described a curve of diminishing returns predicting how much communication would take place with the use of a given level of stimulus intensity (in this case, a given ratio of leaflets per person). Even if one does not follow the mathematics, it is important to see that it is possible: (1) to begin with a specific set of assumptions, (2) to translate these into a formal mathematical statement, and then (3) to derive a testable hypothesis. Such a hypothesis has the advantage of specifying in the clearest possible terms the kinds of data that are needed for the test and the design of the experiment that will be required. We can assume that a community consists of many individuals interacting. We will further assume that the relationship between the intensity of a communication stimulus and the collective response of such a "subject" will show some similarity to the diminishing returns pattern described by Weber's Law. (The pilot study data seemed to suggest that such an assumption had merit.)

A range of stimulus intensities is needed against which to check the corresponding degrees of response that are to be elicited. But the same subject (community) cannot be used over and over because each succeeding leaflet presentation and response measurement would contaminate the experimental situation for the next. An experimental design is required in which a number of communities, selected carefully for their similarity, are exposed to different degrees of message stimulus intensity and in which comparable measures of response are obtained from each.

Given these circumstances, one can define a set of stimulus intensities that start at some arbitrary lower limit and increase by some power, say *two*, by doubling each preceeding intensity. A suitable set of intensities for the leaflet experiment would be to begin with one leaflet for every four people. This can be doubled to one for every two people, redoubled to one per person, two per person, and so on. If this is carried through eight steps of doubling and redoubling, the following set of leaflet intensities would be obtained: 1/4, 1/2, 1/1, 2/1, 4/1, 8/1, 16/1, and 32/1.

Given such a range of stimulus intensities, response measures must also be specified. These can be defined as the proportion of a community's population that performs an observable act as a result of the message stimulation. This act could be learning the message, of course, but it could also be some other form of response such as passing a leaflet on to others or filling out and mailing back a postcard questionnaire attached to the leaflet.

With these measures of stimulus intensity and response defined, we can state the hypothesis (in verbal terms) that the increase in response from one community to the next—where the next higher intensity is used—will be directly proportional to the change in stimulus intensity and inversely proportional to the previous stimulus intensity. We are stating, in effect, that a version of Weber's Law will hold not only for individual stimulation but for the collective case when a community is stimulated to give some form of response, even though that response may depend upon social processes and the individual actions of many persons in the collectivity. (At this point nonmathematical readers may wish to turn to the section on Experimental Procedures on p. 223.)

Deriving the Equation To formulate our hypothesis into an expression suitable for testing, let p denote the proportion of the population who respond as defined, and r denote the measure of stimulus intensity. With a constant of proportionality, a, the above diminishing returns hypothesis can be stated in mathematical form as:

$$\Delta p = \frac{a\Delta r}{r} \qquad [1]$$

Since stimulus intensity increases in powers of two in the series of leaflet ratios chosen, the above can be written: [8]

$$p_{i+1} - p_i = a \qquad [2]$$

The solution to equation [2] can now be written as: [9]

$$p_{i+1} = p_1 + ia \qquad [3]$$

However, for the present development it will help to express p in terms of r, rather than in terms of i. Thus, for i equal to or greater than 1, $r_i = 2^{i-3}$, which may be written as:

$$i = 3 + \log_2 r_i \qquad [4]$$

We may put this into equation [3] to get:

$$p_{i+1} = p_1 + (3 + \log_2 r_i)a = a \log_2 r_i + 3a + p_1 \qquad [5]$$

Equation [5] expressed p_{i+1} in terms of r_i, but it is more desirable to express p_{i+1} in terms of r_{i+1}. This may be accomplished by recalling that each stimulus intensity will be just one-half the next greater one. That is to say, $r_i = \frac{1}{2} r_{i+1}$, and with this we can now write:

$$\log_2 r_i = \log_2 \frac{r_{i+1}}{2} = \log_2 r_{i+1} - \log_2 2 = \log_2 r_{i+1} - 1 \qquad [6]$$

If we put this result into [5] we get:

$$p_{i+1} = a \log_2 r_{i+1} + 3a + p_1 = a \log_2 r_{i+1} - a + 3a + p_1 \qquad [7]$$

This gives a prediction of the extent of response for the (r_{i+1})th stimulus intensity. This can be labeled the typical case and designated as the ith case, rather than the $(i + 1)$th, allowing for the simplification:

$$p_i = a \log_2 r_i + (2a + p_i) \text{ valid for all } i \geq 1 \qquad [8]$$

The expression we are seeking comes out when equation [8] is further simplified by letting $2a + p_i = b$. Thus, we get the formal hypothesis:

$$p_i = a \log_2 r_i + b \qquad [9]$$

It can be noted how similar this is to Weber's Law. As we noted on page 218, Fechner integrated his *fundamental formal* to the expression:

$$R = a \log_e S + b$$

This similarity of form is to be expected. However, equation [9], our formal hypothesis, avoids the assumptions involved in infinitesimal calculus (which would be difficult to justify in this case) and was derived from a different equation. In any case, equation [9] predicts values of response level for the communities that will get each leaflet ratio in the doubling and redoubling series defined earlier.

Ordinary statistical methods can be used to evaluate the differences between the predicted values and the values actually obtained from conducting the experiment. In the present case, chi-square provides a simple procedure for evaluating the goodness of fit between the observed and theoretical data. Note that equation [9] is not confined to leaflet communication specifically. It can be advanced as a testable hypothesis for any medium where measures of stimulus intensity and a level of community response can be obtained.

Experimental Procedures

To test the formal hypothesis stated in equation [9] a rather elaborate experiment was designed around the series of leaflet ratios indicated earlier (p. 221). Eight small communities in western Washington State were chosen as sites for the test. Each was to receive a different leaflet ratio, and interviewing in each town would determine the proportion of the population who had learned the message (or made some other response) within a specified period of time. The actual results obtained can be compared to the theoretical proportions predicted by equation [9].

The communities were selected to be as much alike as possible. Their populations ranged between 1,015 and 1,800. They were relatively stable; all had similar climates and economic bases (lumbering and agriculture); and none was a suburb or bedroom community for a large city.

These eight "subjects" were assigned "treatments" by an elementary randomization procedure. These treatments were, of course, the leaflet drops, using the different ratios described earlier. Table 14 shows the ratio assigned to each community.

As in earlier Project Revere experiments, extensive preparations were completed before the leaflets were dropped. Town authorities were contacted; the cooperation of relevant news media was solicited; maps and aerial photographs were prepared; reconnaisance flights were made over the community to plan the best drop patterns; questionnaires were pretested; and interviewers were carefully trained. All went well. The nine newspapers, three radio stations and one TV station serving the area agreed to the plan. Town officials were most cooperative. The interviewer teams had been thoroughly briefed, and all other details had been taken into account.

The leaflet used was a simple one. It combined the civil defense theme used in the pilot study with the mail-back postcard questionnaire developed in earlier research. The leaflet informed the reader that:

Table 14 Ratios of Leaflets per Person Assigned to the Eight Towns

Leaflets per person	Town	Population	Total Number of Leaflets
1/4	Orting	1,299	325
1/2	Sequim	1,096	548
1/1	Poulsbo	1,306	1,306
2/1	Oak Harbor	1,475	2,950
4/1	Ferndale	1,015	4,060
8/1	Arlington	1,800	14,400
16/1	Darrington	1,052	16,832
32/1	McCleary	1,175	37,600
			78,021

SOURCE: Melvin L. DeFleur, "A Mass Communication Model of Stimulus Response Relationships: An Experiment in Leaflet Message Diffusion," *Sociometry* 19, 1, March 1956, p. 18.

> One raid from an enemy bomber could paralyze radios, telephones, newspapers. *In such a disaster . . .* leaflets like this could be dropped from airplanes to give official instructions. *You* are part of this scientific test to find out how effective leaflets are for spreading vital information to everyone.

The reverse side of the leaflet contained an appeal to "Be a Modern Paul Revere" and pass on extra leaflets to others to "help spread the word." It also asked the recipient to fill out and mail the (self-addressed and postage-free) questionnaire attached to the leaflet in the form of a small postcard. The purpose of the postcard was to provide a measure of *compliance* with the request for a specific action.

All leaflet drops occurred on a Wednesday, commencing promptly at noon in each community. Skilled crews made sure that the leaflets were spread evenly over each site. Three days later, beginning at 9:00 A.M., face-to-face interviews were conducted in every other household in each community. (Previous Revere studies had shown that three days were ample for the message to spread.) The exact person in the household to interview was selected by a special method (often used by the U.S. Census).[10] The data-gathering was designed to determine if the respondents had learned the message, and if so, *how* they learned (via social diffusion or directly from a leaflet); *when* they learned; and what subsequent *action* they had taken on the basis of the requests on the leaflet. Cooperation by the townspeople was excellent in every respect. After the experiment was concluded, local news media described the leaflet drops and their purposes.

The Hypotheses versus the Data

To determine if a given respondent knew the message on the leaflets, his or her verbatim reply to the question "What did the leaflet say?" was carefully recorded by the interviewers. These replies were then independently reviewed by two judges who used previously established criteria to make their decisions as to whether or not a subject should be classified as a "knower" or a "non-knower." The procedure worked well and interjudge reliability was $r = .94$.

The proportion of those interviewed who were classified as "knowers" was plotted by leaflet ratio as shown in Figure 11. By the method of least squares, the curve described by equation [9] was fit through the resulting points. This means simply that the curve predicted by the theory (equation [9]) goes through the observable data points in a manner that minimizes the distance between the empirical data and the points predicted by the curve. The whole idea is shown graphically in Figure 11.

By using chi-square to compare how much the observed data differed from the predictions provided by the hypothesis (equation [9]), a test of good fit was provided. Visual examination of the graph shows that the fit of

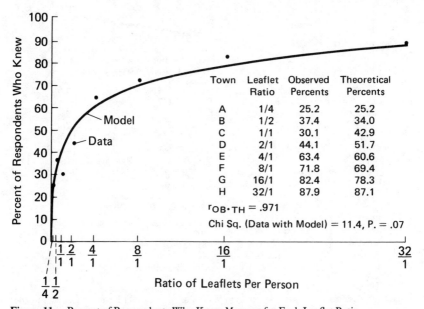

Figure 11. Percent of Respondents Who Knew Message for Each Leaflet Ratio.

SOURCE: Melvin L. DeFleur, "A Mass Communication Model of Stimulus Response Relationships: An Experiment in Message Diffusion," *Sociometry* 19, *1*, March 1956, pp. 21–22.

the theoretical curve to the observed data was, on the whole, quite good. The probability value associated with chi-square indicates that the observed and the hypothesized (theoretical) percents do not differ significantly. The differences between observed and theoretical values could easily have occurred by chance in a universe of such data described by the model. Stated more simply, the curve apparently fits the data, and the outcome supports the formal hypothesis.

A similar test of equation [9] was made with the data shown in Figure 12, obtained from the leaflet postcards that were mailed back. In this case, the curve fits the data pretty well, except in the case of the town that received eight leaflets per person. Here, the mail-back compliance was especially high. It was discovered that in this particular community an active voluntary civil defense group took it upon themselves to see that the "civil defense test" was a success, and these public-spirited citizens made sure that as many people as possible completed the questionnaire and mailed back the postcard. Aside from this understandable aberration, however, the formal hypothesis seemed to predict this form of compliance behavior rather well.

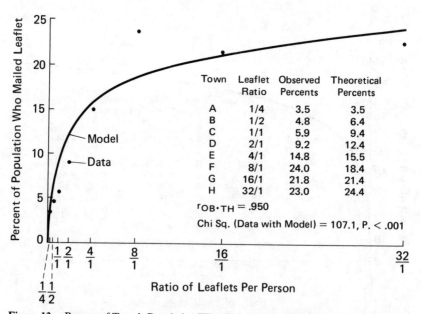

Figure 12. Percent of Town's Population Who Mailed in Leaflet Postcard for Each Leaflet Ratio.

SOURCE: Melvin L. DeFleur, "A Mass Communication Model of Stimulus Response Relationships: An Experiment in Message Diffusion," *Sociometry* 19, 1, March 1956, pp. 21–22.

The conclusion of this study was that the formalized hypothesis (equation [9]) provided a good description of the relationship between the specified stimulus intensity measures and the amount of communication that took place. With the exception of the one deviant case with the active civil defense group, the formal hypothesis also did well in describing the relationship between stimulus intensity and compliance. This version of Weber's Law, in other words, seemed to apply in this communication setting.

Message Diffusion and the Social Structure

The results of the stimulus intensity experiment indicated clearly that the frequency or redundancy with which a message is presented to a target audience is a vital factor in determining the eventual level of communicative and compliance outcome. But a message brought to the attention of the audience will also travel through social channels, as was demonstrated in the coffee slogan experiment. The significance of social diffusion had originally been suggested by *The People's Choice* research (see Chapter 6), which resulted in the discovery of the "two-step flow" of communication. However, at the time of the Revere studies, little was known of the pathways through the social structure which a message would follow as message diffusion took place. The eight-community experiment not only provided data on the Weber's Law hypothesis, it yielded abundant information on what kind of people passed on the message to what other kind of people. In other words, it was possible to sort out the social itinerary followed by the information as it moved through interpersonal networks.

One clear pattern that became apparent was that in a situation of relative *scarcity*, with fewer leaflets available per person, a larger proportion of those receiving the message learned it through social means. When leaflets were relatively *abundant*, on the other hand, that proportion dropped and more people learned by direct contact with a leaflet. For example, among those classified as "knowers" of the message in those four communities with lowest ratios of leaflets per person, 62.9 percent learned by social means. In the four communities with the highest leaflet ratios, the comparable figure was 47.8 percent (a significant difference). It should not be forgotten, however, that in absolute numbers there were considerably larger numbers of knowers in the high-ratio communities. The implications of this pattern are of pragmatic interest in that learning by social means tends to result in relatively inaccurate communication. Therefore, if the intent of the communicator is to reach as many people as possible, high redundancy (stimulus intensity) is required.

The knowers of the message were not evenly distributed throughout the various social categories and subgroups in any of the communities.

Under both high and low stimulus intensity conditions, both *age* and *family size* were significantly related to the probability of learning the message. Children were more likely to know the message than were adults; and adults from large families were more likely to know the message than adults from small families. This suggests that an important aspect of the dynamics of social diffusion (at least in this research) was that a flow of information took place *from children to adults*. More specifically, this flow tended to be from children to their parents. (An analysis of differences by sex showed no significant patterns). Children, then, were more active in picking up the leaflets, learning their content, passing on the message to others, and passing on leaflets to adults in particular.

Further analyses showed that family and friendship ties were important in the process of social diffusion. Among adults, transmitting or receiving the message by any means tended to take place more within the family than among neighbors, acquaintances, or strangers. This was not the case with children, who both learned and transmitted the message more with others outside the family. This was especially true in the case of oral transmission, as opposed to passing on a leaflet. Table 15 summarizes the relevant data.

How can we interpret these findings concerning the penetration of this particular message into the social structure of the communities involved? The following generalizations describe what happened: The leaflets appeared to have a special appeal to children, who picked them up, told other children, or passed on leaflets to their friends, parents, adult neighbors, or

Table 15 The Flow of Information from Various Categories of Leaflet Receivers to Children and Adults

Identity of Message Transmitter	Age Status of Message Receiver							
	Pass-on Diffusion				Oral Diffusion			
	Adults		Children		Adults		Children	
	N	%	N	%	N	%	N	%
Family member	142	49.8	12	22.7	21	35.6	1	3.7
Neighbor	61	21.4	13	24.5	17	28.8	3	11.1
Acquaintance	75	26.3	28	52.8	21	35.6	23	85.2
Stranger	7	2.5	0	0.0	0	0.0	0	0.0
Total	285	100.0	53	100.0	59	100.0	27	100.0

Pass-on: For $3df$, $X^2 = 19.0$, $P < .001$.
Oral: For $2df$, $X^2 = 18.2$, $P < .001$.

SOURCE: Melvin L. DeFleur and Otto N. Larsen, *The Flow of Information* (New York: Harper and Brothers, 1958) p. 178.

acquaintances. This in turn appeared to lead adults to discuss the leaflets and their message with other adults, or to take the requested action and comply by mailing back the postcard. Thus, children were, in a sense, *neutral transmitters* of the oral message, or of the leaflets. The principal role of children, then, was to obtain leaflets, bring them home, pass on the message to others, and thus stimulate action by adults.

CONCLUSIONS AND IMPLICATIONS

The airborne leaflet is obviously a highly specialized medium of communication. As was pointed out, its significance today is as a medium of last resort—as a means by which audiences can be reached during emergencies, wartime, or times of political repression when no alternative channels remain open. Sadly, such situations are as frequent in contemporary times as they were in earlier periods. However, because of the unique qualities of leaflets as a medium, it is appropriate to raise questions about the "generalizability" of the Revere findings to other media and other situations. Would they apply, say, to newspapers, radio, comic books, or television? In addressing this question, one can focus on the differences among these media and wonder if they share *any* common principles. Each conveys its message in a different manner, is attended to as a result of different needs and for varying gratifications. Yet, in spite of these differences, even a moment's reflection confirms that there *are* common principles underlying the process of communication when any of these media are used. Each involves an attempt on the part of communicators to achieve some form of change in their intended audiences. Each depends upon processes of perception and learning. And each is dependent upon the cultural rules of language usage to bring about some paralleling between the intended meanings of the communicator and the interpretations of the recipient.

Beyond these considerations is the fact that communication by any medium includes the two major stages through which information flows from media to audiences, first described as the "two-step flow of communication" in *The People's Choice*. This work became available to the academic community at large in 1948. By the time Project Revere began some three years later, little was known about this form of secondary communication other than the fact that it had been discovered somewhat serendipitously in the Erie County study. Later research on the two-step flow helped fill this gap. It focused on the *people* involved and the *roles* that they played in this form of interpersonal transmission of information and influence. Thus, studies of "opinion leaders" were undertaken, including studies of who their followers were and what topics were involved in such influence (see Chapter 7). In contrast, the Revere studies concentrated on the *quality of the information* that was spread by word-of-mouth through interpersonal networks.

The most significant conclusion from such studies as the coffee slogan experiment was that the person-to-person flow of information resulted in message incompleteness, inaccuracy, and distortion. The implications of this were considerable: The Revere study showed the applicability of the *embedding pattern*, found earlier by social psychologists who had studied "rumoring" by use of the serial retelling strategy, to the word-of-mouth movement of information in the two-step flow. The complex processes of levelling, sharpening, and assimilation were found in the social diffusion of a message through a community. In other words, considerable doubt is cast on the importance of the secondary stage of the two-step flow as a process by which the meanings intended by a mass communicator can be paralleled in the interpretations of the audience toward whom the communication is directed. This issue is even more serious when it is recalled that the message under study was only six words and included only one word of more than one syllable!

The problems posed by the Revere research on message distortion also have a bearing on another line of research that became popular during the mid-1950s and later. The interpersonal diffusion of the news began to be studied intensively by researchers in journalism and communication. Dozens of studies traced time patterns in the spread of important news stories (e.g., Senator Taft's death, Alaska statehood, the Kennedy assassination) as they moved from the media to the secondary stage of the two-step flow. Such time patterns were investigated as part of the Revere studies and were among seven doctoral dissertations and numerous articles in professional journals that appeared during or immediately following the project.[11] However, the significant factor here is that when the news is transmitted from person to person it is likely to be badly distorted, no matter how fast or slow it moves, or how extensively it penetrates the population by word-of-mouth.

If social diffusion is not accurate and reliable, the importance of *direct* contact with the medium by every member of the audience is obvious. At least this was clearly the case with the relatively simple medium used in the Revere studies. This need for direct contact meant that it was important to understand the stimulus intensity issue. How often should the message be presented, with what level of redundancy, to insure that a given level of the intended audience *would* have direct contact with the message? The formal hypothesis based on Weber's Law was an attempt to answer this question. The answers found and the diminishing returns relationship that emerged from the study may have been less important than the opportunity to conduct such research at a level of considerable precision. The mathematical model and its derivation were at a level of formal theory construction not often found in mass communication research, at least up to that time. The large-scale investigation, with eight separate communities carefully surveyed, and with the entire effort aimed at supporting or rejecting a formal mathematical model, was also unusual for the time. In fact, it is not at all clear that research in mass communication has increased its level of precision and theory construction beyond that achieved in Project Revere, even at present.

NOTES AND REFERENCES

1. Melvin L. De Fleur and Otto N. Larsen, *The Flow of Information* (New York: Harper and Brothers, 1948), p. xiv. (This book reports a number of the Project Revere studies.)
2. Melvin L. De Fleur, "Mass Communication and the Study of Rumor," *Sociological Inquiry*, 32, 1, Winter, 1962, pp. 51–70.
3. F. C. Bartlett, *Remembering* (Cambridge, England: Cambridge University Press, 1932); Gordon W. Allport and Leo Postman, *The Psychology of Rumor* (New York: Henry Holt and Company, 1947).
4. Allport and Postman, ibid., pp. 75–115.
5. Ibid., p. 86.
6. Martin F. Herz, "Some Psychological Lessons from Leaflet Propaganda in World War II," *Opinion Quarterly*, 13, 1949, pp. 471–486.
7. Melvin L. De Fleur, "A Mass Communication Model of Stimulus–Response Relationships: An Experiment in Leaflet Message Diffusion," *Sociometry*, 19, 1, 1956, pp. 12–25. (See footnote 3 in this article.)
8. That is, if i denotes the ith increase in stimulus intensity, then $r = 2^{i-3}$ because the lowest intensity ratio in the proposed set was $\frac{1}{4}$ or 2^{-2}; in the next higher, $r = \frac{1}{2}$ or 2^{-1}; and so on through the fourth, $r = 2$, the sixth, $r = 2^3$, etc. In the ith increase, then $r = 2^{i-3}$; and since $\Delta r = r_{i+1} - r_i = 2^{i-3}$ also, then Δr must equal r. This being the case, $\Delta r/r = 1$, yielding equation (2).
9. The expression p_{i+1} merely denotes the response of the community receiving the $(i + 1)$th stimulus intensity. But, if $p_{i+1} = p_i + a$, then it also equals $p_{i-1} + 2a$, $p_{i-2} + 3a$, and so on. By continuing this process we could express p_{i+1} in terms of p_1 plus a certain number of a's. If we want to express p_{i+1} in terms of p_i, it is obvious that one must be added to the subscript of the latter, and it will also be noted that this is precisely the number of a's which must be added to a given p to get p_{i+1}. In general, the number of a's which must be added to a given p to get p_{i+1} is the same as the difference between their subscripts. Thus to p_{i_1} we must add ia's to get p_{i+1}. This situation is summarized in equation (3).

10. Leslie A. Kish, "A Procedure for Objective Respondent Selection within the Household," *Journal of the American Statistical Association*, 44, 1949, pp. 380–387.
11. See pp. 285–293 in *The Flow of Information* for a list of publications and dissertations resulting from Project Revere studies, with special reference to the work of William Catton, Melvin De Fleur, Richard Hill, Otto Larsen, Ørjar Øyen, and Gordon Shaw.

9

seduction of the innocent: the great comic book scare

By 1954, most communication researchers and other social scientists had become complacent in regard to the issues concerning media effects. They considered the matter more or less settled. After all, a number of careful studies, including the milestones presented in Chapters 4, 5, and 6, had indicated that the media had neither dramatic nor dangerous effects. Because the effects of the media had been shown to be so slight, at least some scholars thought that there was no longer any pressing reason even to continue studying them.

These claims about the innocuous nature of media effects were not unchallenged, however. A loud objection was raised by Dr. Frederick Wertham, a noted New York psychiatrist. He claimed that one form of mass communication had practically taken over the minds of our children —silently, very quickly, and without the knowledge of their parents. The villain he referred to was "comic books" and there was, he thought, "nothing funny" about them. Instead, he argued, at their worst they were turning children into dangerous juvenile delinquents; at best, they were giving the children who read them a distorted view of the world.

A few social scientists agreed with Wertham; others disagreed and debated the issue with him in scientific circles; the great majority of social scientists, however, simply ignored him. Not to be denied, Wertham found another audience for his work; he took his argument to the people—to the parents of America. He published articles in widely-read popular magazines such as *Ladies' Home Journal* and *Reader's Digest*. He presented his views on radio and television shows. Wertham thus effectively used other media to condemn comic books. And he succeeded in resurrecting the legacy of fear, at least in the public's mind.

COMIC MAGAZINES AS A CONTROVERSIAL MEDIUM

Comic magazines are offspring of the newspaper comic strips—the "funny papers"—which have a colorful history of their own. They developed during the 1890s when Joseph Pulitzer's New York *World* and William Randolph Hearst's New York *Journal* went all out to lure sensation-hungry readers for their newspapers. Both published lurid stories of murders, scandals involving the rich, tragedies, and disasters. It was said that when news was scarce, neither Pulitzer nor Hearst hesitated to manufacture it. The two newspapers are credited with playing a major role in pushing the country into the Spanish-American War in 1898. They played up atrocities —real and imagined—by the Spanish in Cuba, and whipped up a patriotic fervor against Spain in the United States.

In 1896, a cocky, lovable urchin had quietly begun to entertain readers of the *World* in comic drawings. These were single panels; the comic "strips" would come later. The street kid, who wore a garment resembling a nightgown, began appearing in a bright yellow gown. Suddenly, "The Yellow Kid," the creation of artist Richard Outcault, had boosted the circulation of the *World* ahead of that of the rival *Journal* in their frantic battle for readers. Hearst counterattacked; he hired Outcault away from Pulitzer and began publishing his own comic strip supplement in color. Pulitzer answered this challenge by obtaining the copyright to "The Yellow Kid" and assigning another artist to depict the child's adventures. The "Yellow Kid," however, became immortal; from that strip derives the term "yellow journalism," an epithet used to describe the Pulitzer/Hearst brand of sensationalism in the handling of the news.[1]

Hearst began publishing the first authentic comic strip in 1897, "The Katzenjammer Kids." The strip used a row of panels and dialogue enclosed in balloons to tell the story of two troublesome children and their harried mother and father. The strip set the style for comic strips and was soon followed by others such as "Happy Hooligan," "Little Nemo," and "Mutt and Jeff." The development of the major newspaper syndicates during the early 1900s, including Hearst's International News Service, King Features, United Features, and the Chicago Tribune Syndicate, made it possible to distribute an artist's work throughout the country in scores of newspapers each day. Among the most popular of these syndicated strips were "Bringing Up Father," "Little Orphan Annie," and "Buster Brown," another creation of Outcault, the developer of the original "Yellow Kid."[2] During the 1930s such syndicated comic strips helped millions of Americans to forget temporarily the hard times of the Depression years. It was in this period that such all-time favorite comic characters as "Buck Rogers," "Superman," and "Tarzan" came into their own.

Comic magazines first appeared in the middle 1930s. A New York company, the Eastern Color Printing Company, which already printed Sunday newspaper comic supplements, conceived the idea of printing the comics in book form. They successfully published "Funnies on Parade" and followed it with "Famous Funnies." "Famous Funnies" was distributed through variety stores and proved to be so popular that the publishers began issuing it on a monthly basis. Once the marketability of the comic magazine had been established, many famous comic strip characters began to appear in such publications. "Superman," "Tarzan," "Buck Rogers" and other "action" comics were particularly popular before the outbreak of World War II. They contributed heavily to the success of the comic magazine. And successful they were. In 1941, ten million copies were being sold a month, and by 1947 the figure had risen to 60 million a month.[3] In 1950, a Fawcett Comics Group advertisement was headlined in true comic book style: "The comic books bought each month laid end to end would reach ⅕th the space from the earth to the moon." Comic books had truly arrived—quickly, quietly, and almost unnoticed. The tranquility of the industry was soon disrupted, however. Dr. Wertham brought controversy to the industry and altered the silent acceptance that comic books had enjoyed.

Dr. Wertham was not the first, nor the only professional, to express concern about the effects of comic book reading. However, most of the discussion and disagreement that occurred before his public attack on comic books might be described as a civil war between opposing groups of psychiatrists. The leading critics of comic books, as well as their defenders, were psychiatrists.[4] The critics argued that comic books were "the opium of the nursery" and that they led individual children, who were held spellbound by the crime and horror stories, straight onto the road to crime. Even those children who were not led to criminal behavior were damaged because they were introduced to the comic book world which they accepted as real. The fears of this group of critics were epitomized by the little boy who got a Superman cape for his birthday, wrapped it around himself, and sprang out the window of his apartment house to his death.[5] The defenders, on the other hand, claimed that the comics provided a healthy outlet for the child's violence-play and for his aggressive fantasies. Since children had to suppress this violence and aggressiveness in the presence of adults, both at home and in school, the comics provided a harmless outlet for those forces in their personalities. Comic books and horror stories, they reasoned, were the child's "aspirin and penicillin" for overcoming the painful experience of growing up in a peaceful adult world. This was of course, a simple restatement of the widely-known catharsis theory.

This debate about comic books was waged largely within the confines of the profession of psychiatry, although some of the more active defenders of the comics were also retained as "advisors" by comic book publishers and received lucrative fees for this service. Cynical critics claimed that these "advisors" received their money largely for having their names displayed on the comic books. This, they claimed, amounted to nothing more than a public relations campaign for parents.

Wertham began his public attack on comic magazines in 1948, when he published no fewer than five articles in both professional journals and popular magazines. His position was also stated in some detail in an article written by Judith Crist for *Collier's* magazine. It appeared on March 27, 1948, and was entitled "Horror in the Nursery." The next year, another manuscript entitled "What are Comic Books?" (a study course for parents) was published by the *National Parent Teacher Magazine*. In addition, another article appeared in the *Ladies' Home Journal* under the title "What Parents Don't Know About Comic Books."

Reactions to Wertham's writings by social scientists were mixed. Some vigorously agreed with his conclusions. Others, including the noted sociologist Frederic Thrasher, hotly disagreed.[6] Thrasher, an expert on juvenile delinquency, correctly pointed out that delinquency is a complex phenomenon which cannot be attributed solely to any single cause— whether it be poverty or the media. However, Thrasher's rebuttal was published in a professional journal (*Journal of Educational Sociology*) and was therefore not widely read outside the discipline of sociology.

The public took Wertham's arguments much more seriously. After all, he *was* a well-known psychiatrist and his credentials were impressive. He was Senior Psychiatrist for the Department of Hospitals in New York City (1932–1952). He directed the mental hygiene clinics at both Bellevue Hospital and Queens Hospital Center, and he was in charge of the Court of General Sessions Psychiatric Clinic. For more than twenty-five years, Dr. Wertham had been giving expert opinion in medico-legal cases, and his advice had been sought by defense counsels, district attorneys, judges, and legislators. His views had been discussed before the Supreme Court of the United States. Moreover, he had published many books, including a well-known textbook that was used all over the world, *The Brain as an Organ*.

The most complete treatise on Wertham's position concerning the effects of comic books was published in 1954, under the title *Seduction of the Innocent*. The book received a great deal of attention, both praise and criticism. A condensed version of it was published in *Reader's Digest* under the title "Blueprints for Delinquency" and the book itself was available as a Book-of-the-Month selection in June 1954, for participants in the Reader's Digest Book Club. By publishing in such a forum, Wertham was able to reach the public and to influence a great many people. It is the ideas and findings reported in *Seduction of the Innocent* to which we now turn.

THE RESEARCH PROCEDURES

Wertham's foremost concern was to discover the effects that comic books had on the attitudes and behavior of children. While he studied *all* varieties of comic books, he concentrated on "crime comic books." Crime comics were "those comic books that depict crime whether the setting is urban, western, science-fiction, jungle, adventure, or the realm of superman, horror or supernatural beings."[7] Wertham felt that *all comic books* had undesirable effects (even "Donald Duck"), but he believed that the crime comics were particularly insidious because they had the most virulent effects. Moreover, he made it clear that he was concerned *only* with *comic books* in the study and *not* with *newspaper comic strips*, because he felt that there were fundamental differences between the two types of comics. In the first place, they had different readerships. Comic books were read mostly by children, whereas comic strips had a predominantly adult audience. In addition, the strips that appeared in the newspapers were subject to the strict censorship guidelines of the newspapers' editors and publishers. Those editors sometimes rejected undesirable detail in the strips, or even failed to print whole sequences of the strips. In contrast, no such institutional censorship existed for comic books. No outside agency examined their content for appropriateness or for good taste. Wertham pointed out that even when comic strips were reprinted as comic books they lacked the controls of censorship that existed when they were intended for adults. The publisher enjoyed complete license to print whatever he wanted. He could, and sometimes did, add a semi-pornographic story for the children, and perhaps a gory cover—things from which censorship protected the adult comic strip readers.

The overall methodology of the project consisted of qualitative content analysis of comic books and clinical case studies of children along with the use of psychological testing. Wertham examined thousands of comic books in order to determine the manner in which life, violence, sex, and different groups of people were portrayed. He felt that it was important to describe the contents of comic magazines because he believed that very few adults had any idea what kinds of material they contained. Indeed, he believed that many professionals dealing with child care knew nothing about comic books. Of course, almost everyone knew that children read those little books; they knew about the funny animal stories that children liked to read. Comic books, they assumed, were just reprints of comic strips from newspapers—"like 'Bringing Up Father,' you know"—or other such humorous sequences. Because of this ignorance, Wertham felt that it was necessary to have an adequate description of the contents of comic magazines.

Clinical Research

Because Wertham was a psychiatrist, it is not particularly surprising that case histories were employed. The project reportedly studied a large cross-section of children: This included children from well-to-do families, children from the middle class, and children from the lowest rung of the socioeconomic ladder. Yet, his sample had some unique characteristics: All of the children were seen in mental hygiene clinics. The children who were studied were referred to Wertham by all kinds of public and private child care agencies. Some of them had come to the attention of the juvenile section of the Police Bureau, or to the Children's Court; some were seen in the course of private practice. Some of the children were confined for observation in psychiatric wards for adolescents, while others were confined for physical diseases in pediatric wards or were seen in pediatric clinics. Wertham described a large proportion of these children as being "normal"—children who came to his attention for some social reason. In fact, he pointed out, the sample included some children of superior intelligence who were candidates for scholarships. The upper limit for the age of children included in the study was sixteen; Wertham, however, did not adhere to this limit rigidly. He obtained at least some data from older teenagers and from adults who provided information about their earlier comic-book-reading stage.

It was pointed out that the reasons given why these subjects were brought to the attention of physicians, psychiatrists, psychologists, or social workers usually did not include any reference to comic books. There were, however, a few cases where the reading of comic books was part of the complaint about the child. In these cases, the main complaint was referred to as the "extreme avidity" of their comic book reading. Such children took the comic books to bed with them; they walked along the street on the way to school reading them; they read them in school; and they took them on outings and on vacations. Overall, these children gave an abnormal amount of attention to the comics.

Routine psychiatric examinations were also given to all of the children. A history of the child's development was taken from his or her parents or from those with whom the child lived. As much information about each child was gathered as was possible; Wertham explained:

> Whenever possible, social workers studied the child's social environment, obtained school reports, interviewed teachers, and relayed information from other agencies who had contact with the child or his family. In the same way, pertinent information was obtained from hospitals, private doctors and clergymen. In cases where the courts were involved, probation reports were added to the record or probation officers interviewed.[8]

In cases where children indicated that they belonged to gangs, an attempt was made to talk with other members of the gang. Moreover, an attempt was made to determine the recreational influences to which children were exposed: games, community centers, radio, television, books. It was in that setting and with that perspective that Wertham, with the help of his associates, attempted to ascertain the influence of comic books on children.

Psychological Testing

Several psychological tests were administered since Wertham did not believe that any one test, however valid, was sufficient to make a judgment about children. The *Rorschach*, popularly known as the "ink-blot" test, was routinely used. The test consisted of a series of ten ink-blot pictures; the subject was asked what he or she saw in them. Wertham had been one of the first psychiatrists in the United States to use the Rorschach and he had more than twenty years' experience with it. He noted, from previous research findings, that children often see forms that adults usually do not see. These forms often turned out to be, he argued, related to things that the children had seen in comic books, especially weird and horror comics (e.g., ghost forms, fantastic hands). Wertham cautioned that such forms were likely to be misinterpreted by psychologists as meaning complex-determined anxieties and phobias, whereas actually they were just reminiscences from comic-book illustrations.

The *Thematic Apperception Test* (TAT) was also regularly used. In this test, the child was shown a series of pictures depicting various scenes and then asked to tell stories about them. Sometimes, Wertham found children who were preoccupied with stories of murder and violence. He claimed that this kind of preoccupation occurred much more frequently among avid crime-comics readers than among other children.

The *Mosaic Test* was also routinely used. Here, the children had a choice of a large number of mosaic pieces of different colors and shapes. They were asked to put them on a tray and make any design they wished. Wertham indicated that the Mosaic Test was:

> . . . very useful in a diagnosis for ruling out . . . psychotic conditions, even inconspicuous or incipient ones. These tests revealed in a large series of cases that there is nothing intrinsically abnormal about those children who either became very addicted to reading crime comics or are influenced by such reading to delinquent acts. As a matter of fact, the Mosaic Test—in conjunction with clinical findings—indicated or confirmed the finding that those children who suffer from any really serious intrinsic psychopathological condition, including those with psychoses, are less influenced by comic-book reading.[9]

Intelligence tests and *aptitude tests* were also frequently used. Tests for reading ability were considered to be of crucial importance, because the effects of comic book reading on children's ability to read was a special research question. The *Association Test* was also found to be useful. Wertham believed that word associations could reveal preoccupations and fantasies which cannot be obtained on a conscious level, and certainly not by questioning. Moreover, he claimed that in cases where children were accused of serious delinquencies, the Association Test functioned as a "lie detector" test and could help reconstruct what had actually happened. For example, a ten-year-old boy was referred to Wertham because he had been accused of drowning a younger boy. Another boy had witnessed the act, but the subject denied doing it. The authorities felt, therefore, that it was one boy's word against another's. The Association Test showed a definite blocking to key words—such as drowning, water, little boy, and pushing. Wertham believed the boy to be guilty primarily on the basis of this evidence. The subject also happened to be an avid comic book reader.

Briefly, then, the three major approaches used to study the effects of comic book reading were: (1) content analyses, (2) case histories, and (3) psychological tests.

THE FINDINGS

The major findings can be best summarized by examining two topics: (1) the types and content of crime comics, and (2) the effects of crime comics.

Types and Content of Crime Comics

As indicated earlier, crime comics as a category were of particular interest to Wertham. He found a great deal of violence in this type of comic book. His argument was clear: "It is violence for violence's sake. The plot: killing. The motive: to kill. The characterization: killed." [10] Of particular concern to Wertham was the apparent increase in the popularity of such comics. For example, in 1946–47, crime comics comprised about one-tenth of the total of all comic books sold. By 1948–49, however, they had increased to one-third of the total, and by 1949–50, they made up over one-half of the industry's output. In 1954, the vast majority of all comic books published were crime comics. Wertham felt that this was an ominous trend. He also pointed out that it was necessary to distinguish between the number of comic books printed, published or sold and the number actually read. The last item, the pass-on circulation, he considered particularly important. Many comic books are traded for others after they are sold; others are resold for lower prices. Readership, therefore, may vastly exceed sales. Wertham found that *every imaginable* kind of crime was described *in detail* in the comic books. "If one were to set out to show children how to steal, rob, lie, cheat, assault, and break into houses, no better method could be devised." [11] Furthermore, besides presenting the details of how to commit crimes, he found that the comics also instructed the children how to conceal evidence and how to evade detection. For example, some comic books gave instructions about how to commit robberies. While a child might not attempt a robbery, it is easy and natural, he argued, to translate this crime into a minor key—stealing from a department store instead of breaking into a bank. Other comic books were found to illustrate how a youngster might murder for profit. One book gave a price list for harming people (1954 prices)!

Eyes blackened	$ 4.00
Arm or leg broken	10.00
Whole job	100.00 and up

Other comic books described how to set fires by methods too numerous to enumerate. Some described car thefts in very complete detail. And, of course, all kinds of thefts were described. One frequent depiction was how to steal a woman's pocketbook. According to the stories it could be done skillfully and peacefully—but if that did not work, "just hit them over the head." In addition, numerous "minor" incidents were discussed; skipping school was often described as the "smart" thing to do.

It was also discovered that the comic books often described real crimes that had previously been featured in the newspapers. However, they added many juicy details. In adapting the news story to comic books, the following points were found to be stressed: the daring and success of the criminals; brutal acts shown in detail; sordid details emphasized; and, sexual episodes, if present, featured. An example of this type of story adaptation occurred in 1952. A major newspaper story appeared about three men who escaped from a penitentiary. The story was used by a popular crime comic with descriptive details added. The men stole cars, evaded police, kidnapped people, held up a bank, and were finally caught in New York, where they had been living with three women. In the comic book, the prison break was described as a heroic feat. It was also shown to be easy to steal cars. One of the criminals boasted to a little boy that he had killed 15 or 16 people, "I lost count." Moreover, pictures of half-nude women were featured. There were in this comic book, overall, 76 pictures of exploits by the criminals; in the 77th picture, the police take over with a cheap wisecrack. In other words, crime, violence, and sex were glamorized until the last picture. In that last picture, the action was dull. To Wertham, this finding was typical of all the crime comics he examined. Clearly, crime *does pay*—until the last picture or two.

These crime comics came in many forms; cops-and-robbers dramas were only one type. The vast majority of "westerns," for example, were found to fit into this category. They often described all kinds of crime in vivid detail. One popular western showed a close-up of a dying man with blood streaming from his mouth. The general philosophy expressed by this type of comic was "Since when do we worry about killin' people."

Jungle, horror, and interplanetary comics were a special category of crime comics. Wertham described jungle comics in the following manner:

> Jungle comics specialize in torture, bloodshed and lust in an exotic setting. Daggers, claws, guns, wild animals, well or over-developed girls in brassieres and as little else as possible, dark skinned "natives"; fires, stakes, posts, chains, ropes, big-chested and heavily muscled Nordic he-men dominate the stage. They contain such details as white men banging natives around; a close-up view of the branded breast of a girl; a girl about to be blinded.[12]

While the white people in the jungle books were blonde, athletic, and shapely, the natives were depicted as somewhere between apes and human beings. The dark-skinned people, in short, were characterized as subhuman, while the white people were portrayed as heroes. In addition, amidst all the violence among the slaves, apes, and human beings, the books included big pictures of lush girls, "as nude as the Post Office permitted." The impression of sex plus violence was definite, even to an adult. In the jungle books, the jungle was not a place but a state of mind. And this state of mind was easily transposed to other locales. For example, it was present in outer space in the interplanetary and science-fiction comics. Women were similarly dressed and roughly treated. The torture, however, was more refined. If someone's eye was to be blinded, it was done with some advanced scientific equipment rather than by simply gouging it out.

The "Superman-Batman-Wonder Woman" comics were another variety of crime comics. In this form, a distinction was usually drawn between super-people and sub-people. The latter were usually foreigners. Prejudice against foreigners was a recurrent theme, as the following example demonstrates. A scientist was shown addressing a meeting:

Scientist:	So, my fellow Americans, it is time to give America back to Americans. Don't let foreigners take your jobs!
Member of Audience:	He's right!
Another Applauds:	YEAHHH!

To Wertham, the most dangerous aspect of the superman type of comic book was that these books "present our world in a kind of fascist setting of violence and hate and destruction." [13] They placed too much emphasis on a fascist society and overlooked democratic ideals. In addition to the supermen and superwomen comics, there were superanimal magazines such as "Super Duck." There were also superchildren such as "Superboy." Superboy could slice a tree like a cake, melt glass by looking at it, defeat powerful enemies, and even rewrite American history. For example, in one story he saved the life of George Washington and was even responsible for getting him elected President. Washington was also shown to be crossing the Delaware River with Superboy guiding the boat through the ice floes. It was really Superboy who crossed the Delaware, Washington was simply in the boat!

The love/confession was another type of crime comic. Representative titles included "Intimate Love," "My Desire," "My Love Life," and "Love Scandals." They were merely crime stories with a seasoning of love added. In one of these love comics, a demonstration was given of how to steal a "very expensive gown, Paris original" from a department store.

> "I'll slip it on in the dressing room. They won't notice me!" "I'll put it in that box and walk out, while the saleslady is busy with someone else . . . I walked out, trying to keep calm, trying to look and act natural . . . Nobody has seen me! Ohh! If I can only reach the door!"

The love-confession comics were often very sexy, specializing in highly accented and protruding breasts. They were better known among adolescent boys as "headlight comics." One story, "I was a Spoiled Brat," began with a big picture of an attractive girl looking at herself in the mirror and baring herself considerably. A dash of violence was supplied by hit-and-run driving and by her father's death from a heart attack when he heard about his daughter's wild life. Overall the love comics were found to portray a false picture of love and life.

In summary, the main types of crime comics were: (1) cops-and-robbers comics, (2) jungle comics, (3) supermen comics, and (4) love-confession comics. All of these mixed violence with sex to varying degrees and often added a little sadism as well.

The Effects of Crime Comics

The major concern of this research was the effect that crime comic books had on children. It was discovered, for example, that the "average child" spent two or three hours a day reading comic books. Some, of course, spent much more time involved in such activity. "How," Wertham asked, "can you get a total picture of the child when you leave out entirely what occupies him two or three hours a day?" Ultimately, he felt, reading comics was a "social problem" because the effects of such reading would have repercussions for all of society. Overall, three major effects were attributed to reading comic books in the Wertham study: (1) Comic books contributed to the increase in juvenile delinquency; (2) They presented children with a distorted and dangerous view of life; and (3) They contributed to reading problems. Each effect will be discussed in turn.

Design for Delinquency   While crime comics were certainly not the only cause of delinquency, Wertham believed them to be a major one in many cases, particularly cases involving serious delinquencies. Up to the beginning of the comic book era, he reasoned, there were hardly any serious crimes, such as murder, committed by children under twelve years of age. Yet, in the 1950s he saw younger and younger children committing more and more serious and violent crimes. Indeed, in 1953, *The New York Times* commented in an editorial, "It is difficult to think of children as burglars, gangsters, drug addicts, or murderers. Such has become the reality, however." [14]

The modern and more serious forms of delinquency involved knowledge of technique. As previously illustrated, the crime comics certainly provided this knowledge. Moreover, by showing the techniques, the comic books also suggested the context. The moral lesson provided was that "innocence doesn't pay." Indeed, many delinquents claimed that they had gotten their criminal ideas from the comics as illustrated in the following quotes:

> I got my bad ideas from the comics; stabbing, robbing, stealing guns and all that stuff. In a comic book I read two kids rob a store and steal guns and get away and grow up to be bank robbers. So I did the same thing—only I didn't grow up to be a bank robber—yet!

> I read about a perfect robbery and used parts of it. This was in a crime comic magazine and it said these three men were still at large and didn't get caught, so I figured I could pull the same stuff.

Throughout Wertham's book, there are repeated instances where children imitated violent acts found in crime comics. The following examples illustrate Wertham's claim that "there is a significant correlation between crime comics reading and the more serious forms of juvenile delinquency."

Three boys, six to eight years old, took a boy of seven, hanged him nude from a tree, his hands tied behind him; then they burned him with matches. Probation officers who investigated found that they were reenacting a comic book plot.

A boy of eleven killed a woman in a holdup. When arrested, he was found surrounded by comic books. His twenty-one-year-old brother said: "If you want the cause of all this, here it is: It's these rotten comic books. Cut them out and things like this wouldn't happen."

A boy of twelve and his eight-year-old sister tried to kill a boy of six. They knocked teeth out, stabbed through his hands with a pocket knife, choked him, kicked him, and jumped on him. Both brother and sister were avid comic book readers.

A ten-year-old boy hit a fourteen-month-old baby over the head with a brick, washed the blood off the brick and then threw the baby into the river. He claimed to have gotten the idea from comic books.

When a well-to-do surgeon received an extortion note demanding $50,000 and threatening harm to his young daughter, experts deduced that the note was the work of an "adult male psychopath under emotional strain." As it turned out, it was a fourteen-year-old girl reenacting a comic book plot.

All of these examples are obviously extreme cases. Wertham pointed out that many children who read comic books do not become delinquent; nevertheless, they have been adversely affected by them. When a constant barrage of crime and violence is leveled at young children, he argued, it leads them inevitably to preoccupation with these subjects and subsequently to psychological maladjustment. For example, one frequent theme running throughout many crime comics was that of hanging. So it was not surprising to Wertham that he found many cases of children hanging themselves. Often found beneath the child was an open comic book luridly describing and depicting a hanging. Wertham felt that such cases basically involved the processes of imitation and experimentation in childhood. Even "normal" children imitate, but children who see hanging scenes frequently are more likely to become preoccupied with such behavior. They are thus more likely to "try it out."

In general, Wertham concluded that crime comics were a major factor in delinquency causation, albeit not usually the only factor. Moreover, crime comics often led to psychological maladjustments and preoccupation with crime and violence.

Distorted Perception of Reality   Wertham argued that crime comics altered children's perceptions of reality. A daily dosage of crime, violence and cruelty would often convince the child that this was what the world was really like. Quite often, this view of the world was reinforced in the comic-book reader by the placement of an insert below the book's title. It read: "Every word is true." On the cover of one book bearing this inscription was the picture of a car speeding away. Two men were tied by their feet to the rear bumper and lay face down. One of the men's hands was tied behind his back and the lower part of his face was dragging on the road. The other man's hands were not tied, but his arms were stretched out. The text, enclosed in balloons, indicated that the men in the car were talking.

"A couple more miles oughta do th' trick!"

"It better! These #-**@# GRAVEL ROADS are tough on tires!" "But ya gotta admit, there's nothing like'em for ERASING FACES!" [15]

Next to these balloons is a huge leering face, eyes wide, gloating, and a mouth showing upper and lower teeth in a big grin.

"Superb! Even Big Phil will admire this job—if he lives long enough to identify the MEAT!"

Every word true? That was the claim made on the cover! Not surprisingly, this sort of crime adventure was found to affect children's views about punishment. The reply was frequently that it served the criminal right, whatever the punishment. "He got caught, didn't he?" That was the real crime for these children. The children did not have faith in society's notions of justice. To them, law enforcement officials were no different from the criminals. Whichever side was the strongest, had the most men, would win. "In many subtle and not so subtle forms, the lynch spirit was taught as the moral lesson." [16]

Many children thought that lynching was acceptable behavior and pointed to examples from comic books. In one story, the townspeople get together, hanged the criminal, and finally shot and killed him. The lesson is in the last sentence: "The story of Lee Gillon proves that fearless people banded together will always see that justice triumphs."

It was the superman type of comic book in which the theme of taking punishment, or rather revenge, into one's own hands was most insidiously pursued. This superman ideology ran throughout the stories and can best be summarized as: "the stronger dominates the smaller and weaker." [17] Children often developed what Wertham referred to as the "superman conceit" from reading this type of material. The superman conceit gave children the feeling that ruthless go-getting, based upon physical strength or the power of weapons or machines was the desirable way to behave. Such children expressed a wish for overwhelming physical strength, domination, power, ruthlessness, and emancipation from the morals of the community. As an example of this, Wertham pointed to the "superman-speed-fantasy" in girls. One teenage girl told him that she would go out only with boys who would not let other cars pass them on the road. This was her idea of proper male behavior. Moreover, this girl, along with many others, got this idea from the comics. Wertham believed that children had been poisoned by this "endless repetition" of superman stories. Such stories, he felt, undermined the authority and dignity of ordinary men and women who tried to teach their children community morals and rules of conduct.

Crime comics were also found to interfere with the development of the superego, or conscience, in children. The development of the conscience takes place, Wertham argued, not only on the basis of identification with parents but also with successive parent substitutes. Both the parents and the substitutes represent group demands and are symbols of group responsibilities. "In this sphere, comic books are most pernicious. They expose children's minds to an endless stream of prejudice-producing images." Wertham continues:

> If I were to make the briefest summary of what children have told us about how different people are represented to them in the lore of crime comics, it would be that there are two kinds of people: on the one hand is a tall, blonde, regular-featured man sometimes disguised as a superman (or superman disguised as a man) and the pretty young blonde with the super-breast. On the other hand are the inferior people: natives, primitives, savages, "ape men," Negroes, Jews, Indians, Italians, Slavs, Chinese, and Japanese. Immigrants of every description, people with irregular features, swarthy skins, physical deformities, Oriental features. In some crime comics the first class sometimes wears some kind of superman uniform, while the second class is in mufti. The brunt of this imputed inferiority in whole groups of people is directed against colored people and "foreign born." [18]

Wertham found that children as young as four years old could acquire prejudice from comic books and that six- or seven-year-olds were quite articulate about expressing their contempt for minority groups. Obviously, many of these distorted stereotypes were acquired at home, or in the street. However, they were reinforced by comic book reading. Wertham explained that when a child was shown a comic book that he or she had not read and was asked to "pick out the bad man," the child unhesitatingly picked out bad types according to the stereotyped conception of racial and ethnic prejudice.

Another prejudice-producing situation found in many of the comic books involved the depiction of dark-skinned people in rape-like situations with white women. One picture, which showed a woman nailed by her wrists to trees, with blood flowing from the wounds, could easily have been taken directly from the pages of an illustrated edition of the life of the Marquis de Sade. In another comic, this type of editorial viciousness was carried to the extreme by portraying a white woman being overpowered by dark-skinned people who had tails. Another book showed the hero throwing bombs at a black-skinned individual from his airplane. The hero yelled: "BOMBS AND BUMS AWAY!"

The comic books, moreover, often made a distinction between white and nonwhite females. Pictures of white women with completely bared breasts were taboo while such pictures of dark-skinned women were permitted. Indeed, only brown or black-skinned females had their breasts fully exposed. Wertham thought that this was one of the most sinister methods of suggesting that races are fundamentally different in regard to moral values, and that one is inferior to the other. This, he argued, is where a psychiatric question becomes a social one.[19]

False stereotypes of race prejudice were also found to exist in the "love comics." Children were usually able to pick out unsatisfactory lovers just by their looks. War comics, where war is the setting, also promoted race hatred. For example, Americans were always shown to be good looking with regular features, while people of Asia were depicted as cruel, grimacing, and toothy creatures, often with an unnatural yellow color.

These comics tended to engender two overall attitudes in children: *Either* they viewed themselves as some sort of supermen or superior human being, with the attendant prejudices against those who were subhuman (i.e., members of minority groups), *or* they viewed themselves as really being "submen" and thus were receptive to the blandishments of "strong men," men who would solve all of their social problems for them by the use of force.

Another area where reality was distorted and unhealthy stereotypes were promoted was the depiction of women. Wertham found that women were usually portrayed in one of two ways: *Either* they were scantily dressed *superwomen* flying through the air and outsmarting hostile natives and wicked men, *or* they were *possessions of men*, with no value other than to be sexually used, pushed around, and sadistically abused. Indeed, he claimed, in no other literature for children was the image of womanhood so degraded. Where else, for example, in children's literature besides the comics, would one find a woman called (and treated as) a "fat slut"? In addition, the activities which women shared with men were exclusively related to sex, force, and violence.

The superwoman comics were found to be very popular among delinquent and maladjusted girls. "Wonder Woman," for example, was a horror type. She was physically very powerful, tortured men, and had her own female following. Overall, she was a very frightening figure—and she was created by a child psychologist who argued that it was necessary to create a female character who was alluring and at the same time had the strength of Superman, because "Who wants to be a girl?" To Wertham that was just the point. Not even girls wanted to be girls when they were portrayed as second class citizens.

Not only did the children receive a false concept of womanhood from reading comic books, they also received a false concept of "love." They associated love with brutality, murder, and robbery. For example, one teenage boy discussed the comic book, "Crimes by Women," with Wertham.

> There is one that is sexy! Her headlights are showing *plenty!* She has a smoking gun in her hand as though she had already shot somebody. When you see a girl and you see her headlights and she is beaten up, that makes you hot and bothered. If she will take a beating from a man she will take anything from him.

Another boy, described as a twelve-year-old sex delinquent also discussed his comic book reading with Wertham.

> In the comic book sometimes the men threaten the girls. They beat them with their hands. They tie them around to a chair and then they beat them. When I read such a book I don't get sexually excited all the time, only when they tie them up.

The keynote of the comic books' sexual message was the mixture of sensuality with cruelty. And children were given this message from a tender age. This cultivated, to Wertham, a special kind of perversion, *sadism.* Sadism was defined as "the gratification of sexual feeling by the infliction of or sight of pain." Very young children were especially likely to become confused by a sadistic interpretation of sex, as illustrated in the following example.

> Ronnie, a six-year-old comic book addict attending the clinic, often played with a boy a year or so older who lived downstairs in the same house. One day this playmate took a little girl into his room and proceeded to take off the girl's clothes. Ronnie watched a bit, then ran upstairs excitedly, told his mother all about what he had seen and asked her, "What's he going to do—choke her?" [20]

Graphic descriptions of sexual flagellation of the buttocks were also found in many of the comic books. This sort of illustration, Wertham pointed out, was frowned upon by the Post Office if it occurred in adult books. However, in many children's comic books such erotic scenes were described in detail. Indeed, beatings and brutality were common fare in many comic books. For example, one "typical" book showed the villain (a foreigner) with a half-nude girl in his power. As an appetizer, she is hit in the face. Then she is told:

> I know that you shall love me and shall be loyal after you have taken a dozen or so lashes across your beautiful back.

She is then taken to the cellar, bound by the wrists to a tall post, her breasts conspicuously drawn, where she pleads for mercy. The man stands behind her with a coiled whip in his hand. . . .

Some comic books were found to describe sexual sadism with its morbid psychological refinements. One book, for example, showed a villain making love to a married woman. Her husband, whose leg had been injured by the lover, had to look on helplessly. The villain kisses and fondles the woman, all the while taunting the husband. The result is that the woman becomes sexually excited by this perverse situation. Wertham asked: What kind of message does this story communicate to children?

The drawing of blood from a woman's veins in order to completely overpower her was another morbid fantasy often found in the comic books. According to Wertham, such fully described and depicted perversity was to be found only in one place besides these children's comic books—in the forbidden pages of de Sade himself.

"High heel" literature appeared frequently in the children's comics. This type of literature dealt with the erotic character that high heels have for certain males; often such material appears in pornographic or semi-pornographic literature for adults. It is well known that some men have a fetish for high-heeled shoes; they collect them for erotic pleasure. Such fetishes, however, are often learned during childhood and adolescence; Wertham argued that one source for such learning was the ordinary comic book. Indeed, exaggeratedly high heels were often portrayed in comic books. This type of picture, showing only legs and extremely high heels, was a repeated motif in many different kinds of comic books. Several boys told Wertham that they collected this type of comic illustration and used them to fantasize and for masturbation. One nineteen-year-old described his high-heel fantasy in the following manner:

> I think of girls twisting their heels on my chest and face. My first complete sexual stimulation came from such comic book scenes at the age of about ten or eleven.

Overall, Wertham concluded, the only difference between surreptitious pornographic literature intended for adults and children's comic books was that in the first it was a question of *attracting* perverts, in the other it was a process of *making* perverts. Moreover, all types of crime comics portrayed a link among love, sex, violence, and brutality.

Many of the "love" comics were written to appeal to females. Like other types of crime comics, they played up the angle that what was depicted was real life. "These girls are real people with real problems and real dramatic confessions," states a typical issue. What is it, then, that these real girls wanted? Again the message is clear. "More than anything in the world I wanted glamor, money, adventure. . . ." What were the typical problems these "real" girls faced? the titles of their stories give the answer.

FALLEN WOMAN
RUNAWAY PASSION
PRICE OF PRIDE
FORBIDDEN LOVE
MY FOOLISH MISTAKE
MUST I REVEAL MY PAST?

Wertham believed that crime comics, especially the love-confession variety, played a role in laying the groundwork for childhood prostitution, which he reported to be on the increase. He used the following example to support this argument.

Annie, aged ten, engaged in sex play with men for which she received money. Like most children she was very suggestible. From comic books she absorbed fantasies of violence and sex. . . .

I fooled around with men, young men and old men. They gave me a dollar. I don't have my period yet. They just took down my pants. I meet the men on the docks. They did it in a shady house, a house that has all kinds of tools in it —hammers. I went over there four times a week. I don't like it. Girls don't like it. I did it for the money. Sometimes I would get half a dollar, sometimes a quarter. Some men don't give you anything. Cheap, ain't they!

This girl read about twenty comic books a day. She read some of them three and four times over.

In his investigations, Wertham found that there were a number of obscure stores where children would congregate, usually in back rooms, to read and buy secondhand comic books. As a rule, the proprietors allowed the children to spend a lot of time in their establishments and to pore over the comic books. In parts of some cities, men "hung around" these stores, which sometimes were the foci of childhood prostitution. Evidently, he argued, the books prepared the little girls quite well for prostitution. In addition, they also apparently prepared little boys for childhood homosexual prostitution. For example, Charles, a twelve-year-old, regularly engaged in prostitution. He did not play hooky, but followed the occupation after school hours. He reported:

> I meet the men in office places or places of business. They give me a dollar or fifty cents. I wondered how they'd be so generous. Some men are about thirty-five.

Wertham attributed Charles' behavior to moral confusion, which he believed was caused by the child's avid reading of crime comics such as "Gangbusters" and "True Comics."

The comic books also allegedly contributed to homosexuality in other ways. For example, many pre-adolescent boys pass through a psychological phase of disdainment toward girls. To Wertham, some comic books tended to fixate that attitude and to instill the idea that "girls are good only for being banged around or used as decoys." He felt that homoerotic attitudes were promoted by presenting women in an anti-erotic light. Women were shown as masculine, bad, violent, and witch-like. At the same time, the young male heroes were often presented with pronounced erotic overtones. Wertham pointed out that many adolescents experience vague fears that they might be homosexual but that they often have no one in whom they feel they can confide. He reported finding the following sequence of events in a number of cases. A boy becomes addicted to homoerotic comic books at an early age. Both during and after reading these comics, the boy indulged in fantasies, which were severely repressed. Subsequent life experiences regarding homosexuality produced feelings of doubt, shame, guilt and eventual sexual malorientation.

Some years earlier, around 1950, a California psychiatrist had argued that the Batman and Robin stories were psychologically homosexual. Wertham's research confirmed this finding and he argued:

> Only someone ignorant of the fundamentals of psychiatry and of the psychopathology of sex can fail to realize a subtle atmosphere of homoerotism which pervades the adventures of the mature "Batman" and his young friend "Robin."[21]

In comic books of the Batman type, homosexual relationships were depicted to children before they could even read. The mature "Batman" and the young "Robin" shared adventure after adventure. They constantly rescued each other from violent attacks by an unending variety of enemies. The feeling was conveyed that the men must stick together because there were so many villainous creatures who must be exterminated. At home, they led an idyllic life as Bruce Wayne and "Dick" Grayson. They lived in a beautiful home, with gorgeous flowers in large vases, and a butler—Alfred. Often, they were shown in a romantic setting, such as sitting together on a couch in front of the fireplace. Robin (Dick) was a handsome boy with tremendous energy and he was devoted to Bruce Wayne (Batman). He often stood with his legs spread, the genital region discreetly evident.

It was also significant that in the Batman–Robin stories there were almost no decent, attractive, successful women. A typical female character was "Catwoman," who was vicious and used a whip. The atmosphere was homosexual and anti-feminine. If a girl was good-looking she was undoubtedly the villainess. If she was after Bruce Wayne, she would have no chance against Dick.

In his research, Wertham found that a number of treated homosexuals avidly read Batman stories. One young homosexual stated that he began reading the Batman and Robin stories at the age of eight. He gave the following account:

> At the age of ten or eleven, I found my sexual liking, my sexual desires, in comic books. I think I put myself in the position of Robin. I did want to have relations with Batman. . . . I remember the first time I came across the page mentioning the "secret bat cave." The thought of Batman and Robin living together and possibly having sex relations came to my mind. You can almost connect yourself with the people. . . . I felt I'd like to be loved by someone like Batman or Superman.

Another young homosexual was being treated by Wertham for more than his homosexuality. He and a companion had used a knife to force an eight-year-old boy to undress and have sex with them. Like many other homo-erotically inclined children, he was a special devotee of Batman.

> Sometimes I read them [Batman comics] over and over again. They show off a lot. They live together. It could be that Batman did something with Robin like I did with the younger boy.

However, homosexuality was not only suggested to the male readers of Batman-type comics. The Lesbian counterpart of Batman was found in the stories of "Wonder Woman" and "Black Cat." Whereas Batman was anti-feminine, the attractive Wonder Woman and her counterparts were defi-

MILESTONES IN MASS COMMUNICATION RESEARCH

nitely antimasculine. Like Batman, Wonder Woman had her own following—young girls who were constantly threatened. The stories included mutual rescues and fantasies. Her followers were the "Holiday Girls"; Wertham saw the holiday girls as the gay party girls, or more simply, the gay girls. In one typical story, one character involved in an adventure with Wonder Woman repeatedly referred to "those wicked men." It was clear that the "Wonder Woman" stories were amazingly similar to the Batman ones, except that where Batman was antifeminine Wonder Woman was antimasculine.

In summary, Wertham found that the various types of crime comics influenced children's perceptions of reality in many ways—including the following:

1. They led children to believe that violence is a normal and common-place aspect of everyday life.
2. They instilled in the children prejudice toward minority groups.
3. They portrayed women as either evil or as second-class citizens.
4. They gave children sexually deviant ideas which sometimes resulted in deviant sexual practices, or guilt about such fantasies.

Retooling for Illiteracy   Reading difficulties among children were reported to be increasing. Wertham argued that comic books were an important cause of this increase. He found that a very large proportion of children who could not read well habitually "read" comic books. Moreover, a very high percentage of the worst readers were comic book addicts who spent a great deal of time "reading" comic books. Actually, they were not readers but gazers. That is, they looked at the pictures and managed to pick up a word here and there. They were, in fact, bookworms without books.

The comic books were found to have a negative influence on reading in a number of ways. First, comic book readers were handicapped in vocabulary building because the emphasis in the comics was on the visual image and not on the written word. Children often knew all that they should not know about torture, but were unable to read or spell the word. One detrimental effect comics have is that they hinder the development of fluent left-to-right eye movement necessary for good reading. Reading scattered messages in balloons does not allow for sufficient practice in mastering the skills required for consistent good reading. Moreoever, the spelling in the comic books was often incorrect. "The Case of the Psycopathic (sic) Lady" was not good for children in either content or spelling. The style and language of the comic books' writing was also extremely poor. Editorial comments were hardly better than the text. Consider the example of "cosmic correspondence":

> Greetings, humanoids! Drag over a cyclotron and crawl in! (If we'da known you were coming, we'da baked an isotope!)

Furthermore, the comics had many words that are not words at all. For example, there may be a series of six pictures with violent scenes and no language, just sounds which have no correct spelling. Some of the most common "words" found in the comics were:

OWW	THUNK
ARGHH	YEOW
OOOHHH	UNGH
GLURG	AANGH
UGH	ARRGG
GLHELP	GLUG-UGH

Some of the children called these words "basic American."

The comic books also influenced the creative abilities of the children. Whereas good reading stimulated them to imaginative writing, the comic book influence directed their natural gifts to a cheap whip-the-girl, beat-the-dark-skinned-native mentality.

Overall, Wertham argued that his research offered conclusive proof that comic book reading and reading difficulties went hand-in-hand and that comic books were a causal and reinforcing factor in children's reading disorders. Since reading difficulties were obviously related to failure in school, Wertham also noted the relationship between failure in school and delinquent behavior. (Indeed, even in the 1980s, failure in school remains the *single* best predictor of juvenile delinquency.)

Advertising in Comic Books: Bumps and Bulges

The types of advertisements present in comic books in addition to their actual and potential effects on children were also examined. Wertham argued that it is typical for teenagers and preteens to be very conscious and concerned with their appearance. Comic book advertisements, he claimed, exploited these worries and anxieties with scare tactics that caused many normal boys and girls much grief. Many of the most pernicious ads fell into one of the following categories: "breast ads," "fat ads," "skinny ads," "skin condition ads," "he-man ads," and "weapons ads." Each will be discussed and illustrative examples provided.

Breast Advertisements It is, of course, not unusual for girls to be sensitive about their breasts before and during adolescence. Comic book reading itself could promote this fear through the portrayals of characters with shapely, protruding breasts. The breast advertisements, however, were found to create "sexual hypochondriasis" by promising help for "problem bosoms," "NO MATTER WHAT SHAPE BOSOM YOU HAVE." For example, a typical full-page advertisement addressed to young girls in a popular comic book had photographs of two girls. One girl had average breasts, while the other had markedly protruding comic-book-style breasts. The caption read: DO MEN CHOOSE MARY OR ALICE?

> When Tom H _____ met Mary W_____ and Alice B _____, folks wondered who the lucky girl would be. Both girls were pretty and charming and grand fun, and enjoyed the same interests Tom did. But somehow it was Alice whose lips Tom bent to in the moonlight. . . . it was Alice whose "I do" rose breathlessly at the altar. . . .
>
> Tom's choice was not surprising. For it is the woman with a beautiful, alluring bust contour who most often wins the admiration, popularity and affection every woman desires. And there can be no COMPLETE feminine beauty without a warmly rounded, lovely bust contour, symbol of woman eternal. Look through history. Look around you today. It is the woman with the graceful, appealing figure lines who enjoys social and romantic triumph. Yes, there are many lovely Marys whose wit, charm and friendliness cannot compete with the natural law of man's attraction to beauty fulfilled *completely*.
>
> The _____ Ritual _____ may be able to improve the handicap of unappealing figure lines . . . which may mean the difference between loneliness and thrilling romantic fulfillment! Formerly $2.00. . . . Don't let skepticism or discouragement deny you the opportunity for happiness. . . . Be fair to yourself, to your future as a *woman*.

It was common for this type of advertisement to display "Before" and "After" photographs. The "Before" looked like an average girl; the "After" had noticeably pointed, protruding breasts. Many of these advertisements were directed to growing girls whose busts were just starting to develop and led off with screamers such as "SMALL BUST." Wertham believed that such advertisements caused feelings of inferiority in many young girls and that some carried this emotional burden with them throughout their lives. He cited many clinical cases to support his conclusions.

Weight Advertisements Depending upon their type of body build, many adolescents pass through phases of growth when they are likely to be either too "chubby" or too "skinny." Comic book advertisements played

on this type of fear—all for the sake of increasing their profits. Some typical
"fat" captions included the following:

> Don't suffer humiliation and ridicule by Being FAT!
> You have nothing to lose but Weight!
> RESTORE the RIGHT CURVES in the Right Places!
> How an Unhappy Fat Girl Became a Happy Slim Girl!

Of course, those adolescent girls who pass through a slender growth phase
are not forgotten.

> Skinny Girls are NOT glamor Girls!
> Ashamed of your skinny, scrawny figure?
> SKINNY GIRLS DON'T HAVE OOMPH!

The boys were not ignored in the weight ads, although the slant was toward
body-building.

> Hey SKINNY! Yer ribs are Showing!

Another full-page advertisement illustrated with photos of muscular men
declared:

> From a SKINNY WEAKLING to a MIGHTY MAN. . . .

> I Gained 53 lbs. of MIGHTY MUSCLE. 6½ inches on my CHEST; 3 inches
> on each ARM. You can do it in 10 minutes a day!

Other advertisements tended to make boys feel ashamed of their bodies.

> How to make your Body Bring you FAME instead of SHAME! Are you
> Skinny? Weak? Flabby? . . . I know what it means to have the kind of body
> that people pity! . . . I don't care how old or young you are or how ashamed
> of your present physical condition . . . I can shoot new strength into your old
> backbone . . . help you cram your body so full of pep, vigor and vitality, that
> you won't feel there's even standing room left for weakness and that lazy
> feeling!

Skin Advertisements   Another prime target for scare advertisements
was skin condition. It was, of course, also not unusual for acne, pimples
and blackheads to trouble teenagers and for them to be a major source of
concern. Wertham argued that the comic book ads aggravated this concern
and intensified feelings of anxiety and inferiority. They could make boys

and girls self-conscious about even the slightest blemish; more importantly, the ads promised an instant, miraculous cure.

One full-page advertisement began with this dialogue:

Ask your friend Tom.

Tom, why don't Sis and I get invited to proms and parties?

Frankly, Jim, it's those ugly blackheads.

Then follows the indoctrination with its attendant fear and shame:

What a "black mark" is the blackhead . . . according to men and girls popular enough to be choosy about dates! "Nobody's dreamboat!" "Nobody's date bait!" And that's not all that's said about those who are careless about blackheads. But blackheads ARE ugly! Blackheads ARE grimy! And they DON'T look good in close-ups.

So can you blame the fellow who says, "Sure I meet lots of girls who look cute at first glance. But if, on the second glance I see dingy black—it's *good night!*"

Or can you blame the girl who confesses, "I hate to go out with a fellow who has blackheads, if he's careless about that you're sure he'll embarrass you in other ways, too!

But you—are YOUR ears burning? Well, you've company, and, sad to say, good company. There are lots of otherwise attractive fellows and girls who could date anyone they like if they'd only realize how offensive blackheads are and how easily and quickly they could get rid of them, if they *want* to! . . . The "he-man" who is also clean-cut, will get the breaks wherever he is! . . . Even cute girls get careless . . . so don't take chances, cute though you may be!

Wertham found that some children became so excessively stressed by acne and the repeated failure of comic-book cures that they withdrew socially, to the extent that they were diagnosed as schizophrenic.

Weapons Advertisements Weapons of all kinds were attractively advertised, particularly guns and knives. While some were real (e.g., a .22 caliber rifle) the majority were toys. A typical advertisement contains a big picture of a gun:

Amazing New Gun! Shoots like a real gun.

An accompanying sequence teaches how the gun could be used to threaten people:

You fooled us, kid, I thought that gun was a real one!

Knives of different types were also advertised in the comic books in a glamorous fashion.

FLINGS OPEN FAST. BIG SIZE!
ONLY $1.65

Whittle your enemies down to size.

Peeping Toms and Human Relations   Wertham also discussed a variety of other advertisements, including those for telescopes and "human relations ads." He was particularly concerned with the telescope ads because he had treated a number of youths after they had been arrested as "peeping Toms." Most of them had looked in windows trying to see women undressing. Many of the boys claimed to have gotten the idea from "peeping Tom ads" in the comics. One telescope ad, for example, offered:

Real power and up-close clear view! A 1000 thrills are yours with this powerful imported telescope. Enjoy Life! . . . Bring some scenes so close you feel you can touch them!

Another advertisement for binoculars made the following claim:

You'll get the thrill of a lifetime when you take your first look through these powerful binoculars. It's positively amazing how well you can see . . . You'll be able to see people . . . from a distance and watch what they're doing when they can't see you. Enjoy front row seats from way back!

Other ads explicitly point out that you could even look into "neighbor's" homes.

"Human relations" ads included courses for boys on how to get along with girls.

It's easy to win her! Women are funny—put psychology to work. No more clumsy mistakes for *you* . . . Don't be a Faux Pas! [sic]

Of course there were also courses for girls on how to handle boys.

Wertham concluded that the comic book stories and the advertisements they contained complemented each other. He argued:

Comic book stories teach violence, the advertisements provide the weapons. The stories instill a wish to be a superman, the advertisements promise to supply the means for becoming one. Comic-book heroines have super-figures; the comic-book advertisements promise to develop them. The stories display the wounds, the advertisements supply the knives. The stories feature scantily clad girls; the advertisements outfit peeping toms.[22]

In summary, Wertham concluded that comic books had the following effects:[23]

1. The comic book format is an invitation to illiteracy.
2. Crime comic books create an atmosphere of cruelty and deceit.
3. They create a readiness for temptation.
4. They stimulate unwholesome fantasies.
5. They suggest criminal or sexually abnormal ideas.
6. They furnish the rationalization for these ideas which may be ethically even more harmful than the impulse.
7. They suggest the forms delinquency may take and supply the details of technique.
8. They may tip the scales toward maladjustment or delinquency.
9. Overall, crime comics are an agent with harmful potential. They bring about a mass conditioning of children, with different effects in individual cases.

Wertham further cautioned that even children who did not read comic books could have been influenced by them indirectly through contact with children who were comic book readers (the two-step flow of communication concept). He argued:

Frequently the influence of comic books is not exerted directly, but comes through other children. The influence of children on children is generally underestimated. Parents have sometimes told me that what I have said about comic books may be true, but that doesn't affect *their* children because they do not read such trash. One of my answers to this is generally, "Don't you think your child will later on, either in school or other places, meet other children who have been steeped in comics and have absorbed their attitudes concerning sex, violence, women, money, races and other subjects that make up social life?"[24]

CONCLUSIONS AND IMPLICATIONS

If nothing more, *Seduction of the Innocent* is an important work because of the attention and controversy its claims brought to the comic book industry. Indeed, that attention nearly destroyed the industry! Before we discuss the social significance of this milestone, however, we shall briefly examine its theoretical and methodological importance.

Wertham's research was theoretically inconsistent. At times he clearly specified a theory of selective influence, based upon individual differences. This was evident in his statements that comic books did not affect all children in the same way. Despite this disclaimer, his *real* message came through that comic books did have relatively uniform effects. Children were helpless victims who could not resist the comic books' messages. This was clearly a version of the old magic bullet theory. Indeed, reduced to its simplest terms, Wertham's argument was that (1) comic books were read by a large number of children; (2) since a large component of the comic diet consisted of crime, violence, horror, and sex, (3) children who read the comics were necessarily stimulated to the performance of delinquent acts, cruelty, violence, and undesirable sexual behavior. At the same time Wertham told us that comic books *did* uniformly affect all children, and that they *did not* uniformly affect all children. It appears that he believed the first but felt that it was necessary to acknowledge the second to appear "scientific."

In some discussions (such as those concerning the portrayals of women, blacks, foreigners, and Jews) he anticipated the conclusions of contemporary meaning theory (Chapter 1). Some researchers thought that this was the most important aspect of Wertham's investigation. One researcher, for example, in commenting on the crime comics argued: "The real point is not that the children will tend to resort to violence themselves; it is rather that they begin to *accept* violence, when practiced by others, as 'normal.' "[25] However, in the final analysis, Wertham gave much more coverage and much more attention to what the comics made children "do" rather than to the meaning of all that was done.

The conclusions of *Seduction of the Innocent* may be criticized on many grounds, but the major weakness of Wertham's position is that it is not supported by scientifically gathered research data. The findings are said to be the result of seven years of study conducted by him and eleven other psychiatrists and social workers at the Lafargue Clinic. The claim was made that numerous children, both delinquent and nondelinquent, were studied and that the results of these studies led to the conclusion that the effect of comic books is "definitely and completely harmful."

Wertham claimed to have studied the content of comic books and found that the content of the comics was almost universally one of crime, violence, horror, emphasizing of sexual characteristics, and so on. Of the millions of comic books which Wertham claimed dealt with crime and brutality, he rested his case on the selection of extreme and offensive examples which he made no attempt to prove were typical. No systematic inventory of comic book content was presented, such as that compiled by Edgar Dale for the movies in the 1920s. (See Chapter 2.) Without such an inventory, the conjectures are biased, unreliable, and useless.

Wertham gave the reader numerous examples of comic-book art. One writer even commented that "the most impressive part of the book is its illustration." [26] For example, there was a picture of a baseball game in which the ball was a man's head with one eye dangling from the socket; the bat was a severed leg; the catcher wore a dismembered torso as a chest protector; the baselines were marked with stretched-out intestines; the bases were marked with lungs, liver, and heart; the rosin bag was the dead man's stomach; and the umpire dusted off home plate with the scalp. Another illustration, a comic book cover, was a close-up of a hanged man, tongue protruding, eyeballs turned back, and the break in the neck clearly drawn. Wertham supplied his readers with 35 such "juicy" pictures, pictures which emphasized violence, sex, or both.

Were these scenes representative of comic book illustrations? Although Wertham argued they were, he did not provide systematic evidence to support the argument. His major claims concerning the effects of comics on children rested on selected and often extreme cases of children's deviant behavior where comics were said to have played an important role in producing that delinquency. Although he claimed that he and his associates had studied thousands of children, normal and delinquent, rich and poor, gifted and mediocre, he presented no statistical summary of his investigation. He claimed to have used nondelinquent control groups, but he did not describe these controls, how they were set up, or how they were equated with his experimental groups of delinquents and maladjusted children in order to assess the difference, if any, between the groups resulting from comic book reading and influence. He told us nothing about the specific interviewing techniques used, so we do not know if the interviewers used "leading" questions. In short, his methodology was clinical and speculative, but by no means scientific.

Moreover, Dr. Wertham pursued his argument with a humorless dedication that tended to place all evidence on the same level. Discussing "Superman," he suggested that it would not take much to change the "S" on that chest to "SS" (a reference to the Storm Troopers of Nazi Germany). He told us, with a straight face, of a little boy who, when asked what he wanted to be when he grew up, replied, "I want to be a sex maniac!" (This comment became a chapter title.) He reported the case of a twelve-year-old boy who had misbehaved with his sister and threatened to break her arm if she told anyone. "This is not the kind of thing that boys used to tell their sisters," Dr. Wertham informed us. Dr. Wertham, in effect, took at face value anything children told him, either as evidence of the harmful effects of the comic books ("I think sex all boils down to anxiety," one boy told him; Wertham's response was to indicate that the boy could not have gotten that from anywhere but the comics) or as direct support for his own views. For example, he quoted approvingly a fourteen-year-old boy's analysis of the economic motives which prompted psychiatrists to endorse comic books. It would have been a very dull child, indeed, who attended Dr. Wertham's clinic and did not discover very quickly that most of his or her problem behavior could be explained in terms of the comic books.[27]

Many of Wertham's critics argued that he did not distinguish between "good" and "bad" comic books. Perhaps he was able to ignore this distinction because so many readers found it hard to conceive of what a "good" comic book might be. Yet, in terms of their potential effects, there could be a significant difference between "Donald Duck" or "The Lone Ranger" on one hand, and the comic book from which Dr. Wertham took the picture of the baseball game played with the disconnected parts of a human body. As one observer commented:

> If the Lone Ranger (type of comics) are bad, they are bad in a different way and on a different level. They are crude, unimaginative, banal, vulgar, ultimately corrupting. They are also, as Dr. Wertham claims, violent—but always within certain limits. Perhaps the worst thing they do is to meet the juvenile imagination on its crudest level and offer it an immediate and stereotyped satisfaction.[28]

While this is bad enough, surely it is better (or different) than present raw violence and/or sex.

In critiquing *Seduction of the Innocent*, it should also be noted that Dr. Wertham presented a picture of society and human nature that is not unlike that found in the comic book. His world, like the world of the comic books, was one where the logic of personal interest was inexorable. *Seduction of the Innocent*, as its title and illustrations suggest, is a kind of crime comic book for parents. The book has the same simple conception of motives, the same sense of overhanging doom, the same melodramatic emphasis on pathology, and the same direct and immediate relation between cause and effect. If a juvenile delinquent were found in possession of comic books, the comic books produced the crime. If a publisher of comic books retained a psychiatrist to advise him on the suitability of the content of his publications, it followed that the arrangement was a dishonest one. If no comic book publisher was prosecuted under the laws against contributing to the delinquency of minors, it was not that the laws were not applicable. It was because "no district attorney, no judge, no complainant ever had the courage to make a complaint."[29] In the same vein, Wertham informed us:

Crime comic book writers should not be blamed for comic books. They are not free men. They are often . . . very critical of comics. In every letter I have received from a writer, stress is laid on requests to keep his identity a secret. They are told what to do and they do it—*or else* (emphasis added).[30]

What, perchance, did Dr. Wertham mean by that ominous "or else?" Will the recalcitrant writer be dragged face down over a gravel road in true comic book fashion? Surely not! At *worst*, they faced only the mundane possibility of losing their jobs.

Despite all of the criticism leveled at *Seduction of the Innocent*, it was still important in the history of communication research. It is true that we can criticize its methodology, logic, conclusions and so on. But the book had a tremendous impact on the public's perception of the power of the media. In short, this work reinforced the legacy of fear. As previously discussed, Wertham took his argument to the people in popular forums like *Ladies' Home Journal* and *Reader's Digest*—and a great number of them listened and believed. In many ways, his writings can be said to have sparked the flame which led to Senate hearings, conducted by Senator Kefauver, on the relationship between "juvenile delinquency and comic books." The added publicity focused on comic books because of the hearings spelled doom for the publishers of the most violent and sexually blatant comic books. But a stigma was also placed on the "good" comic books and their circulation began to decline. Other factors, such as the rise of television, contributed to this decline. But Dr. Wertham had had an effect, because in the end, most people agreed! Whatever else they might be— comic books were *not* funny.

NOTES AND REFERENCES

1. For a discussion of this topic, see James P. Wood, "Magazine Publishing Today" in *Mass Media and Communication*, ed. by Charles Steinberg (New York: Hastings House, 1966), pp. 182–183. Also see Melvin De Fleur and Everette Dennis, *Understanding Mass Communication* (Boston: Houghton Mifflin, 1981). See Chapter 2.
2. Norbert Muhlen, "Comic Books and Other Horrors: Prep School for Totalitarian Society?" *Commentary*, Jan. 1949, pp. 80–87.
3. Ibid., p. 81.
4. Ibid., pp. 80–87.
5. Ibid.
6. Frederic M. Thrasher, "The Comics and Delinquency: Cause or Scapegoat," *The Journal of Educational Sociology* 23 (1): pp. 195–205, Sept. 1949.

7. Fredric Wertham, *Seduction of the Innocent* (New York: Rinehart, 1954), p. vi.
8. Ibid., p. 52.
9. Ibid., pp. 57–58.
10. Ibid., p. 111.
11. Ibid., p. 157.
12. Ibid., p. 31.
13. Ibid., p. 34.
14. Ibid., p. 156.
15. Ibid., p. 164.
16. Ibid., p. 96.
17. Ibid., p. 88.
18. Ibid., p. 101.
19. Ibid., p. 105.
20. Ibid., p. 179.
21. Ibid., pp. 189–190.
22. Ibid., p. 217.
23. Ibid., p. 118.
24. Ibid., p. 108.
25. Norbert Muhlen, op. cit., p. 86.
26. Robert Warshow, "Paul, the Horror Comics, and Dr. Wertham," in *Mass Culture*, ed. by Bernard Rosenberg and David White (New York: The Free Press, 1957), pp. 199–211.
27. Ibid.
28. Ibid., p. 207.
29. Fredric Wertham, op. cit.
30. Ibid.

10

television in the lives of our children: the early years

When the movies grew rapidly as a mass medium early in the century, one of the first concerns of the American public was their impact on children. In some ways, the mushrooming growth of television in the immediate postwar years followed a similar pattern. However, its adoption by the public was even more rapid, almost catching everyone by surprise. Suddenly, there was a remarkable new box in everyone's living room, with moving pictures as well as sound. The incredibly rapid pace of the adoption of this device, as well as peoples' growing alarm over its possible effects on the young were factors that helped shape the earliest research directions designed to discover television's role in the expanding system of mass communication.

The television industry exploded across the American landscape during the 1950s; no other mass medium had ever grown so quickly. The extent of this expansion becomes evident when we consider a few facts. In 1948, there were fewer than 100,000 television sets in the United States; one year later, a million sets were in use in American homes—and that was only the beginning! Indeed, by 1959, more than 50 million television sets had been placed in American homes and approximately 88 percent of U.S. households were the proud owners of television receivers. This was a dramatic turnaround from the beginning of the decade, when only about six percent of American households had even one set. Thus, in less than a decade, television had become a pervasive aspect of American life.[1]

Possession of a TV set quickly became a status symbol in the early years of television's diffusion through the American population. Families who could ill afford such a luxury sometimes cut corners on necessities in order to purchase one. Many acquired their sets through installment purchases—the "easy payment plan." In some cases, the urge to own a television and to be identified as an owner was so strong that families were said to have bought and installed antennas in conspicuous locations long before they purchased the sets to hook up and watch. This emergence of television as a status symbol led to occasional public outrage when it was discovered that some people receiving public welfare or other forms of relief possessed sets. Apparently the experiences of those who had lived through the Depression years had been forgotten; at that time, radio sets were welcomed as extremely comforting to people trapped in trying economic circumstances (see Chapter 3).

Television sets might have become a common household item even sooner if it had not been for the intervention of World War II. The technology of television broadcasting had been developed during the 1920s and 1930s, and by 1939, network television broadcasts were already being made in the United States. The World's Fair that year featured demonstrations of that latest scientific marvel, television. President Hoover had experimented with broadcasts, and President Roosevelt even delivered a speech over the new communication medium. The speech's broadcast audience, however, consisted of only a handful of people because commercial manufacturers had not yet begun to mass-produce sets. The Federal Communications Commission approved home television in 1941, on the eve of America's entry into World War II, and the communications industry had already begun to work out plans for its development. At that time, there were approximately 5,000 sets in private hands, mostly around New York City, and several small private stations were broadcasting regularly for two or three hours a day.[2]

World War II, however, abruptly altered this development and postponed the general availability of television until the war had ended. This hindrance to commercial development may account, in some respects, for the extremely rapid growth in both television broadcasting and manufacturing when the country returned to a peacetime economy. For one thing, communications executives had the plans well laid for their expansion into television. In addition, electronics manufacturers had developed new techniques of production during the war which aided the industry in overcoming the problems of mass-producing television receivers. Besides all this, the prewar economic depression had finally ended. In fact, wartime rationing had created an immense pent-up demand for consumer goods and services. Americans, with jobs and money in their pockets, went on a buying spree. With minor fluctuations, the United States entered a period of unprecedented economic growth that was uninterrupted for more than two decades. With this prosperity came an increase in the purchasing power of the average citizen. The purchasing power of the average American family rose to the point that television ownership was within the means of all but the poorest.[3]

By 1960, 150 million Americans had acquired sets and rearranged their lives to accommodate the schedule of television programs presented on their living room screens. This rearrangement appeared to be most striking in homes with children; such homes were more than twice as likely to have a set than homes which did not have children. Television had become the single greatest source of national entertainment; it had displaced radio, comic books, playmates, and babysitters by a wide margin. However, the public knew very little about the effects of this new medium; the legacy of fear persisted among many Americans and there was growing concern about what television might be doing to America's children. Would the new medium stunt or stimulate the growth of children? Was it going to create armies of juvenile delinquents? Would it turn children into passive robots incapable of intellectual creativity? Would it propel children into an adult world of sex, liquor, and violence for which they were unprepared? American parents were deeply concerned about such effects on this crucial segment of the population—from toddlers to teenagers.

The few research projects which dealt with the effects of television in the early 1950s provided no assurances to allay the fears of the public. A series of surveys by the National Association of Educational Broadcasters in 1951 discovered that crime and horror stories comprised ten percent of the programming time in four American cities.[4] While by today's standards this might appear to be a small proportion of the shows, at the time it appeared to be excessive. Other investigations by social scientists revealed that watching television had reduced the amount of time that children spent playing—both indoors and outdoors. Viewing also reduced the amount of time that children devoted to helping out with household chores, such as cooking and cleaning. Children who watched television also spent less time listening to the radio, going to movies, and reading books.[5] Television viewing cut into all of the activities of daily life. No one knew, however, whether television could change attitudes or values. It was unknown whether television could create passivity or aggression, or whether it would enlarge or limit children's intellectual boundaries. Exactly what *was* happening to the tender minds tuned in to the electronic Pied Piper? Clearly, more research was needed to find out television's effects, particularly research focusing on children. In this setting, Professors Wilbur Schramm, Jack Lyle and Edwin Parker undertook the first large-scale investigation of the relationship between television and children in North America. It is to that investigation that we now turn.

THE RESEARCH PROGRAM

The results of the first major study of the effects of television on North American children were reported in *Television in the Lives of Our Children*. It presented the findings and conclusions from eleven investigations carried out between 1958 and 1960, in ten communities in the United States and

Canada. The focus of the project was on the *uses and functions* of television for various categories of children, rather than simply on a straightforward analysis of "effects." The authors believed that the term "effects" was misleading in that:

> . . . it suggests that television "does something" to children. The connotation is that television is the actor; the children are acted upon. Children are thus made to seem relatively inert; television relatively active. Children are sitting victims; television bites them.[6]

Schramm and his colleagues argued that nothing could be further from the truth. Children were not, they emphasized, passive entities being acted upon by television. To the contrary, children were *active agents* who selected material from television which best fit their interests and needs. It was children who used television, not television which used children.

According to Schramm, Lyle, and Parker, children used television to satisfy some need. They drew an analogy between television and a "great shiny cafeteria." From television, as from a cafeteria, children selected only what they wanted at the moment. It was conceded that television's bill of fare contained many dishes heavy in fantasy, that there were large slices of violence and that there was less variety in the menu than some of the patrons might prefer at any one time. But, like the cafeteria, children took and ate only what they wanted from television. Thus, it was argued that in order to understand television's effects, it was necessary to understand a great deal about the lives of children. We needed to know what it was in their lives which made them reach out for a particular experience on television. Only then could we know how their lives interacted with and were influenced by television. This was exactly what they proposed to do.

Research Design and Methodology

As previously noted, Schramm and his associates conducted eleven separate studies between 1958 and 1960. The first study was funded by the San Francisco school system to gain information about the use of television by children in grades one through six. On the basis of the results obtained in the first study, subsequent funding for additional studies was provided, mainly by the National Educational Television and Radio Center. The scope of these studies is briefly summarized below:

Study 1: San Francisco, 1958–1959
In the initial study, the researchers used a total of 2,688 children chosen to serve as representatives of grades one through six, and of the eighth, tenth and

twelfth grades of the public school system. Some of the children were interviewed directly. Many of them, however, completed questionnaires and tests administered in their classrooms. Several hundred students kept diaries. In addition, data were obtained on some of the younger children through questionnaires completed by their parents. The study also included data from questionnaires completed by 1,030 parents, in which they described and reacted to their children's television behavior. The information gathered on each child varied somewhat according to the age of the child, but the researchers tried to learn as much as possible about each child's mass media behavior. Schramm and his associates were interested in what children used the different media for, and what the media meant to them. In addition, they examined what the children knew about public affairs, science, popular and fine art, and other parts of the world. They also learned something about the children's family lives and their relations with children their own age. The research included measures of some of their psychological characteristics, their mental ability, the use they were making of it in school, and so on. In addition to all of this information gathered directly from the children and their parents, the researchers also talked to teachers, school officials, and other knowledgeable persons.

Study 2: San Francisco, 1958
Interviews were conducted with 188 *entire families, as families*. The researchers talked to the parents and the children together so that the subjects could check up on one another and also so that the researchers could observe their interactions. The families were asked chiefly about the use of the media different members of the family made, and what part the media played in family life. In all, 188 mothers, 187 fathers, and 502 children were interviewed.

Studies 3–7: Rocky Mountain Communities, 1959
The entire sixth and tenth grades, or where necessary an adequate sample of them, were interviewed in five communities in the Rocky Mountain area of the United States. In three of these communities, the researchers also included the first grade. In most respects, the information sought about each child paralleled that which had been obtained in San Francisco, although the questionnaires had been expanded and sharpened as the work progressed. In the case of the three first grade cohorts, for example, the researchers administered vocabulary tests to the children. The total sample from the five towns was 1,708 children and 284 parents. As before, local teachers and officials were also consulted as a check on the information.

Studies 8–9: Canada, 1959
Two communities in Canada were studied which were comparable to each other in most respects, except that one of them did not have television. Data were gathered in each community from the first, sixth, and tenth grades using the same materials developed for the Rocky Mountain towns, except that the materials had been improved through use, and somewhat expanded to take into account special characteristics of Canadian mass communication. Again,

MILESTONES IN MASS COMMUNICATION RESEARCH

the first grades were given vocabulary tests. In all, 913 children and 269 parents were interviewed, and as before, the researchers consulted with local teachers and officials.

Study 10: American Suburb
The researchers examined in detail the television behavior, program choice, and time allocations of all of the elementary school children in one school. Data were gathered on a total of 474 children. Again, parents and teachers were consulted.

Study 11: Denver, 1960
This final study examined 204 students in the tenth grade in order to test several hypotheses developed from the results of the previous studies. The information obtained here dealt with the students' media behavior in relation to mental ability and social norms.

To summarize, a total of eleven studies were conducted. Overall, the researchers collected data from 5,991 students, 1,958 parents, and from several hundred teachers, officials, and other knowledgeable persons in ten communities in the United States and Canada. These communities were chosen to be representative of North America and included isolated areas, metropolitan areas, cities, and towns of various sizes. The sample also included industrial, agricultural, and residential communities, and the level of the development of local television ran the gamut then existing in North America—from no television to highly developed, multi-station broadcast areas.

The Functions of Television

Schramm, Lyle, and Parker offered their readers an explanation of why children watched television. They began with the functionalist assumption that every item in a culture exists because it is useful for the members of that culture. Therefore, they reasoned, television viewing must be useful to children. And for it to be useful, it must be meeting certain needs and it must be the *best* way of meeting those needs among the known and available alternatives. What were those needs? The authors posited three primary reasons why children watched television: (1) for entertainment, (2) for information, and/or (3) because of its social utility. Each of these reasons will be discussed below.

Entertainment The most important and most obvious reason why children watched television was to enjoy the passive pleasure of being entertained. They enjoyed escaping from real-life problems and from boredom, and the children enjoyed identifying with exciting and attractive people. And television programming was aimed more at escaping problems than it was at solving them. Watching television is an essentially passive behavior; it is something that the children surrendered themselves to; it is something that they did not have to work for or think about.

Information Most children, when questioned, acknowledged that they learned from television. In many ways the medium served them as had the movies, as reported in Blumer's study (Chapter 2). Girls said that they learned something about personal grooming—how to wear their hair, how to walk and talk, how to choose clothes—by observing the well-groomed mannequins on television. They also learned some of the details of contemporary manners and customs; for example, whether passengers are expected to tip the stewardess on an airplane. Some of the boys said that they learned how other young men dressed in New York or California. Others said that they learned a great deal by watching the performances of good athletes. More than one parent told of a child who learned to swing a baseball bat by watching professional stars on television, and as a result became playground sensations until they began to imitate their young friends instead of the television performers. Typical comments children made about television were: "It helps me to know how other kinds of people live"; or "The news is more real when you have seen where it happens." Many children said that television helped them in school by giving them ideas for themes or topics to discuss.

Social Utility Another attraction television had for children was its social utility. An example of this utility is that, among teenagers, watching television became a social occasion. It provided a handy excuse for boys and girls to enjoy each other's company; it gave them something convenient and inexpensive to do on dates; and it furnished them with a ready-made excuse for sitting close together. In addition, even when they did not watch television in the company of their peers, the previous evening's programs provided a common ground for conversations at school and on dates. If teenagers were not able to discuss these programs, they became out of step with their peers. Hence, watching television had a direct utility in their social lives.

Schramm, Lyle, and Parker reported that some children appeared to be quite compulsive about television. Such children were vaguely ill-at-ease when they missed a favorite program, or when their set was broken, or when some program or performer they particularly liked was off the air. Some children felt uneasy when they were away from television on a summer vacation. When asked to explain this feeling, one girl responded, "It's just as if they were your friends or your family. You miss them when you don't see them." Some children explained that they felt they were missing something, that they were out of step and were not in touch with what their peers were doing. It is evident, then, that watching television was functional for these children beyond the specific benefits of learning and entertainment.

The authors reasoned that any particular TV program might serve all three purposes for a child. A crime program, for example, would be likely to entertain many children. At the same time, however, it might teach some children specific skills and convey information about "what the world is like." In addition, the program provides the child with something to share and discuss the next day. It should be noted, however, that different children might view the same program in different ways. To one child, a news story about a murder trial might be a "whodunit" entertainment program. To another, it might be a commentary on conditions in the real world. For a third child, it could provide a way of learning how to commit murder. The message the child receives from the television show can thus depend upon what the child brings to the TV set—that is, it depends upon the child's personal, social, and psychological characteristics.

Overall, the authors considered the use of television for entertainment and for information to be the most important uses. They argued that the chief needs for which children went to television were the needs for both *fantasy* and *reality* experiences. The authors distinguished between fantasy content and reality content in the following manner:[7]

Fantasy Content:	*Reality Content:*
invites the viewer to take leave of his problems in the real world;	constantly refers the viewer to the problems of the real world;
invites surrender, relaxation, passivity;	invites alertness, effort, activity;
invites emotion;	invites cognition;
works chiefly through abrogating the rules of the real world;	works chiefly through realistic materials and situations;
acts to remove, at least temporarily, threat and anxiety, and offers wish-fulfillment;	tends to make viewer even more aware of threat, perhaps more anxious, in return for better view of the problem;
offers pleasure;	offers enlightenment.

It was thought that the predominant needs that television met for children were fantasy needs rather than reality needs.

THE FINDINGS

The more quantitative and detailed findings of these eleven studies are too numerous and varied to be discussed in any detail. They can, however, be placed into five general categories: (1) how and when children used television, (2) children's learning from television, (3) reality-seeking and social norms, (4) television and social relationships, and (5) the effects of television. Each of these sets of findings will be discussed in turn.

How and When Children Used Television

The first direct experience that a child had with television typically came at age two, although it could not be said that most of the children were "users" at that age. Typically, such children "dropped in" on a program that someone else was watching. Soon after they began to explore the world of television, and by the age of three, many children were making regular use of the medium. In fact, when asked, they were able to name their favorite programs. Figure 13 represents graphically the percentage of children using television between the ages of two and nine.

As can be seen, 37 percent of the three-year-old children were regular viewers, compared to 82 percent of the five-year-olds, 91 percent of those age six, and 96 percent of the nine-year-olds. Thus, by their ninth birthday, only four percent of the children could be considered nonusers!

But how much *time* did these children spend in front of the television set? The "average" three-year-old spent about 45 minutes a day watching television. By the age of five, however, viewing time had increased to a little more than two hours per day. Between their sixth and tenth birthdays,

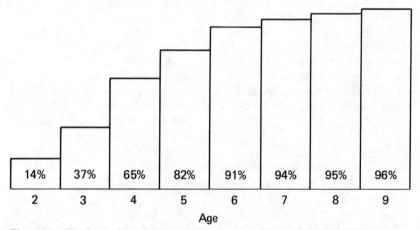

| 14% | 37% | 65% | 82% | 91% | 94% | 95% | 96% |
| 2 | 3 | 4 | 5 | 6 | 7 | 8 | 9 |

Age

Figure 13. The Beginnings of Television Use; Percent of Children Using It by Age.

SOURCE: Wilbur Schramm, Jack Lyle and Edwin B. Parker, *Television in the Lives of Our Children* (Stanford, Calif.: Stanford University Press, 1961) p. 27.

children's viewing time slowly increased to about two and one-half hours each day. When the children reached eleven or twelve, viewing time suddenly jumped to three or four hours daily; at this point, however, it began a slow, steady decline which continued throughout adolescence. It should be noted that these figures were for weekdays. Weekend viewing averages were higher, ranging from half-an-hour to an hour longer. In addition, the authors cautioned that their figures were conservative. Yet they also noted the cumulative situation: They observed that "from ages three through sixteen children spend *more total time* on television than on school. In fact, they are likely to devote more time to television than to any other activity except sleep."[8] (Emphasis added.)

We have indicated that age was an important factor in determining overall viewing time, and that the heaviest period of children's viewing usually came sometime between the ages of 11 and 13. But other factors, especially mental ability and social class background, were also important in determining the viewing habits of children.

The relationship between mental ability, as measured by IQ, and viewing time presented a rather dramatic picture. In the early school years, the children with high IQ scores tended to engage in high levels of television viewing. However, sometime between the tenth and thirteenth years a notable change occurred. The more intelligent children deserted the ranks of heavy viewers. The authors presented interesting data regarding this generalization. In the Rocky Mountain towns, for example, there was no relationship between IQ scores and viewing time among sixth grade students. However, by the time the children had reached the tenth grade, most of the low IQ children had become high viewers, whereas most of the high IQ scorers had become low viewers. The data presented in Figure 14 illustrate these findings.

The chart shows that the percentage of light viewers increased generally between the sixth and tenth grades, but the chief increase was among those in the high IQ group. Data from the other regions paralleled the conditions in the Rocky Mountain towns.

Why did the brighter children stop watching so frequently? Schramm and his associates found that television no longer presented a challenge to those children. Most of them were finding greater rewards in the print media and in social and school activities.

Social class background was also found to be important in determining the amount of time spent viewing. Children of well-educated parents tended to watch less than other children, following the example set by their parents. Children of working-class parents, however, were likely to watch more. The authors speculated that this difference in viewing time between social classes could be attributed to a difference in class norms. The middle

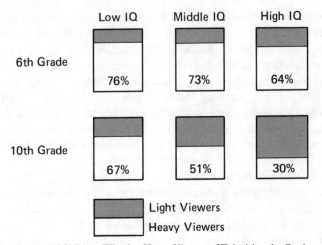

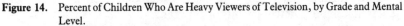

Figure 14. Percent of Children Who Are Heavy Viewers of Television, by Grade and Mental Level.

SOURCE: Wilbur Schramm, Jack Lyle and Edwin B. Parker, *Television in the Lives of Our Children* (Stanford, Calif.: Stanford University Press, 1961) p. 34.

class norms of work, activity, and self-betterment influenced the viewing patterns of the middle class youngsters by giving them incentives to engage in other activities, thereby reducing the time available for viewing.

Schramm, Lyle, and Parker did indicate a note of caution, however. They pointed out that these general patterns did have exceptions and that there were enough exceptions to lead them to believe that some of the most important factors in determining viewing habits must have been missing from their list. They felt that there was something beyond age, intelligence, and family which was affecting the children's viewing patterns. They believed that the missing elements were the child's social relationships and some of his or her personal characteristics.

Social relationships were indeed found to influence a child's use of television. The researchers discovered that children who had unsatisfactory relationships with their families, and/or with their peer groups, tended to retreat from those social interactions into television viewing. When watching television, they could leave real-life problems behind them, at least for a time, and possibly reduce the tension in their lives. The more conflict there was in these children's lives, the more they watched television. It was evident, then, that problems with either the family or the peer group were clearly related to escapist fantasy seeking, and that children with such problems turned to television to escape.

What Children Watched Typically, the first programs that most children identified as their favorites were programs which the broadcasters referred to as "children's programs." The central characters of such programs were usually animals, animated characters, or puppets (e.g., Donald Duck, Huckleberry Hound, Howdy Doody, Rin Tin Tin), although sometimes the children themselves took the role of the sympathetic character. The programs were presented in story form and were full of action, often with a heavy component of slapstick humor. Such programs were traditionally aired in the late afternoon, after school, or on Saturday morning. Programs of this type monopolized the viewing time of preschool children, and their dominance persisted well into the elementary school years, although often in somewhat more mature forms such as "Lassie." By the time the child was well settled in school, however, a new lineup of favorite programs had been established. These consisted of a number of program types created especially for children but modelled after adult programs: children's variety shows, children's adventure programs, children's science fiction, and children's westerns. The Walt Disney programs are examples of the "children's variety shows." The format varied widely, offering cartoons, adventure stories, legends, history, and nature stories; many programs contained a mixture of presentations. The authors offered "Zorro" as an example of "children's adventure programs." In these stories, the tale is told of a simple, strong, "good" hero. This hero is the master of his own fate in spite of the perils he faces in his adventures. The children's "science fiction" and "western" programs were both costume dramas—one set in the future and the other in the past or near past. The stories and characters were uncomplicated and featured adventure and excitement.

Such programs dominated the children's early school years, but soon two new types of program became increasingly important in their viewing—the crime program and the situation comedy. The crime programs were only a short step from the adventure sagas, where the hero righted wrongs by his own strength, skill, and daring. The detective also solved crimes through the use of skill, strength, and daring. Although these programs were generally scheduled during the "adult" programming hours, children usually began watching them in their early school years. The programs' largest juvenile audience, however, was teenagers.

As the children entered adolescence, another type of program became important in their viewing, the popular music variety show. The girls discovered these programs earlier, and watched them faithfully, but such programming eventually became part of most teenagers' viewing. At this point, we have almost the entire line-up of programs watched during the teen years. The crime dramas became more absorbing and the children's westerns were replaced by adult westerns such as "Gunsmoke." Programs like "Disneyland," "Zorro," and "Superman" faded in popularity. Much of the teenager's viewing time was now spent watching crime dramas and popular music shows. By now, little time was devoted to traditional "children's" programs. Interest in public affairs programming came late in this hierarchy. In fact, any use of media other than for entertainment was unusual. Figure 15 summarizes the general pattern that Schramm and his associates described in the growth of the children's program diet. As can be seen, the children learned to watch adult programs very quickly. For example, by the time the children were in the first grade, they were already devoting 40 percent of their viewing time to the kinds of programs which most viewers would term "adult." Moreover, sixth grade children were devoting 79 percent of their viewing time to adult programs and were watching nearly five times as many adult programs as children's programs. This finding led the authors to caution that "networks which believe that they are producing programs for adults might do well to take another look at the age of their audience." [9]

Predicting Children's Taste in Programming It should be made clear that not all children preferred to watch the same types of shows. What

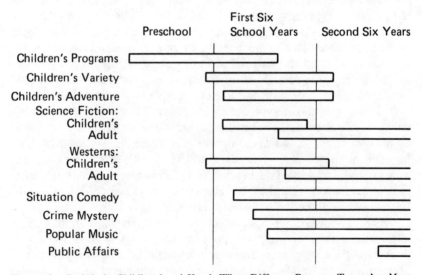

Figure 15. Periods in Childhood and Youth When Different Program Types Are Most Important.

SOURCE: Wilbur Schramm, Jack Lyle and Edwin B. Parker, *Television in the Lives of Our Children* (Stanford, Calif.: Stanford University Press, 1961) p. 39.

were the factors associated with different program preferences? From our previous discussion, it is evident that one important factor was the age of the child. If it was known that one child was nine and another fourteen, other things being equal, it was possible to predict that there would be certain differences in program preferences between them. For example, the younger child would be likely to prefer more traditional children's programs, such as Walt Disney, whereas the older child would likely have more interest in popular music shows and crime dramas. Another important factor was the child's sex. Differences in program preferences between boys and girls were apparent even as early as the first grade. Little girls preferred popular music shows, while boys preferred westerns and adventure programs. This pattern continued throughout the school years—girls preferred "feminine" programs built around marriage and romance (e.g., situation comedies, popular music) and boys preferred "masculine" programs of excitement and adventure. The authors offered one explanation for these differences: Girls developed an interest in adolescent and adult roles at an earlier age than did boys.

Mental ability was again found to be an important factor. Schramm, Lyle, and Parker found that brighter children tried different things earlier. They began watching television earlier and more frequently; then they took the "hard steps" to serious programming sooner, such as watching news programs, educational shows, and documentaries. It was found, for example, that about twice as many of the brighter eighth grade students were watching television coverage of the 1958 Congressional elections, when compared to lower intelligence groups. Moreover, of those who viewed this program, it was the brighter ones who most enjoyed it. The high-IQ scorers were also the ones who were chiefly able to identify faces that had appeared on television for public affairs reasons rather than for entertainment reasons. These patterns of viewing news programs, public affairs commentary, and so on began earlier with the brighter children. They were the first of their age group to turn away from the western and situation comedy shows.

In general, the brighter teenagers were being attracted away from television. Homework and their social lives kept them busier and they had less time for television. In addition, they were becoming more critical and discriminating in their choices of programming, abandoning those offerings which seemed to have less durable value for them. Both the high-IQ scorers and the low-IQ scorers were settling into adult viewing patterns. Thus, the high-IQ category used television less often and more selectively, and turned to print media for much of their serious informational needs. The lower-IQ group, on the other hand, tended to use television more and printed media less. As their teenage behavior suggested, they used television heavily for crime mysteries, situation comedies, westerns, comedy, variety, and popular music programs. In short, sex, age, and mental ability were found to be related to program preference.

Attitudes toward Television   It is not surprising that Schramm and his associates found that most children regarded television with both affection and respect. What is surprising was that they were not alone. Their parents also showed similar attitudes toward television. When the authors conducted interviews in San Francisco with 188 families, each questioned together as a family unit, they asked each member of the family which of the media they would miss the most if they had to do without it. The overwhelming response was television—for the whole family. Overall, television was the most likely to be missed by parents and children alike; and television was the medium mentioned most frequently at every age, even though its relative importance declined during adolescence.

The children were generally enamored of television. When asked, they could find nothing they would change in its content, except that they wanted *more of the same*. Preteen girls, for example, requested more popular music shows and family situations. Boys in the same age group wanted more war stories, sports, crime shows, and more comedy. It was not until the children reached the late high school years that they became critical of television, and even then it was chiefly the brighter children. Those older children who were critical did not have major complaints. Some thought that there were too many commercials; others thought that some television personalities were unpleasant; and a few thought that programming was too repetitive, that it was all the same.

When it came to the parents, however, it was a different story. Overall, they had definite ideas about changes they wanted. Most of them were clearly concerned about the amount of crime and violence on television. This was especially true for the better-educated parents with white-collar jobs. When parents from blue-collar families expressed concern, they tended to be more disturbed about sexual content in programming. In general, however, blue-collar parents were much more likely to express gratitude for television—it kept their children "out of mischief," "off the streets," or was an inexpensive babysitter.

Incidental Learning from Television

The authors argued that most of a child's learning from television was incidental learning. Such learning was defined as "learning that takes place when a viewer goes to television for entertainment and stores up certain items of information without seeking them."[10] In their view, children learned while being entertained; however, the children usually did not seek out television strictly for informational purposes.

A number of conditions were found to be important in determining when incidental learning took place. These included the child's ability to learn, the child's needs at the moment, and what the child paid attention to. The ability to learn was looked upon pretty much as a matter of intelligence. The authors stated that "bright" children learned more from television. Indeed, such children learned more in any learning situation. Other factors, related to attention and needs, were found to be important. For example, children were more likely to pay attention to and learn some particular behavior if it was new to them. The authors discussed, as an example, the impact of a Hopalong Cassidy film in one of their studies. The show produced a considerable amount of learning on the part of younger children, but had very little impact on the older ones. The difference between the two groups was accounted for by the fact that the film was a new kind of experience for the young children, but "old stuff" to the older ones. Because the older children had seen such films many times before, this one did not command their close attention, an effect of familiarity. As children become more familiar with the subject matter, they learn to sort out the material. They note familiar things and set up a pattern of expectation which keeps them from having to pay too much attention to them. In any event, it is the new things, the ones that are not too familiar to them, which they single out for their attention and storage.

On the basis of this familiarity principle, Schramm and his associates posited that the greatest amount of learning from television occurs between the ages of three and eight, when most of the experiences are new to the children. At those ages, those experiences would be especially absorbing to the child. There is, however, another reason why television is an especially effective agent of incidental learning when the child is young. The reason is television seems very real to them. A number of observers have commented that mass media content had greater impact on children if they believed that it had "really happened." The younger children are more likely to think that the events taking place on the picture tube in front of them are real.

The amount of identification that a child has with a television character is another factor which affects the amount of incidental learning that takes place. All parents have observed their children galloping imaginary horses, or seen them acting out an adventure the way their favorite hero would play it. Girls copy the current romantic heroines—mimicking their entrances, their mannerisms, and their seductive manner in love scenes. Many researchers have written about children's identification with characters.

"There is no doubt that a child can more easily store up behaviors and beliefs which he has imaginatively shared with a character with whom he identifies."[11]

A child is also more likely to pick out and remember something from an entertainment program if it is clearly useful to him or her. In this respect the child's needs become important. A girl, for example, is more likely to remember an attractive hairdo, whereas a boy is more likely to remember the techniques a third baseman used when he charged a bunt. If the child notices something he or she can tell to friends, then there is ample reason to remember it—especially if it can evoke laughter. Such "little bonuses" occur all the time in the course of entertainment. Something comes to the child's attention as the program progresses, he or she sees a use for it, and stores it away for the future.

In addition, there is reason to believe that the child will more likely learn and use something when he or she thinks that it will work. When a television character fails at something, it is unlikely that the child will try it. But if the behavior appears to be both rewarding and socially feasible, there is more incentive for the child to store it away and then try it when the proper occasion arises.

Schramm and his associates believed that watching television contributed to a fast start in learning but that the advantage children gained did not last. They felt that children who viewed TV would start school with larger vocabularies than nonviewing children of the same age. Likewise, the authors argued, child viewers would be more familiar with wider worlds and know more (at an earlier age) than nonviewers about adult life, sex, crime, and social problems. In order to test these hypotheses, however, the researchers had to compare two Canadian communities because they could not find an American community that did not have television. As expected, they found that first grade children with television had higher vocabulary scores than similar children living in a community without television. By the sixth grade, however, the difference disappeared. Thus, the advantage gained from watching television did not last. It came as no surprise that IQ scores again emerged as an important factor. Remember our earlier discussions which revealed that brighter children watched more television during their early years but then deserted the ranks of heavy viewers as they grew older. Such factors interact with exposure to television and must be taken into account when we observe that the advantages of television viewing disappear. The authors referred to this interaction pattern as the "principle of maturation." According to this principle, when children mature to a certain point television becomes less attractive and rewarding to them. As a result, they increase the attention they pay to reality-oriented media material, or "material which is at least as useful for its information content as for its entertainment content, if not more so."[12]

Social Norms and Social Relationships

The maturation principle held true for most children, but not for all. While most children decreased their television viewing time considerably during their high school years, others decreased their viewing only slightly, or not at all. Why did this happen? First of all, the pattern of fantasy-seeking and reality-seeking differentiated the children's media behavior more than anything else. Those children who were seeking knowledge or information turned more of their media attention to newspapers, quality magazines, and books. On the other hand, those children who primarily sought entertainment and fantasy/escape remained high users of television fantasy, as well as other media with high fantasy components (e.g., comic books).

The Importance of Social Norms To understand why these patterns of reality-seeking and fantasy-seeking emerged, the researchers divided children into four groups according to the amount of their use of television, books, and magazines. The first group was fantasy-oriented; it was composed of children who were high users of television and low users of print media. The second group, on the other hand, was reality-oriented; it was composed of children who were high users of print and low users of television. The third group was referred to as the "high users" group. It consisted of children with high use levels for both print and television. The fourth group, the "low users" group, consisted of children who were low users of both print and television. In the sixth grade, membership in the reality-oriented group was very small, but by the tenth grade it had grown a great deal. Children who were members of this group differed from the members of the other groups. They had internalized the norms of the upwardly mobile middle class—norms of activity, self-betterment, and deferred gratification. At the beginning of adolescence there was a turning point for a considerable number of children. They left the universal pleasure norm of their childhood for these middle class norms. It was those children, if their mental abilities were sufficient, who became the chief users of print media and educational television. They were also the viewers more likely to select reality programs from commercial television. Social norms, then, had a great deal to do with what kind of use the child made of television.

Television and Social Relationships Another factor that determined how a child used television was social relationships. In general, it was found that children who had unsatisfactory relationships with their families or peer groups tended to retreat to television where they could escape from their real-life problems. However, when we examine some other variables, the relationship is no longer so simple. For example, when children of high intelligence and high social status encountered problems in their social relations, the amount of television they used went up, as expected. Such children turned to television for fantasy and escape, rather than seeking reality in print media, as would be expected from them if their social relationships were satisfactory. But when children of low intelligence and low social status faced similar problems in their social relations, the result was not more use of television. If anything changed, there was less use of television.

The quality of the child's home and peer-group relationships did help to determine the amount of television he or she saw, but also much more. The child who came to television filled with aggression because of the frustrations of these poor social relationships was likely to seek out and remember the violent content of television. The authors concluded that if the child sought violence in answer to his or her own social needs, then he or she was likely to remember and resurrect such violence when real-life needs called for aggression. "In other words, parents, friends, schools have it in their power to make a significant contribution to the healthfulness of a child's use of television by giving him a warm and loving home, and helping him to normal and satisfying friendships with children his own age." [13]

The Effects of Television

The relationship between television and a child can be understood only in terms of the characteristics of both. We have already discussed what a child brings to television (i.e., IQ, social norms, social relationships, and the needs and experiences for which age and sex are partial indicators). Now we turn to the question of what television brings to the child. To examine this, the authors monitored and analyzed a week of television in late October 1960, from 4:00 P.M. to 9:00 P.M., Monday through Friday. Figure 16 summarizes their findings. It can be seen that commercial television brought to children fast moving, exciting fantasy, with broad humor and a considerable amount of romantic interest. The authors considered the content to be "extremely violent." Shootings and sluggings were frequent; in fact, more than half the program hours consisted of programs in which violence played an important part. The authors, it should be pointed out, did not take all of the violence seriously.

For example, the cartoons and slapstick films they deemed were intended to be funny, rather than exciting, were disregarded in the analysis. Nevertheless, in the hundred hours analyzed there appeared:

12 murders
16 major gunfights

21 persons shot (apparently not fatally)

21 other violent incidents with guns (ranging from shooting at but missing persons, to shooting up a town)

37 hand-to-hand fights (15 fist fights, 15 incidents in which one person slugged another, an attempted murder with a pitchfork, 2 stranglings, a fight in the water, a case in which a woman was gagged and tied to a bed, etc.)

One stabbing in the back with a butcher knife

Four attempted suicides, three successful

Four people falling or pushed over cliffs

Two cars running over cliffs

Two attempts made in automobiles to run over persons on the sidewalk

A psychotic loose and raving in a flying airliner

Two mob scenes, in one of which the mob hangs the wrong man

A horse trampling a man under its hooves

A great deal of miscellaneous violence, including a plane fight, a hired killer stalking his prey, two robberies, a pickpocket at work, a woman killed by falling from a train, a tidal wave, an earthquake, and a guillotining.

This picture of the adult world was heavy in violence, light in intellectual exchange, and deeply concerned with crime. Half of the characters in the stories were either involved in enforcing the law, breaking it, or both. There were sixteen detectives, sixteen sheriffs, nine police officers and an

Cartoons	18%	
Westerns	13.0%	
Crime	11.0%	
Feature Films	10.5%	
Dance Parties	10.5%	
Situation Comedies		
News	7.75%	
Slapstick Films	5.0%	
Adventure	3.0%	
Travel Films	2.0%	
Drama	1.5%	
Classical Music	1.25%	

Figure 16. Content of Commercial Television Over 1.0 Percent During the "Children's Hour"—4:00 to 9:00 P.M. Monday through Friday, late October, 1960.

SOURCE: Wilbur Schramm, Jack Lyle and Edwin B. Parker, *Television in the Lives of Our Children* (Stanford, Calif.: Stanford University Press, 1961) p. 138.

assortment of other law enforcement officials. In general, the detectives were more successful than the sheriffs, and the sheriffs were more successful than the police. But despite the presence of all these lawmen, a large part of the crime detection and enforcement had to be carried out by amateurs with steely nerves and a quick draw.

The picture presented of family life was mixed. In some programs, a tolerant, good-humored relationship was shown among the members of the family. Other programs showed conflict, screaming, distrust, and violence within the family. Little attention was paid to how the characters earned a living, so the child seeking career information got little instruction from commercial television fare—that is, unless he or she wanted to be a "private eye," a western sheriff, or a crook. On the other hand, some of the programs, particularly situation plays, went out of their way to offer morals to their stories. Typical examples are: "Don't undervalue your real friends"; "What comes easy, goes easy"; "Don't always believe what you hear."

What kind of variety was there for the child to choose from? About 22 percent of the time a child could have found a reality program other than news somewhere on the four available commercial stations. But for more than half the time, the choice was strictly among different types of fantasy: for example, two crime shows, a cartoon, or a western. This, then, is what television brought to the child.

Television's effects are the result of an interactive process between the characteristics of television and the characteristics of its users. Different children could watch the same television content and the effects could be different. For example, the authors discussed a study done by Fritz Redl, who compared the reactions of disturbed children and normal children to selected TV fare. He found that "ordinary" children would avoid extremely violent and frightening television content. Such was not the case, however, with the problem children. They sought to avoid the "nice" and "sweet" programs which showed loving parents and warm friendly relationships. Those kinds of programs, the researcher argued, were likely to cause the disturbed children to lie awake or to have bad dreams because they reminded the children of what was lacking in their own lives. From this evidence, Schramm, Lyle and Parker concluded: "Thus what would have been soothing (or at least innocuous) for most children was traumatic for these children because of their particular needs and background." [14]

The authors then presented their "inventory" of the effects of television. They felt that they could now discuss the nature of these effects because they had studied the ways in which television entered the life of the child. They placed these effects in the following categories: (1) physical effects, (2) emotional effects, (3) cognitive effects, and (4) behavioral effects. We will briefly discuss what they concluded about each of these effects.

Physical Effects The authors found that the physical effects of television were not very important. Television caused no special eyestrain (when compared to reading) *if* the children viewed under the proper conditions. On the other hand, eyestrain was likely to occur if the child sat too close to the set, looked up at it, and/or viewed it in a dark room. In addition, the authors found little evidence of any serious loss of sleep as a result of television viewing. The average difference in bedtimes between TV and nonTV homes was fifteen minutes later for those who watched TV.

Emotional Effects Television's emotional effects were less innocuous. A television program frightened almost all of the children at one time or another. What chiefly disturbed the children were situations where harm threatened some character or animal with whom they identified. It was particularly acute when the harm involved cutting or stepping into a trap —that is, nonritual violence. The children were frightened when they viewed such violent and stressful programs at too early an age, and many became particularly frightened when they viewed television alone or in a dark room.

In general, the children liked and sought excitement, on the television as well as in real life. However, they did not like the excitement to spill too far over into fear. Children engage in "thrill play" because they seek such excitement, and it has a parallel in television. The authors raised serious questions, however, about the possible effect of the high level of excitement in television, a level which they saw as rising. They questioned what the effects of this excitement would be on the children's perceptions of reality. Would it take the edge off the actual experience and lead children to demand something of real life that it cannot give to them? The authors saw signs that this was happening, but felt that the answer could be found only through long-term research.

Cognitive Effects Television probably helped some children more than others to grow into better-informed adults. It specifically helped those children who chose some of the reality experiences of television. Those children heard important people discuss current issues; they watched demonstrations of the arts and of science. They were "on the scene" in foreign places and observed great events. On the other hand, television was more effective, in all probability, in stimulating interest in the children and contributing to already existing interest, rather than in stimulating creativity or activity. There were cases where television did stimulate some children to read books that had a relation to some program. However, the authors cautioned that the most frequent kinds of activities resulting from TV viewing were either mimicking fads (such as wearing the Davy Crockett hat), or involved adopting details which fit into an already existing interest

—for example, a boy who changes his batting stance following the viewing of a major league game on television.

Some people had hoped that television would raise the level of children's tastes; they wanted television to bring more "highbrow" culture into their lives. There was little sign that this had happened, however. Indeed, there were indications that it was creating a level of taste in children based upon its own common denominator. The authors were particularly disturbed by their finding that children learned to like the programs available to them, even though they would not ordinarily have selected them. Equally disturbing was television's treatment of adult life. They found that television was portraying a "markedly erroneous" picture of adult life. This, they reasoned, was not a positive contribution to the child's socialization process and might require some very tough adjustments later in life. Moreover, such portrayals of life, especially the depiction of sexual behavior and violence, could lead to "premature aging" and even cause children to fear the process of growing up.

Behavioral Effects   The possible behavioral effects of television were the ones which had caused the most concern to both parents and researchers, yet the authors indicated that they were in almost every case controllable through the nontelevision life of the child. The authors addressed the question of whether or not television viewing made children too passive. They concluded that in *some cases* it did and suggested that long-term studies were needed to determine the magnitude and lasting quality of such effects. They also argued that "the way to avoid an excessive passivity in our children is not to give them television as a mother substitute early in life; rather to make them feel loved and wanted at home, and so far as possible to surround them with friends and activities." [15]

The most common and most feared charge leveled against television was that it taught delinquency and violent behavior. The authors argued that it was a contributory cause in some cases. For example, some children confused the rules of the fantasy world with the rules of the real world. The authors explained that a child who wanted to put the ground glass in the stew to see if it worked as on the TV program was merely experimenting in the real world with the tools of the fantasy world. They found too that children who brought aggression to television were more likely to remember aggressive acts portrayed there. The children wanted to be like the successful characters, whether those characters were good or bad. The authors cautioned, however, that little delinquency could be traced directly to television. "Delinquency is a complex behavior growing usually out of a number of roots, the chief one usually being some great lack in the child's life—often a broken home, or a feeling of rejection by parents or peer groups. Television is at best a contributing cause." [16] Schramm, Lyle, and Parker concluded that overall the effects of television pointed as much to the parents as to television. Parents who provided their children with warm, secure relationships and an interesting home life had little to fear from television.

CONCLUSIONS AND IMPLICATIONS

Television in the Lives of Our Children was the first major North American study investigating the effects of television on children and the only large-scale investigation available on that subject until the Surgeon General's Report on Television and Social Behavior in 1972 (see Chapter 12). The basic utility of this milestone is the exhaustive research upon which its findings were based. In many ways it resembled the earlier movie study (Chapter 2). As we have seen, the authors' investigations and findings included a fascinating comparison of children in communities with television and without it, an analysis of the influence of fantasy and reality in the content of programs, a detailed discussion of what children learned from television and the conditions under which they learned it, figures bearing upon homework habits and bedtime hours, a report on the program choices of children, and an exploration of the potential physical, emotional, cognitive, and behavioral problems among children which might result from viewing television. It explained in detail that children exhibited several different patterns in their use of television—patterns which changed as the children grew older. Thus, there were considerable differences among the children in their use of television and these differences were not simply the result of age but also varied in accordance with the child's sex, mental ability as measured by IQ, social class background, and the quality of each child's social relations, both with parents and/or with peer group(s). Moreover, the authors found considerable interaction among these five factors. For example, socioeconomic class and social relations appeared to interact. On the one hand, middle class children who were frustrated by their parents were likely to watch television more than their middle class peers, other things being equal. In addition, they watched television for its fantasy experiences. On the other hand, working class children who were similarly frustrated by their parents were likely to watch television less than their peers. Thus, differences in social class background altered the children's reaction to difficulties in their social relations.

Schramm, Lyle, and Parker suggested, by their very choice of title, that their approach to communication research focused more on the *uses* and *gratifications* of television for various categories of children rather than on actual direct effects. (The uses and gratifications approach, it might be noted, gained increased popularity in the 1970s and 1980s; see Chapter 13.) Indeed, a *leitmotif* which reappears repeatedly in their discussions is: "in order to understand television's impact and effect on children, we have first to get away from the unrealistic concept of what television does to children and substitute the concept of what children do with television." [17]

The authors did note, however, that it was the possible behavioral effects of television that had aroused the most concern in the public. Was television harmful to children? Was TV turning children into delinquents? Or, conversely, was it making them too passive? Schramm and his associates pulled their findings together in the following widely quoted but less-than-precise statement:

> For *some* children, under *some* conditions, *some* television is harmful. For *other* children under the same conditions, or for the same children under *other* conditions, it may be beneficial. For *most* children, under *most* conditions, most television is probably neither harmful nor particularly beneficial. [18]

They also reassured us, more than once, that if a child was given love, security, and healthful activities in his or her nontelevision hours, then there was little chance that television would have negative effects on the child. This assumed, of course, that the child was a normal middle class child who had been properly socialized into the Protestant Ethic. Their statements should have been quite comforting, however, to middle class parents, the principal audience of the book.

Theoretically the research was very diverse; the authors used several theories of selective influence. For example, when they stressed the importance of mental ability in determining the effects of television, they implied a theory of selective influence based upon *individual differences*. The major emphasis of the work, however, was on theories of selective influence based upon *social categories* and *social relationships*. Social categories such as age, sex, and social class all played a role in determining the ways in which children used television, and therefore determined how children were influenced by viewing this newest mass medium. Social relationships, however, were found to be crucial in determining the influence of TV on children. Poor family relationships and/or poor peer group relationships could send a bright middle class child to the tube for fantasy/escape experiences. In many ways, then, social relationships took precedence over social categories in determining the influence of television on children.

The authors anticipated the main tenet of contemporary meaning theory when they discussed the ways in which television could modify children's perceptions of the world. This influence, however, was mediated through such factors as IQ, age, sex, social class, and social relations.

There were some methodological problems with this research, although such a statement could be made of practically any large-scale project. Part of the difficulty seemed to lie in the basic design of the research. Schramm, Lyle, and Parker conducted cross-sectional surveys in several communities, but with a variety of goals in mind. Thus, their findings were not always comparable. In spite of this, the authors attempted to make cross-community comparisons, and the validity of some of their conclusions can be questioned. Overall, this problem points out the difficulty of executing research designs under ever-changing conditions. It should also be noted, however, that this piecemeal approach to planning the research also had a definite advantage, an aspect of the problem which the authors fully utilized. They analyzed the early studies first, then built new measures into the subsequent inquiries to test hypotheses formulated from the results of the earlier segments of the research. This approach allowed them to make the theoretical generalizations more refined than would otherwise have been possible. Thus, we can see that a tradeoff must sometimes be made to achieve research ends. In this case, the researchers traded complete comparability among the various communities surveyed for increased theoretical depth of analysis and for hypothesis testing.

One problem which could have been more easily addressed is the sophistication of the data analysis: it was much too simple. The parts written for general audiences were presented in simple, understandable terms, but the sections of the book intended for more technically sophisticated readers generally did not go beyond simple tabular presentations (although more detailed) of the categories and frequencies of the occurrence. An example of such simplicity is the frequent mention of interaction effects among certain variables (e.g., age, IQ, social class, etc.). Yet these interaction effects were never systematically investigated in the authors' analyses of the data, nor were they spelled out in any great detail: we were simply informed that there was interaction among the variables.

Beyond the questions about data analysis techniques, however, is a deeper theoretical problem. Schramm, Lyle, and Parker consistently made many arguments and drew conclusions about developmental changes in children based upon cross-sectional data. The authors did *not* examine the changes in a group of children over time. Instead, they compared differences among various age-groups surveyed during the same time period and inferred that changes in the young children by the time they reached the age of the older ones would account for the differences. Strictly speaking, these inferences are not appropriate. In order to make such generalizations, they needed longitudinal data—measures of the same, or comparable groups, over time. The authors never cautioned the readers about this; they accepted the differences as developmental differences. In fact, they *assumed* a "maturation effect" rather than discovered it.

Another difficulty in evaluating this research is the authors' desire to go beyond their own data and to present a total picture of the state of the knowledge in the field. In effect, the book becomes, in its conclusions, self-contradictory. At times, the writers appeared to place great importance on the role of television in the lives of children. They informed us that television occupied more time in the first sixteen years of the child's life than anything except sleep. They also indicated that it played a "major part in socializing children" and that it was the "greatest source of common experience in the lives of children." In addition, they believed that television distracted children from the "solution of real-life problems." Yet, in spite of these statements, they also concluded that for most children "television is probably neither harmful nor particularly beneficial." In a similar vein, they argued that television played at most a reinforcing role rather than an initiatory role in the various social ills that popular discussion had linked with it.

In short, some children could be "damned" by exposure to television. Those that could be "saved" were those who enjoyed the WASP world of love, security, and middle class values. These were the simple solutions to the potential problems of television.

Considering the authors' often quoted final conclusion about the effects of television ("*some* children *some* of the time," etc.) it was not surprising that many researchers interpreted this work as supporting the minimal-effects hypothesis. Yet the public was not satisfied. Perhaps it was the conflicting conclusions that bothered many people. How could something that occupied so much of their children's time and was so important in their socialization be so innocuous? Perhaps, also, some had not forgotten Dr. Wertham's heavy-handed argument against comic books (see Chapter 9). Indeed, television was said by Schramm, Lyle, and Parker to be fulfilling the fantasy needs of children that comic books once fulfilled—and doing it *even better*. In any event, the legacy of fear remained alive because in reality the "big" questions about television and its effects on children remained unresolved.

NOTES AND REFERENCES

1. Wilbur Schramm, Jack Lyle, and Edwin Parker, *Television in the Lives of Our Children* (Palo Alto, Calif.: Stanford University Press, 1961), pp. 11–12.
2. Melvin L. DeFleur and Sandra Ball-Rokeach, *Theories of Mass Communication*, 3rd ed. (New York: McKay, 1975), pp. 97–99.
3. Ibid.
4. Eli A. Rubinstein, "Television Violence: A Historical Perspective," in *Children and the Faces of Television*. ed. by Eli A. Rubinstein (New York: Academic Press, 1981), p. 114.

5. Eleanor E. Maccoby, "Television: Its Impact on School Children," *Public Opinion Quarterly*, 15 (1951), pp. 421–444; also Paul I. Lyness, "The Place of the Mass Media in the Lives of Boys and Girls," *Journalism Quarterly*, 29, 1952, pp. 43–54.
6. Wilbur Schramm, Jack Lyle, and Edwin Parker, op. cit., p. 1.
7. Ibid., pp. 63–64.
8. Ibid., p. 30.
9. Ibid., p. 95.
10. Ibid., p. 75.
11. Ibid., p. 78.
12. Ibid., p. 98.
13. Ibid., p. 173.
14. Ibid., p. 143.
15. Ibid., p. 174.
16. Ibid.
17. Ibid., p. 169.
18. Ibid., p. 13.

11

violence and the media: the turbulent sixties

America was bitterly divided in the late 1960s. The social fabric that had bound its people together was being ripped apart by forces that seemed to be uncontrollable on two fronts: The first divisive issue was an increasingly unpopular foreign war; the other was occurring in the streets of America's cities. Many citizens voiced their concern about the justifiability of the United States' involvement in the Vietnam conflict, but people also saw escalating violence at home. They feared rising crime, inner-city riots, campus disturbances, and other forms of civil unrest. In June 1968, President Johnson, in response to concerns about domestic violence and the recent assassinations of Martin Luther King, Jr. and Robert Kennedy, created, by executive order, the National Commission on the Causes and Prevention of Violence. The Commission was charged with investigating violence in America and making recommendations to the President for action. It was to examine "the causes and prevention of lawless acts of violence . . . the causes of disrespect for law and order, of disrespect for public officials . . . of violent disruptions of public order by individuals and groups," [1] and other related matters the President might place before it.

Despite the often violent history of the United States, this domestic turmoil was relatively recent. Indeed, in 1960, sociologist Daniel Bell had commented about America in the 1940s and 1950s:

> A sober look at the problem shows that there is probably less crime today in the United States than existed a hundred, or fifty, or even twenty-five years ago, and that today the United States is a more lawful and safe country than popular opinion imagines. [2]

The country could not understand what had changed this relative tranquility.

The 1960s were years of sometimes violent street demonstrations for a variety of causes. Included among these causes were civil rights, inner-city despair, student activism, and the antiwar movement. Hundreds of people were killed in these confrontations, thousands were injured, and large-scale property damage was inflicted by vandals, looters, and arsonists.[3] In addition, the incidence of crimes unrelated to such disorders soared. The FBI recorded a 100 percent increase in reported violent crimes between 1958 and 1968. Four major political assassinations took place and the new crime of skyjacking literally took off with the times. The first skyjacking (more accurately, air piracy) which involved an American carrier took place on May 1, 1961, when a National Airlines aircraft was diverted to Cuba. Thereafter, such incidents occurred on the average of once a month until 1968, when security systems became widespread. In most cases, the incidents involved persons who wanted to be flown out of the United States, usually to Cuba.[4]

The rising tide of the civil rights movement had begun to crest at the beginning of the decade. The pattern of response which this movement met was a prelude to much of what would later occur—nonviolent militant protest was followed by backlash, with the conflict finally forcing federal intervention when local officials were unable or unwilling to provide effective, equitable protection for the demonstrators. The new President, Democrat John F. Kennedy, had been elected in an extremely close contest in 1960. He had overcome much latent anti-Catholic prejudice to reach the presidency and he sympathized with the civil rights movement and took an interest in its goals. But, as a close advisor, journalist Ted Sorenson observed, "John Kennedy did not start the civil rights movement and nothing he could have done could have stopped it."[5]

A new era of "confrontation politics" had arrived on the American scene. Civil rights activists held marches, rallies, vigils, "freedom rides," "sit-ins," and "lie-downs"—often provoking violent reactions. In 1961, James Farmer led a group of followers on a historic journey from Washington, D.C. to New Orleans by bus. Their objective was to force integration of the transportation system and they focused their attention on segregated bus stations. In Rock Hill, North Carolina, the bus was attacked; in Anniston, Alabama, its tires were slashed. Finally, in Birmingham the passengers were dragged from the bus into an alley and beaten. The group finally arrived in New Orleans, but they came by air. However, they arrived triumphant; they had faced and defeated the lion in its den. Similar confrontations with segregationists, varying in size, occurred all over the South, with consistent gains for the movement. In August, 1963, three hundred thousand people joined Martin Luther King, Jr. in Washington, D.C. in a march for equality and freedom for all—and shared in his dream for democracy.

Political assassinations were a significant factor in the violence of the 1960s. The first jolted the nation on November 22, 1963. President Kennedy was shot as he visited Dallas, Texas. The vibrant young President had been struck down and the effects were profound in all walks of life. Few who witnessed the funeral, either in person, or on television, have forgotten the sights and sounds of the funeral procession—the flag-draped coffin, the riderless horse symbolic of the fallen leader, and the ceaseless deliberate cadence of the drums as the procession moved to Arlington Cemetery. Other prominent men also fell at the hands of assassins: Malcolm X, a black nationalist leader was killed by gunfire in New York in 1965; Martin Luther King, Jr., was ambushed in Memphis in April 1968; and finally, Robert Kennedy was shot in California in June 1968, as he sought the presidency. It seemed that no one in public life was safe from such attack.

Late in the summer of 1964, riots broke out in two black sections of New York: Harlem and Bedford-Stuyvesant. Six days of burning and looting followed. Similar riots and disorders occurred in over 100 cities during the summers of 1965, 1966, and 1967. Thirty-four people died in the Watts section of Los Angeles in August 1965, during a six-day riot. There were riots in Watts again the next summer, as well as in St. Louis, Chicago, Atlanta, and several other cities. In 1967, Newark and Detroit had major riots and several other cities had disturbances attributed to racial grievances. Riots followed the assassination of Martin Luther King, Jr., in 1968.[6] Not only were lives lost, but the destruction of property and the cost to the nation were almost beyond calculation.

Campus protests for student rights and against the war in Vietnam also led to violent confrontations. Protesters at Columbia University and the University of California at Berkeley, led by the militant Students for a Democratic Society (SDS), were particularly effective in drawing attention to their grievances. A wave of bombings and other terrorist acts occurred during the later years of the 1960s, as disaffected groups adopted violent tactics. Groups like the Black Panthers and the Weathermen (a radical faction of the SDS) emerged to carry on the fight. They preached the use of violence in the service of their causes. Protests against the Vietnam war were particularly violent during and after the Democratic Convention in Chicago in August 1968.

While such riots, violent demonstrations, and militant organizations accounted for only a small part of the nation's overall crime, they attracted a great deal of attention and generated considerable public concern. They were responsible for the enactment of tough anti-crime legislation and for a number of police crackdowns. In late June 1968, shortly after President Johnson had created the Violence Commission, Congress passed and sent to him the Omnibus Crime Control and Safe Streets Act of 1968. In spite of his reservations about some of its provisions, Johnson signed it into law. The act was a policeman's program, toughening federal laws, and establishing the Law Enforcement Assistance Administration to provide support for state and local jurisdictions. The government was waging a war on crime.

Besides these new legislative measures, the government also sought to understand the root causes of crime during the 1960s. It searched for ways to deal with the problems of crime through a number of special commissions created to examine particular problems. In November 1963, the President's Commission on Narcotics and Drug Abuse proposed a strategy to control drug traffic and give treatment to drug abusers. The recommendations contained in their report provided the basis for most subsequent drug control measures taken by the federal government.[7] In February 1967, the President's Commission on Law Enforcement and the Administration of Justice submitted more than 200 recommendations that urged sweeping and costly changes in criminal administration. In February 1968, the President's National Advisory Commission on Civil Disorders, created following the Detroit and Newark riots, warned that America "is moving toward two societies, one black, one white—separate and unequal."[8] The report, which followed a seven-month study, placed much of the responsibility for the riots on a century of white racism and neglect. The Commission felt that the deepening racial division was not inevitable, however, and that it could be reversed with a "massive and sustained" national commitment to act. Among the recommendations were sweeping reforms in federal and local law enforcement, welfare programs, employment, housing, education, and the news media. The Commission indicated that implementation of these recommendations would be expensive, but worth the price.

The final such report of the decade, *To Establish Justice, To Insure Domestic Tranquility*, was submitted by the National Commission on the Causes and Prevention of Violence in December 1969. The commission concluded after a year and a half of study that the time had come to reorder national priorities and make a greater investment of resources in the fulfillment of two of the national purposes of the Constitution—establishing justice and insuring domestic tranquility. They concluded that the cures to America's predicament of violence had to be based on two things—doubling the investment currently being made in the criminal justice system and restructuring urban life. Like the recommendations made by previous commissions, these measures could not be undertaken cheaply.

In addition to its final report, the Violence Commission issued a 15-volume series of reports from its seven task forces and five investigatory study teams. One of these reports, *Violence and the Media*, edited by Robert K. Baker and Sandra J. Ball, has become a landmark in the study of mass communication and was indicative of the growing concern that the public had about the relationship between violence portrayed by the media and violence in everyday life. We now turn to an examination of the contents of that volume.

THE MEDIA TASK FORCE REPORT

Violence and the Media is a massive work. It contains more than 600 pages, including 19 substantive chapters and 18 technical appendices. The editors divided the volume into three parts: (I) An Historical Perspective, (II) The News Media, and (III) Television Entertainment and Violence. Parts I and II contain the first nine chapters and seven appendices; the material in this part of the volume provides the groundwork and background for the Task Force-sponsored research and interpretation discussed in Part III. The volume builds upon the work done by other commissions and by individual scholars. It is well-conceived and presented in an understandable manner by a well-qualified staff and a number of special consultants, many of whom were among the leading researchers in the field.

Part I of the Task Force Report contains a summary of the philosophical and historical antecedents which underlie the American tradition of free speech, particularly as it is embodied in First Amendment rights. In Part II, the authors discuss the development, structure, and functions of the contemporary mass media. Among the topics discussed are the functions and credibility of the media, issues about access to the media, media coverage of civil disorders, and media practices and values. The report then draws a number of conclusions and makes recommendations to the government, to the media, and to the public. While limitations of space do not permit full discussion of all of the material presented in these first nine chapters, it is important that we know and understand the perspectives from which the Task Force research was undertaken.

Perspectives on the Study

The Task Force Report noted that much of our heritage regarding free expression stems from the struggle of the press against censorship and regulation. However, even though the press has functioned as reporter and critic for other social institutions, it has shown a marked reluctance to undertake self-analysis and criticism. Because of this reluctance, the Task Force rejected the argument that the government should not be involved in the study of the mass media. It is important, they argued, that we understand what forces shape the media, because the media touch the lives of Americans in ways that are both complex and intimate. Clearly, the Task

Force felt that commercial pressures on the businesses that make up the communications industry did not insure that, in the course of their doing business, the public interest was served. Thus, charges of infringement of free speech and of possible "chilling effects" which might result from government inquiry into media operations and practices did not deny government access to the information it needed to make reasoned judgments about the structure, functions, and possible regulation of the media. In the Task Force's view, it was more likely that public officials would be responsive to citizen need for access to the media channels than that the self-perpetuating corporate management of those media would answer this need. Such corporations already had acquired a highly concentrated ownership of those channels. As the Task Force observed:

> Clearly, then, the media merit study by anyone who would know more about the structure of American society. But when violence becomes the issue, the study is obligatory. For much of what we know of violence in all its forms we understand as observers and students of the mass media, not as participants.[9]

Since the influences of the media are so extensive, it is imperative that we understand how they are doing their job of informing the public. Because of their importance in shaping the public's knowledge and opinions of public affairs, the report focused its attention on media news functions.

Mass Media and the News

When the Task Force turned to the functioning of the news media in American society, it focused particularly on the media's role in intergroup communication and the solution of social problems, particularly media effects on violence. The report, while highly critical of the practices and procedures of the news media, concluded that the news media could be an effective agent in reducing violence if they provided a true marketplace of ideas in which there was enhanced communication between groups. In addition, if they provided increased access to the media by minorities, there might be fewer confrontations that could produce violence in order to gain attention. The Task Force felt that the increased level of violence was due, at least in part, to the slow response of American institutions to demands for social change, and that an important part of this slow response was the failure of the news media to provide routine and peaceful access to new and different points of view. In its opinion, too many news organizations feared social ideas and social action. In addition, because of the failure by the media to report adequately the conditions underlying social protest, the solutions which the media did offer to social problems, and because of their "action-oriented" approach to the coverage of conflict, the media themselves contributed to the widespread use of confrontation in the pursuit of social change.

The report concedes that some groups use violence to exploit press coverage, but such acts were not as common as popularly believed. Besides, the report maintained, violence was not necessary for a group to gain access —dramatizing the conflict was enough to focus attention on the issues. The message was not lost because of the media's tendency to focus on the violence rather than the issues which produced it. The Task Force also endorsed the Kerner Commission's criticisms of the media's handling of civil disturbances. In short, the report called upon the news media to provide the public with the information necessary to have effective democratic action. Journalists, it was felt, needed to reexamine their ways of doing things in order to see if the old ways met modern needs. New approaches were necessary; more emphasis was needed on analysis, opinion, and possible solutions to the problems, once the initial events had been reported. Thus, the news media, in pursuit of these goals, should try to provide a wide variety of such material as a matter of editorial policy. This material should include the full scope of approaches to the subject and should present the views of a wide variety of people. Both experts and non-experts should cover the entire spectrum of opinion.

THE RESEARCH FINDINGS

The third part of *Violence and Media* is concerned primarily with television entertainment and the issue of violence. It contains a large number of papers, written by well-known experts in the field, which summarize past research dealing with the subject of violence and the mass media. The most significant presentation in this portion of the volume, however, is the section covering the new research that was prepared especially for the Media Task Force. Specifically, this new research consisted of: (1) a content analysis of portrayals of violence in prime-time television programs, and (2) a nationwide survey of the actual violent experiences of Americans. Once these studies had been completed, a comparison of the two worlds of violence—television portrayals versus real-world experiences—could be undertaken and the accuracy of the media ascertained.

The Content Analysis

The Media Task Force was concerned not only with the quantity of violence on television entertainment but also its quality. In other words, how was violence portrayed? Who killed? Who was killed? Were the killings shown to be justified or unjustified? Were the aggressors in these situations rewarded or punished? The Media Task Force considered these inquiries and others to be important in addressing the issue of how violence was portrayed on television. To answer such questions, they contracted with Professor George Gerbner and his staff at the Annenberg School of Communication to do the content analysis. Gerbner, it should be noted, was then and remains a well-known expert both on the research technique of content analysis and the general area of the study of media effects.

The Annenberg/Gerbner content analysis of the television world of violence examined the entertainment programs during prime time viewing hours (4:00 to 10:00 P.M.) and Saturday morning viewing hours (8:00 to 11:00 A.M.) during the weeks of October 1–7, 1967 and 1968. The analyses were conducted by pairs of trained coders who viewed videotapes of the programs which had been supplied by the networks. A standard recording instrument for analyzing acts of violence was used by all analysts.

Gerbner and his staff had been given an important research goal: "To provide an objective and reliable analysis from which the Task Force could deduce the messages about violence which were communicated to the audience."[10] Since different individuals may perceive different messages from the same content, effects cannot be inferred directly from that content. However, knowledge of the content is a necessary starting point in the study of media effects. If certain messages are repeated over and over again, it was argued, they might be influencing a significant portion of the audience.

Since people do not agree on the boundaries of what constitutes violent behavior, it was obviously important that one and only one definition of violence be used in the content analysis. For example, while most people would agree that killing is an act of violence, many might not extend the concept to include verbal assaults. Therefore violence was defined, in the Gerbner research, simply as "the overt expression of force intended to hurt or kill."[11] The Annenberg staff undertook the study with the understanding that they would produce a "bare bones" report; that is, they were to provide a report which contained little interpretation of the data. Later, the Media Task Force itself examined these data and provided further analysis and interpretation. Thus, the Task Force's treatment of the content analysis can be further divided into three sections: (1) the extent or quantity of violence on television, (2) the qualitative characteristics of television violence, and (3) the Task Force interpretation of the content analysis.

Extent of Violence   It was found that generally the network entertainment presented in 1967 and 1968 was filled with violence. Approximately 80 percent of all programs contained one or more violent incidents —for both years (see Table 16).

Furthermore, the total amount of violent programming on the three networks did not decrease between 1967 and 1968. The highest percentage of violent programs (90.9 percent) was broadcast by ABC in 1968, and that network had ranked second highest in 1967 (88.6 percent). If a person who watched ABC wanted to avoid programs containing violence, it would have been difficult in 1967, but more so in 1968. CBS, on the other hand, had the lowest percentage of programs which contained violence in both years, although the percentage increased from 1967 to 1968. Even though their programming ranked lowest in violence among the networks, a regular CBS viewer would have experienced difficulty finding programs that did not contain violence. NBC programming was the only network programming to register a decline from 1967 to 1968, from 89.7 percent of their programs to 80 percent. Nevertheless, a regular viewer of NBC programs who wanted to avoid violent programming during the prime-time hours, was in a position comparable to the viewers of CBS and ABC.

On the other hand, if persons sought out violent programs, as was entirely possible, they probably would have been able to find them during all of prime-time television. In short, those who wished to avoid violent programming had an almost impossible task, while those who desired violence had little trouble finding it.

The researchers recognized that various types of programs would probably contain different kinds of violence and varying levels of violence; in some programs violent acts would appear more frequently than in others and might also be more brutal in nature. For the purposes of this research, the investigators classified each of the entertainment programs into one of three categories: (1) crime-western-adventure-style programs, (2) comedy-tone programs, and (3) cartoon-format programs. As we might expect, the

Table 16   Programs Containing Violence (Percent of Total Programs Presented)*

	All Networks		ABC		CBS		NBC	
	N	Percent	N	Percent	N	Percent	N	Percent
1967	(78)	81.3	(31)	88.6	(21)	65.6	(26)	89.7
1968	(71)	81.6	(20)	90.9	(27)	77.1	(24)	80.0
Total	(149)	81.4	(51)	89.5	(48)	71.6	(50)	84.7

* N = Number of violent programs

SOURCE: Robert Baker and Sandra Ball, eds., *Violence and the Media* (Washington, D.C.: Government Printing Office, 1969, p. 327.

crime type programs were the most likely (96.6 percent) to contain violent incidents. Cartoon shows, however, followed closely (93.5 percent), while comedies were the least violent. Nevertheless, 66.3 percent of all comedies contained violence during the two years analyzed. Thus, the researchers concluded that not only was violence prevalent in crime-style programs and cartoons, but "violence plays a significant role in television comedy." [12]

Overall, the researchers examined 183 programs. The analysis of these programs included some 455 major characters—more than half of whom (241) were violent. In addition, a total of 1,215 separate violent encounters were recorded! It was clear that violent content was easy to find in the programs and extremely difficult to avoid.

The Qualitative World of Television Violence Most of the violent episodes were portrayed as serious in intent, rather than as "funny." Humorous intent (slapstick, sham, etc.) was apparent in only two out of every ten violent acts. Violent acts were usually performed at close range, and more often than not, a weapon was used to inflict the pain. Typical weapons ran the gamut from knives and handguns to machine guns and explosives to elaborate devices for mass destruction. Portrayals of violence between members of the same family were rare (two percent); more than half of the time, violence occurred between or among strangers.

The violence shown, however, produced little visible pain, and the gory details of physical injury (such as blood gushing from a wound) were shown in only 14 percent of all programs. In addition, the violence generally took an entrepreneurial form; in other words, it was undertaken in pursuit of some self-interest, often solely for personal gain rather than performed in the service of some (worthy or unworthy) cause. It is interesting to note that the "good guys" inflicted just as much pain and suffering as did the "bad guys," but the good guys usually triumphed in the end. Such good guys are, by definition, those who achieved a happy outcome. The losers (bad guys) came to an unhappy end. Generally, the good guy killer did not suffer negative consequences for his acts of violence. Of the 54 killers who were major characters in the programs, 46 did not "pay" for their act with their own lives, nor even suffer much punishment. Indeed, it is significant that the major characters who did die were all bad guys. Not one good guy character who killed was a victim of such violence himself!

While across all age groups at least one character in three was guilty of violent conduct, it was the young or middle-aged, unmarried male who was the most typical violent character. These characters committed more than their share of the television violence; in nine out of ten cases, such characters were the killers, and in eight out of ten cases they were the fatal victims. Race and ethnic heritage also played an important part in the portrayal of violent behavior. Nonwhites and foreigners committed more than their share of violent deeds, and were usually the villains. However, unlike their white American counterparts, for nearly every life taken such killers paid with their own. Violence was observed between members of different races, nationalities, or ethnic groups in 28 percent of all violent episodes; in about another third of the episodes the violence occurred between opponents who shared the same ethnic background. However, such relationships could not be determined in the remaining incidents.

The police and other law-enforcement officials were portrayed in the crime shows to be nearly as violent as the criminals. There was, of course, one difference—violence by the police rarely cost them their lives. Police brutality was not usually portrayed; in eight out of ten instances, the level of violence employed by officers of the law was portrayed as no more than was necessary to get the job done. The problem was that the officers had to deal with "bad guys" who initiated violence. However, the law-enforcement officers were depicted as initiating the violence 40 percent of the time. The violent criminals were infrequently turned in for trial, conviction, and sentencing; the elements of due process of law were portrayed to be a consequence of violence in only 20 percent of the cases. Instead "shoot 'em up" solutions were the norm—with the bad guys losing.

The researchers pointed out that it was difficult to observe witnesses to crimes portrayed on television. "Frequent close-ups and medium shots tended to exclude them." [13] Even when witnesses are assumed to be present, showing them and their reactions adds to the cost of production and complicates the scene; it is therefore done only if showing them is necessary to make a specific point in the story. In half of the episodes where violence was shown, no witnesses appeared. When witnesses were shown, they were usually passive. In one-third of the violent episodes witnesses were present but did not react to the violence. The witnesses assisted in or encouraged the violence in nine percent of the episodes, and in only eight percent did they attempt to prevent it. In general, violent behavior in the television dramas was rarely overtly objected to by witnesses and rarely punished.

The historical period or setting of the drama was another significant factor in the violence. Seventy-four percent of all contemporary (the 1960s) programs contained violence. However, this frequency paled when compared to those that were set in the past or in the future. Dramas that were set in the past contained violence 98 percent of the time, while those that were set in the future *always* contained violence. Overall, the researchers found that the television dramas portrayed America as a violent country filled with many violent strangers. Indeed, America was shown as a nation with a mostly violent past and present but the worst was yet to come; the future seemed likely to be totally violent.

Interpretation of Content Analysis   The Media Task Force examined and interpreted the content analysis data seeking to determine what messages were being broadcast over the airways to the viewing public. Once they had identified these various messages, the Task Force went beyond the data and inferred from them the social norms concerning the appropriate use of and proper context for violent behavior portrayed on television. The process they used for these inferences was one of identifying the substantive meaning of a televised event on the basis of incomplete information. As an illustration of the process, suppose that a boy had been turned down by a girl three consecutive times when he had asked her for a date. Might he not draw the inference that she was not interested in dating him? Although the girl had never come right out and said so, he could easily draw such a conclusion and stop asking her out. Thus, the boy "gets the message" and makes an inference based upon incomplete information.

The members of the Media Task Force argued that they used a similar procedure in deciphering the norms of violence implied in the messages contained in the television programming. Their problem was to infer the substantive meanings of these violent messages (i.e., What were the television norms containing violence?) Since under these circumstances it was likely that more than one norm could be inferred from the same message, it was conceivable that one investigator's inference might not agree with another's. It was even possible for them to draw contradictory inferences. The fact that the inferences involved judgment meant that, within reasonable limits, two or more investigators could legitimately differ in their interpretations. To illustrate this, return for a moment to the boy–girl dating situation previously discussed. One inference that the boy who received three consecutive refusals could legitimately make was that the girl was not interested in him. However, based on these same facts, he could also have concluded that she was simply a very popular girl and that if he kept trying she might have time to fit him in. In this view, he would eventually get a date with her if he persisted. Remember, however, that practical factors limit the scope of such inferences. For example, the boy would not have been able to conclude, based upon these facts, that the young lady had been patiently waiting by the telephone for him to call, eagerly expecting a date with him. It is evident that, when the researchers of the Task Force interpreted the messages in the television violence, their inferences were not haphazard, nor were they based upon whim. Their inferences consisted of a process of attributing meaning to events on the basis of factual, although admittedly incomplete data, using logic and trained judgment.

Using this attribution process, then, the Media Task Force set forth a number of the norms concerning violence in television. Among them were:

1. Unmarried young and middle-aged males are more violent than others.
2. Violence can be expected more from nonwhites and foreigners than from whites and Americans.
3. Situations in which strangers are encountered at close range are particularly dangerous; violence is to be expected more from strangers than from family, friends, or acquaintances.
4. Middle-aged men and nonwhites are most likely of all groups to be killed when they become involved in violence.
5. Law-enforcement personnel are just as violent as the most violent citizens.
6. The past and present may have been saturated with violence, but the future will contain even more.
7. While the use of violence may lead to death, the inflicting of physical injury does not cause discomfort or pain.
8. Witnesses to violent behavior seldom intervene.
9. Persons who engage in violent behavior do not need to be concerned about punishment.
10. The use of violence is consistent with being a "good guy" because violence is a legitimate and successful means of attaining a goal. "Good guys" use violence just as much as "bad guys."

Overall, the report concluded that violence was a predominant characteristic of life in television programming. Violence, as portrayed, was useful as a means of conflict resolution and to promote the achievement of personal goals. Violent behavior was a particularly successful means of reaching personal goals, especially when the individual had been cast in a "good guy" role, because that violence was not usually punished. On the other hand, alternative means of conflict resolution—such as cooperation, debate, and compromise—were notable for their absence in television programming. Even when they were present they were shown to be relatively ineffectual.

The Violence Commission National Survey

The Media Task Force did not limit itself to an examination of the world of violence portrayed on television. They also investigated the actual world of violence as it was experienced by residents of the United States. There are two reasons why this examination of the real world was important. First, it was necessary for the Task Force to compare the fictional world of television violence with the real world of violence—the major objective of the new research. Second, it was likely that persons who had experienced direct exposure to violence would be affected by exposure to television violence differently from those who had not experienced it directly. Thus, the Task Force reasoned that: "Experience with violence may be both an independent source of learning and an intervening factor between exposure to and the effects of violence on television." [14]

To examine this "real world" of violence, the Task Force contracted with Louis Harris and Associates, a well-known public opinion research firm. Harris and Associates designed and conducted a national survey using professional interviewers and an area probability sample to estimate the total adult (18 years of age and older) and teenage (14 to 19 years of age) populations of the United States. The area probability sampling procedure required a random selection of census tracts, of clusters within those tracts, of household units within the clusters, and finally of respondents within each household. In total, the samples consisted of 1,176 adults and 496 teenage respondents representing households within the United States. The respondents were considered representative of the total adult and teenage populations of the country.

The Louis Harris researchers collected detailed information about respondents' demographic characteristics in addition to the substantive information in three important areas: (1) the respondents' norms concerning violence, (2) the extent and nature of their actual experience with violence, and (3) the media habits and preferences of the respondents. Each of these areas will be examined and the major findings discussed.

Norms about Violence   Norms set standards for behavior and define the limits of that behavior; they separate the acceptable and the unacceptable in social interaction. Moreover, norms have an explicit controlling function over behavior; conformity to them is rewarded but deviance is punished. Thus, it is generally assumed that most persons seek to act in accordance with established norms.

The survey sought to ascertain adult and teenage norms concerning violence. All respondents in both samples were asked to answer a series of questions which posed hypothetical situations. These items were intended to draw out their norms concerning the use of violence. In all, the respondents were confronted with 16 different situations which involved eight different assailant–victim relationships and two levels of violence (minor violence and major violence). The eight different role relationships used in the hypothetical situations were:

1. A parent and a child who was at least one year old and healthy.
2. A husband and a wife.
3. A wife and a husband.

4. A public school teacher and a student.
5. A male teenager and a female teenager.
6. A man and an adult male stranger.
7. A policeman and an adult male.
8. A judge and a citizen.

In each situation the first party was the assailant and the second was the victim. The questions were administered in the following format where situation A represented an example of minor violence, while situation B contained major violence.

A. Are there any situations that you can imagine in which you would approve of a policeman striking an adult male citizen?
   (1) YES   (2) NO   (3) NOT SURE

B. Are there any situations that you can imagine in which you would approve of a policeman shooting an adult male citizen?
   (1) YES   (2) NO   (3) NOT SURE

The findings were similar in both the teenage and adult samples, although the teenagers were more likely to approve of violence. The findings are presented in Table 17. As can be seen, only two role relationships won approval from a majority of the American adult population regardless of the severity of the violent act. These were a policeman and an adult male and a judge and a citizen. Thus, the police and judges may engage in minor and major acts of violence with the general approval of a majority of adults. Parents, teachers, teenagers, adult males, husbands, and wives, on the other hand, may engage only in acts of minor violence within these role relationships with varying degrees of approval. Severe acts of violence, however, are disapproved within these role relationships by a majority of the adult population.

What distinguishes policemen and judges in these role relationships from the other characters studied is that they possess an institutionalized authority to engage in violence. For example, the police officer is authorized to use whatever force is necessary to apprehend lawbreakers, including violence. Judges, on the other hand, have the authority and responsibility of meting out punishments which are consistent with the provisions of the law. Such punishments may involve acts of violence: public whipping, the death penalty, and so on.

Interestingly, the role relationship in which the occurrence of violence is least approved is that of husband and wife. The vast majority of adult Americans disapproved of even the use of minor violence between spouses, no matter which of them was the instigator.

Table 17 The Adult Responses to the General Question of "Are There Any Situations That You Can Imagine in Which You Would Approve of X Doing B to Y?" are:

		Yes	Percent Not Sure	No
1.	Parent spanking his or her child assuming the child is healthy and over a year old..................	93	1	6
2.	Parent beating his or her child........	8	1	91
3.	Husband slapping his wife's face	20	2	78
4.	Husband shooting his wife	3	0	97
5.	Wife slapping her husband's face	22	2	76
6.	Wife shooting her husband	4	0	95
7.	Public school teacher hitting a student	49	4	47
8.	Public school teacher punching or beating a student	5	2	93
9.	Policeman striking an adult male citizen.....................	73	5	22
10.	Policeman shooting an adult male citizen.....................	71	5	24
11.	Teenage boy punching another teenage boy...........................	66	4	30
12.	Teenage boy knifing another teenage boy...........................	3	0	97
13.	Man punching an adult male stranger......................	52	5	43
14.	Man choking an adult male stranger...	24	4	72
15.	Judge sentencing a person to one or more years of hard labor	84	6	10
16.	Judge sentencing a person to death....	53	7	40

SOURCE: Robert Baker and Sandra Ball, eds., *Violence and the Media:* (Washington, D.C.: Government Printing Office, 1969) pp. 343–44.

It should be noted that a small minority of both samples (less than 15 percent), adults as well as teenagers, gave general approval to the use of high-level violence. The adults who were most likely to approve of high-level violence were male residents of metropolitan areas who were between 18 and 35 years of age and who had attained less than a college degree in their education. Among the teenagers who approved of high-level violence, the greatest proportion were black males between 16 and 19 years of age who lived in metropolitan areas.

Briefly stated, the major findings of the national survey were: Adult and teenage Americans approve of violence only when it is carried out by legally constituted authorities. That is, judges and police authorities may use a high level of violence when it is legally permitted. Low-level violence, however, is much more broadly approved of by the majority of both adult and teenage Americans. The only exception to this is the husband–wife relationship; there, even low levels of violence such as slapping the spouse's face is disapproved for either partner.

Actual Experience with Violence   The survey respondents were also asked about their direct experience with violence. They were questioned about personal experiences with any of five violent encounters. Had they, the interviewer asked, experienced them as either the victim, the assailant, or as an observer. The questions asked are presented below:

Victim–Observer Questions

Victim: Have you ever been (repeated 1–5)	(1) slapped or kicked
	(2) punched or beaten
	(3) threatened or actually cut with a knife
Observer: Have you ever seen another person (repeated 1–5)	(4) threatened with a gun or shot at
	(5) choked

First, the respondents were asked if they had been a victim, then if they had observed someone else being victimized, and finally, in a different series of questions, if they had been the assailant. Since it was strongly suspected that very few persons would willingly admit that they had committed a severe act of violence against someone else, a slightly different procedure was used to measure experience with violence as an assailant. Some of the questions were changed so that they implied self-defense rather than aggression. The questions about whether or not the respondents had used a gun or knife were placed in the context of self-defense in order to improve the willingness of the respondent to give an honest answer. It should be noted, therefore, that use of a knife or gun for reasons other than self-defense are not reflected in the answers to the questions.

Assailant Experience Questions

Have you ever (repeated 1–4)	(1) slapped or kicked another person
	(2) punched or beaten another person
	(3) been in the situation in which you had to defend yourself with a knife
	(4) been in the situation in which you had to defend yourself with a gun

The data obtained from the responses to the experience questions are presented in Table 18. It is clear that for both adults and teenagers the most common experience with violence was as an observer. While low level violence such as being kicked or slapped was a fairly common occurrence in their lives, more severe forms of violence were rarely observed, much less experienced, either as a victim or an assailant. Overall, the vast majority of Americans have not had direct personal experience with severe violence. The Task Force thus concluded that: "Direct personal experience is not a source of learning about severe violence for the majority of the American adult and teenage populations." [15]

Who, then, were the "violents" in the actual world of violence? That is, who were the people who had experienced severe violence such as choking or threat with a knife or gun—as either victim, assailant, or observer? In the first place, it was found that a person who was a "violent" in one role was likely to be violent in the other two roles. That is, many of the violents in the victim role were also violent as assailants and as observers. Adult violents were mainly males between 18 and 35 years of age, who lived in metropolitan areas and who had obtained less than a college education. Although there were some variations among the teenage violents, the researchers concluded that: "In general, both adult and teenage demographic subgroups with the highest proportion of violents are strikingly similar to the adult and teenage groups with the highest proportion of approvers of violence." [16] This fact, the Media Task Force argued, strongly supported

Table 18 Percent of Adults and Teens Who Have Had Experience with Violence as the Victim, Assailant, and Observer

Violent Acts	Adults			Teens		
	Victim	Assailant	Observer	Victim	Assailant	Observer
Slapped or kicked	0.54	0.30	0.57	0.72	0.49	0.83
Punched or beaten	.30	0.16	.45	.42	0.38	.64
Threatened or cut with a knife	.13	NA	.17	.11	NA	.19
Threatened or shot at with a gun	.12	NA	.16	.06	NA	.14
Choked	.08	NA	.13	.16	NA	.22
Self-defense: Knife	NA	0.05	NA	NA	0.03	NA
Self-defense: Gun	NA	0.09	NA	NA	0.01	NA

SOURCE: Robert Baker and Sandra Ball, eds., *Violence and the Media* (Washington, D.C.: Government Printing Office, 1969) p. 355.

the assumption that norms about violence are directly related to experience with it. They found further evidence of the relationship between norms and experience in the fairly strong statistical association between the two. In short, people who were violent in experience also tended to be approvers of high-level violence, and vice versa. Thus, the Task Force argued that it had presented evidence which indicated that norms approving violence was one factor related to the probability of actually experiencing violence.

Media Habits and Preferences   The national survey conducted for the Violence Commission contained several questions dealing directly with the issue of the respondents' media habits and preferences. It was not surprising to learn that for Americans television was the medium most often used by both adults and teenagers for entertainment and relaxation. More interesting were the respondents' answers to the items relating to media preferences. One question, for example, inquired:

> How do you feel about the amount of violence portrayed in television programs today, not including news programs—do you think that there is too much, a reasonable amount, or very little violence?

Of those responding to this question, 59 percent said that there was too much violence in television programs, 32 percent indicated that there was a reasonable amount, while only four percent thought that there was very little, with another four percent undecided. The Media Task Force concluded, on the basis of these data, that "a majority of adult Americans think there is too much violence on television." [17]

Another question asked:

> Apart from the *amount* of violence, do you generally approve or disapprove of the *kind* of violence that is portrayed on TV?

Only 25 percent of those questioned approved of the kind of violence portrayed on television, while 63 percent disapproved, and 12 percent were not sure. On the basis of these data, it was concluded that: "Americans may not be getting what they want in television programming when the issue is the kind of violence portrayed." [18] Yet 25 percent of the adult sample indicated their approval of the kind of violence shown on television. When we examine the characteristics of these respondents, we discover that they are males between 18 and 35 years of age who live in metropolitan areas and have attained less than a college education. Thus, we can see that the demographics of those who approved of television violence were the same as those of the adult "violents" based upon actual experience. In the teenage sample, 53 percent approved of the kind of violence portrayed on television. And again the category with the greatest proportion of approvers was black males between 13 and 15 years old who lived in metropolitan areas. In short, there is almost a complete overlap between the "approvers" of television violence and the actual "violents" in both the adult and teenage samples.

The limitations of such demographic data should be recognized. Even with the substantial overlap between actual "violents" with respect to norms and experiences, and the categories who approve of and prefer violent television content, we cannot infer a cause-and-effect relationship. In other words, we cannot conclude that viewing television violence causes violent norms and behavior; nor can we say that having violent norms and experiences "causes" a preference for violent shows. Because survey data is cross-sectional, it can yield only correlations between characteristics; this allows us to speak of statistical association between the characteristics but not of causality.

Another important limitation of the comparisons of these demographic data is that the unit of analysis is a category, not an individual. It is not possible to make reliable inferences about individuals from collective or central tendency data. If a demographic category has a large proportion of its members classified as "violents" and "approvers" of television violence, it does not mean that all or even most of the individuals who have the same demographic characteristics also have the same norms, experiences, and preferences with respect to violence. The reverse inference would be equally untrustworthy. Unfortunately, those who prepared the report were apparently unaware of this *non sequitur*.

Comparison of the Two Worlds

Thus far in our discussion of the content analysis and the national survey, the television world of violence and the actual world of violence, respectively, have been described in terms of the extent and nature of their violence. When they are compared, however, the differences between the two worlds are quite noticeable. Clearly, the television world of violence does not accurately reflect the real world in many significant aspects. First of all, television exaggerates the probability of being directly involved in violent acts. Additionally, whereas in real life legality is a prerequisite for the approval of violence, in television programs illegal violence is often approved. In real life, most violence occurs between family members, friends, or acquaintances, while in TV-Land the majority of the violence occurs between strangers. In addition, the most frequent type of violence in the television world involves the use of a weapon. But the great majority of adult and teenage Americans have never experienced this type of severe violence. The most common role in the television world of violence is the assailant and the least common is the observer or witness. In real life, however, the situation is reversed; the observer is the most common and the assailant is the least common role. The television world of violence is often set in a time and place other than contemporary America. However, no attempt was made in this study to demonstrate that TV programs accurately or inaccurately reflected the actual world of violence in the American past or the conditions in foreign countries.

It must be kept in mind when comparing the two worlds of violence that a major concern of the Media Task Force was to examine the kinds of implied norms that were depicted by television and the effects of such messages. The Task Force wanted to know if the norms of television modified or changed the actual norms of the viewing audience (especially its younger members) so that violence became commonplace, or, worse, an acceptable method of obtaining a goal. What exactly were the audience members learning? The Task Force concluded that the high degree of overlap between preferences for violent media content and real-life violent experiences (coupled with norms in support of such acts) suggested that: "The television world of violence has the capacity to reinforce the 'violents' in the beliefs and actions in the real world." [19] They further hypothesized that the long-term effect of television violence on the "violents" would be in the direction of unrestricted approval of actual violence. They specifically argued that this group might be expected to act violently in conflict situations, when enforcing the law, and when attempting to achieve personal ends. The Task Force further cautioned that long-term exposure to the patterned world of TV violence could affect the norms and behavior of "normal" individuals; there would be an increase not only in the likelihood of their acceptance of violence but also in the probability that these individuals would use violence themselves. In short, the Task Force concluded that watching television violence could both reinforce violent behavior and cause it.

CONCLUSIONS AND IMPLICATIONS

The major conclusion of the Media Task Force was not particularly surprising. They found that television portrayals of violence were "one major contributory factor which must be considered in attempts to explain the many forms of violent behavior that mark American society today." [20] While the research concentration had been on television programming, the Media Task Force did not let the other media off the hook. They too were guilty, but the Task Force believed that television, as the most popular medium, had the most powerful and hence most dangerous effects. However, all of the media had to share in the blame for helping to make American society into a more violent one.

Although the Task Force came to many specific conclusions concerning the effects of the media, these effects can, for convenience, be categorized as either short-term or long-term effects. Simply stated, the overall evidence from the many papers contained in *Violence and the Media* indicated that the major short-term effects were two-fold: (1) Audiences that are exposed to mass media portrayals of violence learn how to perform violent acts; and (2) Audience members are more likely to exhibit that learning if they expect to be rewarded for violent behavior and/or encounter a situation similar to that portrayed. It must be remembered, however, that these conclusions about the short-term effects of media were derived from papers which summarized earlier research; the Media Task Force did not conduct research on the above issues. More importantly, it should be noted that the conclusions they drew concerning short-term effects were already well-established in the scientific literature.

The Task Force's numerous conclusions about long-term media effects, however, contained many more new insights and in many ways anticipated research trends that would become prominent in the late 1970s and early 1980s (see Chapter 13). For example, the researchers stated: "Exposure to mass media portrayals of violence over a long period of time socializes audiences into the norms, attitudes, and values for violence contained in those portrayals."[21] They further added that the probability of such socialization increased as the age of the viewer decreased; the probability also increased as the number of alternate or competitive sources of socialization into violence decreased. The Task Force also noted that persons who had been effectively socialized in this manner by mass media portrayals of violence could be expected to act in accordance with their beliefs. While this view has many implications, a few are quite blatant. First, these persons could be expected to resolve conflict in their lives through the use of violence; hence, the value of nonviolent means of problem solving would be diminished. Such persons would also be likely to use violence as a means to obtain desired goals, and when they engage in violence would probably use a weapon. In addition to engaging in violence, they would probably observe passively when exposed to violence between others. Indeed, it is likely that individuals who have been influenced by the television world of violence would develop the attitude that it is not the responsibility of individual citizens to help each other out of violent or violence-threatening situations. Thus, long-term exposure to mass media portrayals of violence might make members of the audience insensitive to or emotionally neutral to real acts of violence.

Other important long-term effects were also discussed. They included:

1. To the extent that mass media portrayals of violence contain rigid "good-guy"–"bad-guy," right–wrong, and either–or distinctions, young audiences are likely to develop and maintain psychological rigidity.
2. Inaccurate portrayals of class, ethnic, racial, and occupational groups in the mass media can be extremely damaging to communication between groups. When a group is portrayed as violent, members of the group may emulate the portrayal; nonmembers, however, may react to members with hatred, fear, or other emotions, creating additional intergroup conflict and violence. Such portrayals are especially potent if members have no personal contact with one another.
3. Both the extent and intensity of mass media portrayals of violence, especially on television, probably have the effect of creating and/or supporting a view of the world as totally violent. This world view tends to promote widespread toleration of violence, and a feeling that it is hopeless to try to control it, and the belief that individuals must be violent in order to survive in a violent world.

These were the major conclusions reached by the Media Task Force. However, they were marred by an important consideration: They were not inferred solely from the research and summary papers contained in the volume. The Task Force did a great deal of extrapolation and often outran the data; that is, there are many conjectures and suppositions in the conclusions. However plausible they may seem, it is difficult to separate them from the research findings. In short, the major conclusions of the study were not directly based on the research conducted, or even on the previous research summarized for the volume. This is the major flaw in the volume as a whole.

Nevertheless, important issues were summarized in the volume and the research that was conducted did give concrete information concerning the violent content of television. The networks could now no longer delude us with claims that they had been reducing the violence in their programming, as they had said for years. The data clearly contradicted them. Additionally, the content analysis showed that the television world of violence was a patterned one in which violence was portrayed in an unrealistic but potentially dangerous manner.

The Harris survey also added to our knowledge. We learned that a majority of Americans said that they did not approve of either the amount or kind of violence that was portrayed on TV. The American public, it appeared, was not getting the type of programming it wanted. Moreover, it was clear that those persons who watched and approved of violent shows, and those individuals who were violent in actual behavior shared certain characteristics. They were males between 18 and 35 years old, who lived in metropolitan areas, and who had an educational level of less than a college degree.

But what did these data really tell us that we did not already know at the time? Not much! As we discussed previously, we can infer no cause-and-effect relationships. We cannot draw reliable conclusions about individuals from grouped data. However, even if we were able to make causal statements about individuals from the survey findings, how much would we really learn? There was nothing new in the demographic descriptions of the "violents"—their characteristics had long been known. Perhaps the most important finding from the survey was that most Americans did not experience violence directly. For the most part, what Americans know about violence they learn from portrayals on TV. Thus, the implications for television's role in providing constructions of reality and socializing the audience about violent behavior are truly significant.

Finally, the comparison of the two worlds of violence showed how different they were—and how unrealistically violence was portrayed on TV. Yet the comparison raises the concern that if television can influence attitudes, values, and behavior, then the two worlds might one day be much more similar.

The editors, Baker and Ball, used a social learning theoretical approach to structure the interpretation of both the research conducted and the research summarized. However, it was not the simplistic stimulus–response assumption that characterized the old magic bullet theory. Indeed, Baker and Ball made this quite clear.

> Common sense and observation refute the claim that exposure alone makes all people think and act violently. We know that millions of adults and children are exposed daily to television entertainment programming but a majority of them do not espouse violent norms or behave violently.[22]

Although the volume discussed both short-term (direct) and long-term (indirect) effects, the editors emphasized the long-term and indirect effects. For example, they stressed the role that television may play in socialization. After all, their findings indicated that teenagers were more approving of violence on television than were adults. This is not surprising given that the teenagers of 1968 had grown up with television, while the majority of the adults of that decade had not.

Baker and Ball also discussed the concept of identification and its relationship to social learning. "Identification occurs when an individual emulates another, seeking to be like that person in appearance and behavior." [23] By 1968, the importance of the process of identification for personality and attitude formation was already well-established in scientific literature. Baker and Ball observed that in both the televised and the real worlds of violence, young and middle-aged males dominated the violence. Thus, they concluded that the potential for identification with characters in the television world of violence was greatest for young males. They noted that a common problem in the maturation process of males is the establishment of a male identity. If the young males seized upon "violents" in television portrayals in their search for masculinity, then they would be more likely to imitate the attitudes and behavior of the television world of violence, particularly if young males lack other role models.

Identification may act as an intervening factor between exposure to television violence and the learning of violent attitudes and behavior from this exposure. Thus, young males are more likely than young females to learn violent attitudes and behavior from exposure to the television world of violence. By stressing the long-term and indirect effects rather than the short-term direct effects, the editors were able to contribute to a theoretical approach that remains significant in the 1980s.

In terms of methodology, the research in *Violence and the Media* receives mixed reviews at best. Both the content analysis and the survey sampling were well done. However, when interviewing people in person there are certain factors that become particularly important. One of these is the tendency for respondents to give socially desirable responses to sensitive questions. This could at least partially explain why a majority of respondents said they disapproved of violent shows while at the same time they watched them with pleasure. Asking respondents questions which required them to rely on their memory (e.g., have you ever seen . . . ?) can also be a problem. In addition, particularly in questions like those administered in this survey, there are problems of demand characteristics. That is, the respondent answers the questions in the way the interviewer seems to want it answered.

Moreover, the measurement of the role of assailant was not adequate. The questions concerning severe violence were conducted in terms of self-defense; the use of a knife or a gun for other reasons was never addressed. The researchers assumed that the respondents would not be honest about violent uses of guns and knives, so they did not bother to ask. Not measuring the assailant role is a major problem because we cannot make any assessment of the effects of behavior on norms and attitudes.

Additionally, the data accumulated by the Media Task Force were composed entirely of descriptive statistics. The content analysis and national survey were discussed solely in terms of frequencies and percentages, rankings, demographic groupings, and averages per program or per hour. Trends and tendencies were often noted simply by "eyeballing" the data. In short, the research analysis was descriptive; no inferential statistics were utilized. The discussions overgeneralized from the findings, particularly given the absence of inferential techniques. The analyses simply outran the data.

Yet, *Violence and the Media* has become a classic in the field of mass communication for several reasons. For a number of years (since the 1940 Presidential voting study in Erie County, Ohio) many social scientists had argued that the primary effect of the media was reinforcement. In their discussions reinforcement had taken on the unique meaning of "no effect." Thus, they argued that mass media presentations did not create attitudes, norms, and values among the audience, but rather simply supported or reinforced attitudes, norms, and values already held. This was no effect? Indeed, even if the reinforcement effect *were* the only influence of the mass media, it would have to be viewed as extremely significant, given the widespread exposure that people have to the media in today's society. This was one of the major contributions of *Violence and the Media:* it forced social scientists to reevaluate the importance of the reinforcement effect. In addition, the work forced social scientists to consider that the reinforcement effect and the "causality argument" go hand in hand. In other words, television portrayals can both *create* and *reinforce* attitudes, values, and behavior. Indeed, a portrayal might do several things simultaneously. For some people it may reinforce attitudes, while for others it could help to form and shape attitudes and values, even if those attitudes and values differ from the portrayal. Because ours is such a heterogeneous society, different members of the audience can see different things in the same portrayal, perhaps focusing on different aspects of it and selectively ignoring others.

The public, unlike social scientists, received only a superficial coverage of the research and conclusions. The media chose not to make this book and its contents a subject of public discussion. Nevertheless, *Violence and the Media* had an impact if only because it raised more questions than it answered. Furthermore, those questions were of deep concern to Americans. In fact, the clamor for answers on the issue of television violence and its effects was to grow louder and louder until it could be heard even by politicians.

NOTES AND REFERENCES

1. Executive Order 11412, in *To Establish Justice, To Insure Domestic Tranquility,* Final Report of the National Commission On the Causes and Prevention of Violence (New York: Award Books, 1969), p. vii.
2. Daniel Bell, "The Myth of Crime Waves," in *The End of Ideology* (New York: Collier Books, 1960), p. 151.
3. Robert W. Peterson, editor, *Crime and the American Response* (New York: Facts on File, Inc., 1973), p. 23.
4. Ibid., p. 74.
5. Theodore Sorenson, *Kennedy* (New York: Bantam Books, 1966), p. 528.
6. Robert W. Peterson, op. cit., p. 23.
7. Ibid., p. 43.
8. Ibid., p. 45.
9. Robert Baker and Sandra Ball, editors, *Violence and the Media* (Washington, D.C.: Government Printing Office, 1969), p. 3.
10. Ibid., p. 312.
11. Ibid., p. 314.
12. Ibid., p. 328.
13. Ibid., p. 321.
14. Ibid., p. 341.
15. Ibid., p. 356.
16. Ibid., p. 358.
17. Ibid., p. 332.
18. Ibid., p. 333.
19. Ibid., p. 367.
20. Ibid., p. 375.
21. Ibid., p. 376.
22. Ibid., p. 375.
23. Ibid., p. 368.

12

television and
social behavior:
the surgeon
general's report

The ink was scarcely dry on the Report of the President's Commission on the Causes and Prevention of Violence when a large-scale research program was funded by the Congress to probe the issue of televised violence more thoroughly. The President's Report had identified the relationship between violence in media content and violence in society as a potentially important and disturbing one, but available data on the role of media content left many questions unanswered. Meanwhile, by the late 1960s, the issue of violence in American society had reached new levels of concern: The urban riots had created confusion and anxiety; street crime had continued to rise sharply; the nation's campuses were in chaos over the Vietnam war and related issues. Most of all, the assassinations of President Kennedy, his brother Robert, and of Martin Luther King, troubled Americans deeply. In the midst of all of these events, television became the nation's most widely attended-to medium. At the same time, the suspicion was well-established in people's minds that the portrayal of violence in mass communication was a cause of violence in everyday life.

Political leaders are always alert to public issues that can have an influence on elections. Violence was just such an issue, and it proved to be a subject that linked research to politics. It was perceived by Senator John O. Pastore (Democrat of Rhode Island) as a problem that might be posing a "public health risk" for members of the American society. If TV violence prompted children to be more aggressive, he reasoned, some sort of political action might be required to modify the practices of the medium.

But what action might be needed? Outright censorship was out of the question, but careful research, showing the facts linking televised portrayals of violence to aggressive behavior, might be enough to change the programming of the industry. After consultation with the research community, it was clear that such facts were not yet clearly available. An impelling case could be made, therefore, that the federal government had a responsibility to provide the funds necessary to resolve the issue once and for all. It was this political situation that prompted the U.S. Congress to take a deep interest in social science research to probe the linkage between violence portrayed in mass communication and aggressive behavior among its consumers. This interest led the Congress to appropriate a million dollars to fund research studies on violence portrayed on television and the behavior of children and adolescents.

After a massive research effort, five volumes of results (plus a summary volume) were published. Popularly (if incorrectly), they are collectively referred to as the "Surgeon General's Report." It is the task of the present chapter to review the highlights of these efforts and to place this massive project into perspective as a milestone in mass communication research.

The so-called "Surgeon General's Report on Television and Social Behavior" is a monumental collection of more than 40 scientific papers; it includes specially commissioned research in addition to extensive reviews of the relevant literature. Collectively, these independently prepared papers are referred to as the "technical report" and they are divided into five volumes according to their common subject matter and/or their empirical orientations. In addition to these volumes of sponsored research, The Surgeon General's Advisory Committee itself prepared a report (*Television and Growing Up*), in which the Committee states its conclusions about the relationship between viewing televised violence and social behavior. The Committee's argument is that the conclusions it makes were drawn from earlier research and from the papers and reports contained in the five volume "technical report." It is important to note that this summary volume, *Television and Growing Up*, was released weeks before the technical report and that the conclusions that the Committee draws in that volume were the ones that made headlines.

In evaluating the Committee's work, we should note that its title, The Surgeon General's Advisory Committee on Television and Social Behavior, emphasizes *more* than the issue of violence and the impact of televised violence on the attitudes and behavior of children. The issue of televised violence and its effects, was, however, the central focus of the research program, even though the research conducted for the program examined such diverse topics as television advertising and viewer reaction to it, the amount of time spent watching television, activities displaced by television viewing, the learning of specific information, and the comparative effects of black-and-white versus color television on the information learned from the television program. A wide range of social science methods were used in these studies, including: content analyses, laboratory experiments, field experiments, observation studies, and opinion surveys. Nevertheless, despite the diversity of topics examined and the multiple methods used, it is clear that the product of this research program does not cover the *entire* range of the subject of television and its influence on social behavior, nor was such a claim made by the Committee.

As we noted, the impetus for the Committee's work was provided by a request from Senator John O. Pastore, then Chairman of the Senate Commerce Committee's Subcommittee on Communications. This committee provides legislative oversight to the Federal Communications Commission (FCC). In a letter of March 5, 1969 to Robert Finch, then Secretary of Health, Education and Welfare, Pastore indicated that he was "exceedingly troubled by the lack of any definitive information which would help resolve the question of whether there is a causal connection between televised violence . . . violence and antisocial behavior by individuals, especially children."[1] It was as though the recently completed review of the subject by the National Commission on the Causes and Prevention of Violence—both extensive and expensive—had never taken place.

Surgeon General William H. Stewart (on orders from President Nixon) announced on March 12, 1969 that his agency would immediately embark upon a study to "help resolve the question" and that a committee comprised of distinguished men and women from appropriate disciplines would be appointed to study the issue. The job of the committee would be to establish scientifically, insofar as possible, what harmful effects, if any, violent television programs have on children. Stewart also announced that a one million dollar budget was being assigned to the project from otherwise undesignated funds in the budget of the National Institute of Mental Health (NIMH) and a report was promised in approximately one year. In addition, NIMH provided staff for the work of the Committee and was responsible for screening proposals, selecting those which would provide the most valuable data, and monitoring the implementation of the studies.

To aid in the selection of members of the Advisory Committee, the Surgeon General sent letters to a variety of academic and professional associations, including The American Psychological Association, The American Sociological Association, and The American Psychiatric Association. He also wrote to the three major national networks: The American Broadcasting Company (ABC), The Columbia Broadcasting System (CBS), and The National Broadcasting Company (NBC). A letter was also sent to the National Association of Broadcasters (NAB). All of these groups, as well as distinguished social scientists and government officials, were asked to recommend "knowledgable scientists" for membership on the Advisory Committee.

A list of 40 "recognized experts" in the behavioral sciences and mental health disciplines was compiled by the Surgeon General's office from the names received. Then, in a step retrospectively described as "it seemed like a good idea at the time," the Surgeon General sent the list to the presidents of the three networks and the NAB asking them to indicate "which individuals, if any, you believe would *not* be appropriate for an impartial scientific investigation of this nature."[2] CBS declined to offer any advice, but ABC, NBC, and the NAB named seven persons on the list as unsuitable. Eleven members were chosen from the remaining names and another member was chosen whose name had not been on the original list. The reason given for this addition was that representation in one of the scientific disciplines needed to be strengthened.

OVERVIEW OF THE RESEARCH REPORTS

The Committee began its work on June 16, 1969. The recent comprehensive examination of the existing evidence in the area of televised violence made by the National Commission on the Causes and Prevention of Violence, and the reaction it received, reinforced the original decision to sponsor new research. Between August 1969 and April 1970, 40 formal research proposals were submitted and reviewed for possible funding. Those applications selected to receive financial support had to pass a formal review system similar to the one usually used by NIMH to evaluate research proposals. For the Television and Social Behavior Program, groups of four to seven senior scientists in the researchers' field of expertise met, on nine occasions, to review proposals. Each review committee consisted largely of social scientists in the field who were not affiliated with the Television and Social Behavior Program, and senior staff members. In addition, one or two members of the Scientific Advisory Committee itself were present at most meetings. The Committee as a whole did *not* select the research projects. In all, 23 independent projects were funded, providing a multidimensional approach to the assessment of television's effects. These 23 projects —many of which involved more than one study and sometimes more than one report—form the basis of the technical report.

Volume I: Media Content and Control

Volume I contains the results of six studies, although one of the studies incorporates the separate efforts of many investigators and is the object of discussion in five papers. Overall, a total of 11 reports and papers are contained in the volume and they are all concerned with the *content* of television and how it comes to be what it is. These reports are *not* concerned with effects. The focus is almost exclusively on content intended as entertainment, rather than on news or educational programs; prime-time evening television and those programs designed specifically for children are dealt with extensively.

Content Analyses of Televised Violence Some continuity was maintained with earlier research. For example, in Chapter 11 (pp. 304–307) we noted the work of George Gerbner, who had done a content analysis for the National Commission on the Causes and Prevention of Violence, he did a similar one for the Surgeon General's Committee.[3] Gerbner analyzed one week of Fall prime-time and Saturday-morning programming in 1969, and compared the results with the analyses done in 1967 and 1968. In all three studies he used trained coders who enumerated and classified violent incidents by watching videotapes of selected network programs. He defined an instance of violence as "the overt expression of physical force against others or self, or the compelling of action against one's will on pain of being hurt or killed."[4] Note also that he was concerned not only with the quantity of violence but also with its quality or character.

The overall results of the quantity of violence studies displayed, at best, a quality of irony. Killing, compared to 1967 and 1968, declined sharply. But the presentation of aggression, harm, and threat did not. These remained about the same throughout all three years. Thus, the *prevalence* of violence did not fluctuate much from 1967 through 1969. In fact, in each of the three years eight out of ten dramatized entertainment programs contained violence; violent episodes occurred regularly at the rate of eight per hour. Therefore, overall—considering killing and other types of violence together—there was only a slight decrease in violence in prime-time television.

In children's cartoons, however, violence increased. The "children's viewing hours" were the *most* violent of all television hours in 1969 and they were increasing their lead over other types of programs. Violence in cartoons did vary by network; CBS was always lowest. The three-year average was about the same for ABC and NBC, with NBC greatly increasing the level of violence in its cartoons during 1969. It is evident that any overall decline in violence over the three years is attributable to a reduction in violent programming aimed at *adults*. As Gerbner notes:

> It is . . . clear that children watching Saturday morning cartoons had the least chance of escaping violence or of avoiding the heaviest saturation of violence on all television . . . Of all 95 cartoon plays analyzed during the three annual study periods, only two in 1967 and one each in 1968 and 1969 did *not* contain violence. The average cartoon hour in 1967 contained more than three times as many violent episodes as the average adult hour . . . By 1969 . . . the average cartoon hour had nearly six times the violence rate of the average adult television drama hour. . . .[5]

As previously noted, the content analyses dealt not only with the quantity of violence but also with its quality or character—that is, when and where it occurs, who participates, and in what ways different kinds of people are involved. The major findings were: Violence was usually excluded from the familiar; it occurred with much greater frequency when the setting was the past (e.g., westerns) or the future (e.g., space adventure), rather than the present, and when the setting was remote or nonidentifiable. Violence was *least* common in urban settings, as compared to rural, small town, and remote settings. A particularly interesting finding was that, in 1969, violence was typically presented with an absence of suffering.

Violence, and television action in general, tended to be the prerogative of males free of responsibilities. Roughly three-fourths of all leading characters were "male, American, middle and upper class, unmarried, and in the prime of life." Most male roles involved violence. In addition, most televised killings occurred between strangers or slight acquaintances, which is certainly not the case in the real world. Nonwhites, foreigners, and persons of low socioeconomic status, where shown, were portrayed as likely to become involved in violence; but they usually ended up on the "losing side." Women were depicted as lacking social power and influence and much more likely to be the objects of victimization. Between 1967 and 1969, female involvement (as the aggressor) in violence dropped sharply. In fact, this accounts for the slight overall decline in violence in prime-time television. Even though women characters were less violent, men were as violent as ever.

This discussion of the content analyses can be summarized best by noting that the most striking aspect of television violence is its unreality. People, relationships, settings, places and times all depart from real life. Why is violence so portrayed in TV Land? Perhaps placing violence in such uncommon settings and involving people who are strangers is a device that makes violence itself less disturbing to the average viewer and hence more acceptable. In any event, two implications of these unrealistic portrayals can be noted: (1) The reflection thesis, which maintains that television simply mirrors the world as it is, receives little support; and (2) As a guide for attitudes and behavior, television cannot be said to provide much accurate information about real life.

Interviews with Television Professionals   As part of the research, television professionals were interviewed to gain insight into how television content comes to be what it is. Two reports discuss these interviews; Cantor[6] interviewed 24 script writers and producers involved in the production of children's programs, while Baldwin and Lewis reported on the production of drama intended for adults.[7] While the two studies differ in many ways, the picture they convey is largely consistent.

Television professionals see violence as synonymous with action and hence as the best way of holding the attention of both children and adults.

They claim to attempt to confine violence to situations where it is appropriate—essential to the plot or character. The television professionals were generally unsympathetic with criticism of television violence. They asserted that violence accurately reflects life (a contention which the content analyses did not support) and that it prepared the young for adulthood. They rebutted critics by citing influences on viewers other than television. They criticized parents for ignoring their responsibilities and argued that the high ratings of certain violent programs indicated parental support. Cathartic benefits of watching television were cited (even though the weight of the evidence did not support this theory).

The professionals *did* admit that television might adversely influence a "disturbed" viewer, but they did not believe that the television industry could be overly concerned with this segment of the population. They suggested that television might be a scapegoat when poverty, racial hostility, distrust of government, and alienation should be the true focus. They argued that on television violent acts were shown as immoral unless they were in self-defense, or on behalf of national security or law enforcement. They argued that the heroes of violent programs used violence only when necessary and in accordance with the law. In sum, television professionals generally believed that violence on the part of viewers was inhibited— either (1) because of cathartic emotional release, or (2) because violence was always shown as either justified or punished.

Cantor found an overall indifference on the part of the producers regarding the possible harmful effects of television on children. "While the shows are in production, producers rarely consider the effects they may have on children; most believe those considerations are the networks' responsibility, or maybe the parents', but not theirs."[8] The creators of children's week-night programs expressed a similar indifference.

> Those producing adventure stories deny that they are making shows for children, although these programs are categorized as children's programs by the National Academy of Television Arts. One producer, whose program's ratings and demographic survey data show a large number of children under ten as part of the audience, said, "We are not making a children's story. I don't think anyone in the business knows who their audience is. I think it is presumptuous of anyone to claim they know this. Kids don't know anything. They are not discerning. As long as we are on the air, I don't care."[9]

Networks, of course, do have broadcast standards departments. Each network has a director and about eight staff members who are collectively referred to as "the censors." The general attitude of the "censors" concerning the work of social scientists on the effects of television violence is best summed up by the words of one chief censor: "We laugh at them. I don't see how the work accomplished so far by social scientists is of practical value." [10]

Many network people, in contrast to script writers and producers, verbalized to the researchers interest in reducing violence but the researchers felt that there was little chance that it could be substantially reduced given the methods of production. What else could be as popular and as effective in holding the attention of both children and adults as violence?

Comparisons with Other Countries   Last in Volume I is an interesting group of papers concerning the social processes and institutional structures through which television content is organized and controlled in the United States, Great Britain, Israel, and Sweden. Michael Gurevitch [11] compares these findings and notes that the proportion of violence in American entertainment programs is greater than that broadcast in any of the other three nations. Yet there is some tendency toward an Americanization of world television; a substantial proportion of the violence on the television of other countries is provided by American programs. However, the relative lack of governmental involvement in broadcasting separates the United States from other countries. In Great Britain, Israel, and Sweden broadcasting is much more tightly controlled by governmental and other public institutions. In addition, in those countries broadcasters gain support either through subsidies or by the licensing of receivers. In the United States, governmental influence is minimal; broadcasters support their enterprise by the sale of advertising and access is free once the viewer obtains a television receiver. Thus, this report gives support to the view that television violence is encouraged and perhaps made inevitable by the competitive economic structure of the American broadcast industry. For the future, however, perhaps public television represents a potential means of altering television content in this country, since public television's content is not dictated by audience size.

Volume II: Television and Social Learning

The second volume of the report consists of six papers: Two are essentially reviews of the literature while the other four report the results of experimental studies. The reports are organized around determining the nature and extent to which social learning occurs as a result of children watching television. More specifically, the reports are concerned with the nature of observational learning, or modeling; that is, the way in which the behavior of children changes as a result of observing the behavior of others. In this case, the children are observing the behavior of actors in television programs.

Modeling and Observational Learning Virtually all social scientists have acknowledged that attitudes, values, and behavior of any individual may be developed, at least in part, through observational learning. Research studies have shown that simple observation of others can be very effective in changing widely varied aspects of the behavior of children or adults. For example, children's observations of others in films, or on television, have been shown to produce: an impressive level of learning of unfamiliar behavior; an increase in willingness among children to aid others and to share with others; and even a reduction of phobic reaction (e.g., seeing another individual pet a dog in a film may reduce the observer's fear of dogs). These are only a few examples from the impressive body of evidence that supports the conclusion that learning by observation is a critical aspect of the social learning process.

In discussing observational learning, a distinction must be made between *acquisition* of new behavior and *acceptance* of that behavior. In other words, we must distinguish between the ability to reproduce previously unfamiliar behavior (acquisition) and the actual performance of behavior that is the same or similar to that which has been observed (acceptance). A child may *observe and remember* novel behavior without necessarily performing that behavior. If the child can reproduce or describe the behavior he has witnessed (i.e., when asked to do so) the *acquisition* of new behavior has occurred.

The possibility that behavior can be acquired through observation and retained without necessarily being performed *immediately* (or ever) has important implications for our understanding of the effects of television. If a child has acquired some new behavior, he clearly possesses the potential to produce it, particularly if he finds himself in a situation in which such a performance might appear to be useful or desirable (for example, one similar to the situation from which he learned the behavior). Thus, although learning does not necessarily lead to action, it makes more probable the performance of otherwise unlikely responses.

The learning changes the potential range of behaviors a child may display when provoked or when under stress—especially in a new situation. Therefore, the process of observational learning can be seen to involve three stages:

1. The observer must be exposed to the behavior of another individual, either a "live" model (direct exposure to other persons) or a symbolic model (the behavior of others as observed in television and other media);
2. He must acquire and be able to reproduce what he has seen or heard; and,

3. He may or may not accept the model's behavior as a guide to his own actions.

Relating this to the viewing of televised violence, there is no doubt that children are exposed to violence (Stage 1); nor is there any doubt that they can learn by viewing television (Stage 2). What is missing is an adequate explanation describing the conditions under which an observer will accept a model's behavior as a guide to his own actions. Even today, the answer to this question remains an elusive one.

Experimental Studies of Aggression   The experiments reported in this volume take as their starting point a study carried out by Bandura in 1965; they represent variations and refinements of that classic work. In his project Bandura had children watch a model perform a series of aggressive acts against a plastic Bobo doll.[12] One group of children observed the model rewarded for this behavior; another group observed the model receive no consequences; and a third group observed the model punished. When the children were subsequently placed in a play situation, those who had viewed the model rewarded or perform without consequences for the behavior showed a high level of direct imitation (i.e., they hit or kicked the Bobo doll in the manner the model had done). Not surprisingly, those who observed the model punished showed relatively few imitative or aggressive responses. Nevertheless, when the children in *all* groups were later asked by the experimenter to reproduce as many of the model's aggressive acts as they could—and were offered attractive rewards for doing so—all groups showed a remarkably *high and uniform* degree of learning.

Note that this evidence does not tend to support the argument advanced by network spokesmen that the depiction of violence has no harmful effects on young viewers so long as violent behavior is ultimately punished. We see that children learn the aggressive behavior and can reproduce it when the situation encourages such behavior.

One point should be clarified. The laboratory experiments concerned with the effects of violence or aggressiveness portrayed in films or on television have focused primarily on two different, although often related, kinds of effects: imitation and instigation. Imitation occurs when what is observed is copied or mimicked. This was shown in Bandura's study of the Bobo doll. There is no longer any doubt that a child may learn a new aggressive or violent form of behavior through observation and imitation. Bandura's work, in addition to the research of many other investigators, has thoroughly documented that fact. As previously discussed, the ability to imitate does not always translate into the performance of actual imitative behavior. Whether or not what is observed will be imitated depends upon a variety of situational and personal factors.

Instigation, on the other hand, occurs when what is observed is followed by a generalized increased aggressiveness. After viewing a boxing match on TV a child might exhibit increased aggressive behavior—some of which is the result of imitative behavior and some a result of instigation. In other words, the child's aggressive behavior after watching the TV program can be quite different in quality and character from the aggressive behavior displayed in the television program.

Since the fact of imitation was so well-established, no research in the Television and Social Behavior Program was concerned solely with imitation. Instead, the research attempted to provide more precise and extensive evidence about the capacity of televised violence to *instigate* aggressive behavior in children. For the most part, these studies utilized the classic design developed by Bandura in studying imitation.

The study, "Short Term Effects of Televised Aggression on Children's Aggressive Behavior," done by Liebert and Baron,[13] is representative of this approach. The purpose of the study was to determine whether the willingness of children to engage in aggression against other children would be affected by the viewing of violent televised material. One hundred and thirty-six children (68 boys and 68 girls) participated in the study. Sixty-five children were five or six years of age; the remaining 71 subjects were either eight or nine years old. The children were randomly assigned to one of two groups. Both groups of children were shown brief excerpts from publicly broadcast television shows. One group, however, observed the first three-and-one-half minutes of a program from a popular television series, *The Untouchables*. The story line contained a chase, two-fisted fighting scenes, two shootings, and a knifing. In contrast, children in the control group viewed exciting, but nonaggressive, sporting events (e.g., hurdle races, high jumping, and so on).

After viewing one of these two programs, children in both groups were placed in a series of situations where they could either *hurt* or *help* another child by pushing one of two buttons. The children were told that if they pushed the green button they would help the other child win a prize; however, if they pushed the red button they would hurt the other child's chances. They were also told that the longer they pushed the button the more they helped or hurt the other child.

The results of this experiment are startling. Witnessing the aggressive episodes increased the willingness of the children to be an aggressor. But the primary effect of the exposure was that those who had observed the violent scenes pushed the red button for a significantly longer period of time than those who had observed the nonaggressive sporting events. It was the magnitude of the hurting response that was increased. It should be noted that *not all* of the young children became more aggressive. Yet the fact remains that most of these "normal" children acted in a much more aggressive manner after a very brief exposure to violence. We do not know how long such effects last, but we cannot overlook this evidence.

Robert Liebert summarized the research reported in this volume and related it to 54 *earlier* experimental studies.[14] His conclusion was that continued exposure to violence is positively related to the acceptance of aggression. Children who view programs or films in which aggression is rewarded are subsequently more violent in their own behavior. According to Liebert, the accumulated evidence shows that

> . . . at least under some circumstances, exposure to televised aggression can lead children to accept what they have seen as a partial guide for their own actions. As a result, the present entertainment offerings of the television medium may be contributing, in some measure, to the *aggressive behavior of many normal children*. Such an effect has now been shown in a wide variety of situations. (Emphasis added)[15]

In general, the studies contained in Volume II were methodologically sound and generally consistent in their findings of a cause-and-effect relationship between viewing televised violence and subsequent aggressive behavior in children. The major criticism directed at these studies has been the fact that they were laboratory experiments. Laboratory experiments are probably the *most* efficient means of obtaining information, but critics charge that such studies represent an *artificial* situation that seriously restricts the possibility of generalizing the experimental findings to everyday life. Statistically significant effects may be obtained from events that occur in the laboratory, but will they, critics ask, have any relation to the behavior of young children in the "real" world *and* over long periods of time? Will aggressive effects present minutes after viewing the program persist one month or one year later? There is no doubt that laboratory studies do give us insight into cause–effect relationships that exist under *specified* conditions, but critics argue that laboratory studies are incapable of providing conclusive evidence about what happens in the "real-life" world. Questions about generalizing from laboratory experiments to the real world remain a subject of controversy.

Volume III: Television and Adolescent Aggressiveness

The question of whether aggressive behavior by adolescents can be attributed, in some degree, to viewing violent television programming is the focus of the research reported in Volume III of the technical report. Eight studies, plus review and commentary, all report analyses of the answers given by *adolescents* to questions asked of them in *surveys*. Note that the methodological focus shifts from small-scale laboratory experiments involving preadolescent children to field studies which examine the attitudes and behavior of adolescents in real-life settings. Thus, these studies address some of the questions of generalizability raised in objection to the experiments. It should also be noted that in some respects it is easier to study adolescents than any other age group. One reason is that, unlike adults, they can be found in groups at schools rather than singly or in pairs at home. Moreover, as subjects they have a distinct advantage over children —they can usually understand and answer questions.

Generally, the studies in this volume all address three problems: (1) the measurement of adolescent television use, (2) the measurement of adolescent aggressiveness, and (3) the correlation or association between viewing violence and aggressive behavior. Even with this common focus, however, the sophistication of the concepts, measures, samples, and modes of analysis vary widely among these studies.

Adolescent Television Use   Three different measures of adolescent viewing behavior were used: (1) total time spent viewing television, (2) program preferences, and (3) frequency of viewing recurrent programs. Total time spent viewing was usually measured by asking the respondent to estimate how much time he or she watched television on an "average" day. Program preferences were usually measured by asking the respondents to list their favorite show; this measure can also serve as an indicator of whether the individual prefers violent or nonviolent programs. Recurrent viewing was usually measured by providing the respondent with a checklist of recurring programs and asking how often he or she watched each. This indicator also served as a measure of how *often* the individual watched violent programs.

Although each of these measures has something in common, it is obvious that they are *not* measuring exactly the same thing. Therefore, they do not produce consistently similar results. While it might appear that adolescents who view television more frequently would also see more violence than those who view it less often, this is not always the case. An individual who watches a great deal of television may view only as much violence as another individual who watches less often overall but who has a distinct preference for violence.

The most general and consistent finding concerning adolescent use of television was that the amount of time spent watching *decreases* throughout adolescence. Children's viewing is the heaviest during the sixth grade;

thereafter, the amount declines steadily. Many factors account for the diminishing of the "TV habit" during this age period. Generally speaking, teenagers increasingly discover other activities which compete with television for their time. Such a tendency is, in fact, particularly evident among those adolescents who have the greatest potential for involvement in other activities—the brighter and more socially skilled, and members of more affluent social groups.

While age is indeed an important factor when considering viewing time, it appears *not* to be much of a factor when it comes to preference for violent programs. If there is any tendency, it is for older adolescents to be slightly more likely to name a violent program as their favorite. It is somewhat surprising, given the decline in viewing time among teenagers, that the average amount of time spent viewing by half of all American adolescents on a given day is *three hours or more*. While some do not watch at all, a substantial number watch twice that amount. Overall, a general impression is conveyed that many teenagers spend hours in front of a television set.

Another consistent finding was that of a negative relationship between television use and mental ability. Almost all of the studies reported that intellectually brighter adolescents watched less television and, moreover, were less likely to prefer violent programs. A negative correlation between both I.Q. and/or academic performance, and viewing time was obtained consistently. In addition, socioeconomic status also tended to be negatively related to the time spent viewing. Those adolescents whose parents' occupation and education levels placed them in the lower socioeconomic strata spent more time watching television than did those in the higher socioeconomic levels; they also indicated more of a preference for violence.

Adolescents saw the violent shows as being "highly realistic"; they thought they were even more realistic than news or documentary programs. Both boys and girls reported emotional involvement with television violence. But the boys were more likely to identify with violent characters. It must be remembered, however, that the girls lacked aggressive female role models; this alone could explain their failure to identify with violent or aggressive characters.

Adolescent Aggressiveness   Both the measures of aggression and the conceptualizations underlying it were numerous and varied in these studies. This is understandable, even defensible, in view of the fact that there is no simple or uniform consensus definition of aggression. For convenience, the measures of aggression can be placed into four categories:

1. Reports of aggression by others—usually parents, peers, or school officials.

2. Self-reports of aggression and delinquent behavior.
3. Self-reports of aggressive feelings and attitudes.
4. Self-reports of cognitive and affective reactions to aggression.

Some of the studies use a combination of these measures of aggression, while others do not.

The two most general findings about adolescent aggressiveness were: (1) Boys, not surprisingly, reported a higher incidence of aggressive behavior than did girls; and (2) Aggressive adolescents were more likely to have come from low socioeconomic-status homes and to have received low grades in school.

Relationships between Viewing Televised Violence and Aggressiveness The studies in this volume were primarily concerned with the relationship between exposure to televised violence and aggressive tendencies. As previously discussed, some studies used total viewing time as an index of exposure; others employed preference for violent programs; and some used the amount of violence viewed. Most of the relationships obtained were positive, but were of low to modest magnitude. This is particularly true in regard to the strength of the relationship between both total viewing time and preference for violent programs, and aggressive behavior. Stronger relationships, however, were obtained between *amount* of violence viewing and aggressive behavior.

What do these correlations indicate about the relation between viewing televised violence and aggressive behavior? There are three general possibilities:

1. The viewing of violence leads to aggressive tendencies.
2. Aggressive tendencies lead to the choosing of violence viewing.
3. Aggressive tendencies and the viewing of violence are both products of some third condition or set of conditions.

An example of the third alternative is a child who, as a result of certain personality characteristics, may be predisposed toward aggressive behavioral tendencies and toward a preference for violent programs. It should be noted, however, that these three alternatives are not necessarily mutually exclusive. The demonstration that one of the three processes exists would not preclude the occurrence of the others. Each may have an independent effect. In an attempt to find the most *plausible* explanation for the obtained correlations between measures of viewing and aggressive behavior the study "Television Violence and Child Aggression: A Follow-up Study," by Lefkowitz and his associates will be examined in detail.[16]

The Lefkowitz study is somewhat unusual because it was a ten-year longitudinal study. Children in Columbia County, New York, were first tested in their third grade classrooms (in 1959–60) and again ten years later as a part of the Television and Social Behavior Program. There were 436 respondents for whom both third grade and "thirteenth grade" data were available. The subjects were asked to respond to essentially the same questions on both occasions. The researchers had the children rate each other on aggression and then also interviewed their parents in order to establish aggressive tendencies both inside and outside the home. The subjects also made self-reports on their own behavior.

It was found that the popularity of an eight-year-old child in the third grade turned out to be a good predictor of that child's popularity ten years later. The child who is unpopular in the third grade tends to watch television more as he gets older, and continues to be unpopular. More important, the television habits that had been established by the age of eight were found to have influence on the boys' aggressive behavior throughout childhood and into their adolescent years. The more boys viewed violence in the third grade, the more aggressive their behavior was at that time and ten years later. In fact, the relation between third grade TV-watching and later behavior is even stronger than that between third grade TV-viewing and third grade aggressive behavior. Lefkowitz and his associates thus argue that the effects of television violence on behavior is cumulative. Since they also found that there was no relation between later television preferences and earlier aggressive behavior, the authors also argue that this finding supports the claim that frequency of violence viewing is causally related to aggressive behavior ten years later. Although many of these same relationships were also found for girls, they were much weaker and less pronounced.

Another interesting finding was that the more an individual watched violent shows, the more likely he or she was to judge that the situations depicted in television western and crime stories were realistic representations of life. Such a violent and hostile view of the world might lead these subjects to see their own aggressive behavior as normal and a perfectly proper method of solving problems.

Overall, the authors concluded that their findings, over a ten-year period, strengthened the conviction that there was indeed a real relation between viewing violence and behavior. Viewing violence *regularly* appears to lead to aggressive behavior. The significance of the studies in this volume was that they contribute to selecting among the three alternative explanations of the association between violence viewing and aggression. And there is considerably more support for the "viewing induces aggressiveness" position. If the association were due to the initially more aggressive youths preferring violent programs, then there would have been a stronger association between preference and aggressiveness than between exposure and aggressiveness, but this is not the case.

What about the third alternative? Is this relation between exposure to violence and aggressiveness due to some third set of conditions which affects both preference and exposure? When the researchers examined the relationship and took into account a variety of other variables, the relationship between exposure to violence and aggressiveness was not significantly diminished. Neither poor performance in school, nor low socioeconomic status, where norms of aggressiveness are more prevalent, explained any of the relationship. Nor did a variety of other additional variables. It should, however, be kept in mind that there is a multitude of additional factors which might account for the correlation. Noted communication researcher Steven Chaffee, however, concluded:

> There is clearly a preponderance of evidence in these studies to support the conclusion that adolescent aggressiveness and the viewing of violent television programs are statistically associated.[17]

He further clarifies this statement by pointing out that a significant positive correlation was found more often than not and that there was no negative correlational evidence. The correlation held up consistently in varying samples, with different sexes, age levels, and locations, and with a variety of measures of aggressiveness. It remained no matter what variables were controlled.

Yet, overall, these correlations were of modest strength. What can we conclude from the studies we have reviewed in this volume? The best summary is probably as follows: Regular or frequent viewing of violent television programs may cause aggressive behavior. This conclusion should not be surprising, since it would be terribly naive to expect that regular or frequent media experiences would have no influence on the social behavior of developing children. But television violence is only one of many factors that lead to aggressive behavior. It cannot by itself explain aggressive behavior; but its influence cannot and must not be ignored.

Volume IV: Television in Day-to-Day Life

The primary purpose of the eight projects and 18 papers reported in Volume IV was to provide a current picture of what kind of television people watched in the early 1970s. The projects included field studies, surveys, and laboratory experiments. Discerning these patterns of television use is important, since most people have access to *at least one* television set. The research contained in the volume dealt primarily with households containing children or adolescents; between 98 and 99 percent of these households reported that they had sets, with nearly half of those surveyed watching color sets.

In the early 1970s, television remained primarily a family experience were multiple family members viewed the same set. This was changing, however, because of the increasing number of multi-set households. In homes with two sets, one was usually designated "the children's set." While having such a set reduced parent–child conflicts over program selection, it increased sibling conflict. It is not surprising that viewing time for both mothers and children was higher in multi-set homes than in single set homes.[18] One study, however, did report that children were influencing their parents to watch the violent programs rather than the other way around.[19]

Viewing and Age Individuals follow an overall pattern of viewing consistent with their age levels. Children begin frequent viewing at about age three and their level of watching remains quite high until age 12, when it begins to decline. As people marry and begin having their own families they again begin to spend more time viewing; the level stays rather stable throughout their early- and middle-adult years. After middle-age, when the children have grown and left home, the level rises again.[20]

The studies in this volume reported that most children did watch television every day and that most watched for at least two hours. Many, of course, watched considerably longer. One study found that the viewing time of first grade Negro boys varied between five and 42 hours weekly.[21] Another study, involving nursery school children, documented an average weekly viewing time of 34.55 hours for boys and 32.44 hours for girls.[22] This represented well over one third of these children's *total waking hours* during the week. In yet another study, Lyle and Hoffman reported that "most elementary school pupils watch television before and after school as well as in the evening."[23] Older children (sixth grade and above) also watch through most of the evening prime time as well as during the earlier "family viewing" period. Children became purposive viewers long before they start school; they have regular viewing times and favorite programs. It is also interesting to note that sex differences in program preferences were evident by the time the children began school. Males showed a preference for violence; indeed, such violent programming, excluding cartoons, increased in importance as the children grew older. The children were found to be very consistent viewers; only two percent did not view on any given day.

LoSciuto reported that most adult Americans watch television daily and that they watched for at least two hours.[24] For adults, however, as much as 20 percent of the population did not watch on a given day. Women tended to watch more than men, probably because more women than men had the opportunity to watch during the day.

The studies in this volume clarified somewhat the relationship between viewing television and socioeconomic status. Before the Television and Social Behavior Program had begun, several studies reported that children of low socioeconomic status tended to spend more time watching television than did children of higher socioeconomic status. One study in the Program supported this conclusion.[25] Lyle and Hoffman, however, in a replication of the classic, *Television in the Lives of Our Children,* found results reminiscent of the 1959 data reported by Schramm, Lyle, and Parker: "At the sixth grade level, bright students tended to be among the heaviest viewers, but at the tenth grade level their viewing was more likely to be somewhat lower than that of their peers."[26] Overall, the viewing differences based upon socioeconomic status were not nearly as great as those found in 1959. It thus appears that there has been some leveling of comparative viewing among children. Several of the researchers (Lyle and Hoffman; Murray) suggest that the brighter children showed more variation in their program preferences. Such diversified program preferences were also related to higher socioeconomic status. Generally, children from higher socioeconomic groups and those who had higher IQ's watched less violence than their age-peers. This may not, however, have been their own choice, since their parents were also more likely to restrict program selection. For most children, however, there was little parental control of television viewing; indeed, despite what many mothers said, most children actually "viewed at will."

The data on adult viewing interestingly parallels that reported for adolescent audiences. Men watch more violence than women. Negroes watch more than Caucasians. The poor and less educated watch more than those who have gone to college. Male high school dropouts were reported to have a particularly high rate of violence viewing. This group is, of course, also higher than average in reports of actual violent behavior.[27]

Family Patterns of Viewing It should be pointed out that many of the studies in this volume made use of individual or family diaries. One member of the family, usually the mother, recorded for the whole family the amount of time spent viewing and the programs watched. LoSciuto,[28] for example, interviewed a national sample of 252 families and had them keep television diaries. The study is interesting because of some of its peripheral findings indicating that only one-third of the programs watched were viewed all the way through by people who had tuned in. Two out of every five viewers reported that they had watched the program only because it happened to come on the channel they were watching, or because someone else in the family wanted to see it. The diary records for the individuals showed a daily average of one hour, 59 minutes, but the respondents said that they watched three hours and 20 minutes on the average day. Other studies report the same discrepancy; the conclusion was reached that Americans consistently tend to overestimate generously the time they spend viewing and feel little social pressure to conceal television viewing.

The obvious problem with diaries as a measure of viewing, however, is that people may neglect, for one reason or another, to record all of the programs viewed. This is especially true when one individual attempts to record the viewing of all family members, often with multiple television sets. It is likely that some omissions will occur. This explanation was often given to clarify the discrepancy between recorded viewing time and verbal estimates of viewing time.

Another interesting study, conducted by Bechtel and associates, examined the validity of such reports of viewing time. They wished to learn whether the viewing habits of individuals were more in line with what they say or with what they report in their diaries. A small sample of 20 families participated in the project for a period of six consecutive days. Each household had a camera installed so that actual behavior in front of the set could be filmed. While this is an intriguing idea, there is little doubt that the presence of the camera affected the subjects' behavior and, in fact, several so reported. But whatever effect the presence of the camera may have had, it recorded only three hours of actual viewing time for every four hours viewing reported by the same individuals in a diary. This gives more credibility to the idea that Americans often overreport their viewing time.

A more interesting finding was that the level of attention to the television screen was constantly varying. The researchers divided the activities they saw while the television set was on into six levels of attention:

1. *Participation* (actively responding to the set or to others regarding content from the set).
2. *Passively watching* (doing nothing else).
3. *Simultaneous activity* (eating, etc.).
4. *Positioned to watch* but reading, talking, or attending to something else.
5. *In the viewing area* but positioned away from the set in a way that would require turning to see it.
6. *Not in the room* and unable to see the set.

Bechtel et al. indicate that as much as half the time the television sets were on, the viewers were doing something which placed them in one of the last three categories. This means that they did not actually "watch," even though they may have later reported that they watched the program. These researchers catalogued an extensive list of activities in which the people who "did watch" were simultaneously engaged. These ranged from eating and talking (the most frequent) to activities such as sleeping, smoking, dancing, preparing meals, dressing and undressing, doing exercises, and crawling.

The data presented by Bechtel et al. are important because they raise some important questions about the nature of television viewing. The most important question is whether viewing time is restricted to "eye contact" time. The authors developed their study from the standpoint of eye contact time, but is that necessarily appropriate? Does a person who performs household chores with the television set on, watching when something catches their interest, qualify as a viewer? The results of the Bechtel study emphasize the problem of establishing the validity of measures of viewing.[29]

Robinson advances this thesis a step further, arguing that viewer time is a continuum of short periods of full attention interspersed with periods of non-attention, or only partial attention. The viewer is alerted to things of interest to him or her by cues from the program itself. If Robinson is right, then the viewer may see only small segments of a program. The viewer may see violence without punishment, victims without criminals, as he or she tunes in and out of the program. What can we then say about the effects of portrayals of violence? Do those who prefer violence see only the violent segments, while those who do not prefer it tune them out?

Considering all of the studies contained in this volume, it appeared that several changes had occurred during the 1960s in the public's attitudes toward, and use of, television. The evidence indicated that more time was spent in the company of television sets than in the 1950s, but that the level of attention fluctuated greatly. Viewers were no longer "glued" to the set; in fact, it appeared that the set was often simply left on with the viewer tuning in and out as the programs changed. This raises the possibility that while television has become even more interwoven with our daily lives, its hold upon our attention has perhaps been reduced. Indeed, one might ask if the public's general affection for television has perhaps fallen despite apparent increases in "viewing time."

Moreover, the public has become more critical of television in one respect. The data gathered showed a high level of antagonism toward commercials. This antagonism was not only in regard to frequency but to their content. The public showed a strong tendency to reject them as deceitful, if not flatly untrue. And this antagonism was stronger among teenagers than among adults.

Overall, the new research indicated that while individuals do spend a great deal of time viewing television, they are primarily seeking relaxation.

This in itself does not turn viewers into "escapists, social isolates, or deviants."

Volume V: Television's Effects

The final volume of independent research prepared for the Commission contained a mixed bag of 13 different papers and reports. Unlike the first four volumes, there was no common substantive theme which united the papers except that all of them were based upon ongoing research. The author cautioned that their conclusions were tentative, that the data presented were undergoing further analyses, or that follow-up studies were in progress. In all cases, the reports were not intended to be definitive.

Some of the papers did, however, explore the role of televised violence in some new and interesting ways. For example, Ekman and associates[30] videotaped the faces of 65 five- and six-year-old children while they watched television (30 boys and 35 girls). The hypothesis was that the facial expressions displayed by the children while watching televised violence would reflect emotional reactions. The researchers also believed that certain types of facial reactions would be associated with subsequent behavior. They posited that child viewers whose faces expressed happiness or interest while watching violence would be more aggressive than children whose faces expressed sadness, disgust, or fear. Two different measures were used. The first involved a laboratory procedure where the children pushed "help" or "hurt" buttons in the manner previously discussed in the Liebert and Baron study (Volume II); the second was conducted in a more natural play situation.

The researchers found that facial expressions of emotions shown during the viewing of televised violence did indeed predict later aggressive behavior—but for boys only. They concluded, therefore, that it is not the mere presence of televised violence but the boys' emotional responses to it which predict later displays of aggression. However, the question remains: Why did the authors fail to obtain the same success with girls? The authors speculated that the differences may have been due to the fact that the violence shown was male-oriented; in other words, it involved male actors and male roles. There were no female aggressors for the girls to identify with. In addition, we should also consider female socialization in regard to attitudes toward violence. Overall, the girls may have been more frequently censored or punished for approving of aggressive behavior whereas the boys were not. The authors concluded that more studies were necessary to test these possibilities—studies that should include female role models and take into account female socialization.

Another interesting and even more perplexing study was conducted by Foulkes and his associates.[31] They examined whether pre-sleep viewing of a violent program, in contrast to a nonviolent one, affected (reduced or increased) the vividness, pleasantness, aggression, or anxiety components of dream content. Each subject participated in two experimental sessions seven to nine days apart. After arriving at the sleep laboratory, they changed into bed clothes, had electrodes attached to their face and scalp, were exposed to either the violent or the nonviolent film, and slept. The experimental procedure was to awaken each subject after ten minutes of "Rapid Eye Movement" sleep. The subject was interviewed and instructed to go back to sleep after each awakening.

This study was repeated three times, with three separate groups of subjects. Different results were obtained each time. The results of the first experiment indicated that dreams recalled after watching violence were more exciting, more interesting, and more imaginative. There was *increased* general activation. The results from the first replication of this experiment, however, indicated that the exposure to the violent film produced less imaginative and exciting dreams. There was *reduced* general activation. Because of this conflict in results, a second replication was funded by the Commission as a part of the Television and Social Behavior Program in an attempt to resolve the question. The results of this second replication indicated that there was *no difference* whatever in the content of dreams between viewing one of the two films before sleep. The authors indicated that follow-up studies were being planned to further clarify the issue.

The other studies reported in this volume were all projects "in progress" and the papers prepared for the volume were essentially progress reports on these continuing projects. Because of their in-progress status, those papers will not be examined.

Summary Volume: Television and Growing Up

The report prepared by the Surgeon General's Scientific Advisory Committee, entitled *Television and Growing Up*, contains a summary of the technical studies previously reported, recommendations for future research, and the Committee's "definitive" statement about the relationship between the viewing of televised violence and aggressive behavior in children.[32] As previously noted, this volume was the one most often read by scholars and laymen alike; unfortunately, the five volumes of technical research are neither light reading nor, with rare exceptions, particularly enjoyable.

Since the technical reports have already been summarized above, we will turn our attention to the recommendations made by the Surgeon General's Committee. The Committee qualifies its report at the outset by stating their unhappiness with the "narrowness" of the focus of the research program. "Exposure to violence," they argue, "does not exist in a vacuum." They further indicate that the narrowness of concentration "has severely hampered the interpretation of the results."[33] However, in any scientific investigation narrowness of focus is somewhat mandatory. It is this approach which is taught to students in their courses on research methods. No social scientist has yet been able to study all influences on behavior simultaneously. Moreover, the investigators do manage adequate interpretations of their data. That the evidence is not clear, convincing, and irrefutable is not unusual—scientific answers are never absolute or final. A Committee composed of "recognized experts" should have been cognizant of this, but they seemed not to be. Definitive answers can be sought as a goal, but such answers are unlikely to come out of a single series of investigations. In fact, it is widely viewed that definitive answers will perhaps never be found in social investigations. And it should be noted that most scientific studies have a more narrow focus than did the Television and Social Behavior Program.

The Advisory Committee recommended that future research concentrate on the following areas:

1. *Television should be studied in the context of other mass media.* The members of the Committee argued that a positive relationship exists between an individual's use of television and use of other mass media. (This has not been found to be the case.) They thus believed that attempts to isolate the effects of television exposure on social behavior resulted in "possible confounding of attributions."

2. *Television should be studied in the context of the **total** environment, particularly the home environment.* The question posed was: "To what extent does what the young viewer brings to the TV screen determine what he carries away—which is another way of asking where the television ranks among all other aspects of a child's environment?" The members of the Committee indicated that they were particularly interested in identifying the predispositional characteristics of children who displayed an increase in aggressive behavior in response to televised violence.

3. *Studies should be conducted to distinguish between functional (useful) and dysfunctional (damaging) aggressive behavior.* The Committee pointed out that the "realities of life require a certain set or readiness for aggressive behavior" and that the lines which distinguish between aggression and vigorous competition are often blurred. Even in the early 1970s, most boys were being taught to "stand up

for your rights and defend yourself." Thus, the argument is that the viewing of certain aggressive behavior (e.g., vigorous competition) may be beneficial for some viewers, especially perhaps for the shy, timid viewer.

4. *Modeling and imitation of prosocial behavior should be studied.* The Committee argued that if children imitate aggressive acts, they may also imitate prosocial acts; furthermore, this imitation of positive prosocial behavior may balance any negative effects.

5. *We should examine the symbolic functions of violence on television.* Violent content in fiction may sometimes be a vehicle for presenting "messages" to a general audience about important social and cultural issues. Without the use of this violence, it may not be possible to examine these issues.

The Advisory Committee also called for a "more humane definition of violence." While violence was defined primarily in a physical sense in the research program, the Committee argued that it should be expanded to include the "experience of [all its victims]." These victims include those who have been killed or disabled by unsafe drugs which have been approved for public use. (Prescribing birth control pills would thus be defined as an act of violence.) Pollution of the air and water, impure foods, the operation of a factory (if a death or disability occurs) are all violence. The Committee goes so far as to say that the "casting of a vote in Congress, or the signing of an Executive Order" should be defined as violent when such acts have adverse effects "on a few people or a multitude of people." They then suggest that television should be used as a social force to modify society's definition and awareness of violence.

Finally, we come to the Committee's conclusion concerning the relationship between viewing televised violence and aggressive behavior. When the Committee began its work in 1969, it took as the starting point the conclusions derived from a well-known 1961 study (which we discussed in Chapter 10), *Television in the Lives of Our Children:* "For *some* children, under *some* conditions, *some* television is harmful. For *other* children under the same conditions, or for the same children under *other* conditions, it may be beneficial. For *most* children, under *most* conditions, most television is probably neither harmful nor particularly beneficial." [34] To see just how far we have come from these findings, the Committee summarized its findings and conclusions:

Thus the two sets of findings (laboratory and survey) converge in three respects: a preliminary and tentative indication of a causal relation between viewing violence on television and aggressive behavior; an indication that any such causal operation operates only on some children (who are predisposed to be aggressive); and an indication that it operates only in some environmental contexts. Such tentative and limited conclusions are not very satisfying [yet] they represent substantially more knowledge than we had two years ago.[35]

It cost the American public 1.8 million dollars to gain this "increase" in our collective knowledge. Such is the price of progress.

As a result of this report and the above conclusions and observations, the Committee has been charged with having become an apologist for, and defender of, the broadcast industry. Given the industry's input into the Committee's makeup, the charge is not surprising; the controversy surrounding the Committee and its report will now be examined in detail.

THE FIRESTORM OF CRITICISM AND THE SENATE HEARINGS

In many ways, the real impact of this research came not from the studies themselves but from the controversy which followed the publication of the Committee's report. Even before the Committee's work had been completed, the manner in which the Advisory Committee was selected became a topic of heated controversy.

The May 22, 1970 issue of *Science* magazine contained a report which publicized a previously unknown fact: ABC, NBC, and the National Association of Broadcasters had blackballed seven social scientists distinguished for their past research and expertise on the subject (Albert Bandura, Leo Bogart, Leonard Berkowitz, Leon Eisenberg, Ralph Gerry, Otto Larsen, and Percy Tannenbaum). In response to this revelation, several members of the Advisory Committee threatened to resign but were persuaded to continue serving.

The notoriety prompted an explanation from Robert Finch, Secretary of Health, Education and Welfare. He argued that the same procedure had been used with the earlier Advisory Committee on Smoking and Health. That is, the tobacco industry had been asked to approve the composition of that Committee in order to forestall any subsequent charge that it had been biased against the industry. In both cases, Finch indicated, the purpose of seeking such advice was to enhance the Committee's credibility and to secure the cooperation of the industry whose product was under scrutiny. What Finch neglected to note at that time was that in the Smoking and Health Advisory Committee, organizations on *both sides* of the controversy had been asked to identify unsuitable parties. Moreover, no individual had been allowed to serve on the committee if he represented any organization or group with an interest in the outcome.

The Advisory Committee appointed to investigate the television question consisted of four psychologists, three sociologists, two psychiatrists, a political scientist, an anthropologist, and an educator. However, all three of the sociologists who served were affiliated with CBS! (Ira H. Cisin and Harold Mendelsohn were active consultants with CBS; Joseph T. Klapper headed the network's Office of Social Research.) Furthermore, two of the psychologists had network affiliations (Thomas E. Coffin was the Research Director at NBC and Gerhardt Wiebe was a long-time research executive for CBS.) Not only was the broadcast industry given veto power over prospective members but it also placed five of its own people on the Committee.

The reaction from social scientists was immediate and hostile. Leo Bogart's remarks are typical:

> The idea that an industry should not only be represented directly in a scholarly inquiry into its activities, but should also exercise a veto over the membership of the investigating panel, is too stupid and scandalous to escape commentary. It cannot be permitted again in future government-sponsored research on public matters that affect established interests.[36]

In addition to the five persons closely affiliated with the networks, four others were decidedly unfamiliar with the empirical studies of communication effects, although each was well-known and expert in his own field. This left only three persons (a political scientist and two psychologists) who could be said to both possess the necessary technical expertise and be free of affiliations with the television industry. Indeed, the Committee has been described as consisting of "the network five, the naive four, and the scientific three."[37]

Why was the Committee so composed? It might be thought that an ideal investigative team would be a "scientific twelve." The presence of the four members from outside disciplines, however, was the result of a standard policy requiring heterogeneous representation in such panels. But their presence was compromised by the broadcast industry personnel whose participation was considered by many to be a simple function of the power of the industry and the hesitancy of the Nixon Administration to offend it unnecessarily.

While the composition of the Committee provided minimal affront to broadcasters, the shabby treatment of eminent social scientists shocked the scientific community. The blackballing of widely recognized experts *because of* their past work and professional expertise created a deep hostility among social and behavioral scientists. The irony was that it was the broadcasters who paid the price. The broadcast industry made a preemptive strike in a conflict that need never have occurred. In the end, it was the broadcasters who were bloodied.

In addition to the issue of committee composition and selection, the report issued by the Advisory Committee (*Television and Growing Up*) also sparked a controversy. Many of the independent investigators whose works were included among the papers in the technical volumes claimed that their findings had been "irresponsibly distorted" in the Committee's report. Another charge was that "some highly pertinent studies demonstrating that violence viewing causes children to behave aggressively were not even mentioned."[38]

This storm of protest was the impetus for Senate Hearings, chaired by Senator Pastore, March 21–24, 1972, before the Subcommittee on Communications of the Commerce Committee. It became clear from the testimony offered that the final Advisory Committee document reflected a considerable amount of drafting and redrafting, and that this redrafting was largely the work of the two network research directors—those with the most at stake in the outcome. Indeed, George Comstock, a member of the NIMH staff, testified that "as much as 90 percent of the report revision was made at the insistence of Klapper."[39]

Besides the more blatant errors and abuses, there are many statements in *Television and Growing Up* which were clearly misunderstood by those untrained in the social sciences. For example, in social science research a call for further study is almost always necessary—to confirm and elaborate findings. However, to reporters untrained in the social sciences this meant that the study failed to prove that violent television presentations had harmful effects. And since *Television and Growing Up* was released prior to the technical reports, the conclusions contained in it were the ones which made news headlines. *The New York Times*, for example, ran a front page story under the headline: "TV Held Unharmful to Youth." Other newspapers and magazines reported the Committee's findings under similar headlines. The cautious and carefully worded conclusions of the Committee were reported in such a way in the news media that the meaning of the Committee's language may have been distorted. The more cynical reader might infer that the carefully drafted wording was intended to mislead the technically unsophisticated.

Because of all the problems associated with the Advisory Committee report, Senator Pastore elected to bypass that report and to examine directly the five volumes of technical research during the hearings. The object —to arrive at an independent conclusion about the relationship between viewing televised violence and aggressive behavior.

Before the end of the hearings, all those who testified before the Senate Committee—even the presidents of the three major national networks—agreed (although it must be admitted, some under heavy pressure from the Committee) that television violence had an adverse effect on children. No one who testified claimed that television violence was the sole cause of aggressive behavior. Indeed, many testifying wished to address other pertinent causes. However, Senator Pastore indicated that the issue at hand was determining the relationship between television violence and aggressive behavior. He pointed out that no one was naive enough to posit a single cause.

The most definitive and incisive testimony given at the Hearings was probably that offered by the Surgeon General himself, Jessie L. Steinfeld:

> While the Committee report is carefully phrased and qualified in language acceptable to social scientists, it is clear to me that the causal relation between televised violence and antisocial behavior is sufficient to warrant appropriate and immediate remedial action. The data on social phenomena such as television and social violence will never be clear enough for all social scientists to agree on the formulation of a succinct statement of causality. But there comes a time when the data are sufficient to justify action. That time has come.[40]

Dr. Steinfeld might just as easily have said: "Warning: the Surgeon General has determined that viewing television violence is dangerous to your child's health."

CONCLUSIONS AND IMPLICATIONS

What are we to conclude from all of this? Can we, or should we, separate the research from the controversy surrounding it? The importance of the Television and Social Behavior Program obviously lies in the five volumes of technical reports and not in the Advisory Committee report. The most appropriate way of looking at that report is as the product of a three-way process of interaction—among government, the TV industry, and social science. From this perspective, what was studied and why becomes almost as interesting as what was learned. We can draw three main conclusions from the five volumes of research:

1. Television content is heavily saturated with violence.
2. Children and adults are spending more and more time exposed to violent content.

3. Overall, the evidence supports the hypothesis that the viewing of violent entertainment increases the likelihood of aggressive behavior. This evidence is derived from both laboratory experiments which permit causal inference, *and* from surveys which provide evidence of real-life associations in everyday events.

Not all social scientists will agree with the third conclusion. It is easy to criticize most of the studies on an individual basis. For example, in some of the laboratory experiments the samples studied were quite small. In many of the experiments and all of the surveys there was an overconcentration on the more articulate and responsible older children and an underrepresentation of younger children (who appear to be especially susceptible to the influence of television). However, the methodological flaws of one study do not usually apply to another. Taken as a whole, the consistent accumulation of evidence allows us, as social scientists, to feel reasonably comfortable with the conclusions reached.

The major problem of the Television and Social Behavior program of research is the way in which the research problem was posed. The Advisory Committee chose to frame the question in terms of direct effects: Does exposure to violence lead children to specific acts of antisocial behavior? As far as the broadcast industry is concerned, this is probably the most acceptable formulation. We must, however, consider the possibility, or probability, that television's most profound influences may be indirect. How does the presentation of life in television programming alter the socialization process, if it does? Does it change the world view of those who are regular viewers? Does it make violence a more common phenomenon in familiar contexts to more people and thus make it more acceptable? Or does the presentation of violence simply make for a more timid, fearful populace? How does the continual flow of violence in the media affect our beliefs, attitudes, and values, and the quality of life in our country? We do not really know what the long-term effects are for individuals or for society.

What, then, should be done about violence on television? Should it be eliminated? No, because violence *is* a part of life, and of art. Besides, the real issue is not the use of violence that honestly reflects the conflicts of the times, "the issue is the deliberate use of cliché violence, violence contrived to formula, violence as a commodity that can be packaged for sale." [41] When violence is packaged in an "acceptable" format, and is presented as real, it distorts reality, and it distorts the perceptions of those who must live in that reality. Violence contrived for the sake of violence—for comic effect, for amusement—without meaning or purpose, does no service to the viewer. It may beguile the audience, but in the end the play may become real—and painful.

In conclusion, *Television and Social Behavior* has an assured place in the history of applied social research. That place is secure because of the large budget, the controversy surrounding the project, and also the broad public and journalistic interest in the wider questions it raises. The reader should be cautioned that this chapter can only hint at the rich detail of the specific findings, theoretical insights, and heterogeneity of research methods and techniques employed. The *Television and Social Behavior* project remains one that is unique in its size, scope, and focus. In many ways, it is a noteworthy exemplar of communication research. Unfortunately, it is also a document that has been discussed much more often than it has been read.

NOTES AND REFERENCES

1. Surgeon General's Scientific Advisory Committee on Television and Social Behavior, *Television and Growing Up: The Impact of Televised Violence*. Report to the Surgeon General, United States Public Health Service (Washington, D.C.: U.S. Government Printing Office, 1971), p. 14.
2. Ibid., p. 15.
3. George Gerbner, "Violence in Television Drama: Trends and Symbolic Functions," in G. A. Comstock and E. A. Rubinstein, eds., *Television and Social Behavior, Vol. I, Media Content and Control* (Washington, D.C.: U.S. Government Printing Office, 1971).
4. Ibid., p. 31.
5. Ibid., p. 36.
6. Muriel G. Cantor, "The Role of the Producer in Choosing Children's Television Content," in G. A. Comstock and E. A. Rubinstein, eds., *Television and Social Behavior, Vol. I, Media Content and Control* (Washington, D.C.: U.S. Government Printing Office, 1971).
7. Thomas Baldwin and Colby Lewis, "Violence in Television: The Industry Looks at Itself," in G. A. Comstock and E. A. Rubinstein, eds., *Television and Social Behavior, Vol. I, Media Content and Control* (Washington, D.C.: U.S. Government Printing Office, 1971).
8. Muriel G. Cantor, op. cit., p. 19.
9. Ibid., p. 20.
10. Ibid., p. 21.
11. Michael Gurevich, "The Structure and Content of Television Broadcasting in Four Countries: An Overview," in G. A. Comstock and E. A. Rubinstein, op. cit.
12. Albert Bandura, "Influence of Models: Reinforcement Contingencies on the Acquisition of Imitative Responses," *Journal of Personality and Social Psychology*, 1965, 1, 589–95.
13. Robert M. Liebert and Robert A. Baron, "Short-Term Effects of Televised Aggression on Childrens' Aggressive Behavior," in J. P. Murray, E. A. Ru-

binstein, and G. A. Comstock, eds., *Television and Social Behavior, Vol. II, Television and Social Learning* (Washington, D.C.: U.S. Government Printing Office, 1971).

14. Robert M. Liebert, "Television and Social Learning: Some Relationships Between Viewing Violence and Behaving," in Murray, Rubinstein, and Comstock, op. cit.
15. Ibid., pp. 29–30.
16. Monroe M. Lefkowitz, et al, "Television Violence and Child Aggression: A Follow-up Study," in Comstock and Rubinstein, eds., *Television and Social Behavior, Vol. III, Television and Adolescent Aggressiveness* (Washington, D.C.: U.S. Government Printing Office, 1971).
17. Steven H. Chaffee, "Television and Adolescent Aggressiveness," *in* Comstock and Rubinstein, op. cit.
18. Jack Lyle, "Television in Daily Life: Patterns of Use," in Rubinstein, Comstock, and Murray, eds., *Television and Social Behavior, Vol. IV, Television in Day-to-Day Life: Patterns of Use* (Washington, D.C.: U.S. Government Printing Office, 1971).
19. Bradley S. Greenberg, Phillip M. Ericson, and Mantha Vlahos, "Childrens' Television Behaviors as Perceived by Mother and Child," in Rubinstein, Comstock, and Murray, op. cit., 1971.
20. Jack Lyle, op. cit.
21. John P. Murray, "Television in Inner-City Homes: Viewing Behavior of Young Boys," in Rubinstein, Comstock, and Murray, op. cit., 1971.
22. Aletha Stein and Lynette Friedrich, "Television Content and Young Childrens' Behavior," in Murray, Rubinstein, and Comstock, op. cit. (Vol. II), 1971.
23. Jack Lyle and Heida Hoffman, "Childrens' Use of Television and Other Media," in Rubinstein, Comstock, and Murray, op. cit. (Vol. IV), 1971.
24. Leonard A. LoSciuto, "A National Inventory of Television Viewing Behavior," in Rubinstein, Comstock and Murray, op. cit. (Vol. IV), 1971.
25. Jennie J. McIntyre, and James J. Teevan, "Television Violence and Deviant Behavior," in Comstock and Rubinstein, op. cit. (Vol. III), 1971.
26. Jack Lyle, and Heida Hoffman, op. cit., p. 138.
27. Harold Israel and John P. Robinson, "Demographic Characteristics of Viewers of Television Violence and News Programs," in Rubinstein, Comstock and Murray, op. cit. (Vol. IV), 1971.
28. Leonard A. LoSciuto, op. cit.
29. Robert B. Bechtel, Clark Achepohl, and Ronald Akers, "Correlates Between Observed Behavior and Questionnaire Responses on Television Viewing," in Rubinstein, Comstock, and Murray, op. cit. (Vol. IV), 1971.
30. Paul Eckman et al., "Facial Expressions of Emotion While Watching Televised Violence as Predictors of Subsequent Aggression," in Comstock, Rubinstein, and Murray, *Television and Social Behavior, Vol. V, Television's Effects: Further Explorations* (Washington, D.C.: U.S. Government Printing Office, 1971).

31. David Foulkes, Edward Belvedere, and Terry Brubaker, "Televised Content and Dream Content," in Comstock, Rubinstein, and Murray, op. cit., 1971.
32. Surgeon General's Scientific Advisory Committee on Television and Social Behavior, op. cit.
33. Ibid., p. 113.
34. Wilbur Schramm, Jack Lyle, and Edwin B. Parker, *Television in the Lives of Our Children* (Stanford, Cal.: Stanford University Press, 1961), p. 13.
35. Surgeon General's Scientific Advisory Committee on Television and Social Behavior, op. cit., p. 11.
36. Leo Bogart, "Warning, the Surgeon General Has Determined That TV Violence is Moderately Dangerous to Your Child's Mental Health," *Public Opinion Quarterly*, 1972, 36, pp. 491–521, p. 520.
37. George A. Comstock, *Television in America* (Beverly Hills, Cal.: Sage, 1980), p. 100.
38. Hearings Before the Subcommittee on Communications, of the Committee on Commerce, United States Senate, March 21st through 24th, 1972 (Washington, D.C.: U.S. Government Printing Office, 1972), p. 11.
39. Ibid., p. 41.
40. Ibid., p. 42.
41. Leo Bogart, op. cit., p. 519.

13

pathways of the past and the journey ahead

The eleven studies we have reviewed show clearly that researchers today have at their command a remarkably rich accumulation of concepts, generalizations, and theories about the effects of mass communication. Our rich base of concepts, theories, and generalizations was certainly not available to those who undertook the first scientific studies of the media. Contemporary investigators can also use statistical techniques, research designs, computing technology, and methodological strategies that would have amazed the pioneer communication researchers. Many of these theoretical and methodological advances were developed as part of the milestones in mass communication research that we have reviewed here. Others were borrowed from a number of disciplines to become a permanent part of the communication research tool kit. Perhaps the simplest description of what has happened to the scientific study of mass communication over the last half century can be summed up in the flippant phrase from the advertising world that proclaims, "you've come a long way, baby!" At the same time, anyone familiar with science in general and the study of mass communication in particular would hasten to add, "you've still got a long way to go!"

In some ways the accumulated body of research findings regarding the effects of mass communication is an embarrassment of riches. There have been so many conclusions advanced; later findings contradict earlier ones, and more recent data offer still different interpretations. Today we have an almost hopeless jungle of contradictory claims about how it all works. How does one sort through this maze of inconsistent and often unrelated knowledge to reach some sense of closure on how mass communication influences individuals and society? The present chapter tries to address this difficult question—first by reviewing the major findings that have emerged from the eleven milestone studies that we have reviewed, and then by relating these efforts of the past to several emerging theoretical perspectives that are guiding new research efforts. These new approaches appear to hold great promise for the future.

THE LESSONS OF THE MILESTONES

Clearly, there are important lessons to be learned from the past—not only from the studies reviewed in the previous chapters, but from thousands of other smaller studies that have yielded important additional findings and insights. The past is always the principal guide used by science for the future. It is not an infallible guide; sometimes the past represents blind alleys that need not be trod again. But most of the time it represents the foundation on which the cutting edge of current conceptualization rests as knowledge presses forward. On rarer occasions the past becomes irrelevant as a totally new direction is conceived by an innovator. We have seen all of those uses of the past as we moved from the late 1920s to the 1970s in our analysis of the most significant studies over the last half-century.

But what about the present as a guide to the future? Currently, a number of very promising theoretical issues and directions are being pursued. These represent all three of the relationships to the past outlined above. In sections that follow, these trends and relationships will be noted. Obviously our review of both past and present must be brief, but comments on at least the most salient developments will provide some minimum sense of continuity.

We can never reach a state of complete closure on understanding the effects of mass communication. A characteristic of science is that its truths tend to be temporary. The best explanations of today are likely to be discarded in the future as new insights are gained, new data are assembled, and new explanations are formulated and tested. Furthermore, special difficulties confront the scientist who sets out to study any *social* process such as communication. Unlike the more invariant world of physical science, mass communication takes place in a constantly changing social and cultural milieu that can alter both the process and its consequences. We have seen in our review of major studies a number of seemingly convincing generalizations about media effects that may have been valid in their time. As new media were widely adopted and as our society developed new habits of using mass communication, those generalizations became obsolete and untrustworthy. *Thus, as society and the media change, their effects can be expected to change.*

These difficulties with the study of the effects of mass communication need not imply that it is not worthwhile or that no lasting conclusions can be obtained from prior research. It does mean that all generalizations about mass communication and its consequences for human activities must be continuously reexamined and retested against the realities of a changing social world.

Media Research in the Context of Society

Systems of mass communication operate within and are a part of the broader institutions of society. There exists, in other words, a state of *interdependence* between the institutionalized structure of society at any point in history, the various media that exist at that time, and the contemporary human populations that they serve as audiences. All three of these components undergo constant alteration as the flow of history continues. In the present book we have attempted to show how each of the milestones in communication research was to some degree a product of its times. Clearly, theoretical considerations from the parent disciplines of psychology and sociology played a role in guiding the investigations of the early researchers. Earlier studies also had at least *some* theoretical influence on those that followed. Yet, each study was shaped to a very substantial degree by ongoing trends or events of major significance in the society.

In our first chapter we noted the master trends—industrialization, urbanization, and modernization. These were the fundamental social changes in western societies. The rise of the media within those societies was a part of the master trends. We noted also that as the media spread, their audiences came to believe more and more firmly that they served as *causal agents* in creating a number of unwanted personal and social conditions. Whether such fears were justified or not, they were a major factor in providing social approval of and monetary support for mass communication research. Yet, as always, those who pay the piper call the tune. As we have seen, major research efforts in the study of mass communication were largely restricted to those questions that the *public* wanted answered. For example, time and time again, the people in the society wanted to know what some new medium—movies, horror comics, television—was doing to their children. Also, time and time again, people wanted to know how the media could be used to manipulate others for prosocial purposes—to improve military morale, to reduce prejudice, or to teach children in an easier way. The advertising industry, of course, had a deep interest in manipulation as did many political leaders, or would-be leaders. No doubt all of these were worthy questions for research and they remain so today. At the same time, they are not the most pressing of the basic *theoretical* issues that could have been explored in seeking to understand the nature and functions of mass communication. Thus, the same high interest in communication research shown by the public and by special interest groups who controlled research funds may also have been a major force holding back its maturation as a scientific discipline.

More specifically, how have particular historical events provided significant influences on mass communication research; and how have particular concerns of the public influenced lines of research at various times in the past?

A central proposition of the sociology of knowledge is that in the search for new understanding, the problems that are investigated, the strategies used in their study, and even the conclusions reached, are heavily influenced by the times in which the knowledge is sought. These conditions appear to hold whether such understandings are pursued within the framework of science or within some totally different perspective (e.g., religion, magic, and so on).

The above proposition seems well-illustrated in the field of mass communication research. The continuously evolving capacities of science, and even the general social structure and culture bore heavily on the processes by which knowledge about media effects was generated. As various media appeared, their effects were studied within the framework of the social or behavioral sciences available at the time. However, they were also studied against the background of unfolding history. The disturbing new behaviors of the "flaming youth" of the 1920s focused public attention on the need to study the new moving pictures. Limited public understanding of the background of the second world war was the major factor prompting the Army studies of the use of films for military orientation. A widely shared concern in the postwar world about the need to persuade people to adopt more prosocial attitudes and behavior was a factor motivating Hovland's search for the magic keys. Project Revere was obviously prompted by the Korean War. And on it goes: the research done for the Violence Commission grew out of concerns about crime, assassinations, and urban upheavals; Dr. Wertham's unusual study of comic books resulted from parental fears that the medium was harmful to the young; the Schramm et al. study of the way children used television came about because the medium was new and seemed threatening; the Surgeon General's Report was prompted by continuing public concerns about rising violence among the young. All of these studies illustrate the principle. In other words, like all sciences, the study of communication developed mainly because people wanted answers to questions that seemed urgent within the social and cultural context of the time; they were willing to foot the bills for such research; and there were qualified people at hand who were willing to do the job on those terms.

We noted earlier that the scientific study of the process and effects of mass communication began in earnest when the motion picture quickly emerged as a major medium of family entertainment. In the space of two decades, this new phenomenon changed from an amusing novelty of the penny arcade to a significant factor in the lives of almost all Americans. The society was experiencing a rapid erosion of Victorian morality codes during the 1920s. This erosion was reflected in the so-called emancipation of both youth and women that characterized the period. It is little wonder that the legacy of fear, already well developed among the public, assumed new proportions. People grew increasingly concerned over the impact of the movies on children.

This kind of sequence—the emergence of a new medium, along with increases in behavior forms that are widely deplored, has been a familiar pattern in stimulating research on the mass media. Variations in this pattern underly the *Invasion From Mars* research (fear of the great power of radio); the *People's Choice* research (concern over the use of media rather than rational discussion of the issues to control an election campaign); Wertham's frightening *Seduction of the Innocent* (fear of the seemingly powerful influence of horror comics), and so on up to the research studies of today. Indeed, many of the contemporary directions in mass communication research that will be reviewed later in this chapter are textbook examples of how the events of history and concerns of the public continue to shape the questions addressed by contemporary mass communication researchers, just as they did a half-century ago.

Improvements in the Tools of Analysis

A review of the methodological tools used in the milestones shows that research on mass communication became increasingly less cumbersome. It also became less restricted by limitations in methodology and statistics as time went on. Not only was there a considerable expansion in statistical procedures available for description and hypothesis testing, but other research tools also became more and more sophisticated. The techniques and strategies of content analysis and the availability of computers provide good examples.

Statistics   The last half-century has seen a tremendous growth in the field of inferential statistics. When the Payne Fund Studies were undertaken, statistical analysis in the social sciences was in its infancy. For example, in the late 1920s a great debate was in progress concerning the place of quantitative techniques in social and psychological research. Many professionals at the time held that introducing numbers and measurement into such research would rob it of its human qualities. We saw that Herbert Blumer's contribution to the Payne Fund Studies ("The Movies and Conduct," pp. 46–54) was a *qualitative* rather than quantitative effort. He described what he found in verbal terms and "let the facts speak for themselves." In contrast, in the same series of studies, Peterson and Thurstone reported their findings concerning the influence of movies on children's attitudes (pp. 41–46) in terms of *quantitative* indices—differences between means and the standard errors of such differences. In fact, at the time, their statistical procedures seemed very precise and on the cutting edge. In retrospect, however, because of their lack of adequate controls, their procedures now seem somewhat naive and their conclusions open to rather serious questions.

As time went on, increasingly sophisticated use was made of an ever-improving logic of method. The before–after designs with control groups from the Army's use of films represented a considerable advance over earlier research strategies. By the time Hovland did his research on the keys to persuasion he and his associates were able to make use of laboratory designs with numerous controls over a variety of conditions. Still later, the panel design used in the Erie County study represented an important innovation in survey methodology. The panel technique is still being used today in large-scale and sophisticated studies of the impact of mass communication on elections.[1]

And so on it went. The various studies of the Surgeon General's Report made use of almost every imaginable variation of laboratory experiment, longitudinal study, and survey methodology that existed in the late 1960s. Today, more and more research depends on multivariate procedures such as linear models, analysis of variance, and rotated versions of factor analyses. Tools are still being invented and improved. Statisticians are not yet through innovating in the field of inferential statistics and we can confidently look forward to improvements in tools of analysis and decision making.

Content analysis   This form of analysis, somewhat unique to communication studies, has played a central role in media research from the beginning. Early efforts were restricted largely to simple classifications and counting. The Payne Fund researchers, for example, classified movies according to their predominant themes—love, sex, crime, and so on. Later, more elaborate procedures were developed so that reliability and validity could be assessed as analysts made more refined judgments concerning the categorization of media messages. Various kinds of indices were developed for measuring and counting different units of content. Sampling procedures were adapted to the problems of content analysis. Still, it was a laborious procedure, characterized by the need to make a great many subjective judgments. The arrival of television, with its rapidly moving subject matter, made content analysis even more difficult. However, when the video recorder became available a new era was begun in quantifying the content of programs that appear on the screen. Off-the-air broadcasts can be recorded and replayed repeatedly on a moment-to-moment basis for more refined analyses. Complex content reports such as Gerbner's annual "violence profiles" are now routinely accomplished.[2]

Computers The span of time between the Payne Fund Studies and the Surgeon General's Report saw a revolution in the technology of calculation. First, reliable electric calculating machines replaced paper and pencil or slide rule technologies for handling relatively large sets of numbers. During the 1950s electronic computers found their way to American campuses. The availability of these devices provided a tremendous stimulus to the development of more complex techniques and procedures for statistical analysis. For example, working out a factor analysis with a matrix of 15 to 20 zero-order correlations is now a matter of a few moments of calculation by the computer, once the data are on the disc and the computer program is ready. Various procedures for rotation are almost routinely applied with the use of prepared software. In the early 1950s, just before computers became available, such a problem took two to three months of steady calculation, even with an electric machine, on an eight hours per day, 40 hours per week basis. To give a concrete example of how computer technology has speeded up the research process, recall that the *Personal Influence* study (pp. 184–200) was begun in 1944, but its final report did not reach print until 1955. Many of the analyses of the study were complex comparisons of subjects with different social characteristics. They had to be sorted into subcategories for such comparisons, where their behavior could be contrasted by this means of partialling. Even though electric card-sorting machines were available, it was still a laborious task. Today, such comparisons and partialling are little more than elementary problems that can be accomplished in many alternative ways very quickly with standard SPSS programs or other prepared software.

The new wave of microcomputers promises to speed things up even more. It is not that they calculate faster, but their availability on the desk of the researcher cuts down on delays involved in waiting for turnaround at the computing center. What has often taken overnight can now be accomplished immediately, with tables and other results printed out on the spot. No one can forecast the degree to which improvements in statistics, content analysis, and computers will pay off in more insightful research on mass communication. However, if the past is any guide, improvements in such supporting technology will continue to expand our ability to do needed research.

Changing Conclusions about Media Effects

Our accumulated understandings of the process and effects of mass communication have undergone rather substantial revisions over the last half-century. The milestone studies we have reviewed played a central role in this transition. In the early days, just before the scientific study of the media began, mass communication was seen as being able to produce very powerful effects on audiences. We have noted earlier that mass communication seemed capable of: persuading nations to rally behind war efforts; maintaining animosities toward enemies portrayed as savages; stimulating vice; and driving youth into lives of crime and delinquency. The media were feared as agents of social control that could be used by demagogues to shape the behavior of the masses. They were thought to be causing a lowering of esthetic tastes by their shameless exploitation of the elite art forms to produce cheap mass culture. In short, their effects were seen as powerful and often antisocial.

Then scientific research began. As findings accumulated, the interpretation of the role of the media in modern society began to undergo change. At first, the worst suspicions of the critics of the media seemed confirmed. But as investigators gained the ability to probe deeper into the question of media effects with better and better controls and measures, the picture grew more complicated.

The Case for Powerful Effects   The first large-scale research efforts to study mass communication within the perspectives of science seemed to give strong support to the magic bullet model. Beginning in the late 1920s, the Payne Fund Studies showed that children of that time were profoundly influenced by motion pictures. While being entertained by the new medium, youngsters "incidentally" learned a tremendous amount of information about social life and other aspects of the world around them. Movies appeared to be capable of changing audiences' attitudes toward various categories of people unlike themselves. The movies showed versions of social reality that seemed to the investigators to erode the standards of morality that had been maintained by the older generation. The movies provided material that was used for fantasy, escape, daydreaming, and emotional stimulation. Finally, there seemed little doubt that the overt behavior of children was shaped greatly by what they saw in the films. Their play was influenced. Their manners, mannerisms, dress, speech, and interpersonal relationships were all touched by the messages on the silver screen.

To the public, the great power of the media seemed adequately demonstrated. Never mind about the squabbles of research specialists over points of methodology. The public neither understood nor cared about such debates. The bottom line for the ordinary citizen was that a number of experts had studied the films scientifically and had confirmed that movies were an unwholesome influence on children. Because of this, the makers of films ought to be forced to make improvements. Indeed, that is precisely what happened. The movie industry was scared. The motion picture producers developed a self-policing system in the 1930s that imposed rigid scrutiny and powerful moral censorship on their products.

Meanwhile, radio was fast becoming a household medium. By the mid-1930s this new form of communication had developed into a major entertainment industry supported by its advertising messages. Many people suspected that it too had great power. Certainly its increasing use by politicians was creating anxiety in many quarters, and its obvious efficiency as a means of persuasion in the advertising world was very clear. Then came the invasion from Mars. The new medium that brought such pleasant music, drama, and sports bared its teeth and bit hard—it seemed to show the great power it was capable of. Over a million Americans were duped into mindless panic by a single broadcast. In reality, the War of the Worlds broadcast and the chaos it created can be regarded as a classic example of "Murphy's Law" in action—every unlikely thing that could go wrong did, and in the worst possible way. The broadcast was intended to be harmless. There was no plan to trigger a panic. Nevertheless, its consequences reinforced the convictions of many people that radio was a medium of great power with considerable potential for evil in the wrong hands.

Generally as the 1930s came to a close, the new media of the 20th century, motion pictures and radio, were seen by the public as even more powerful than the venerable newspaper. Mass communication was the tool of propaganda, with which the minds of millions could be controlled. Even seemingly harmless entertainment content, as in the movies and radio plays, had a darker side. The media were capable of insidious erosion of moral standards; of persuading people to spend their money on goods and services they didn't need; and they presented dreadfully distorted views of the world to their audiences, who confused them with reality. If such conclusions were true, any thinking person had ample grounds to fear the powerful effects of such media.

The Perplexing Results of Further Research The study of the power of the media continued both during and right after World War II. However, the results from the major studies of the time were not like earlier ones. For example, the findings from the study of the 1940 presidential election (*The People's Choice*) were in many ways a disappointment. The media used in that election campaign—newspapers, radio, and magazines, for the most part—had had only limited influences on the voters. In spite of massive efforts on the part of the media, only a handful of people were persuaded to convert from one party to another, from one candidate to another. The effects that were found were anything but powerful. The media campaign had activated some people's predispositions and it had reinforced those whose loyalties were already committed. But such limited effects were not the stuff of which the legacy of fear had been born.

A second large-scale study also failed to confirm powerful media effects. Completely unrelated to the sociological study of the presidential election were the Army's experiments on the use of films to inform and persuade soldiers. Proceeding on the assumption that films were an effective device for shaping people's beliefs, opinions, and attitudes, the psychologists assessed the degree to which motion pictures produced by Hollywood's top talent could strengthen the motivation and morale of troops undergoing orientation and training. The experiments showed that the effort was a flop. Even though tight controls were used, measurements were sophisticated, and statistical analyses were flawless, the films never achieved the objectives for which they were designed. This was not a case of methodological shortcomings in the research process. The experiments were cleverly designed and effectively executed. The problem was that the motion pictures used simply did not have the kind of power that had been assumed. It was true that, from exposure to the films, the soldiers learned new facts. In some cases their opinions related to those facts were reshaped. However, their more general attitudes and motivational commitments were not influenced in any substantial way. Far from having immediate, direct, and powerful effects, the films had only minimal influences.

As the war came to a close it was not apparent to the research community that thinking about the effects of the media would have to be considerably revised. The search for the factors that could produce effects on demand pressed on. Identifying the magic keys to persuasion through research remained a great challenge. The world was in need of change, and doing it with carefully designed campaigns of psychological persuasion seemed a far better way than using the terrible tool of war. The professors who had conducted research for the military forces returned to their universities and continued their efforts to find the factors that made a difference—the variables that were significant in changing people's opinions, attitudes, and behavior through the use of persuasive communications.

What began to emerge from the new studies was not a simple picture. People's beliefs about the nature of the communicator and his or her purposes seemed to make a difference. The emotional appeals built into the message made a difference. The structure of the message made a difference.

The initial attitudes of the audience member made a difference. The entire personality of the receiving person made a difference. Almost everything and anything, it seemed, made some kind of difference. In other words, a host of variables and factors were in some way related to the process of changing people's opinions, attitudes, and behavior. The old idea that people could be readily influenced in some uniform way by a single communication had to be abandoned.

Adding greatly to the complexity of the emerging picture of the effects of mass communication was the discovery of the part played by interpersonal relationships among members of the audience. Earlier, researchers had focused on the individual audience member and his or her responses to message stimuli. Social relationships among members of the audience were either ignored or seen as irrelevant. However, the *Personal Influence* study, following the leads opened by the Erie County election research, probed "the part played by people" in the movement of information and influence from media to mass. The two-step flow turned out to be far more complex than anyone had imagined. The specifics of the process changed from one topic to another. The position of the person in the life cycle, and in the whole social web of community life, were related to whether that person would be a leader or a follower. Clearly, the two-step flow was a reality that had to be better understood.

Complicating the emerging picture of the process of mass communication were the Project Revere studies. Originally designed to test the capacities and limitations of leaflets as a medium of last resort, they also focused on the process of "social diffusion." Such diffusion is interpersonal message transmission—word-of-mouth telling and retelling of a message originally obtained directly from a medium and then passed on to other people. This is a more detailed way of describing the two-step flow of information. The importance of the Revere research to the emerging picture of the two-step flow process was that it showed it to be a dreadfully inaccurate means of communication. As a message moved from person to person through a community it was shortened, reshaped, and distorted in an embedding pattern virtually identical to that found in laboratory studies of rumor transmission. Thus, the two-step flow and the message diffusion process more generally were shown to be ineffective in spreading information accurately.

These various studies, done during the 1940s and 1950s, plus an increasing accumulation of smaller projects, had all but laid to rest the old magic bullet theory. However, no clear alternative formulation had emerged. Instead, the research community had been forced to the conclusion that mass communication had only limited effects on some people under some circumstances. Those circumstances were very difficult to sort out. By 1960, the dream of discovering some set of magic keys to persuasion that could change people in ways desired by communicators also began to seem unreal. The scientific study of mass communication had led, not to clear insights into strategies for using the media for prosocial purposes, but to an accumulation of confusing and often contradictory findings that seemed to cloud understanding of the media more than to clarify it.

Television had been widely adopted by 1960, and the first major study of the impact of the medium on children seemed to confirm the idea that it had only minimal effects. *Television in the Lives of Our Children* showed that the medium provided for a great deal of incidental learning, and that children used its contents in their fantasy life. There were even positive influences on vocabulary for some children. Yet, no dramatic or threatening influences were identified. Certainly nothing was found that even remotely resembled the conclusions of those who first studied the influence of the movies on children decades earlier. The conclusion that television produced only minimal effects was widely accepted by the research community. If negative effects did sometimes occur, it was among children who already had problems. Middle class children in emotionally supportive homes were relatively immune.

As the 1960s moved on, television assumed its position as the nation's dominant medium. Because of the public's mounting concerns over TV's influences, it became the focus of increasing research attention. By comparison, little research was being done on newspapers, radio, or even film. With the increasing focus on television, the pace of communication research quickened enormously. A number of new journals were started to provide places to publish the ever growing flood of articles and reports. Even so, the field floundered in a state of theoretical disarray. The older simplistic formulations had been abandoned, but no clear explanations had taken their place.

But if the research community was uncertain about the effects of mass communication, the public was not. Dr. Wertham had seen to that! Virtually single-handedly he had revitalized the magic bullet theory and strongly reinforced the legacy of fear. His "clinical" studies of the powerful effects of horror comics proved what every parent secretly suspected: Those awful comic books were turning America's youth into psychological cripples. It is difficult to calculate with precision the impact of *The Seduction of the Innocent* on public thinking about the mass media. Certainly, it was more widely read than any other report of research on mass communication. As such, it must be considered a factor in reinforcing the conviction of the public that mass communication has powerful bad effects on youthful audiences. This factor in turn produced a willingness to provide support for further research. At least communication researchers could thank Dr. Wertham for that.

The rise in urban violence in the late 1960s had a significant impact on media research. Rising crime rates, urban riots, and political assassinations seemed to the public to have something to do with the swift rise of television usage in our society. The President's Commission on Violence looked into the matter of how much aggressive behavior was portrayed on television. They were disturbed by what they found. The medium was filled with portrayals of violence. Calculations of how many murders a child had seen on TV by age 16 were alarming. Violence, it seemed, was being championed by the medium as a means of settling disputes of almost every kind. No wonder, people concluded, that the kids were running wild in the streets. The legacy of fear remained alive and well in the suspicions of Americans concerning what television was doing to them.

It was that legacy that provided the political base for the federal government's commitment of a million dollars to support the research that was ultimately published as the *Surgeon General's Report.* In many ways, the whole project was simply "more of the same." There were no new ideas explored in the numerous studies that made up the commissioned projects. Some of the investigations represented methodological improvements over earlier efforts, but the experiments, content analyses, surveys, and longitudinal studies that were done showed once again that it is very difficult to sort out the influence of one medium over a relatively short period of time.

Perhaps the most important lesson to be obtained from the project is that research on a topic of deep concern to the public will almost certainly be caught up in a web of complex political controversies. The networks, Congress, the researchers, and various segments of the public all had something at stake in the outcome. For that reason, the results were interpreted and reinterpreted over and over in ways supportive of the values of a given set of special interests. It seems reasonably clear that televised portrayals of violence have some undesirable influences on at least some categories of children. Yet, that conclusion still remains clouded by claims and counterclaims. A more recent report developed by the National Institute of Mental Health, entitled *Television and Behavior: Ten Years of Scientific Progress and Implications for the Eighties,* has summarized research on the issue of violence and a number of other topics—research that has appeared over the ten years since publication of the Surgeon General's Report. Numerous additional studies seem to confirm the conclusion that at least some normal youngsters become more aggressive as a result of heavy exposure to portrayed violence. Once again, this conclusion has stirred controversies and vigorous debates among researchers, politicians, media managers, and the public.[3]

The Search for Indirect Influences In overview, the 11 milestone studies analyzed in the present work represent the major directions that have been taken during the last half-century in the search for an understanding of the effects of mass communication. Out of those historically significant studies, and literally thousands of other smaller efforts that have explored the same or closely related issues, have come the major turning points in methodology, conceptualization, and explanation of the influence of mass communication on those who attend to them. As can be seen, the central preoccupation of the research scholars who created that history has been with the potential negative impact of the media on children. Always, however, it has been the conviction that mass communications have the power to *change* people, to cause them to behave in ways either desired by someone or deplored by someone else, that has motivated an ever-increasing effort to understand what the media do and how they do it.

From the standpoint of today, the major problem with the conclusion that the media have only minimal effects is that it appears to be wrong! To be sure, it is what the research up until recently seemed to indicate, but there is a growing belief among communication scholars that the problem lies with the research rather than the reality. This does not mean that the public had the right idea all along and that the media operate in the manner of the magic bullet. What it does mean is that the strategies of research used in the past may not have been adequate to demonstrate empirically what influences the media actually have. As we have made clear, those strategies have focused mainly on short-term, immediate, and direct effects. The media were seen as stimuli, shaping and molding people's responses. Experiments and surveys sought to link specific messages or types of content with specific patterns of belief, attitudes, and behavior. More and more, media scholars have come to believe that the influences of mass communication are long-term, indirect, and accumulative. If this is indeed the case, the influence of the media may be profound rather than trivial. Such subtle but powerful influences cannot be expected to show up in research strategies modeled after those of physical science, where a limited number of factors are measured and controlled. This limitation does not rule out science as a means of studying mass communication. Obviously, new scientific procedures must be invented. Long-term, large-scale, accumulative, and subtle processes can be studied. Charles Darwin's methods and conclusions regarding the evolution of species provide a clear case in point.

But if the research strategies to be used in the years ahead are not entirely clear, some of the theoretical directions that will be followed in the short term are somewhat more predictable. Some of these directions will be extensions of conceptual paths that are already being followed. Others can be seen only dimly as emerging directions for research.

CONTEMPORARY TRENDS AND EMERGING DIRECTIONS FOR RESEARCH

Research efforts aimed at understanding the effects of mass communication continue to make use of concepts, frameworks, and theoretical paradigms drawn mainly from psychology, social psychology, and sociology. Such investigations also make use of the methodological and epistemological systems that characterize those fields. In the sections that follow, research trends that are based on all of these general disciplines are summarized briefly but selectively.

The Psychological Approach

During the early years of this century, scholars tried to use the psychological theories of the time to understand the propaganda effects of mass communication. Unfortunately, psychology was still looking for biological explanations of human behavior in such concepts as *instincts* and *conditioned reflexes*. These concepts are now obsolete as bases for explaining complex human activity. As psychologists became increasingly sophisticated about the role of learning as a basis of habits of attention, perception, and selective response patterns, these concepts began to play a central role in theories about mass communication's effects. Such factors as beliefs, opinions, attitudes, and values were explored as influences on motivation, perception, and selective learning. Literally thousands of studies and scholarly treatises have been published on how such variables shape the way in which people select media content, interpret that content, and organize their behavior as responses to their interpretations of the content. Today, the psychological approach continues full force as a major strategy for understanding the influences of mass-mediated messages on individual behavior.

One feature of the psychological approach that must be kept in mind is its clear focus on the *individual*. Psychologists seek to understand the connative, cognitive, and affective organizations, "inside the head," so to speak. They search for variables and generalizations that can explain what motivates individuals to act, what leads a person to behave in new ways, and what maintains patterns of responses already established. These are critical questions for understanding the activities of individual human beings. Naturally, such focus has its limitations. It is unlikely to lead to an understanding of complex social systems or of the kinds of shared behaviors that make up much of a culture. Both individually-oriented and socially-oriented strategies are needed to investigate fully the overall effects of mass communication. In any case, two somewhat independent lines of research are now at the forefront of psychological studies of media influences. These are the *uses and gratifications* approach—actually an old idea that continues to be important—and the study of *fantasy* as a significant part of the individual mass communication experience.

Uses and Gratifications   The term "uses" implies that the member of the audience is not a passive but rather an active part of the mass communication process. Such active participants seek content selectively, commensurate with their needs and interests. They incorporate that content into their activities instrumentally to obtain fulfillment of those needs or interests. Generally speaking, the word "gratifications" pertains to rewards and satisfactions experienced by an individual. As used in the study of mass communication, it refers to satisfying or rewarding experiences provided by attending to media content. Such gratifications are important in establishing habits of selection of media content and in understanding motivations that underly attention to mass communications.

In the early decades of media research, the needs and interests of individuals were seen as significant "intervening" variables between apprehension of the stimulus and the elicitation of responses to media messages. A substantial number of studies were done around the "appeals" of radio, such as the "rewards" provided by attention to soap operas. A number of studies probed the "motivations" underlying reading of the comics in the newspapers, attending movies, and so on.[4] Research in this tradition continued sporadically through the 1950s and early 1960s. With the development of television, interest in uses and gratifications research has been considerably revived. At least one theory has been developed around the idea that mass communications are a form of "play" in our society, providing the kinds of gratifications that the term implies.[5]

In 1974, Blumler and Katz attempted to set forth the status of needs and gratifications research at that time.[6] Generally, they described the uses and gratifications approach as one concerned with the nature and origins of people's needs that play a part in leading them to different patterns of media exposure. Such exposure presumably gratifies those needs and stabilizes habits of selecting media content. The approach has obvious policy and commercial implications. If the form of content that satisfies the needs of a particular segment of the audience (e.g., middle-class housewives, the elderly, single males, blacks, and so on) can be identified, media presentations incorporating that content can be used to capture and hold the attention of such segments. If the content gratifies their needs, such presentations would appear to be dependable vehicles for the presentation of advertising messages, political campaigns, or other appeals. In this sense, needs gratifications research is relevant to the use of the media for deliberate persuasion.

A host of studies has attempted to set forth lists of the needs satisfied by media content, or typologies of motivations and functions involved in attention to mass communication. Unfortunately, such lists and typologies vary greatly from one investigator to another. No agreement exists, at least up to now, why people select particular content, what needs a given form of content satisfies, or how such gratification leads to behavioral consequences. Nevertheless, research continues to try to find answers to these questions. In many respects, this approach represents a modern version of Hovland's search for the magic keys to persuasion.

Typical of recent efforts to study how motivations produce different patterns of viewing and use of media content is a study by Rubin.[7] The principal focus was on the relationship of motivations underlying TV viewing and the age of the audience member. He studied 626 people; some were as young as four years and others were oldsters approaching 90. Most were somewhere between these extremes. By asking people why they viewed (whatever they had selected) he was able to identify nine claimed motivations. These were: viewing to pass time, for companionship, for arousal or excitement, to see particular program content, for relaxation, to obtain specific information, to escape or forget, for entertainment or enjoyment, or as a basis for interacting with other people. While some of these reasons seem related or even overlapping, these were the reasons given by Rubin's subjects for turning to their sets.

One might raise the objection that such subjects may not be aware of the underlying motivations that draw them to particular kinds of content. What they claim in lay terms may have little to do with their "true" motivations because these motivations may not be understood at the conscious level. One can also ask whether age, sex, socioeconomic status, and other such common variables of social research are the ones that should be given priority in gratifications research. The answers to these issues are not at all clear. It is for such reasons that the future of uses and gratifications research is not clear. Above all, the approach needs to be brought together from its present fragmented and uncoordinated state into a more integrated theoretical formulation. If this can be done effectively, the approach will become a more significant guide for research in the future. Perhaps the hidden keys to persuasion will eventually be revealed after all!

Learning from Media Portrayals An important theoretical framework for the study of the effects of mass communication on individuals is *social learning theory*. It is a derivation of more general paradigms that describe or explain the relationship between what psychologists call reinforcement and acquistion of new forms of behavior by an individual. Social learning theory has been developed by Bandura and his associates.[8] Essentially, it presents explanations of how subjects acquire new response patterns by seeing these patterns acted out or otherwise displayed in social settings. The media obviously provide one kind of social setting. When response patterns are acted out on television, or in the movies, for example, they are said to be "modeled" by the actors portraying the behavior. In other words, the more general idea of social learning theory becomes "modeling theory" when applied to acquisition of new behavior forms from exposure to portrayals of action in mass communication content. Although, presumably, behavior can be modeled in print, the theory seems far more relevant to accounting for influences on individuals from film and television. Virtually all of the research done thus far within this theoretical perspective has focused on television.

Modeling theory was discussed in some detail in Chapter 1 as an important emerging theory of media effects. As such, it remains one of the more significant guides to research in the future. Individuals do pick up new ideas, action patterns, and modes of psychological orientation by attending to mass communication. This was clearly pointed out by Blumer in his early studies of the influences of the movies on children (Chapter 2). In fact, if this formulation had been available to him at the time he would probably have used it heavily to interpret his findings. Many aspects of modeling were rediscovered years later as "incidental" learning by Schramm, Lyle, and Parker in the first truly large-scale study of the impact of television on children (Chapter 10).

There are several issues that are significant regarding modeling theory for the future. First, the lessons that can be learned by the media are increasingly being revealed through systematic and detailed content analyses. Gerbner's Violence Profiles provide an excellent example. In addition, technical journals reporting mass communication research are devoting more and more attention to content analyses of media-portrayed behavior patterns related to such issues as minorities, women, the elderly, or to sex, drugs, the use of alcohol, and a host of other issues. Thus, what is being modeled is becoming much better understood.

Content analyses are important in their own right insofar as they do reveal the modes of behavior that are available for people to imitate in their own individual activities. Findings from such analyses have often been dismissed in the past as relatively unimportant if it could not be shown convincingly that the content under study had some immediate and direct influence on a particular audience. As our review of changing perspectives on media theory has shown, such immediate and direct influences cannot easily be demonstrated because it is highly unlikely that they exist. Much more significant are the long-range, accumulative, and indirect influences that are provided by modeled behavior. These may be very difficult to demonstrate by research procedures currently in use. Nevertheless, patterns of behavior shown by media models to be appropriate for relating to various categories of people, or for coping with controversial issues, if shown over and over in much the same way, may be very influential in establishing or confirming *norms* that appear to the audience to govern certain situations. In other words, behavior forms repeatedly seen on the television or movie screen may come to be interpreted as the manner in which such activities "should" be performed. This would be especially true where viewers lack what psychiatrists call "reality checks" that correct inappropriate interpretations. Unfortunately, there are many children who spend a great deal of time viewing in the absence of parental guidance. For such children, whose adult interpretations remain to be formed, behavioral norms modeled on the screen may have a cumulative influence of considerable importance.

For the most part, research within the framework of modeling theory has not addressed long-range, accumulative influences. Many studies have established the fact that modeling effects *do* occur, but much research is still needed even at a basic level. Much remains to be uncovered regarding the conditions under which a subject will find a form of modeled behavior attractive, will identify with the actor, or find some other motivation for adopting the behavior, and then make the behavior a permanent part of his or her habit patterns. Once such issues have been clarified, the long-range influences of modeling can be better understood. In general, modeling theory provides an excellent theoretical framework for the future study of accumulative and indirect influences on the behavior of individual members of the audience.

Fantasy as Personal Experience A complex psychological perspective is developing around the issue of *mental processing* of content that takes place within the cognitive processes of the individual as he or she attends to a medium. Central questions concern the depth of attention given to the content, whether the individual actively and selectively synthesizes the incoming stimuli with other cognitive content of which the person is already aware, or whether attending to the media is a more passive experience. This is very difficult research. No one can monitor a person's internal subjective experiences during a movie, while watching TV, or while reading a book. However, various research efforts suggest that fantasy experience plays a considerable role in the processing of media content. There is a relationship, in other words, between the pictures on our screens and the pictures in our heads. Fantasy appears to play a considerable part in structuring those inner interpretations.

This perspective is well-illustrated by (but not restricted to) the study of fantasy behavior that takes place when viewers process television content. Those who pursue these studies are convinced that such mental activities and mental processes may provide important keys to understanding the psychological influences that television has on its audiences.

The main psychological theories related to the process and consequences of fantasy have been ably summarized in a recent article by Lindlof.[9] Clearly, there are many perspectives and methodologies to choose from in the study of this type of mental functioning. Generally, however, viewing television in the fantasy mode must be learned. It also involves a low level of attention or task demand. It remains to be established how fantasy viewing provides positive reinforcement for the viewer, or whether there is incidental learning as another outcome. In any case, the importance of fantasy as a part of the media experience has been a topic of study ever since Blumer discussed "emotional possession" as a consequence of watching exciting movies, and the manner in which children incorporated movie-derived themes into their patterns of play. Currently, there are no claims that fantasy experience provides a high level of stimulation to engage in specific forms of overt action (as is implied in the studies of televised violence). At the same time, there appear to be adequate grounds to hypothesize that, over a long period of time, selective viewing of specific forms of content, accompanied by repetitive forms of fantasy experience, could influence overt behavioral decisions. As yet, however, no compelling evidence supports this hypothesis. The role of fantasy experience in the mass communication process remains an interesting line of research that has yet to make its important contribution.

The Social Construction of Meaning

One of the most promising directions for future research lies in attempting to assess the role of mass communication in establishing, modifying, and reinforcing the meanings people share about the nature of the world around them. Central to shared meanings are the common symbols of language. Such meanings for words are used collectively and individually whenever people try to interpret and respond to any aspect of social or physical reality.

There can be little doubt that mass communication plays a key role in providing people with interpretations of reality, either deliberately or unwittingly. It is easy to see this in perspective if one reviews the events of the 1982 hostilities between Great Britain and Argentina over the Falkland Islands in the South Atlantic. Americans who followed the comparative interpretations of what was taking place in the Argentine and British media during the fighting were perplexed by how they could be so different. The reality constructed by the officially controlled Argentine news media was that the whole series of events was a glorious victory for that South American country and a bitter, humiliating defeat for the British. The Argentine people, depending almost exclusively upon their own media, had no other interpretations and believed their media completely in a surge of great nationalistic pride. Much the same happened in Great Britain. As the battle unfolded, British official sources reported quite a different picture via the media. Their courageous armed forces were dislodging an aggressor and restoring British rule to their illegally seized territory. That version was accepted by the British people as the correct interpretation of what was happening, and they took great pride in their county's victories. The question is not which of these versions of reality was correct, but the nature of the processes by which they were constructed and accepted. The British and Argentine constructions were deliberate products of official policy. Similar events happen in the U.S. Also, American media present versions of every conceivable aspect of reality daily with no particular intent other than making a profit. Such unwitting constructions of meaning are every bit as important as those produced by official control of media content.

The pace of research on the role of the media in providing meanings and interpretations of reality increased dramatically during the decade following the Surgeon General's Report. The search for the implications of the media's role in the construction of meaning is now one of the most important directions of present and future investigation. This line of research may provide very important interpretations of how mass communication can be used to build systematically the kinds of shared beliefs that are necessary as a basis for persuading people to take or support large-scale collective action. Such beliefs are critical when new political policies shift a nation from one direction to another, when significant new social programs need widespread consensus, or when one country makes war on another. In retrospect, these theoretical orientations may even enable us to understand why domestic propaganda was so successful in earlier wars.

The study of the relationships among communication through language, the sharing of meanings made possible by cultural conventions, and the influences of meaning systems on both individual and social behavior has ancient roots. These issues have concerned not only philosophers but all of the social sciences for well over a century. Students of mass communication began to be concerned with such issues in the early 1920s. Walter Lippmann, writing about the role of the press in shaping public opinion, noted that the newspapers selectively portrayed "the world outside" and by so doing created "pictures in our heads." These in turn, he maintained, shaped our thinking and behavior toward outside events. He also noted that any relationship between what was being described by the media and what was really taking place was purely coincidental.[10] He would not have been surprised at all by the differences between the British and Argentine versions of the battles for the Falkland Islands.

Today, there are three independent branches to the efforts to formulate theories that can guide research into the area of meanings provided by the media. One is the study of the *agenda-setting* functions of the news media; another is the investigation of the *cultivation effects* of television on people's beliefs; and the third is the *meaning theory of media portrayals*. At first glance, these independently developed approaches to the study of media effects may seem to have little in common. On closer analysis, however, they are in many respects focusing on similar underlying issues. All three are concerned in some way with the role of the media in shaping people's interpretations of the world around them. They differ primarily in terms of the media on which they focus and in their scope.

Agenda Setting The basic idea of agenda setting is usually traced to a brief passage in a book by political scientist Bernard Cohen. In 1963 he wrote that "The press may not be successful much of the time in telling people what to think, but it is stunningly successful in telling its readers what to think *about*."[11] The idea that the press provides surveillance of the environment, and that the news media selectively present ideas to the public, has long been well-known. Presumably the news media do so in a pattern that brings the public to attach the most importance to those given the most prominent attention in the press. Noted communication researchers McCombs and Shaw put it this way:

> Audiences not only learn about public issues and other matters from the media, they also learn how much *importance* to attach to an issue or topic from the emphasis the media place upon it.[12]

This is the agenda-setting hypothesis. It concerns the news media rather than mass communication in general, and its dependent variable is the level of importance audiences attach to topics and issues given various coverage by the press. The degree of importance is, of course, a significant dimension of the meaning that people attach to the reports they encounter in the press. Therefore, the agenda-setting hypothesis is concerned with one somewhat limited but nevertheless significant dimension of meaning.

An important part of the agenda-setting function of the press is the process by which certain topics are selected by the media for presentation in news coverage from those available. Another important part is the way in which various factors in news organizations shape the nature of the final report to the public. Such matters are usually investigated under the general heading of the "gatekeeping" process (letting some information through while keeping some out in the formulation and editing of news reports). While there is a substantial accumulation of research available on the way in which news organizations shape their content, the links between this process and the influence on the public in terms of a hierarchy of perceived importance remains to be thoroughly investigated.

Another issue closely related to the agenda-setting function of the press is the degree to which the meanings attached to issues by the public (e.g., perceived importance) play a part in formulating public policy. In other words, if the press emphasizes a given topic to a point where the public comes to believe that it is truly important, do political leaders then take action to "do something" about the issue? There is reason to suspect that such an hypothesis may be viable. The classic example is Watergate. The news media gave the Presidential indiscretions involved in those events maximum possible exposure for months. Eventually, the term was on the lips of virtually every American. Whether they truly understood the realities of the case or not is an open question. It is clear, however, that the topic was increasingly seen as important to a point where a U.S. President left office in disgrace and under threat of impeachment.

In more recent times, the press has shaped the interpretations Americans have given to the Iranian hostage matter, the Soviet invasion of Afghanistan, the space shuttle flights, the bleak economy, crime in the streets, and the Argentine/British conflict over the Falkland Islands. Whether these are the issues that have shaped our nation's destiny or the lives of most people remains to be seen. However, we can agree that the press has told us what to think about. In any case, research interest in agenda setting appears to be increasing; but while this trend is clearly an important one, the great studies remain to be done.[13]

Cultivation Analysis   The study of television as a major influence on people's beliefs has largely focused on the issue of violence. Recently, a number of other issues have been explored. In an insightful article reviewing a number of published and unpublished papers on the study of TV's role in the social construction of reality, Hawkins and Pingree point out the main thrust of these efforts and the difficulty of such research.[14] However, the best-known work is that of George Gerbner and his associates. We have noted earlier that Gerbner et al. began to probe the nature of portrayed violence on American television in the 1960s, but they had not systematically developed an underlying theoretical base. In its early phases their work was a large-scale but atheoretical accounting of what was happening on the television screen in the way of portrayals of violence. Nevertheless, the work was very helpful in understanding the medium. Their content analyses and "violence profile" were an important part of the report of the President's Commission on Violence (see Chapter 11, pp. 297–323).

Since the time of the Violence Commission report, Gerbner et al. have continued to expand their concern with TV's role in portraying violent social relationships. In recent times, however, they have developed a somewhat more elaborate theoretical framework within which to interpret their work. This framework has been expanded a number of times, but it is now converging on the relationships between symbols, their meanings, and patterns of individual and social action.[15] These relationships have been widely studied and have rich theoretical traditions from work earlier in this century in anthropology, philosophy, semantics, social psychology, and sociology. By 1976, Gerbner and his associates had identified their work on television's role in shaping people's beliefs with the traditions that are often referred to collectively as the study of the "social construction of reality":

> The environment that sustains the most distinctive aspects of human existence is the environment of symbols. We learn, share, and act upon meanings derived from that environment.[16]

In their empirical studies, Gerbner and associates have explored these relationships in terms of television's role in influencing people's beliefs, particularly their beliefs about *violence*. The term they use to identify this role is *cultivation effects*. They have completed a number of investigations that they feel demonstrate the central role of television in "cultivating" people's beliefs:

> Television is likely to remain for a long time the chief source of repetitive and ritualized symbol systems cultivating the common consciousness of the most far-flung and heterogeneous mass publics in history.[17]

In their study of cultivation effects, Gerbner and his associates have been concerned mainly with the way in which violence shown on television exaggerates the fears people have about crime in their neighborhoods. To provide empirical evidence that this is the case, they have devised a measuring procedure called "the cultivation differential." This is essentially a forced choice procedure for constructing and using questionnaire items used in surveys. An item is posed to a subject, such as "During any given week, what are your chances of being involved in some type of violence?" (in your neighborhood). Factually speaking, that chance is very small (certainly less than one in a hundred even in a relatively high-crime neighborhood). However, reason these researchers, if the respondent has watched a lot of violence on television, and if this experience has shaped that viewer's beliefs, the chances of being so involved may appear subjectively to be much higher (e.g., one in ten). Thus, "one in ten" can be posed as the *television* answer to the questionnaire item while "one in a hundred" can be the *reality* choice. The prediction is that if the viewer's beliefs have been "cultivated" by violence shown on television, he or she will choose the television answer.

Data assembled with the use of the cultivation differential approach seem to show that at least some people who view a lot of television have exaggerated fears about the level of violence they expect to encounter in their neighborhoods. Unfortunately, much of the research thus far has raised methodological questions and remains controversial. Investigators who have tried to replicate the findings have not found their data in support of the hypothesis that television has shaped people's fears of their neighborhoods. Instead, the level of actual crime in the neighborhood seems to be a more important factor, at least in some cases. Because of these conflicting findings, cultivation analysis has become quite controversial.[18] Nevertheless, it is an effort to explore an important tradition concerning the role of language and meaning in shaping human affairs and it holds high promise for the future in attaining a better understanding of the role of television in our individual and social lives.

The Meaning Theory of Media Portrayals   Numerous theories of human communication have been proposed. Many are complex and sophisticated.[19] However, for the study of the effects of the media, a general theory of human communication that includes mass communication is essential. Mass communication is a part of the totality of communication processes that shape human affairs; it is not something separate and distinct that operates according to principles unique to television, newspapers, film, and so on. Communication that is mediated by some device, such as a television transmitter and a receiver, or a movie camera, screen, and projector, depends on the same neurobiological, psychological, semantic, cultural, and sociological process as those processes involved in purely oral exchanges. Therefore, theories of human communication that make no place for mass communication have limited value in today's world. Such a general theory of communication is implicit in the several theoretical traditions from the social and behavioral sciences that emphasize the link between human behavior and shared human understandings for symbols. In a recent work, DeFleur and Plax have proposed a *biosocial* theory of human communication that synthesizes a number of these earlier traditions. From that biosocial theory, a *meaning theory*, of the consequences of the portrayal of reality in mass communication content, can be derived. That theory has been set forth in some detail in recent works by DeFleur and Dennis and by De Fleur and Ball-Rokeach.[20] Its main concepts were discussed briefly in Chapter 1 (pp. 28–29). However, it needs to be discussed in more detail.

The biosocial theory and the derived meaning theory of mass media portrayals treat mass communication as but one part of the more general processes of communication by which societies develop and maintain an organized group life, and by which individuals within societies are socialized and otherwise develop the ability to think, remember, communicate, and guide their behavior according to social expectations. Thus, the meaning theory stresses the manner in which words and symbols are linked by portrayals of reality in print, film, and broadcasting to meanings that the members of a given language community share as part of their culture. In other words, the media provide specific meaning functions in the societies in which they are present. These functions can be referred to as *establishment* (of new meaning conventions), *extension* (of existing meanings), *substitution* (of different meanings for existing ones), and *stabilization* (of meanings already established as conventions). Each of these functions can be illustrated.

By presenting a new symbol/meaning linkage that is not already a part of the language culture, a media portrayal can *establish* new habits of thinking, understanding, and communicating. Recent examples are provided by the terms "Rubik's cube," "Reaganomics," and "Pac-Man." These terms for an amusing puzzle, a presidential economic policy, and a funny character in an electronic game were not part of our nation's system of symbols and meanings a decade ago. They have clearly been established in our collective repertoire of symbols and meanings by their repeated use by the media in recent times.

Similarly, the media *extend* existing meanings. For example the term "ecology" was at one time a technical word used mainly by a restricted scientific community to refer to a system of balanced relationships between organisms in a local environment. Its popularization via mass communication has added more general meanings, vaguely implying concern for protecting the physical environment from degradation.

The media also *substitute* new interpretations for earlier ones. We mentioned the term "Watergate" earlier. At one time it referred merely to a fashionable apartment and hotel complex beside the Potomac River in Washington, D.C. Massive publicity about misdeeds associated with the Nixon administration transformed the meaning of the term into one implying scandalous events that rocked the nation's political structure.

Finally, the media *stabilize* our language as well as change it. Indeed, this may be one of their most important functions. As people read newspapers, listen to their radios, watch television, and so on, they get constant reminders of the shared meanings of language symbols. For example, they can see acted out on their television screens the behavioral meaning of "being in love," of "police brutality," "housewife," "old person," "mentally ill," and so on. Descriptions in newspapers and the content of other media provide similar functions.

The contribution of mass communication to our shared meanings is both complex and profound. These are not the kinds of effects and influences that are easily demonstrated by some quick laboratory experiment, or by a cleverly designed social survey. Indeed, there may be no existing research methodology that can be employed to test the assertions of the meaning theory in a definitive study. In other words, the functions of media portrayals are subtle, long-range, accumulative, and nearly impossible to sort out from other kinds of communication processes. Nevertheless, they are critical parts of the processes by which human beings in modern media societies construct shared meanings that enable them to organize their social lives and conduct their individual affairs.

If research solidly confirms the role of mass communication in shaping people's meanings, their interpretations of reality, and therefore their subsequent actions in attempting to cope with that reality, such confirmation will have truly profound implications. For one thing, such a confirmed role of the media could have significant *legal* consequences. Those who control the content of the media will be seen to have a special responsibility that they do not now accept. If people's meanings and interpretations are shaped in ways that unfairly create *harm* (in the precise legal meaning of that term) to persons because of negligently inaccurate portrayals of them or their situations, new kinds of litigation could follow. The issue is somewhat similar to the current situation of *libel* except that prosecutions for libel must show "deliberate intent" to create harm. However, if scientific research solidly establishes the meaning-creation functions of media portrayals, even the "negligent" use of such power could be a subject of legal suits. Such an idea is speculative, of course. But in view of the fact that our system of laws is constantly changing, particularly with respect to mass communication, it is not beyond the realm of possibility. Only the results of further research will answer the question.

In overview, the development of new perspectives on the role and influences of mass communication in modern societies shows that we do indeed "have a long way to go." For the most part, these newer perspectives have outstripped our ability to study them definitively in empirical research. Yet, these new theories and the limited, even controversial, research associated with them seem to suggest that we are indeed leaving behind the era of "limited effects" interpretations of media influences, and entering a time when we believe that they have "powerful effects," even though they are very difficult to study and demonstrate.

NOTES AND REFERENCES

1. Thomas E. Peterson, *The Mass Media Election: How Americans Choose Their President* (New York: Praeger, 1980).
2. Numerous works are now available on the techniques, procedures, and problems of content analyses. The following have been widely used: George Gerbner et al., *The Analysis of Communication Content* (New York: John Wiley & Sons, 1969). See also: Ole Holsti, *Content Analysis for the Social Sciences and Humanities* (Reading, Mass.: Addison-Wesley, 1969).
3. *Television and Social Behavior: Ten Years of Scientific Progress and Implications for the Future*, Volume I, Summary Report, National Institute of Mental Health, 1982.
4. Herta Herzog, "What Do We Really Know About Daytime Serial Listeners?" in Paul F. Lazarsfeld and Frank N. Stanton, eds., *Radio Research, 1942–1943* (New York: Duell, Sloan, and Pierce, 1944), pp. 3–33. See also: Bernard Berelson, "What Missing the Newspaper Means," in Paul F. Lazarsfeld and Frank N. Stanton, *Communication Research, 1948–1949* (New York: Harper and Row, 1949), pp. 111–129.
5. Walter Stephenson, *The Play Theory of Mass Communication* (Chicago: University of Chicago Press, 1967).
6. Jay G. Blumler and Elihu Katz, *The Uses of Mass Communication: Current Perspectives on Gratification Research* (Beverly Hills: Sage Publications, 1974).
7. Alan M. Rubin, "An Examination of Television Viewing Motivations," *Communication Research*, 8, 2, April, 1981, pp. 141–1665.
8. Albert Bandura, *Social Learning Theory* (Englewood Cliffs, N.J.: Prentice-Hall, 1977).
9. Thomas R. Lindlof, "A Fantasy Construct of Television Viewing," *Communication Research*, 9, 1, January, 1982, pp. 67–107.
10. Walter Lippman, *Public Opinion* (New York: Macmillan, 1922).
11. Bernard Cohen, *The Press and Foreign Policy* (Princeton, N.J.: Princeton University Press, 1963), p. 13.
12. Maxwell E. McCombs and Donald L. Shaw, "Structuring the 'Unseen Environment,' " *Journal of Communication* 26, 2, Spring, 1976, p. 18.
13. Several researchers have taken the lead in formulating and investigating agenda setting. See, for example: Maxwell E. McCombs and Donald L. Shaw, "The Agenda-Setting Function of Mass Media," *Public Opinion Quarterly*, 1972, pp. 176–187; also J. McLeod, L. Becker, and J. Byrnes, "Another Look at the Agenda-Setting Function of the Press," *Communication Research*, 1974, pp. 131–166.

14. Robert P. Hawkins and Suzanne Pingree, "Using Television to Construct Social Reality," *Journal of Broadcasting*, Vol. 25, 4, Fall, 1981, pp. 347–364.
15. George Gerbner and Larry Gross, "Living with Television: The Violence Profile," *Journal of Communication*, 26, Spring, 1976, pp. 173–199. See also: George Gerbner et al., "The Mainstreaming of America: Violence Profile No. 11," *Journal of Communication*, 30, Summer, 1980, pp. 10–29.
16. Ibid., p. 174.
17. Ibid., p. 176.
18. Anthony N. Doob and Alen E. MacDonald, "Television Viewing and Fear of Victimization: Is the Relationship Causal?" *Journal of Personality and Social Psychology*, 37, 2, 1979, pp. 170–179.
19. Frank E. X. Dance, *Human Communication Theory: Comparative Essays* (New York: Harper and Row, 1982).
20. Melvin L. De Fleur and Everette E. Dennis, *Understanding Mass Communication* (Boston: Houghton Mifflin, 1981). See also: Melvin L. De Fleur and Sandra Ball-Rokeach, *Theories of Mass Communication*, 4th ed. (New York: Longman, 1982).

name
index

subject
index

Reinforcement, 102–104, 110–111
Repetition experiment, 217–227

Scientific Advisory Committee, 328
Selective influences, theory of, 174
  and comic books, 262
Senate hearings, 352–353
Sharpening, 214–215
Sleeper effect, 45, 128, 158
  and persuasion, 173
Social relationships, 111, 145
Society, mass, 3–11, 111
  defined, 10–11
  traditional society, master trends of,
    4
S-R learning, 153–154
Stabilization, concept of, 384
Statistics, beginnings of, 21
  development of, 32–33
Stimulus intensity, vs. response, 218
Student activism, 297
Substitution, concept of, 384
Suggestibility, 77
Surgeon General's Advisory Commit-
  tee, 326, 355n, 357n
Surgeon General's Report, 326–355,
  371, 379

Television:
  adolescent use of, 337–338
  behavioral effects of, 290–291
  cartoons and violence, 329
  and children's attitudes toward, 282
  and children's tastes, 280–281
  cognitive effects of, 289–290
  content analysis of, 303–309
  early years of, 268–270
  effects on children, 270–294
  emotional effects of, 280
  as entertainment, 273–274
  and family patterns, 343–344
  growth of, 16–17
  and incidental learning, 282–285
  and individual differences, 292
  as information, 274
  and long and short term effects of,
    310–321
  and magic bullet theory, 320
  and maturation effect, 293
  and meaning theory, 292

  and modeling theory, 333–334
  and observational learning, 333–334
  physical effects of, 280
  programs for children, 279–280
  and quantities of violence, 306–308
  and social categories, 292
  and social norms and social relation-
    ships, 285–286, 292
  social utility of, 274–275
  uses and functions, 271, 273–275
  viewing and age, 342–343
  viewing and levels of attention, 344
  and violence, 286–287, 304–309,
    329–330
  and violence, main conclusions,
    353–354
  violence, and network programming,
    305–306
Theory:
  biosocial theory of human communi-
    cation, 383–384
  of indirect influences, 24–26
  of individual differences, 262
  magic bullet, 23, 262
  modeling, 27, 376
  of selective influence, 24–26, 262
  of uniform effects, 22–24, 262
Training films:
  audience evaluation of, 129–131
  and factual knowledge, 119–120,
    124–125, 127
  and general attitudes, 125, 127
  long term effects, 138
  and morale, 120, 124–125, 127
  and opinions, 120, 124, 127
  short term effects, 138
Training, military, 115–116
Two-step flow of communication,
  108–111, 179, 201, 229, 230

Urbanization, 7–9, 361
Uses and gratifications, 374–375

Validity, 188
Values, 184
Violence:
  and actual experience with, 314
  national survey of, 309–316
  and network programming, 305–306
  norms of, 310–313

and personal experiences with, 314
and television, 286–287, 304–309
preferences for, 315–316
on TV and aggressiveness, 339–341,
349–350
and TV cartoons, 329
on TV and comparisons with other
countries, 332
on TV and effects of, 329–331
on TV, main conclusions of, 353–
354
quantities of on TV, 306–308

on TV vs. reality, 316–317
television world of, 316–317

War of the Worlds, 60–70, 82–83, 367
Watts riot, 299
Waverers, 101
Weber's Law, 218–223, 227, 230
Why We Fight films, 117–119

Yale Communication Research Program, 150–175
Yellow journalism, 235

Melvin L. De Fleur is now at the University of Miami in Coral Gables. There, he is Chairman of the Department of Sociology and Professor of Communication. His well-known text *Sociology: Human Society* (written with others) has just been published in its third edition. Among his new books in communication are *Understanding Mass Communication* (with Everette C. Dennis) and the fourth edition of *Theories of Mass Communication* (with Sandra Ball-Rokeach), another Longman Inc. publication.

When he is not chairing a department, teaching, doing research, or writing, he continues his interest in flying and regularly pilots his Cessna Centurion to professional conventions and meetings. For recreation he turns to rod and reel. He has forsaken the trout of the Pacific Northwest for the sailfish and other denizens of the deep in the Gulf Stream, pursuing them avidly in his boat, the *Emile Durkheim*. He is also a scuba and snorkle enthusiast, spending as much time as possible in the Florida Keys and the nearby Bahamas. He claims that many of his best ideas come to him while his boat is anchored in a quiet cove where the telephone lines cannot reach.

Shearon A. Lowery received her Ph.D. from Washington State University in 1979. Since then she has been teaching in the Department of Sociology and Anthropology of Florida International University in Miami. She has done research on television soap operas, focusing on the manner in which they portray the use of alcohol and how this may influence their viewers. In addition she has published articles and chapters on various forms of deviant behavior.

Since she was a child she has had a deep affection for animals. She began to ride almost as soon as she could walk. She is especially fond of thoroughbred horses and this leads her to spend as much time as possible riding or at the track where she can watch her favorites in action. Her love of animals naturally includes both dogs and cats. At home she lives with two German shepherds and a big mean Siamese cat named Memphis Tiger who keeps the dogs in line.

DATE DUE

FEB 2 5 1985 F		
JUN 4 1985		
OCT 5 1985		
OCT 1 6 1985		
OCT 2 9 1985 RENEWED		
NOV 1 2 1985 Grant F		
DEC 1 8 1985		
JAN 1 0 1986		
SEP 1 0 1986 F		
SEP 2 4 1986		
SEP 2 9 1989		
NOV 5 1989		
DEC 05 1988		
Nov 16 05		